# Tokyo TARAREBA GIRLS 2

### AKIKO HIGASHIMURA

## TODAY'S RECOMMENDATIONS

ACT
Ex
BONUS COMIC
169

Special
Chapter
CHOCOLATE IS ALWAYS SWEET TO ME
160

ACT
8
PUNCH-DRUNK WOMEN
119

ACT
7
SHIMESABA WOMAN
079

ACT
6
CONVEYOR-BELT SUSHI WOMAN
039

ACT
5
THE DESERTER WOMAN
003

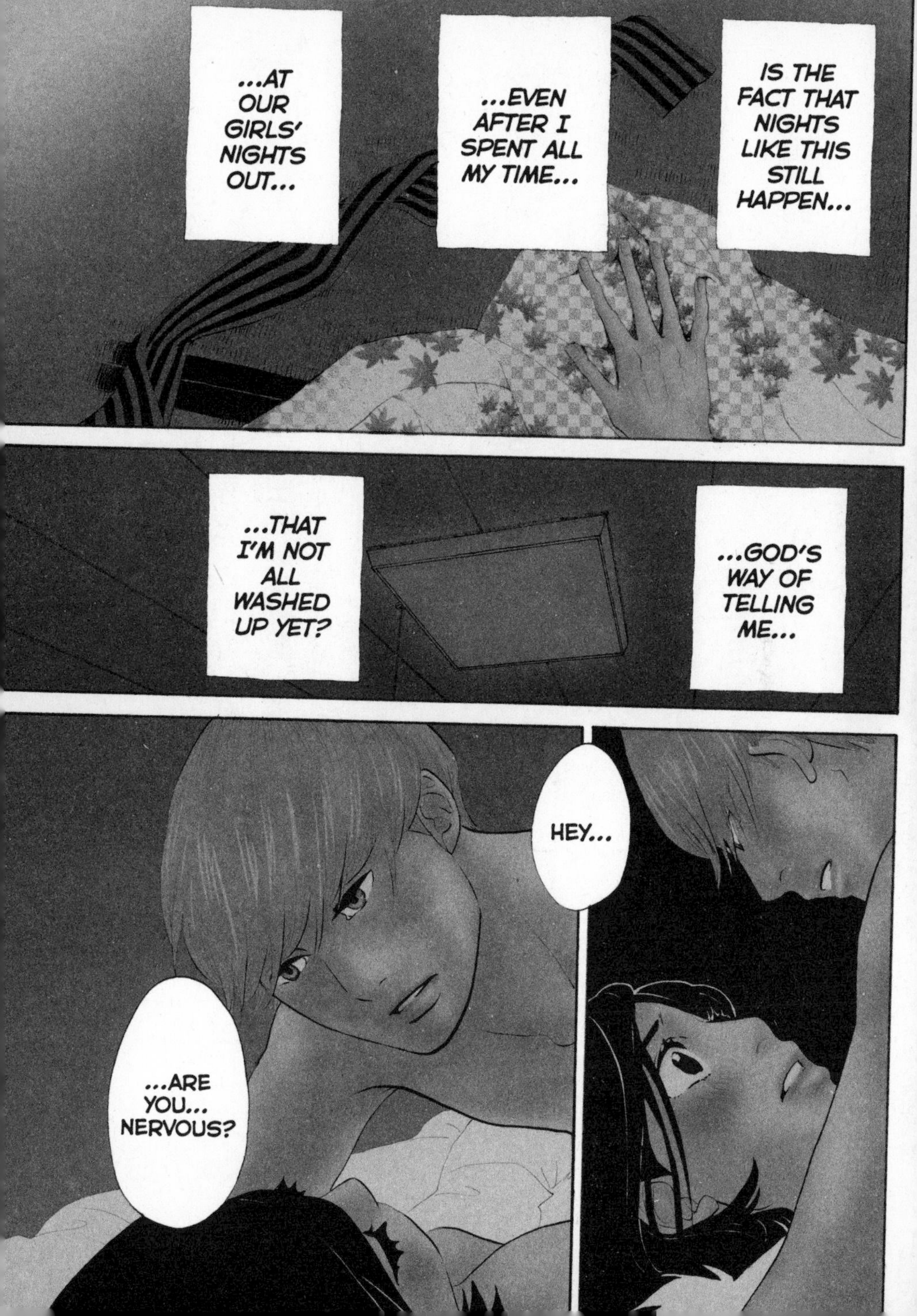
IS THE FACT THAT NIGHTS LIKE THIS STILL HAPPEN...
...EVEN AFTER I SPENT ALL MY TIME...
...AT OUR GIRLS' NIGHTS OUT...
...GOD'S WAY OF TELLING ME...
...THAT I'M NOT ALL WASHED UP YET?
HEY...
...ARE YOU... NERVOUS?

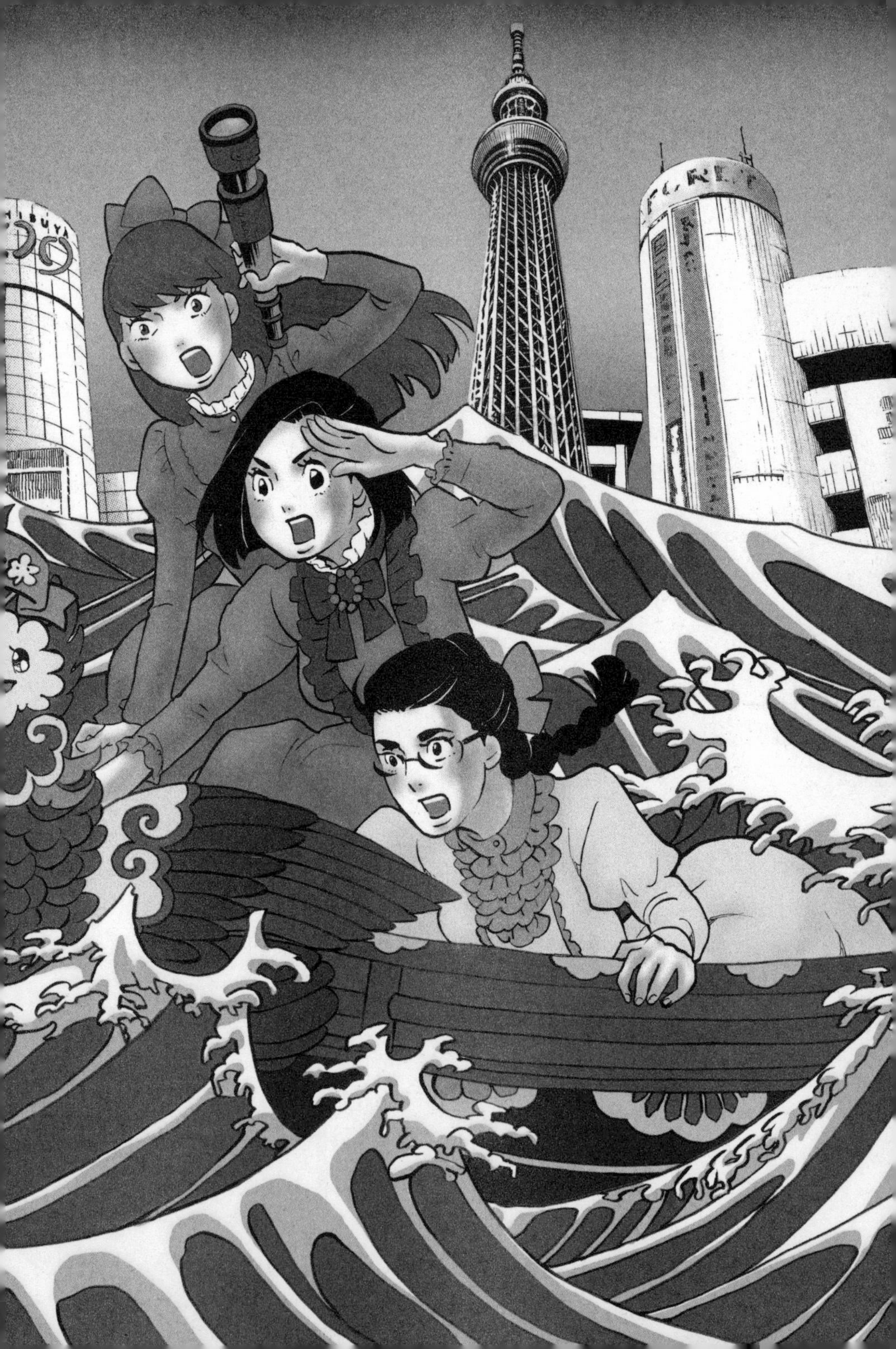

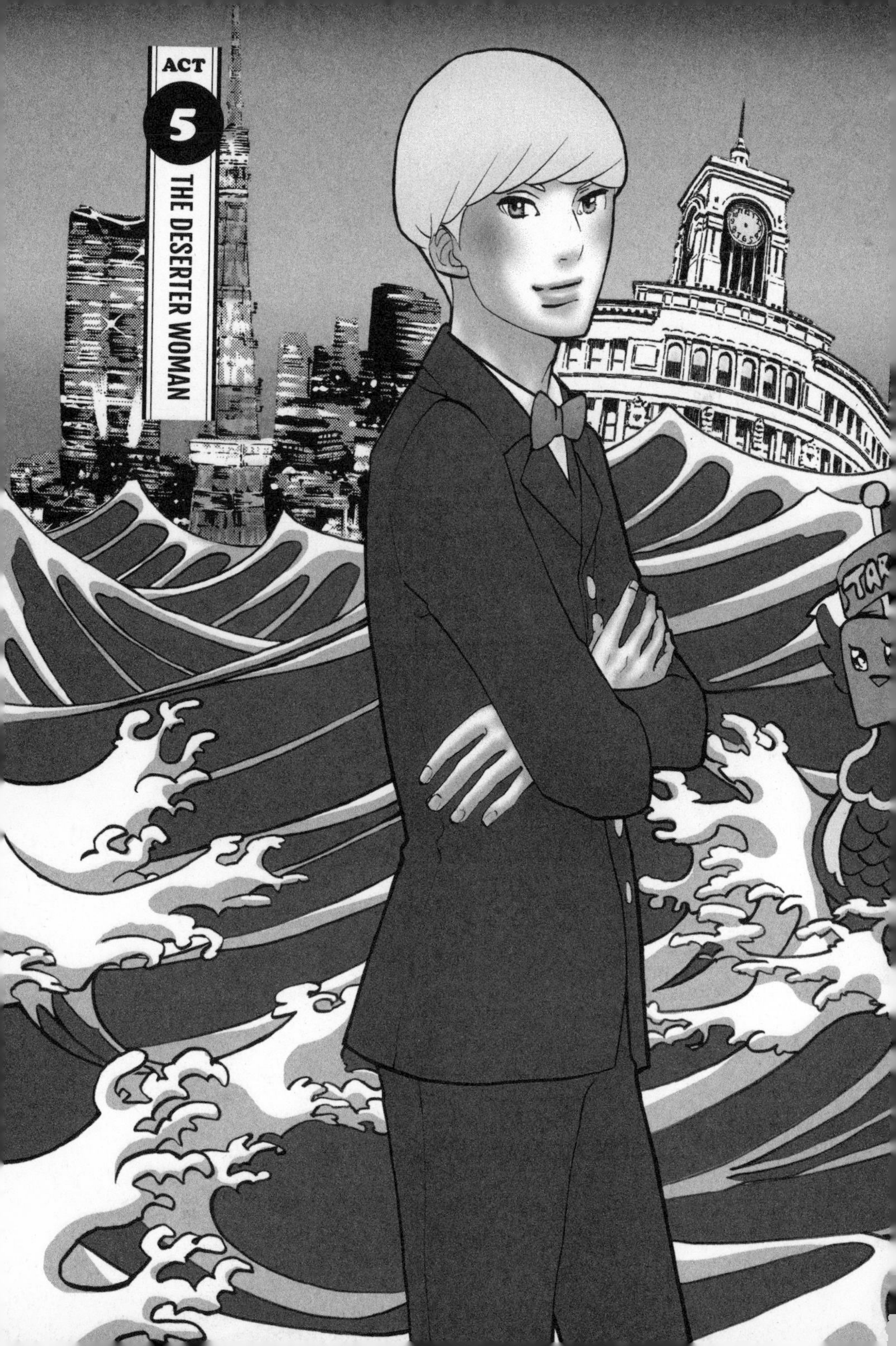
ACT
5
THE DESERTER WOMAN

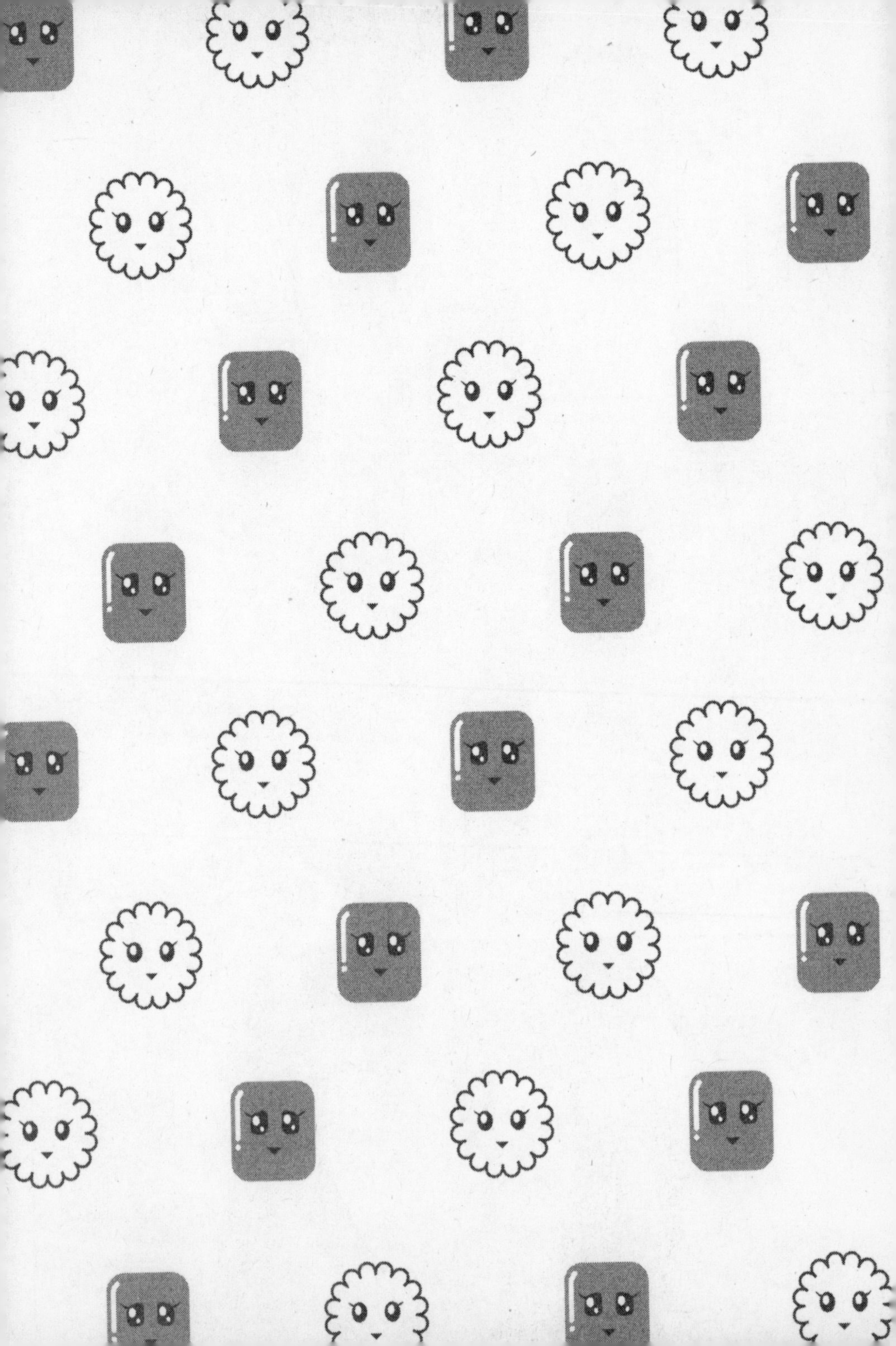

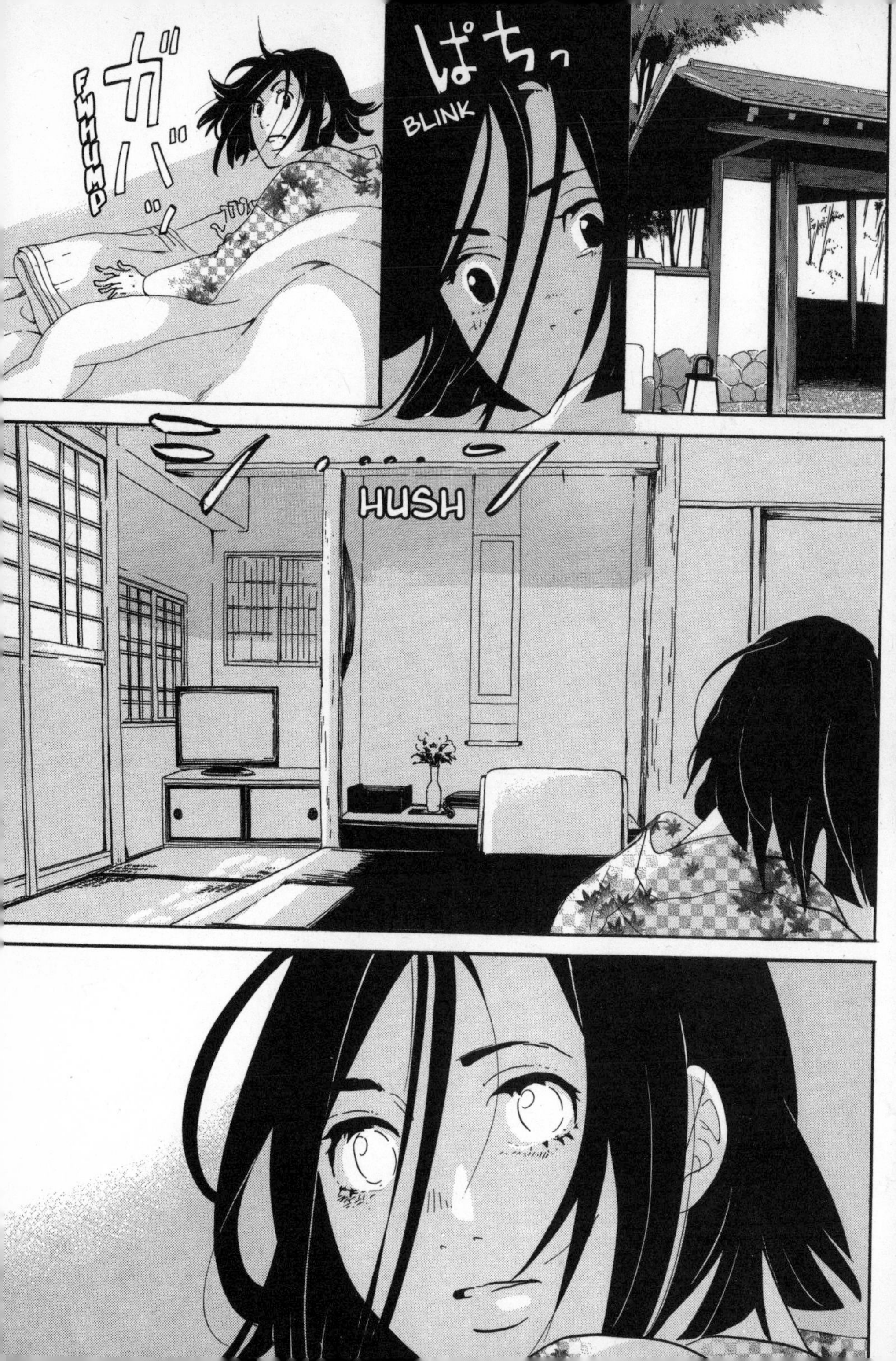
ぱちっ
BLINK
ガバッ
FWHUMP
HUSH

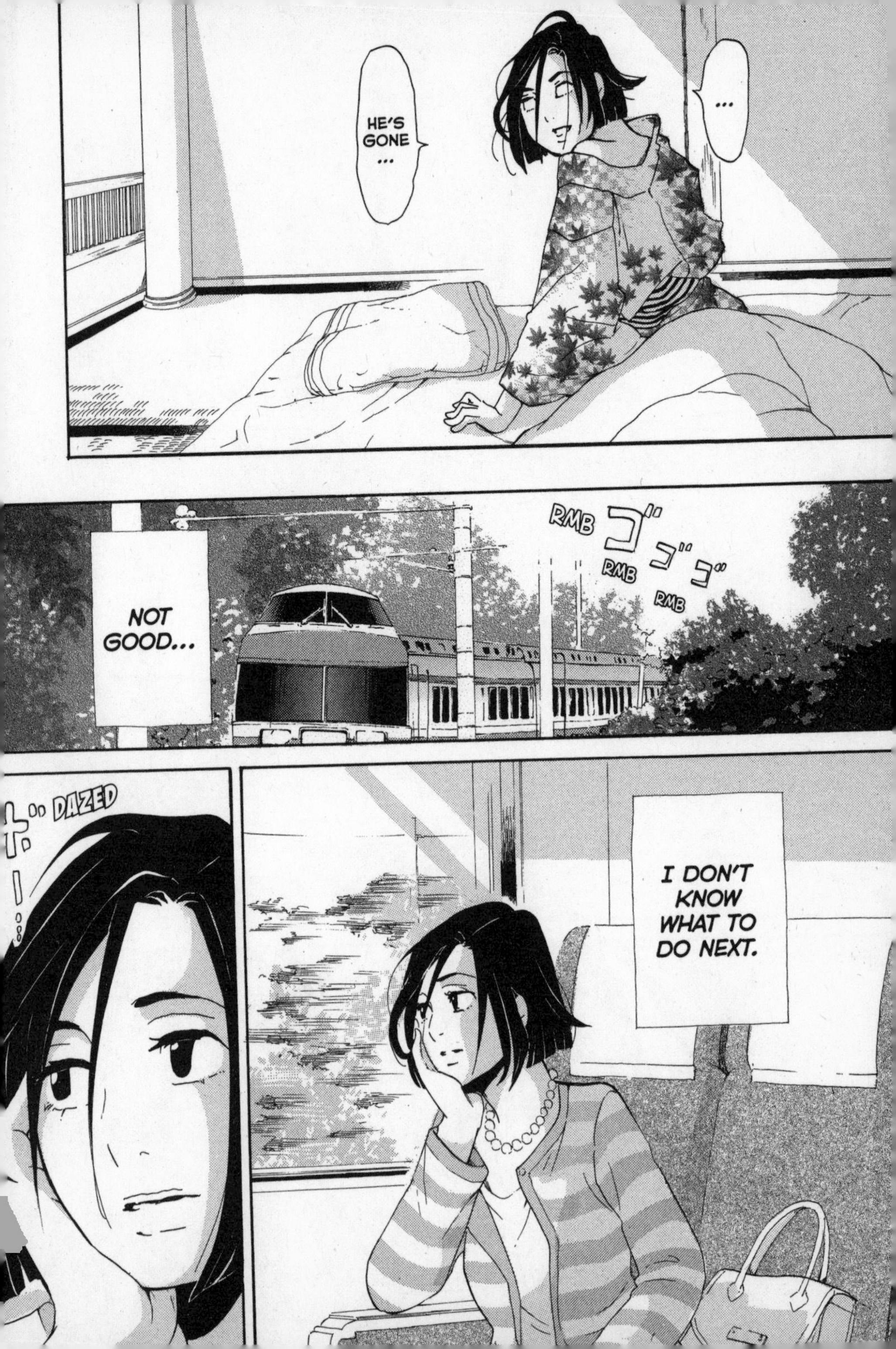

...
HE'S GONE ...
RMB
RMB
RMB
NOT GOOD...
I DON'T KNOW WHAT TO DO NEXT.
DAZED

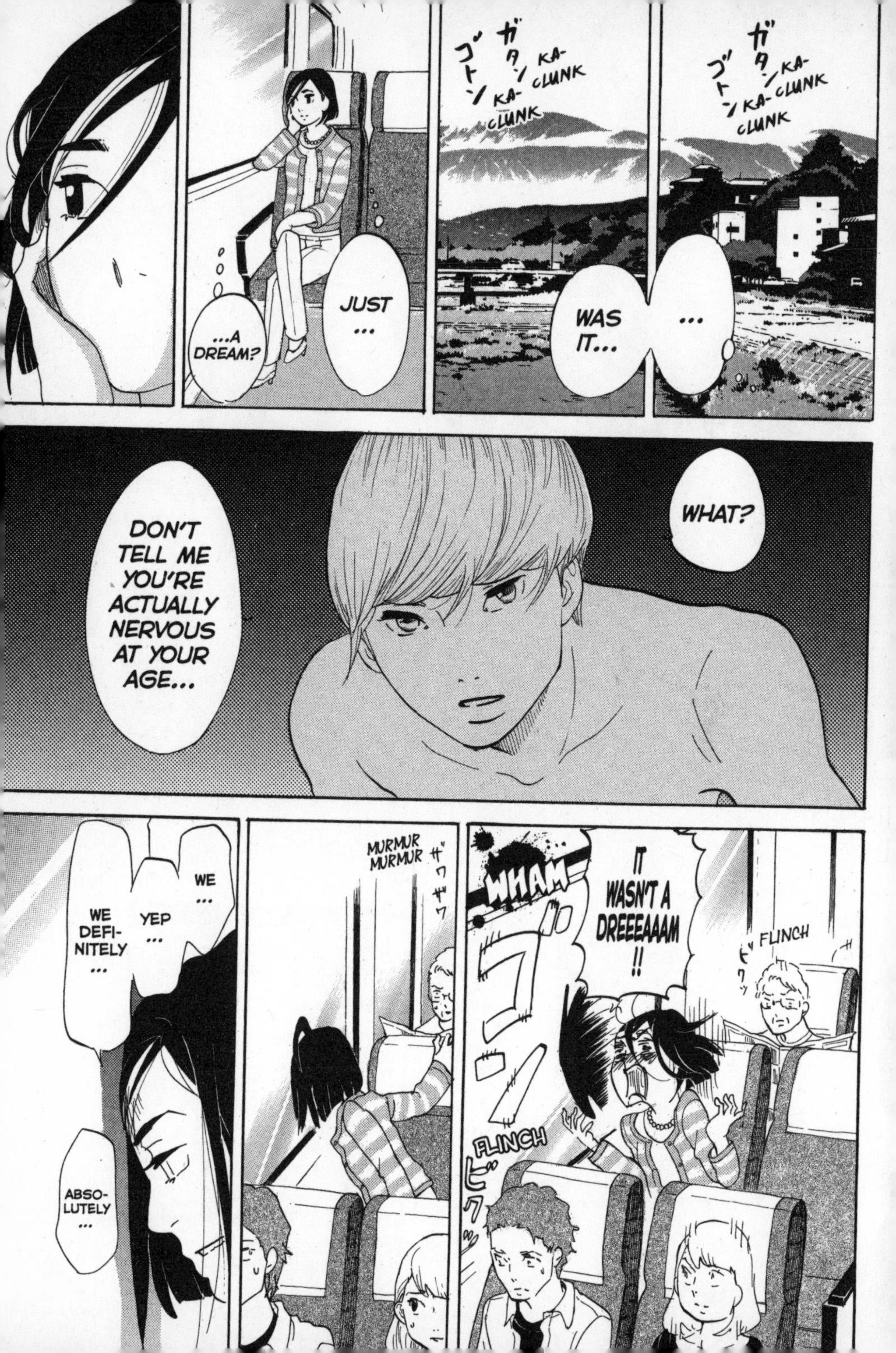
ガタン
ゴトン
KA-CLUNK
KA-CLUNK
...
ガタン
ゴトン
KA-CLUNK
KA-CLUNK
WAS IT...
JUST ...
...A DREAM?
WHAT?
DON'T TELL ME YOU'RE ACTUALLY NERVOUS AT YOUR AGE...
WHAM
IT WASN'T A DREEEAAAM !!
ビクッ
FLINCH
FLINCH
ビクッ
MURMUR MURMUR
ザワザワ
WE ...
YEP ...
WE DEFI-NITELY ...
ABSO-LUTELY ...

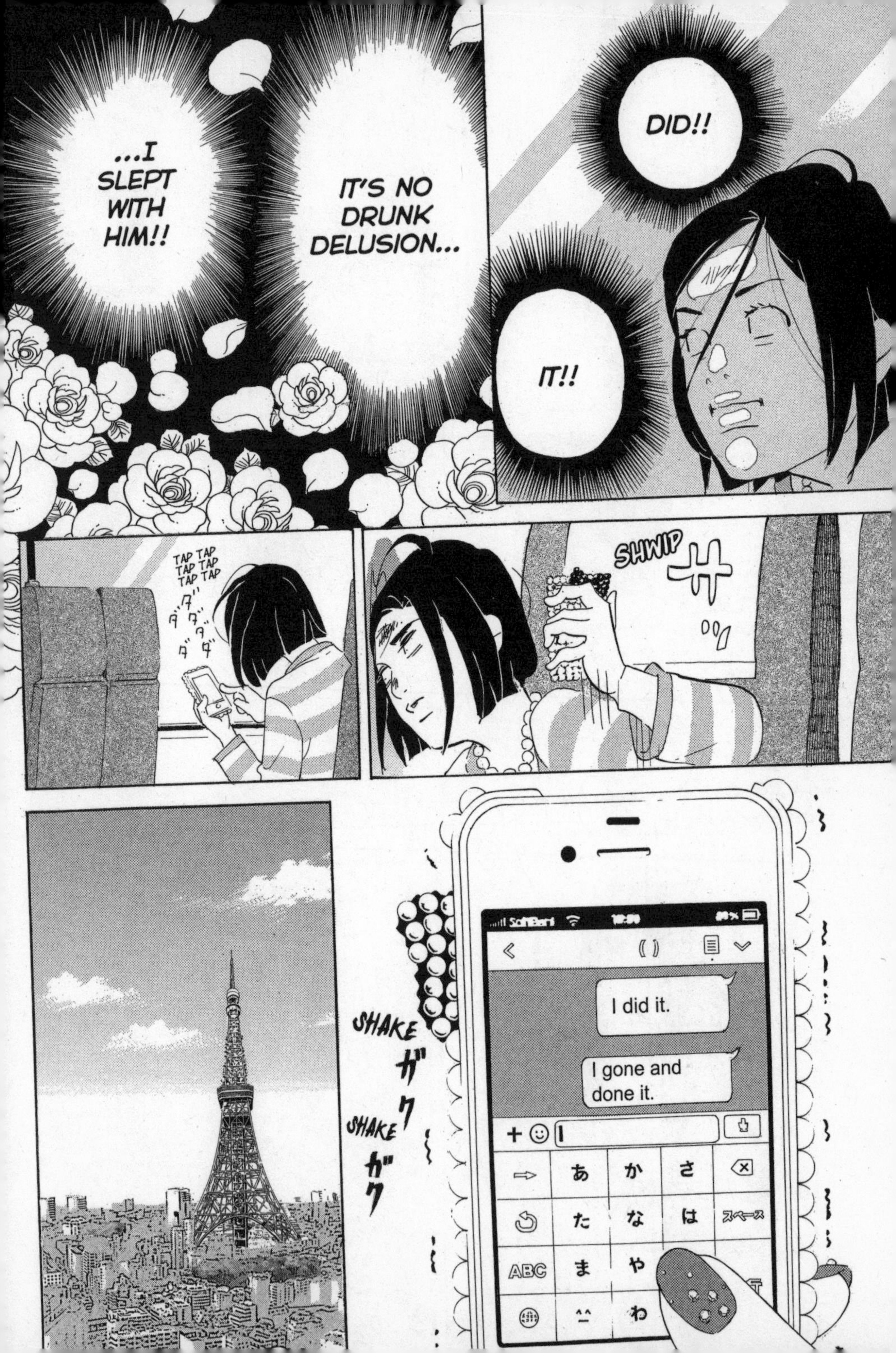
DID!!
IT!!
IT'S NO DRUNK DELUSION...
...I SLEPT WITH HIM!!
SHWIP
TAP TAP TAP TAP TAP TAP
I did it.
I gone and done it.
あ か さ
た な は スペース
ABC ま や
わ
SHAKE
ガク
SHAKE
ガク

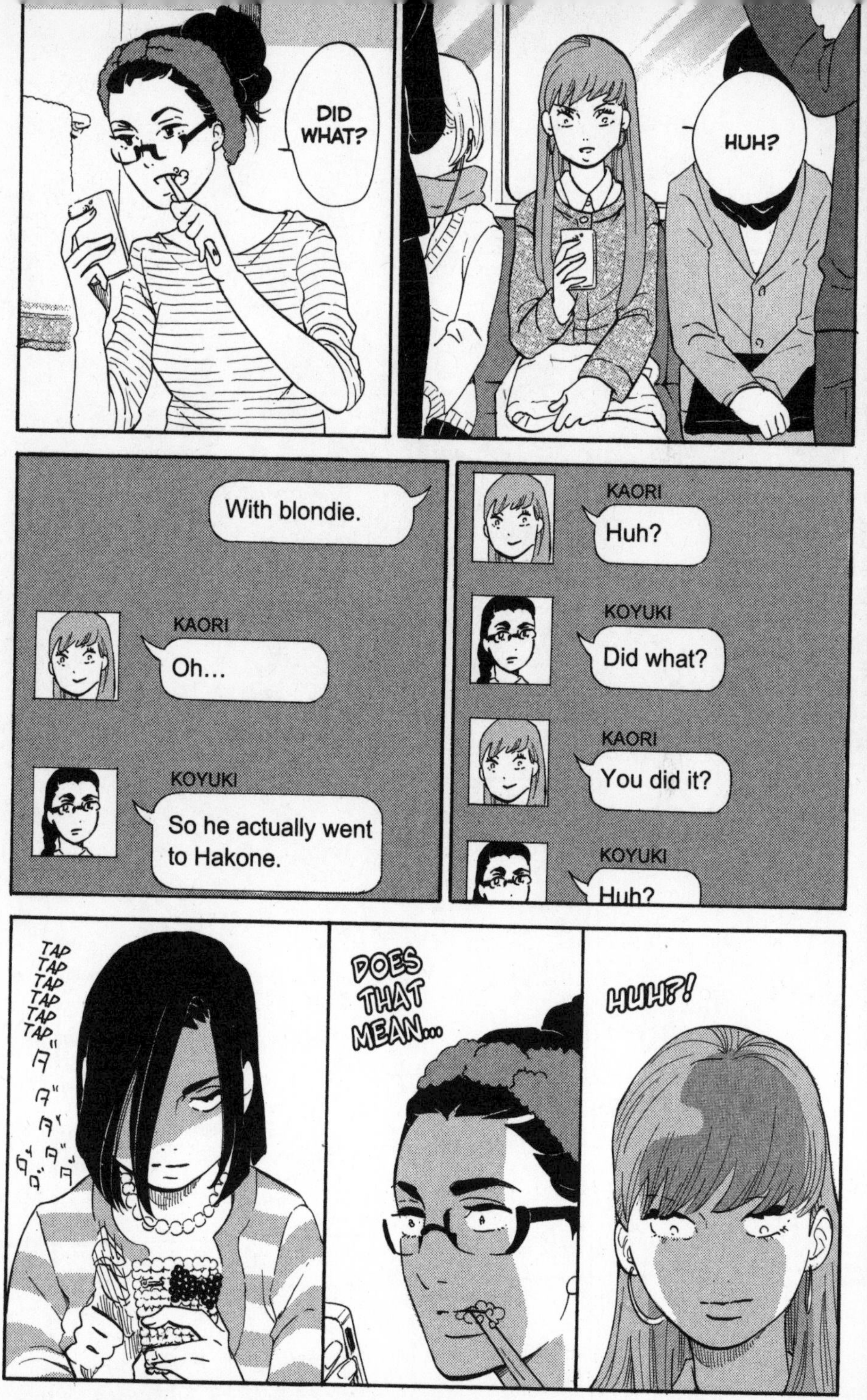
HUH?
DID WHAT?
KAORI
Huh?
KOYUKI
Did what?
KAORI
You did it?
KOYUKI
Huh?
With blondie.
KAORI
Oh...
KOYUKI
So he actually went to Hakone.
HUH?!
DOES THAT MEAN...
TAP TAP TAP TAP TAP TAP

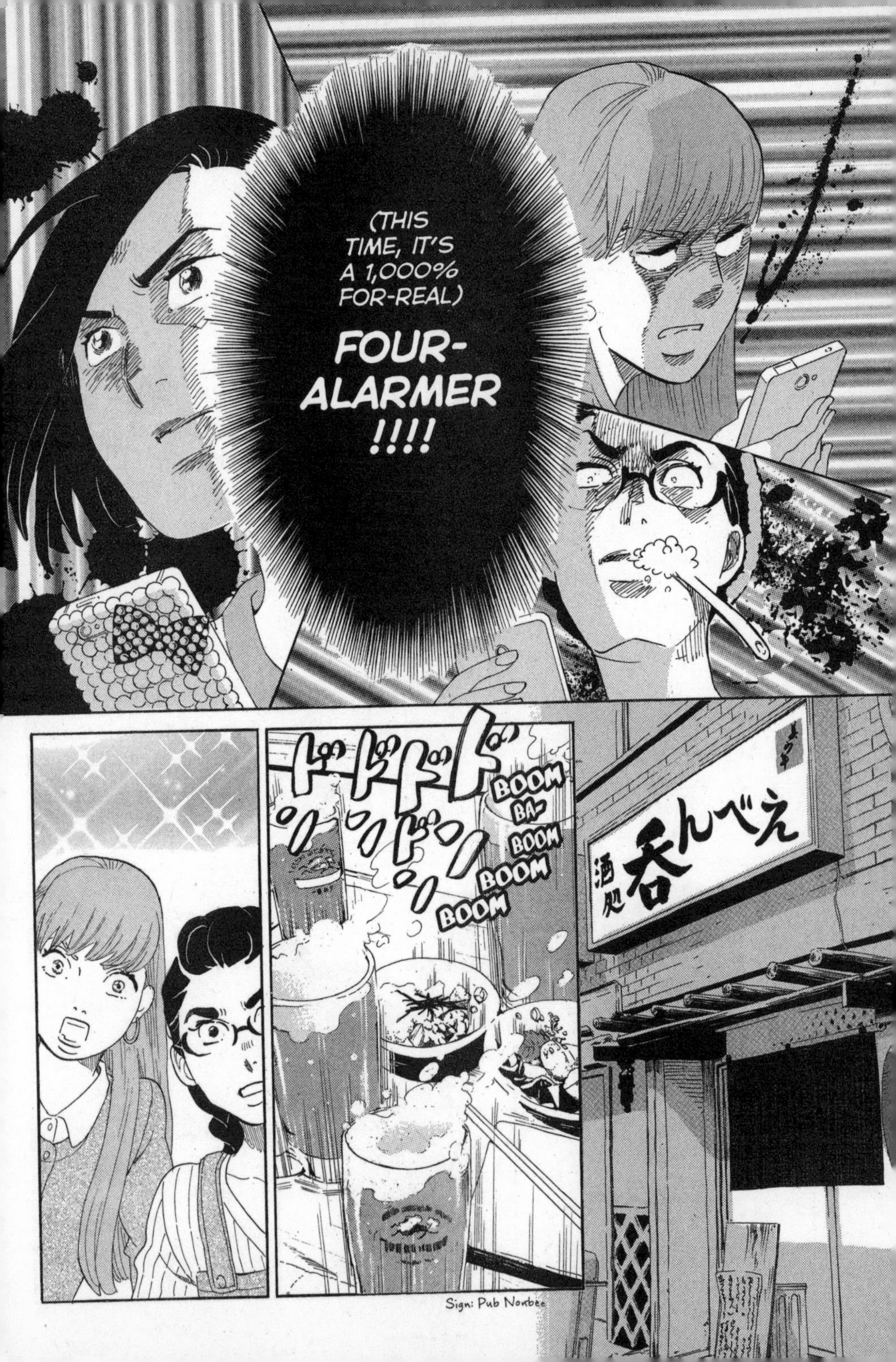
(THIS TIME, IT'S A 1,000% FOR-REAL)
FOUR-ALARMER !!!!
酒処 呑んべえ
ドドドドド
BOOM BA-BOOM BOOM BOOM BOOM
Sign: Pub Nonbee

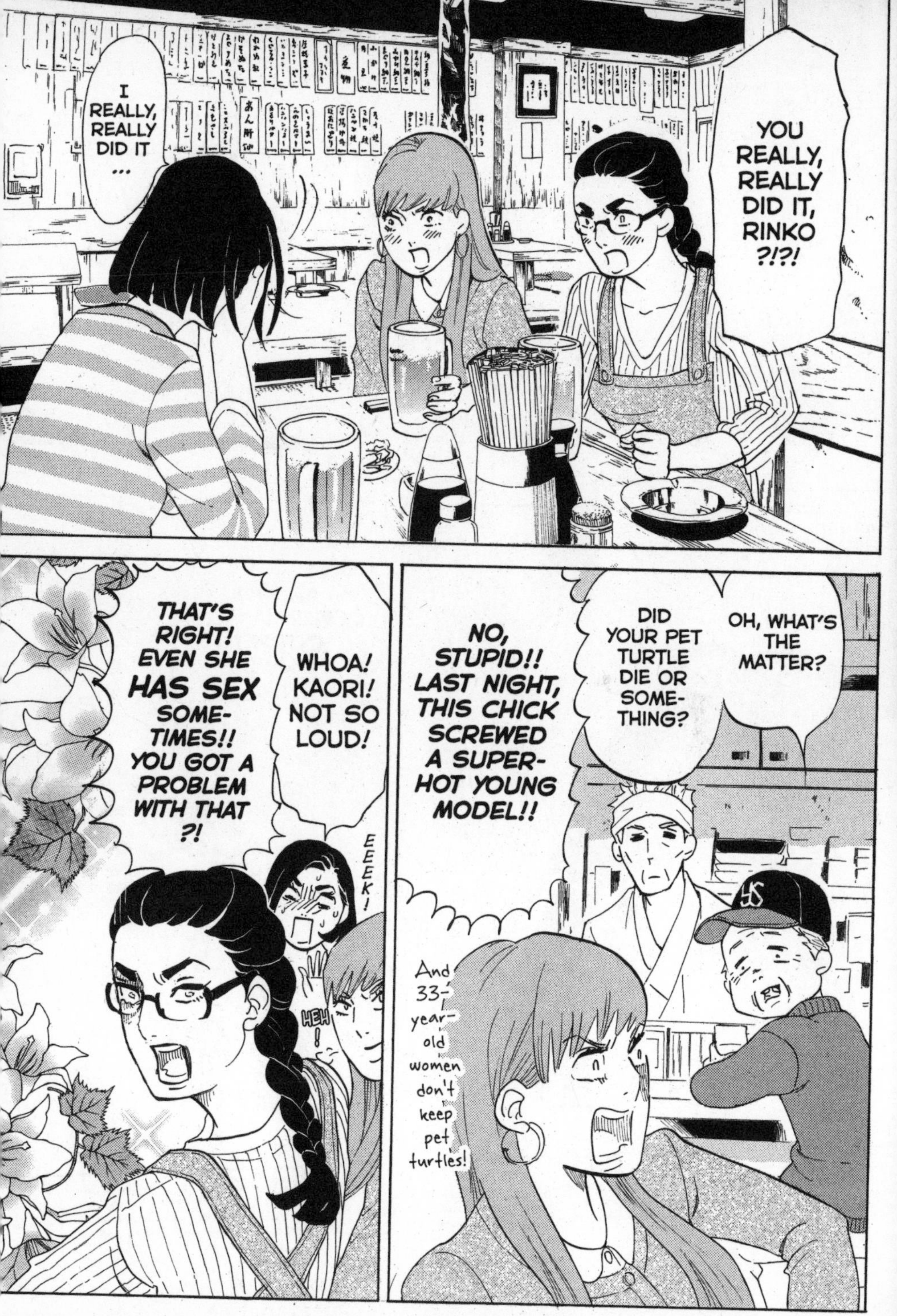
YOU REALLY, REALLY DID IT, RINKO ?!?!
I REALLY, REALLY DID IT ...
OH, WHAT'S THE MATTER?
DID YOUR PET TURTLE DIE OR SOME-THING?
NO, STUPID!! LAST NIGHT, THIS CHICK SCREWED A SUPER-HOT YOUNG MODEL!!
And 33-year-old women don't keep pet turtles!
WHOA! KAORI! NOT SO LOUD!
EEEEK!
THAT'S RIGHT! EVEN SHE HAS SEX SOME-TIMES!! YOU GOT A PROBLEM WITH THAT ?!
HEH!

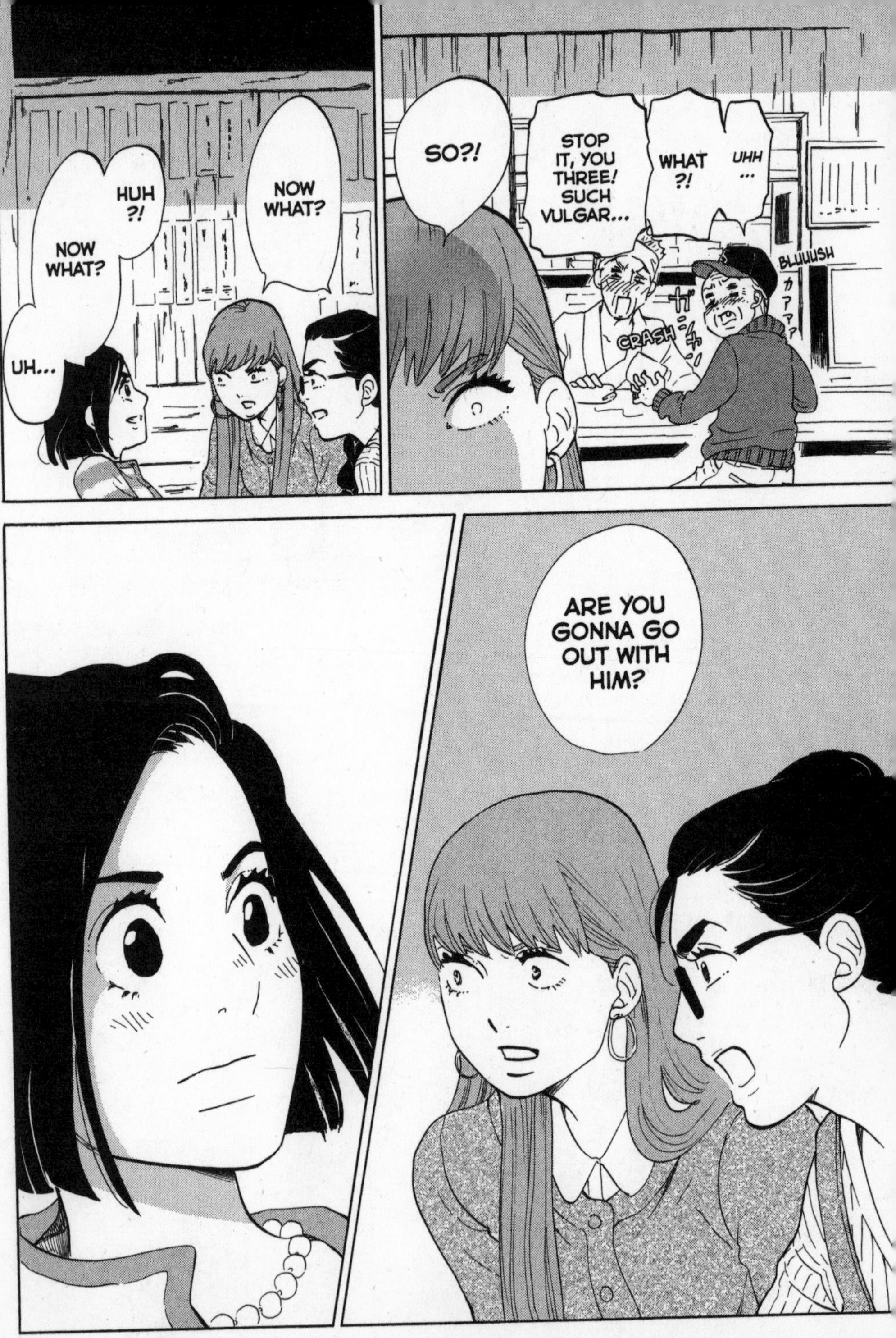
UHH...
WHAT?!
STOP IT, YOU THREE! SUCH VULGAR...
SO?!
BLUUUSH
CRASH
NOW WHAT?
HUH?!
NOW WHAT?
UH...
ARE YOU GONNA GO OUT WITH HIM?

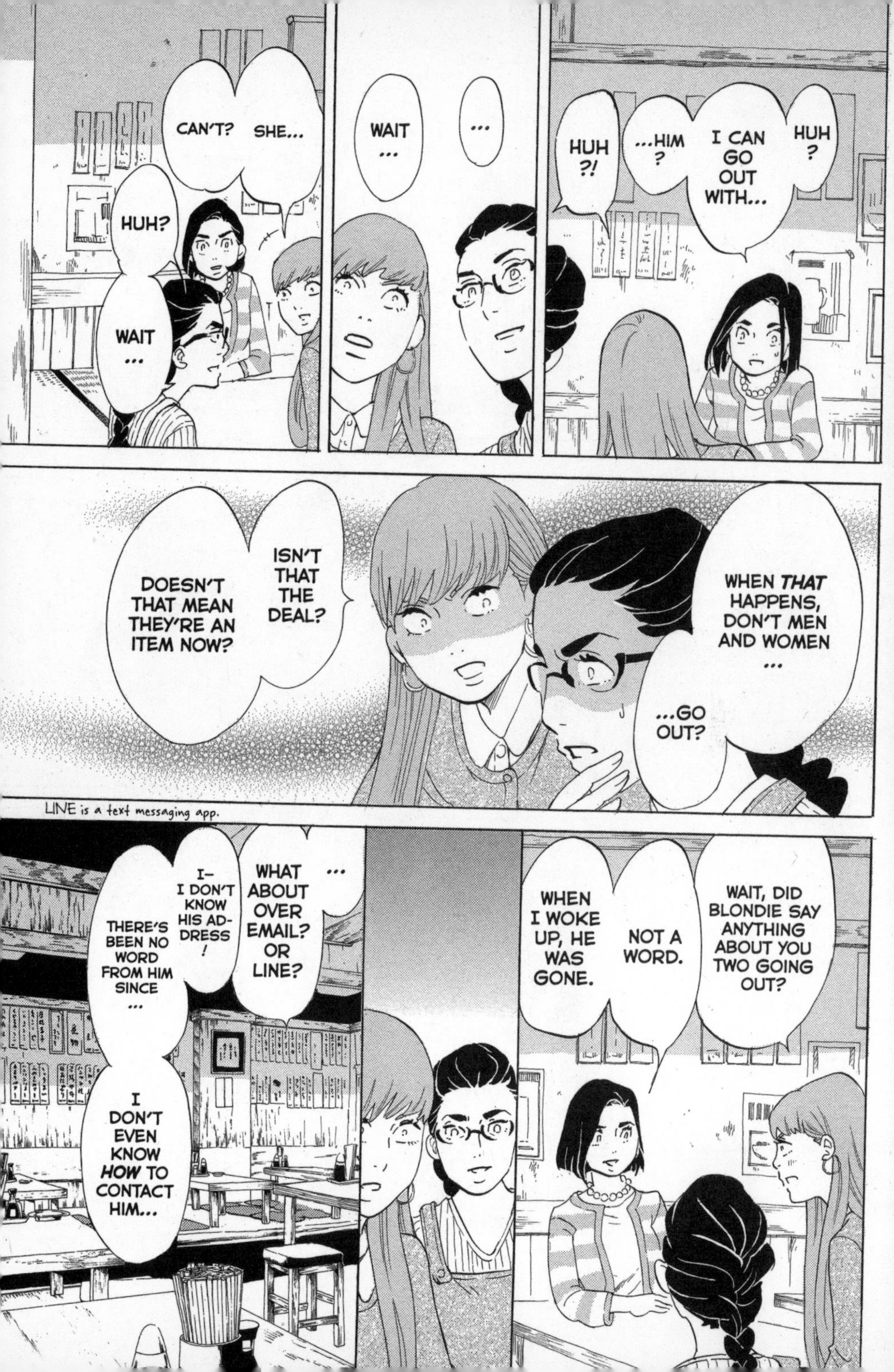
HUH?
I CAN GO OUT WITH...
...HIM?
HUH?!
...
WAIT...
SHE...
CAN'T?
HUH?
WAIT...
WHEN *THAT* HAPPENS, DON'T MEN AND WOMEN...
...GO OUT?
ISN'T THAT THE DEAL?
DOESN'T THAT MEAN THEY'RE AN ITEM NOW?
WAIT, DID BLONDIE SAY ANYTHING ABOUT YOU TWO GOING OUT?
NOT A WORD.
WHEN I WOKE UP, HE WAS GONE.
...
WHAT ABOUT OVER EMAIL? OR LINE?
I– I DON'T KNOW HIS ADDRESS!
THERE'S BEEN NO WORD FROM HIM SINCE...
I DON'T EVEN KNOW *HOW* TO CONTACT HIM...

LINE is a text messaging app.

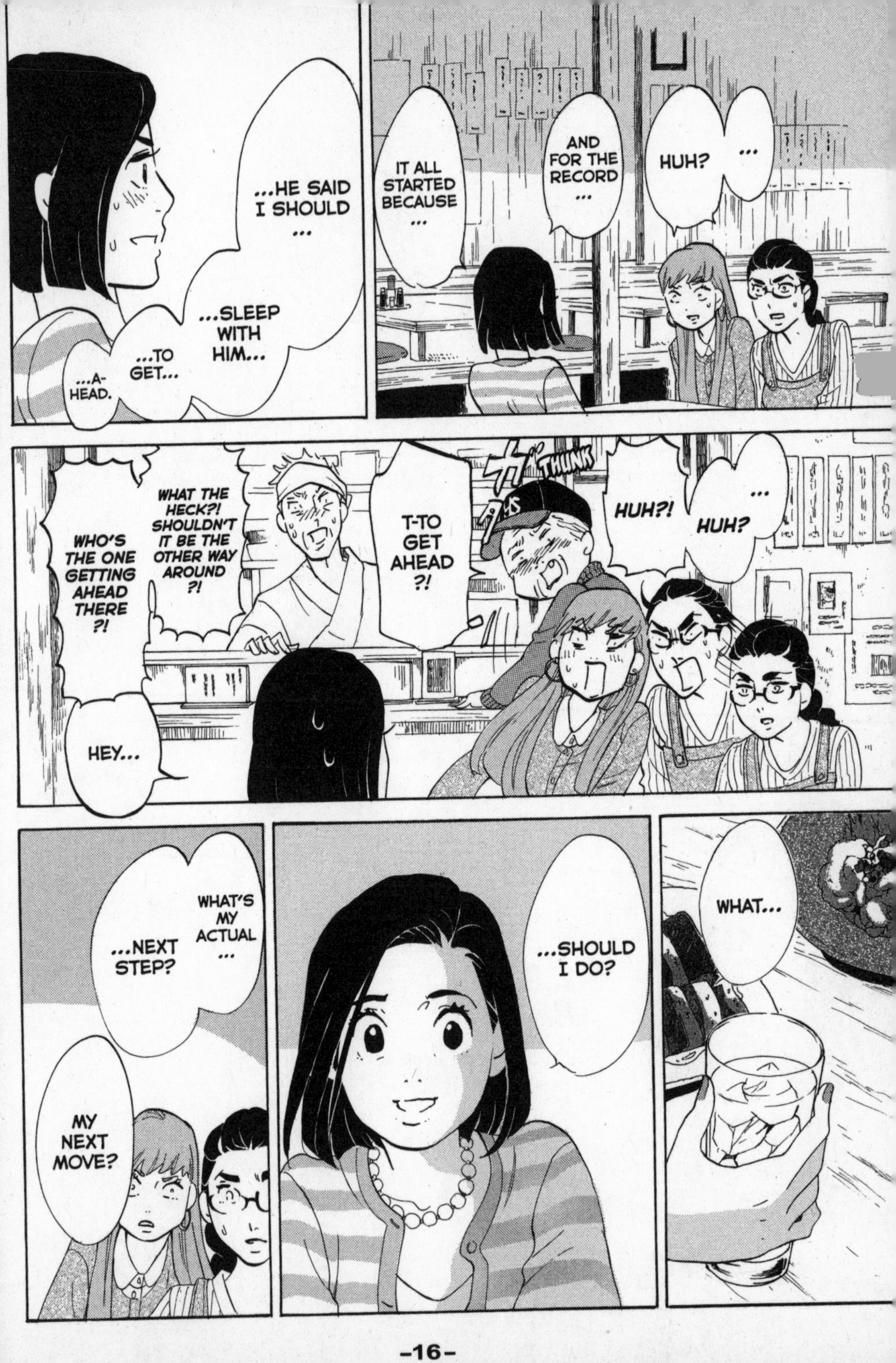
...
HUH?
AND FOR THE RECORD ...
IT ALL STARTED BECAUSE ...
...HE SAID I SHOULD ...
...SLEEP WITH HIM...
...TO GET...
...A-HEAD.
...
HUH?
HUH?!
THUNK
T-TO GET AHEAD ?!
WHAT THE HECK?! SHOULDN'T IT BE THE OTHER WAY AROUND ?!
WHO'S THE ONE GETTING AHEAD THERE ?!
HEY...
WHAT...
...SHOULD I DO?
WHAT'S MY ACTUAL ...
...NEXT STEP?
MY NEXT MOVE?

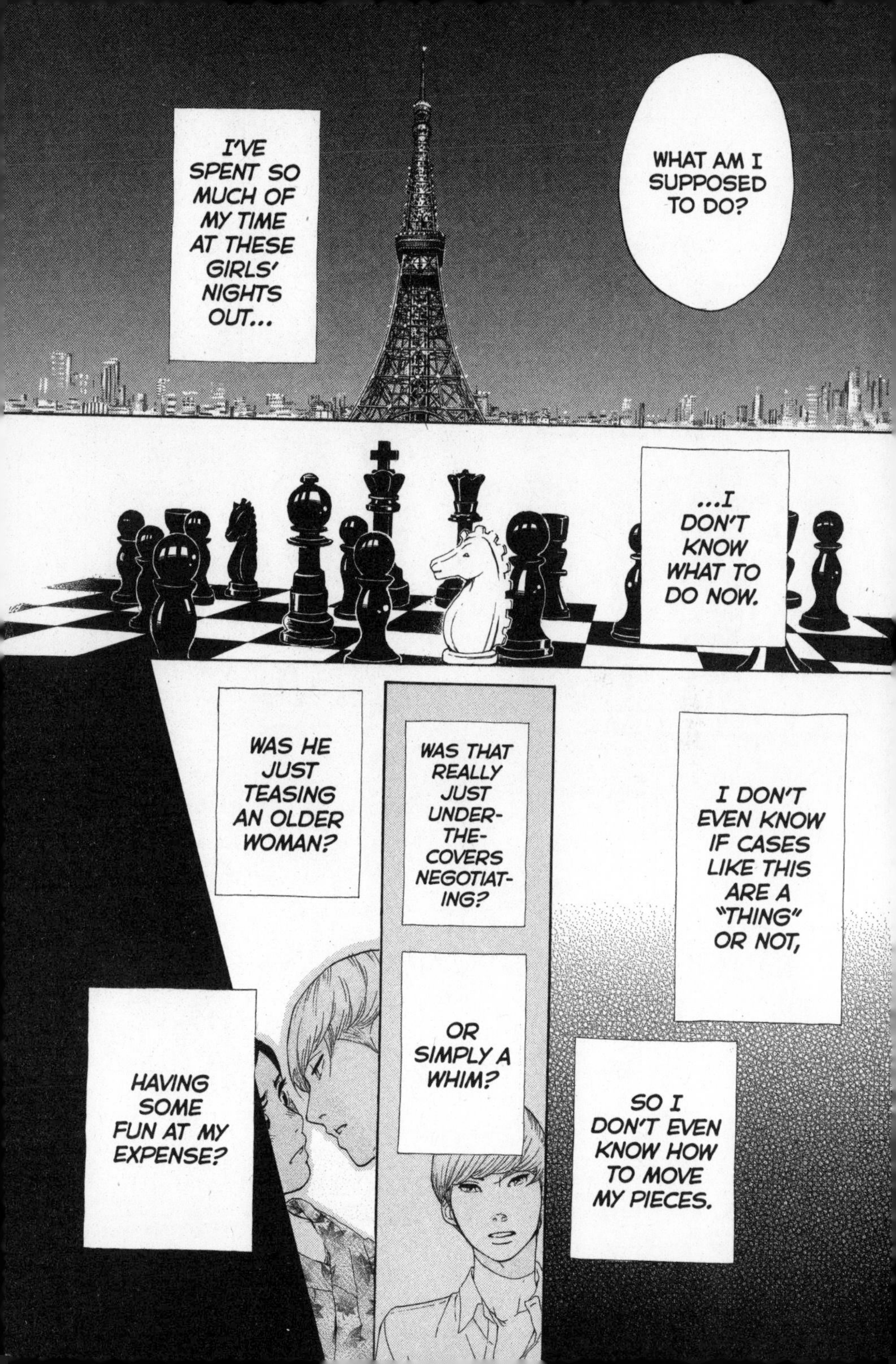
WHAT AM I SUPPOSED TO DO?
I'VE SPENT SO MUCH OF MY TIME AT THESE GIRLS' NIGHTS OUT...
...I DON'T KNOW WHAT TO DO NOW.
I DON'T EVEN KNOW IF CASES LIKE THIS ARE A "THING" OR NOT,
SO I DON'T EVEN KNOW HOW TO MOVE MY PIECES.
WAS THAT REALLY JUST UNDER-THE-COVERS NEGOTIATING?
OR SIMPLY A WHIM?
WAS HE JUST TEASING AN OLDER WOMAN?
HAVING SOME FUN AT MY EXPENSE?

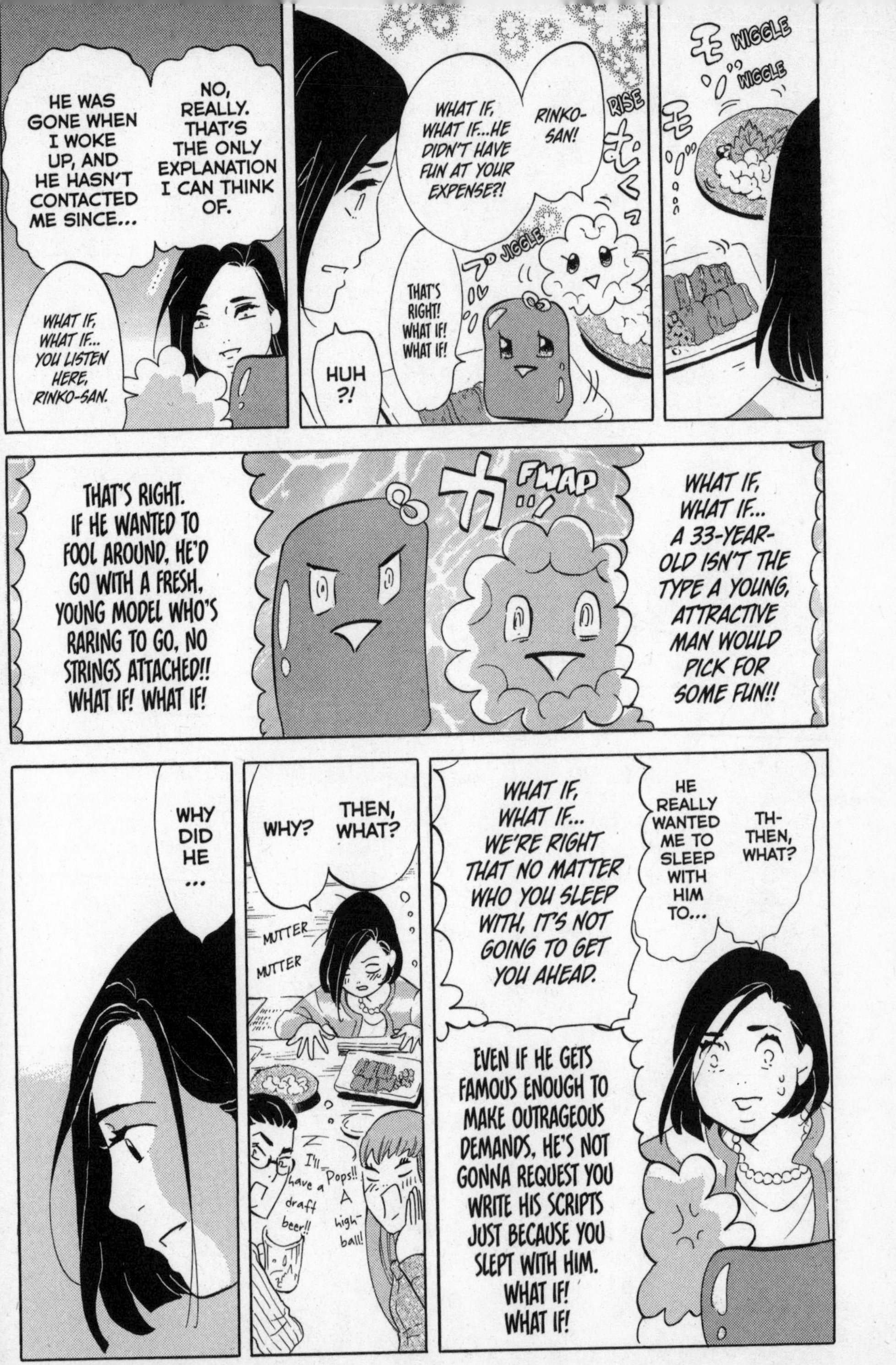
WIGGLE
WIGGLE
RISE
RINKO-SAN!
WHAT IF, WHAT IF...HE DIDN'T HAVE FUN AT YOUR EXPENSE?!
JIGGLE
THAT'S RIGHT! WHAT IF! WHAT IF!
HUH ?!
NO, REALLY. THAT'S THE ONLY EXPLANATION I CAN THINK OF.
HE WAS GONE WHEN I WOKE UP, AND HE HASN'T CONTACTED ME SINCE...
WHAT IF, WHAT IF... YOU LISTEN HERE, RINKO-SAN.
WHAT IF, WHAT IF... A 33-YEAR-OLD ISN'T THE TYPE A YOUNG, ATTRACTIVE MAN WOULD PICK FOR SOME FUN!!
FWAP
THAT'S RIGHT. IF HE WANTED TO FOOL AROUND, HE'D GO WITH A FRESH, YOUNG MODEL WHO'S RARING TO GO, NO STRINGS ATTACHED!! WHAT IF! WHAT IF!
TH-THEN, WHAT?
HE REALLY WANTED ME TO SLEEP WITH HIM TO...
WHAT IF, WHAT IF... WE'RE RIGHT THAT NO MATTER WHO YOU SLEEP WITH, IT'S NOT GOING TO GET YOU AHEAD.
EVEN IF HE GETS FAMOUS ENOUGH TO MAKE OUTRAGEOUS DEMANDS, HE'S NOT GONNA REQUEST YOU WRITE HIS SCRIPTS JUST BECAUSE YOU SLEPT WITH HIM. WHAT IF! WHAT IF!
THEN, WHAT?
WHY?
MUTTER
MUTTER
Pops!! A highball!
I'll have a draft beer!!
WHY DID HE ...

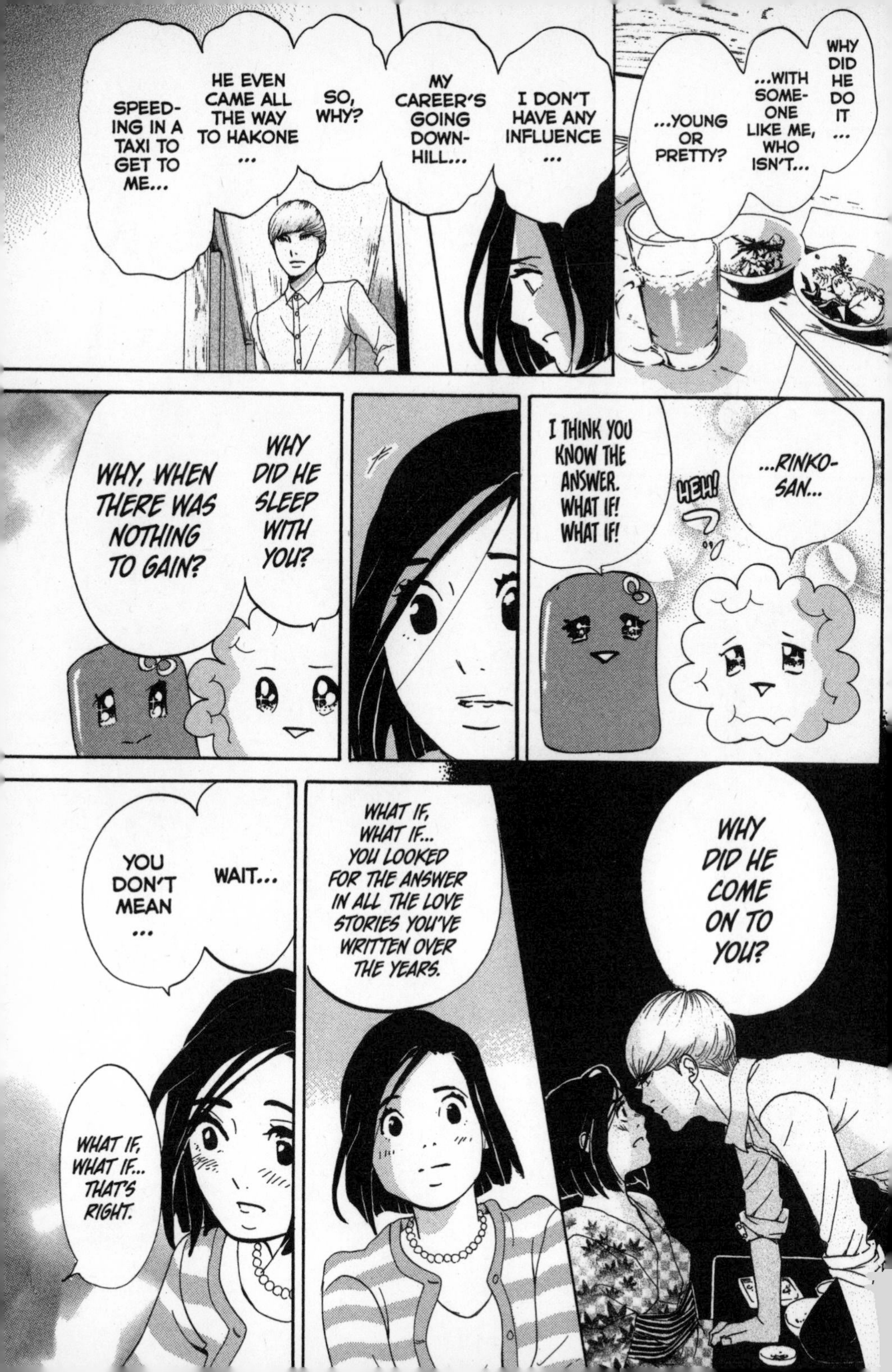
WHY DID HE DO IT ...
...WITH SOME-ONE LIKE ME, WHO ISN'T...
...YOUNG OR PRETTY?
I DON'T HAVE ANY INFLUENCE ...
MY CAREER'S GOING DOWN-HILL...
SO, WHY?
HE EVEN CAME ALL THE WAY TO HAKONE ...
SPEED-ING IN A TAXI TO GET TO ME...
...RINKO-SAN...
HEH!
I THINK YOU KNOW THE ANSWER. WHAT IF! WHAT IF!
WHY DID HE SLEEP WITH YOU?
WHY, WHEN THERE WAS NOTHING TO GAIN?
WHY DID HE COME ON TO YOU?
WHAT IF, WHAT IF... YOU LOOKED FOR THE ANSWER IN ALL THE LOVE STORIES YOU'VE WRITTEN OVER THE YEARS.
WAIT...
YOU DON'T MEAN ...
WHAT IF, WHAT IF... THAT'S RIGHT.

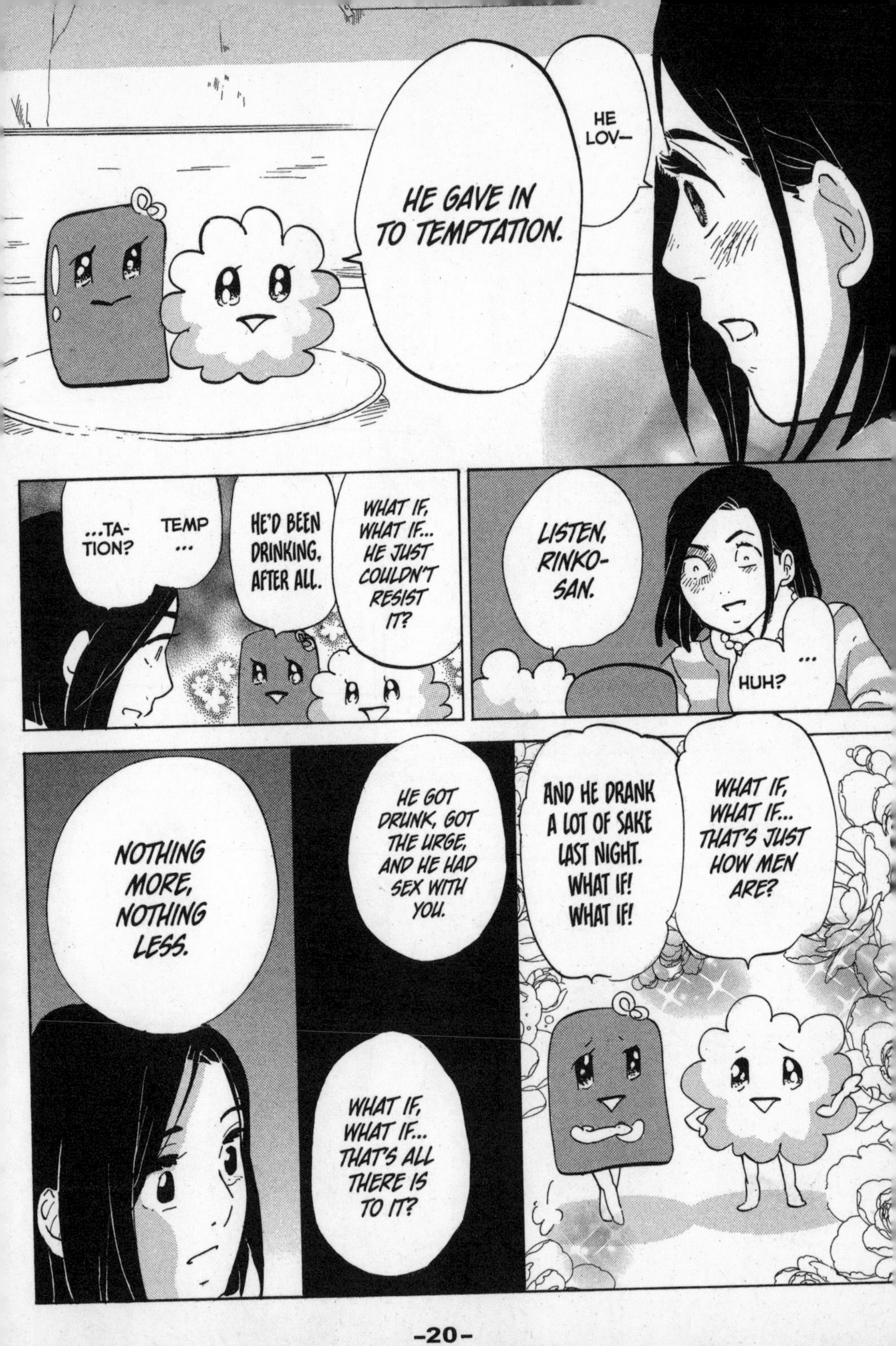
HE LOV—
HE GAVE IN TO TEMPTATION.
LISTEN, RINKO-SAN.
... HUH?
WHAT IF, WHAT IF... HE JUST COULDN'T RESIST IT?
HE'D BEEN DRINKING, AFTER ALL.
TEMP ...
...TA- TION?
WHAT IF, WHAT IF... THAT'S JUST HOW MEN ARE?
AND HE DRANK A LOT OF SAKE LAST NIGHT. WHAT IF! WHAT IF!
HE GOT DRUNK, GOT THE URGE, AND HE HAD SEX WITH YOU.
WHAT IF, WHAT IF... THAT'S ALL THERE IS TO IT?
NOTHING MORE, NOTHING LESS.

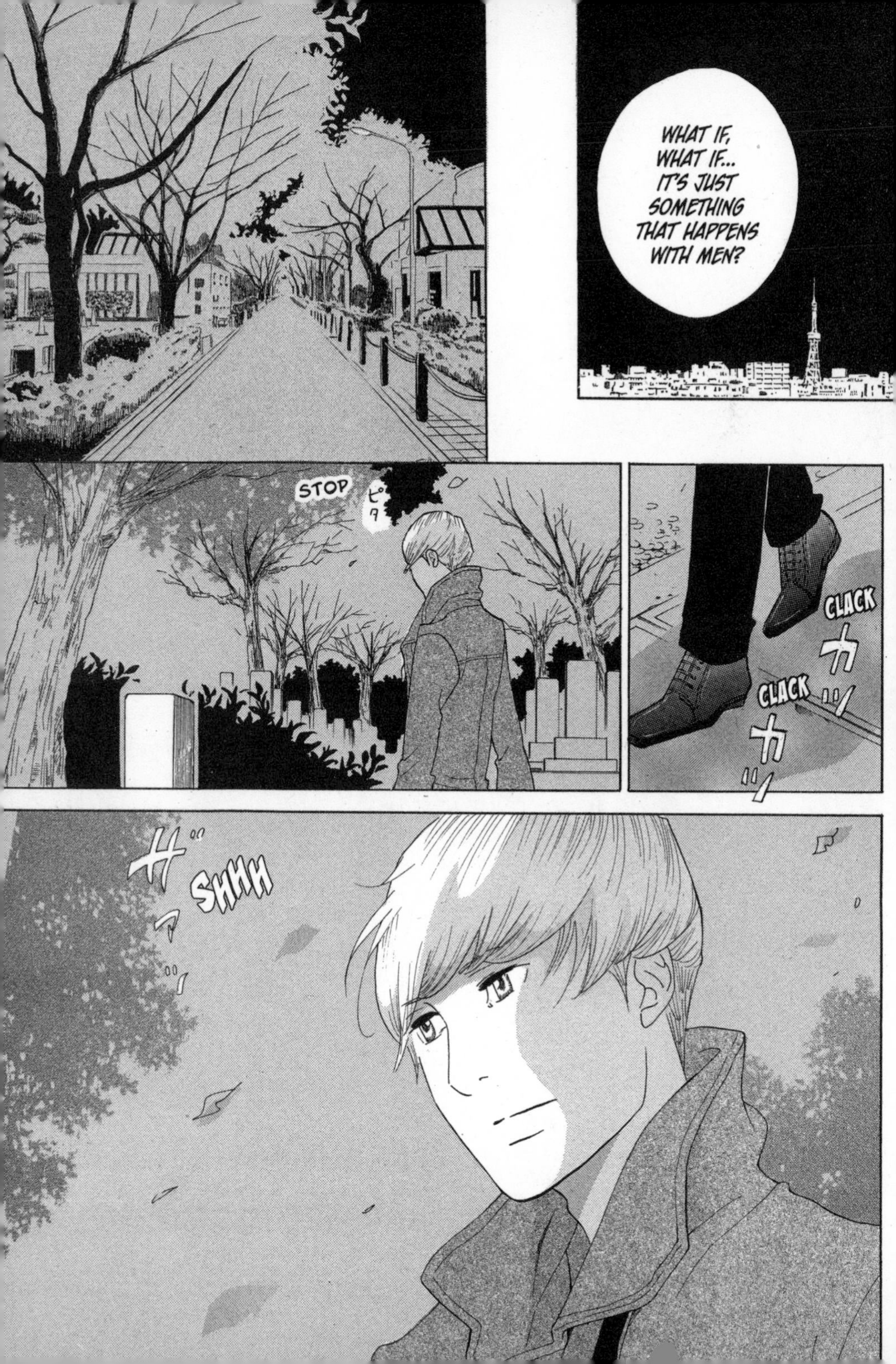
WHAT IF, WHAT IF... IT'S JUST SOMETHING THAT HAPPENS WITH MEN?
CLACK
カツ
CLACK
カツ
STOP
ピタ
SHHH
ザァッ

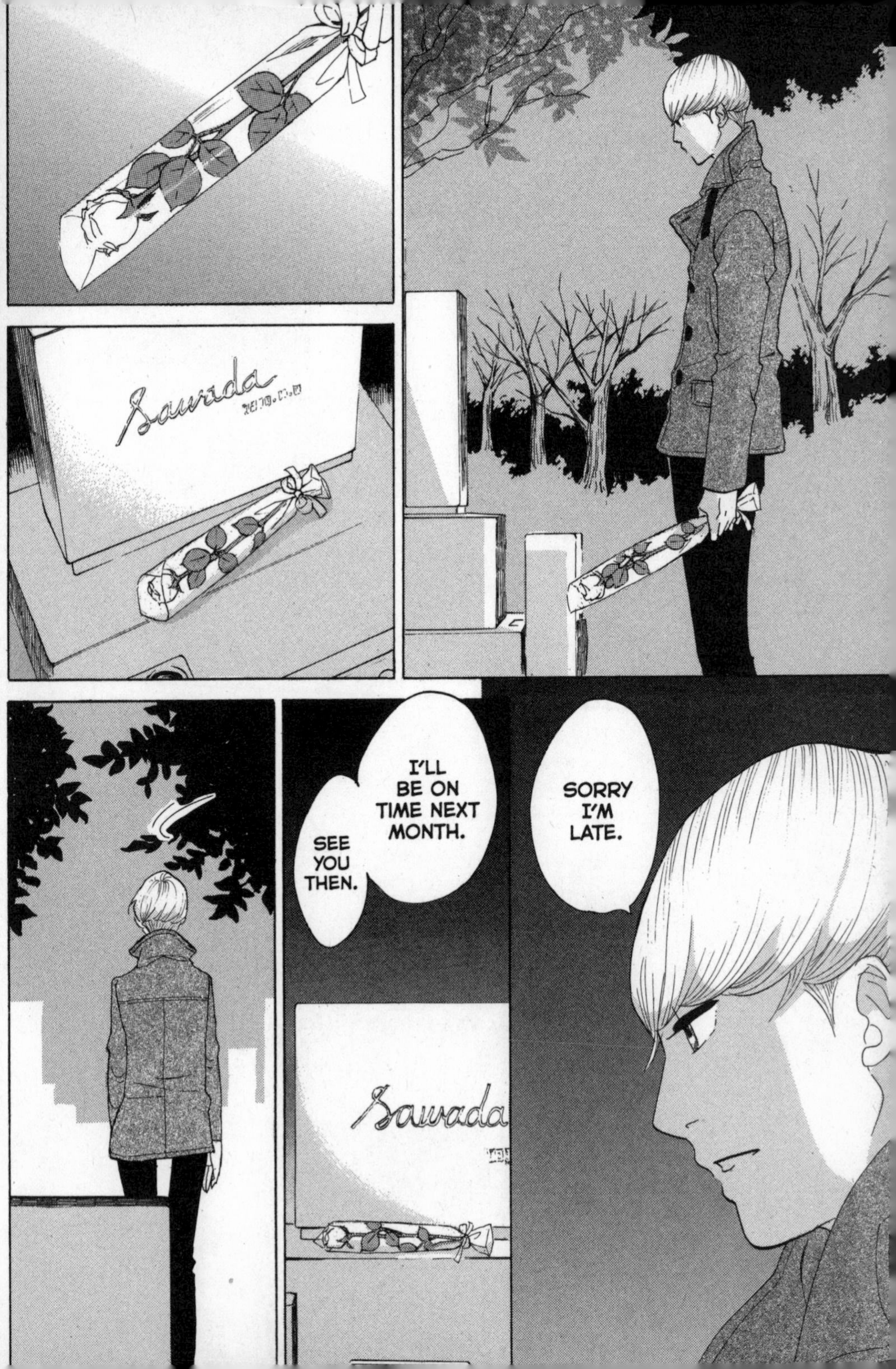
Sawada
SORRY I'M LATE.
I'LL BE ON TIME NEXT MONTH.
SEE YOU THEN.
Sawada

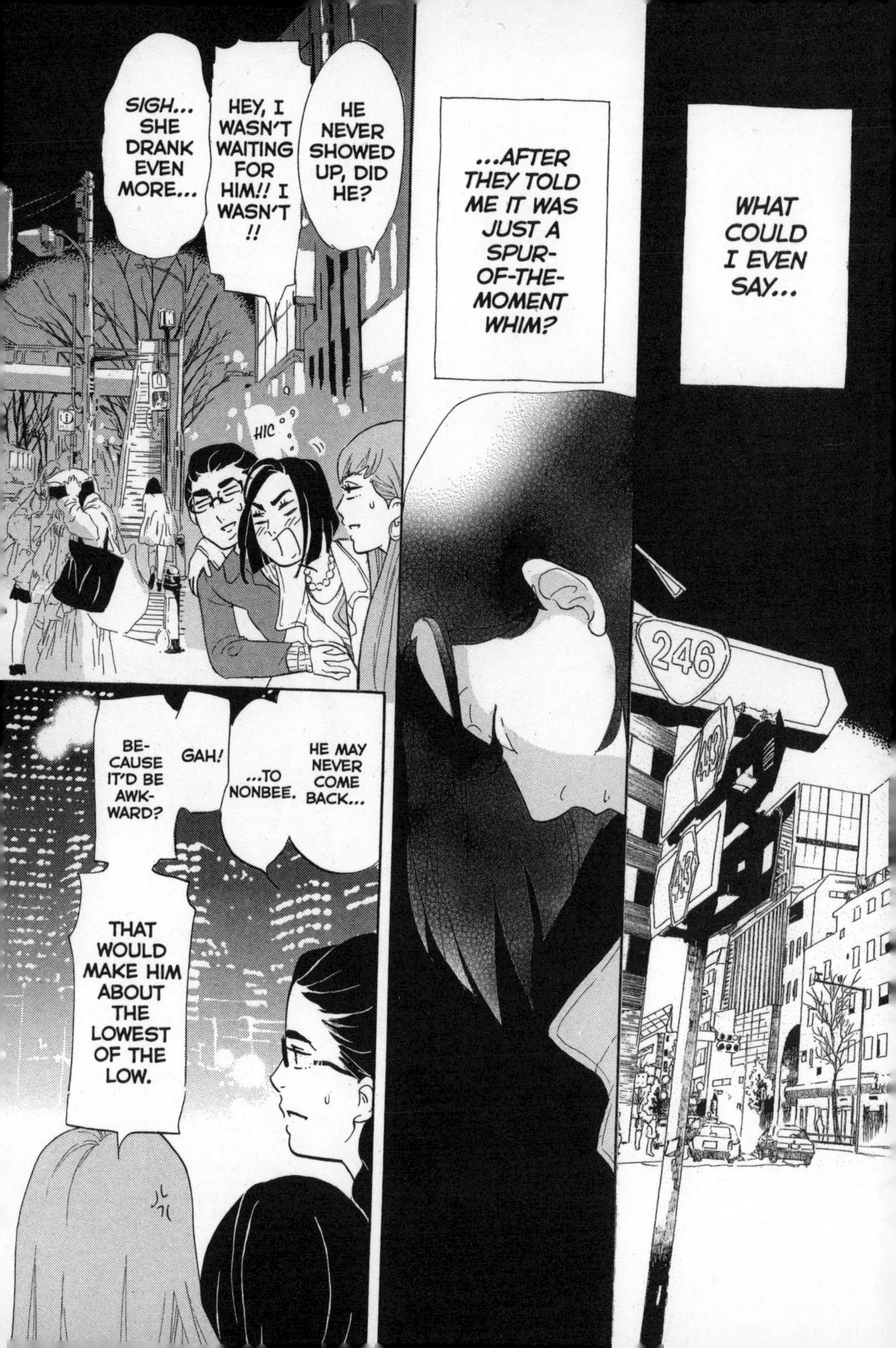
WHAT COULD I EVEN SAY...
...AFTER THEY TOLD ME IT WAS JUST A SPUR-OF-THE-MOMENT WHIM?
246
HE NEVER SHOWED UP, DID HE?
HEY, I WASN'T WAITING FOR HIM!! I WASN'T !!
SIGH... SHE DRANK EVEN MORE...
HIC
HE MAY NEVER COME BACK...
...TO NONBEE.
GAH!
BE-CAUSE IT'D BE AWK-WARD?
THAT WOULD MAKE HIM ABOUT THE LOWEST OF THE LOW.

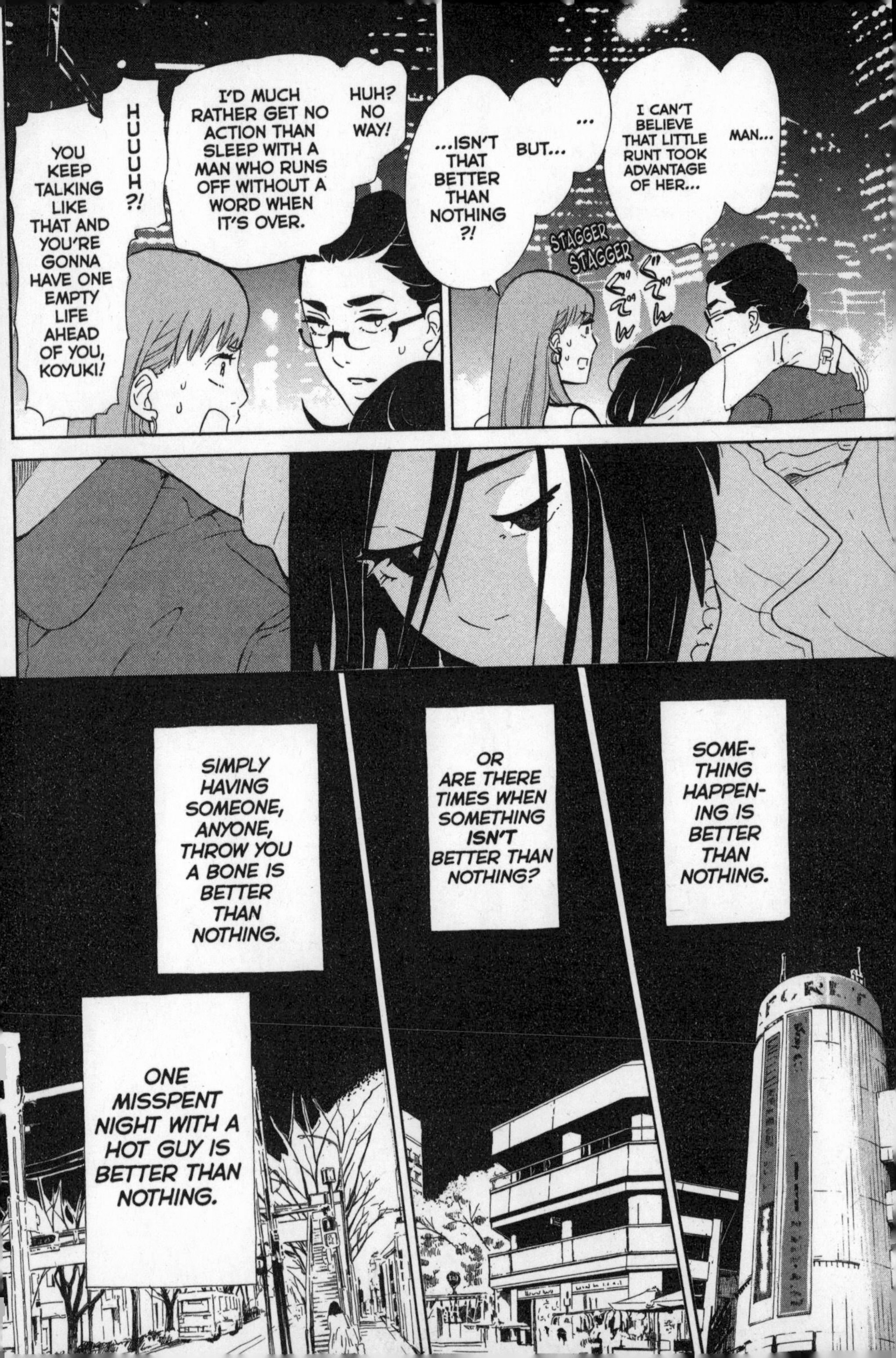
MAN...
I CAN'T BELIEVE THAT LITTLE RUNT TOOK ADVANTAGE OF HER...
...
BUT...
...ISN'T THAT BETTER THAN NOTHING?!
STAGGER STAGGER
ぐでん ぐでん
HUH? NO WAY!
I'D MUCH RATHER GET NO ACTION THAN SLEEP WITH A MAN WHO RUNS OFF WITHOUT A WORD WHEN IT'S OVER.
HUUUUH?!
YOU KEEP TALKING LIKE THAT AND YOU'RE GONNA HAVE ONE EMPTY LIFE AHEAD OF YOU, KOYUKI!
SOME-THING HAPPEN-ING IS BETTER THAN NOTHING.
OR ARE THERE TIMES WHEN SOMETHING *ISN'T* BETTER THAN NOTHING?
SIMPLY HAVING SOMEONE, ANYONE, THROW YOU A BONE IS BETTER THAN NOTHING.
ONE MISSPENT NIGHT WITH A HOT GUY IS BETTER THAN NOTHING.

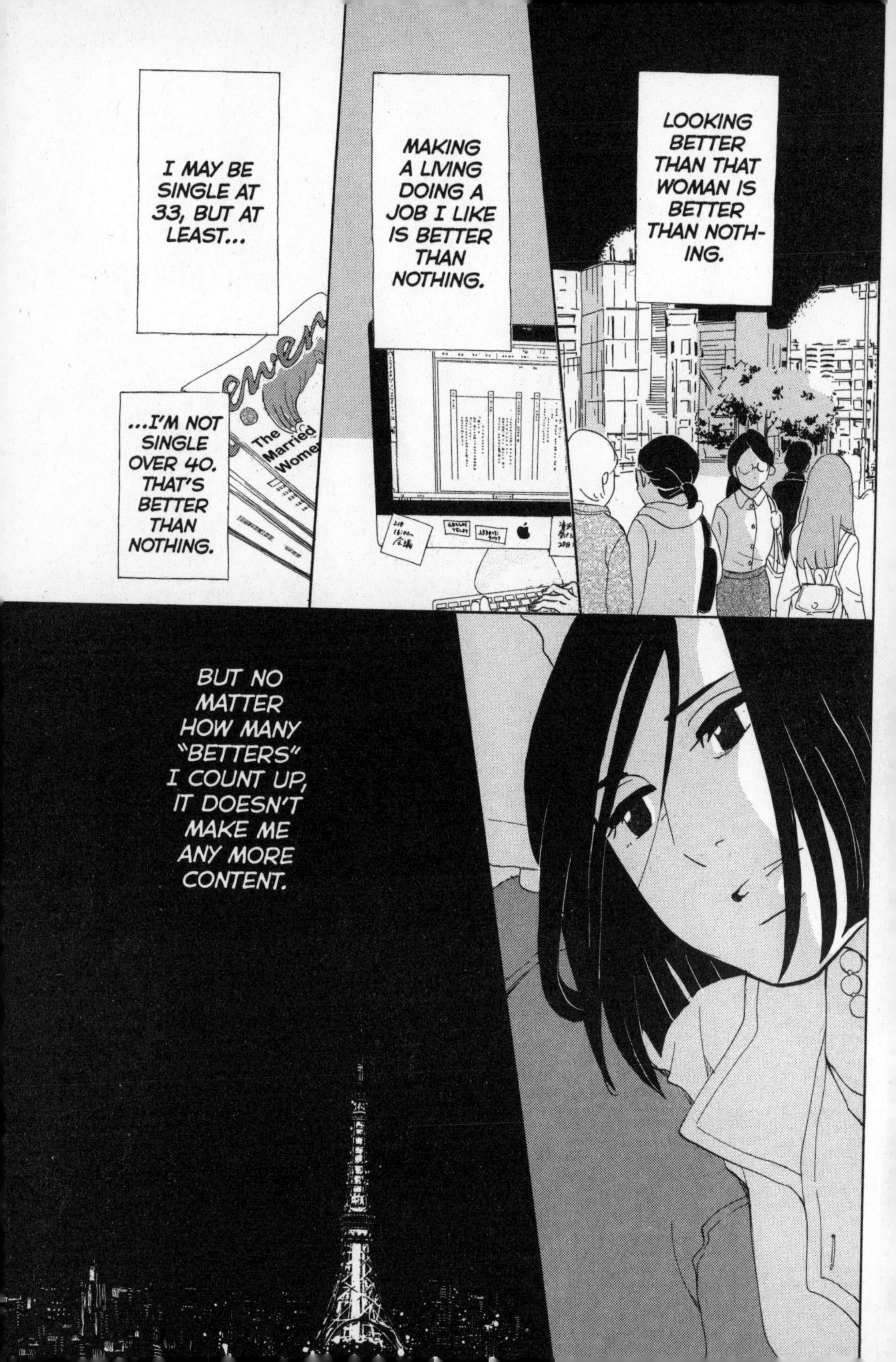
LOOKING BETTER THAN THAT WOMAN IS BETTER THAN NOTH-ING.
MAKING A LIVING DOING A JOB I LIKE IS BETTER THAN NOTHING.
I MAY BE SINGLE AT 33, BUT AT LEAST...
...I'M NOT SINGLE OVER 40. THAT'S BETTER THAN NOTHING.
BUT NO MATTER HOW MANY "BETTERS" I COUNT UP, IT DOESN'T MAKE ME ANY MORE CONTENT.

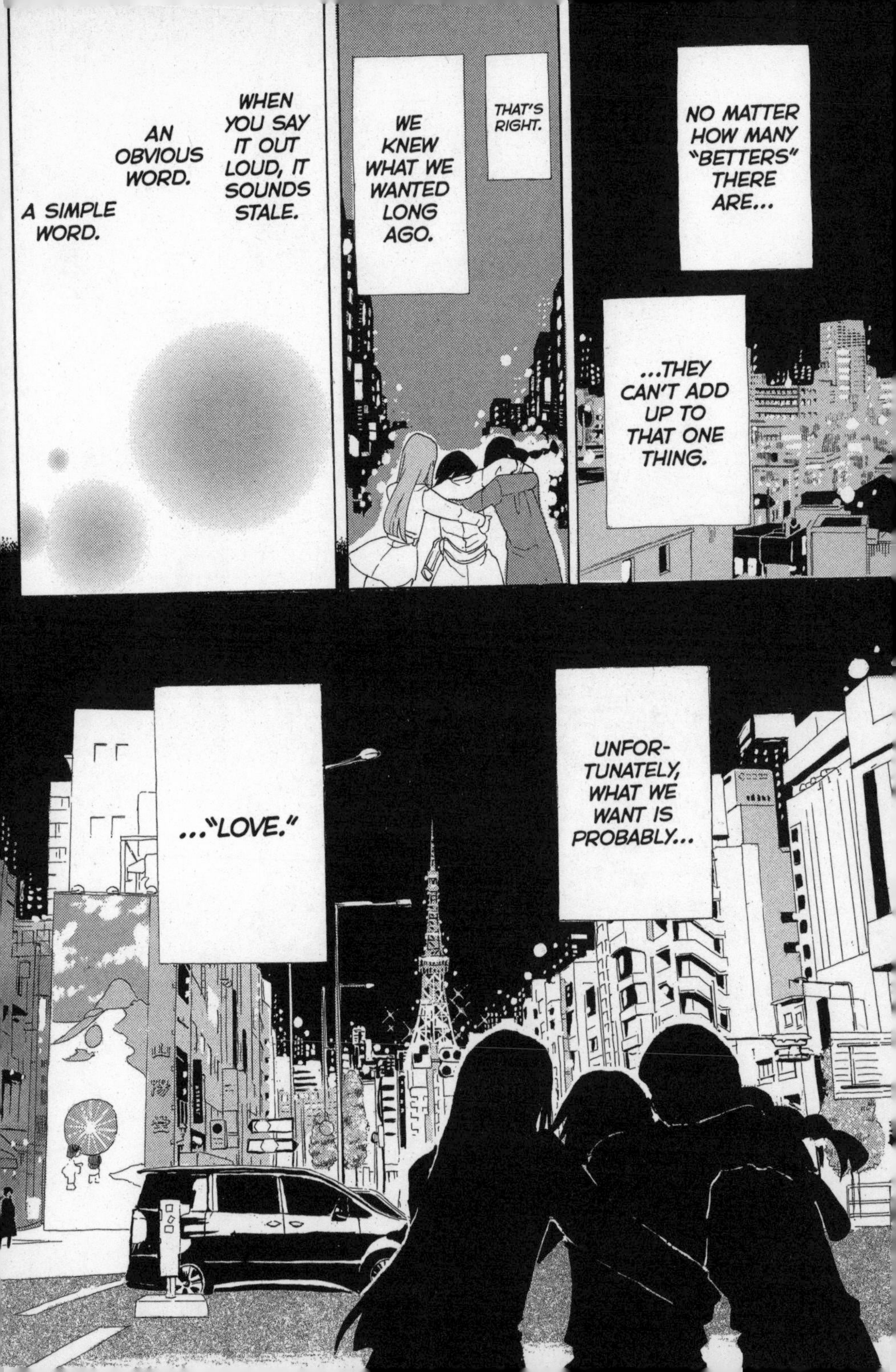
NO MATTER HOW MANY "BETTERS" THERE ARE...
...THEY CAN'T ADD UP TO THAT ONE THING.
THAT'S RIGHT.
WE KNEW WHAT WE WANTED LONG AGO.
WHEN YOU SAY IT OUT LOUD, IT SOUNDS STALE.
AN OBVIOUS WORD.
A SIMPLE WORD.
UNFOR-TUNATELY, WHAT WE WANT IS PROBABLY...
..."LOVE."

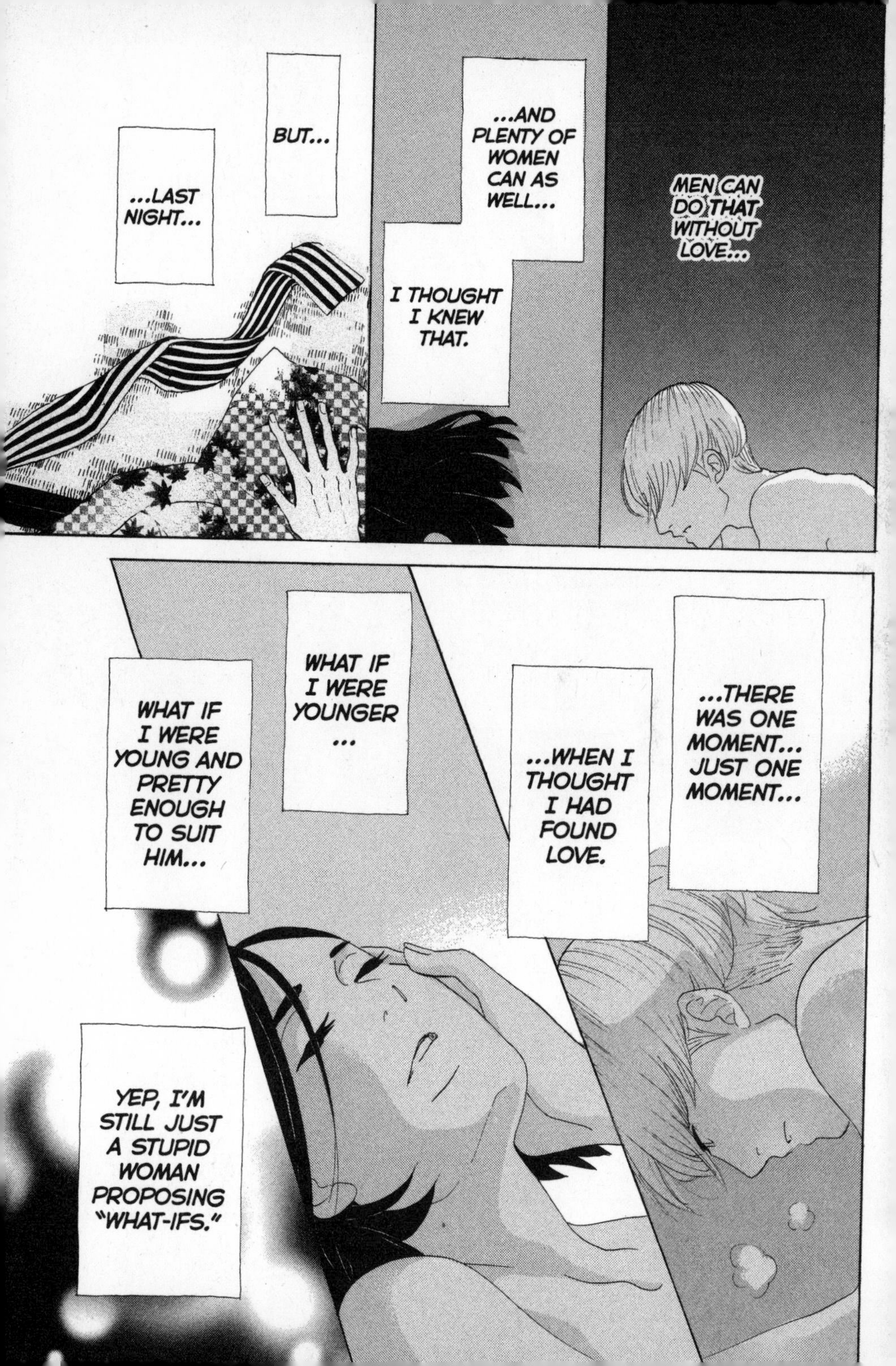
MEN CAN DO THAT WITHOUT LOVE...
...AND PLENTY OF WOMEN CAN AS WELL...
I THOUGHT I KNEW THAT.
BUT...
...LAST NIGHT...
...THERE WAS ONE MOMENT... JUST ONE MOMENT...
...WHEN I THOUGHT I HAD FOUND LOVE.
WHAT IF I WERE YOUNGER ...
WHAT IF I WERE YOUNG AND PRETTY ENOUGH TO SUIT HIM...
YEP, I'M STILL JUST A STUPID WOMAN PROPOSING "WHAT-IFS."

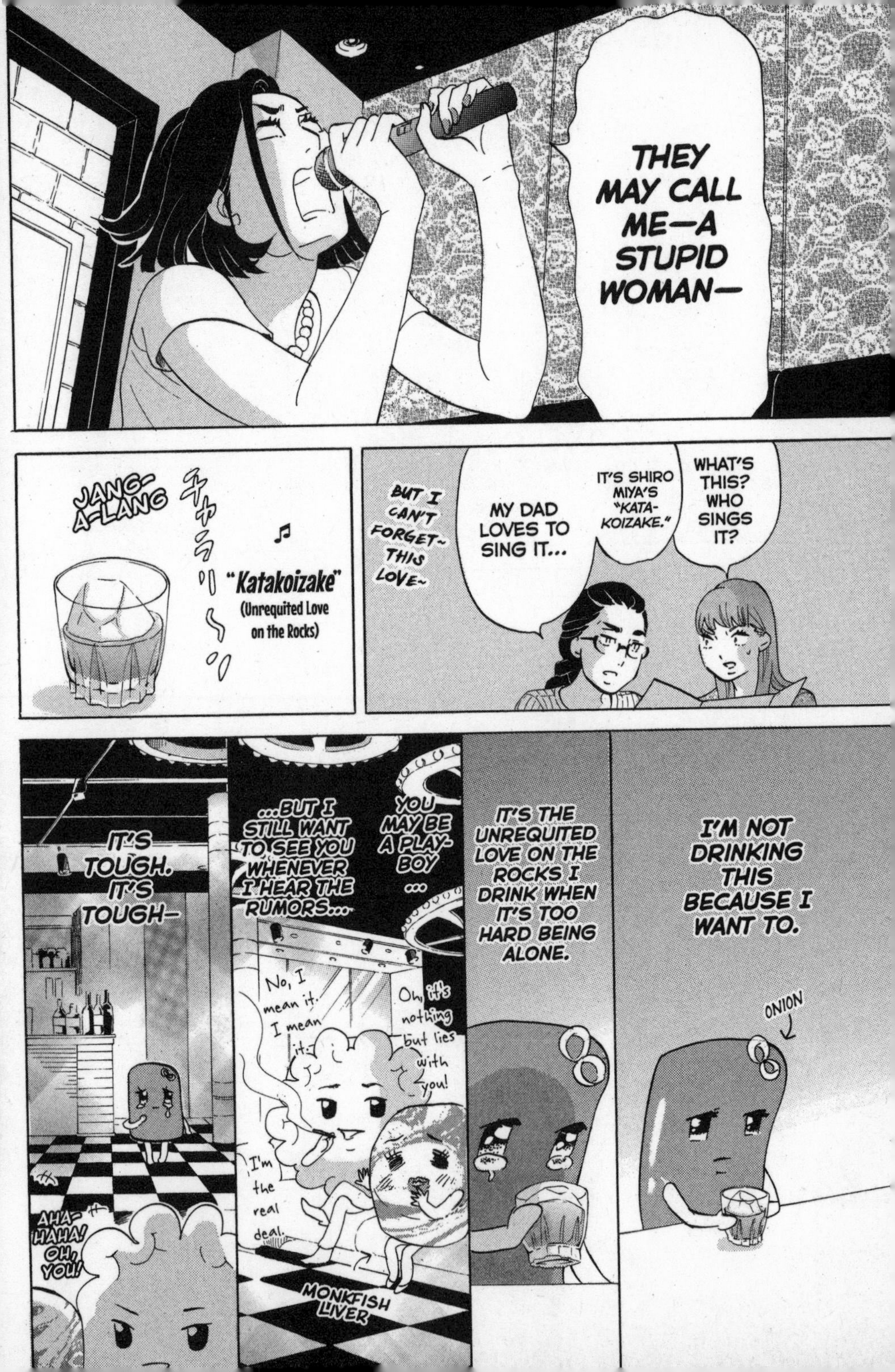
THEY MAY CALL ME—A STUPID WOMAN—
WHAT'S THIS? WHO SINGS IT?
IT'S SHIRO MIYA'S "KATA-KOIZAKE."
MY DAD LOVES TO SING IT...
BUT I CAN'T FORGET~ THIS LOVE~
JANG-A-LANG
♫ "Katakoizake"
(Unrequited Love on the Rocks)
I'M NOT DRINKING THIS BECAUSE I WANT TO.
ONION
IT'S THE UNREQUITED LOVE ON THE ROCKS I DRINK WHEN IT'S TOO HARD BEING ALONE.
YOU MAY BE A PLAY-BOY...
...BUT I STILL WANT TO SEE YOU WHENEVER I HEAR THE RUMORS...
Oh, it's nothing but lies with you!
No, I mean it. I mean it.
I'm the real deal.
MONKFISH LIVER
IT'S TOUGH. IT'S TOUGH—
AHAHAHA! OH, YOU!

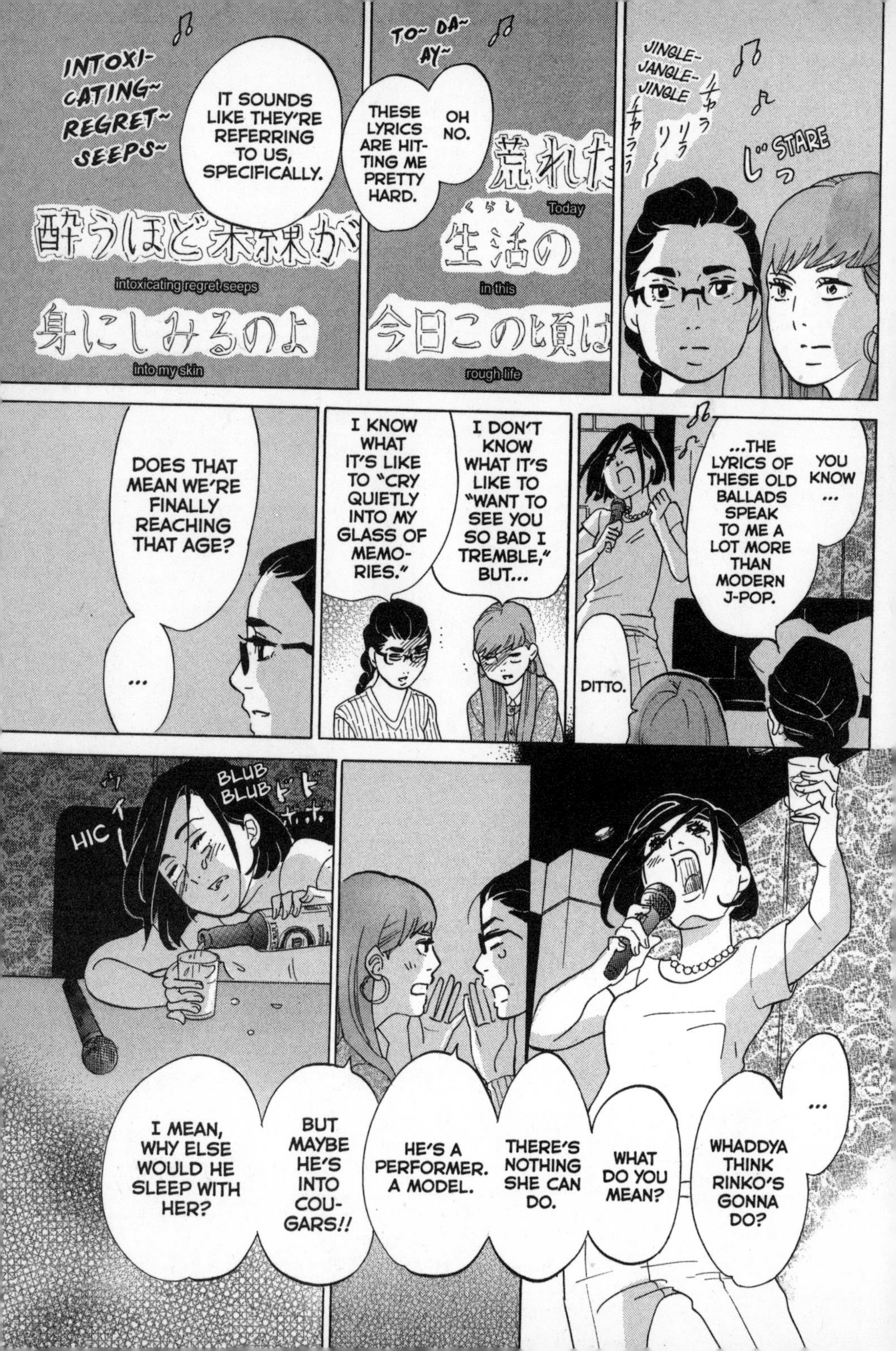
JINGLE-JANGLE-JINGLE
STARE
TO~ DA~ AY~
OH NO.
THESE LYRICS ARE HIT-TING ME PRETTY HARD.
荒れた
Today
くらし
生活の
in this
今日この頃は
rough life
IT SOUNDS LIKE THEY'RE REFERRING TO US, SPECIFICALLY.
INTOXI-CATING~ REGRET~ SEEPS~
酔うほど未練が
intoxicating regret seeps
身にしみるのよ
into my skin
YOU KNOW...
...THE LYRICS OF THESE OLD BALLADS SPEAK TO ME A LOT MORE THAN MODERN J-POP.
DITTO.
I DON'T KNOW WHAT IT'S LIKE TO "WANT TO SEE YOU SO BAD I TREMBLE," BUT...
I KNOW WHAT IT'S LIKE TO "CRY QUIETLY INTO MY GLASS OF MEMO-RIES."
DOES THAT MEAN WE'RE FINALLY REACHING THAT AGE?
...
...
WHADDYA THINK RINKO'S GONNA DO?
WHAT DO YOU MEAN?
THERE'S NOTHING SHE CAN DO.
HE'S A PERFORMER. A MODEL.
BUT MAYBE HE'S INTO COU-GARS!!
I MEAN, WHY ELSE WOULD HE SLEEP WITH HER?
BLUB BLUB
HIC

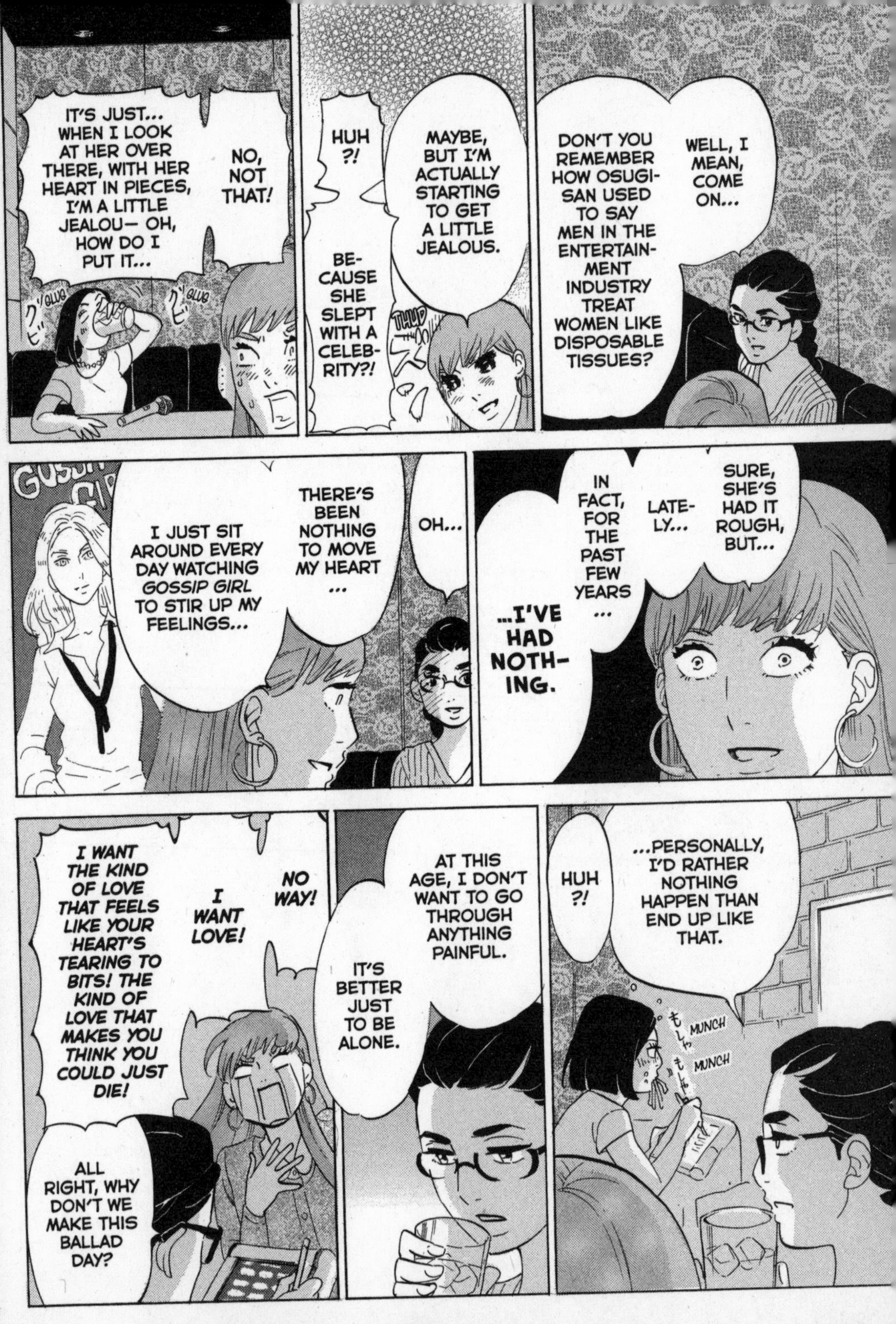
WELL, I MEAN, COME ON...
DON'T YOU REMEMBER HOW OSUGI-SAN USED TO SAY MEN IN THE ENTERTAINMENT INDUSTRY TREAT WOMEN LIKE DISPOSABLE TISSUES?
MAYBE, BUT I'M ACTUALLY STARTING TO GET A LITTLE JEALOUS.
HUH?!
BECAUSE SHE SLEPT WITH A CELEBRITY?!
THUD
NO, NOT THAT!
IT'S JUST... WHEN I LOOK AT HER OVER THERE, WITH HER HEART IN PIECES, I'M A LITTLE JEALOU— OH, HOW DO I PUT IT...
GLUG
GLUG
SURE, SHE'S HAD IT ROUGH, BUT...
LATELY...
IN FACT, FOR THE PAST FEW YEARS...
...I'VE HAD NOTHING.
OH...
THERE'S BEEN NOTHING TO MOVE MY HEART...
I JUST SIT AROUND EVERY DAY WATCHING *GOSSIP GIRL* TO STIR UP MY FEELINGS...
...PERSONALLY, I'D RATHER NOTHING HAPPEN THAN END UP LIKE THAT.
HUH?!
MUNCH
MUNCH
AT THIS AGE, I DON'T WANT TO GO THROUGH ANYTHING PAINFUL.
IT'S BETTER JUST TO BE ALONE.
NO WAY!
I WANT LOVE!
I WANT THE KIND OF LOVE THAT FEELS LIKE YOUR HEART'S TEARING TO BITS! THE KIND OF LOVE THAT MAKES YOU THINK YOU COULD JUST DIE!
ALL RIGHT, WHY DON'T WE MAKE THIS BALLAD DAY?

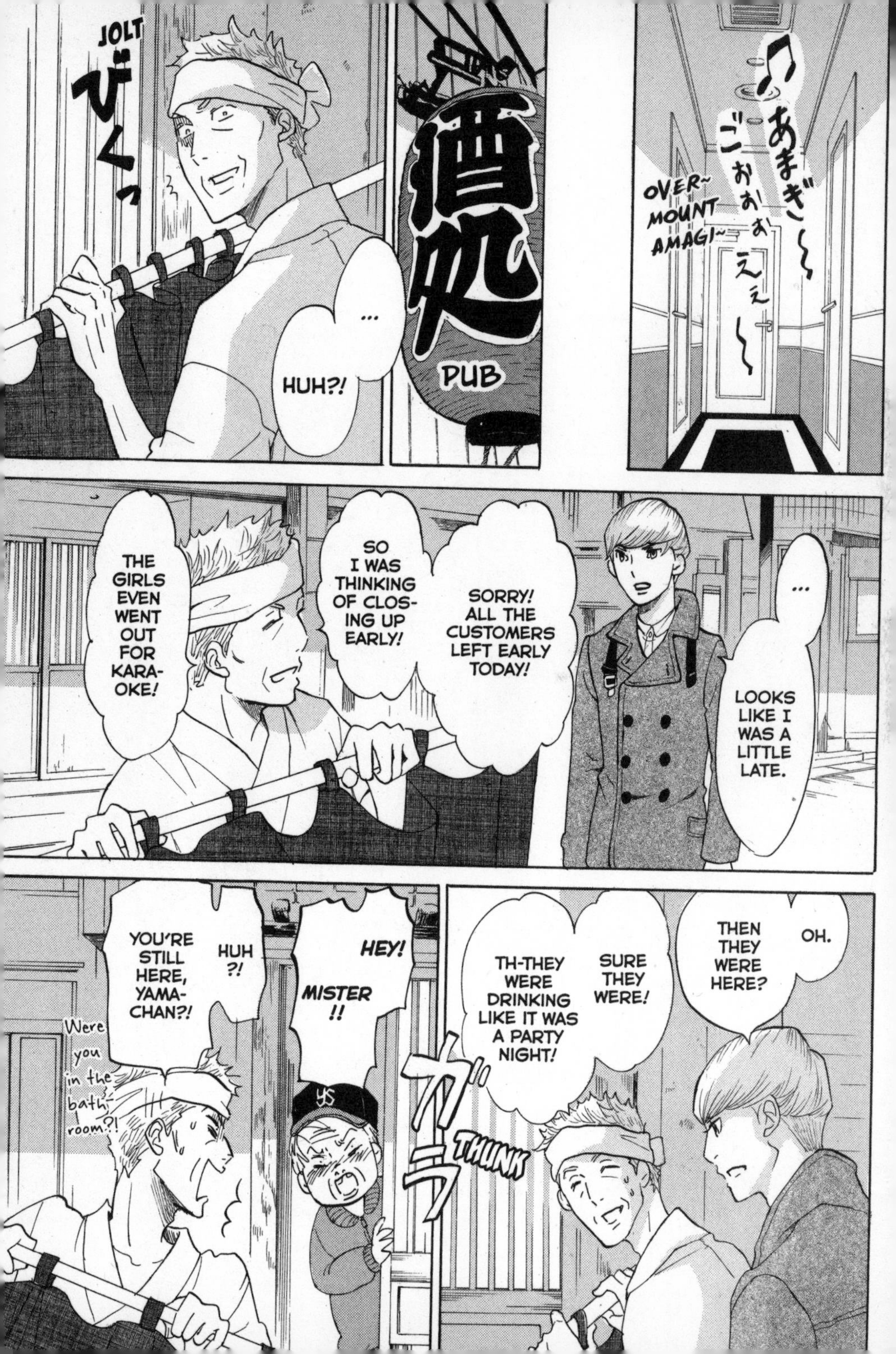

♪あまぎ～
ごおおおえぇ～～
OVER~ MOUNT AMAGI~
酒処
PUB
...
HUH?!
JOLT
びくっ
...
LOOKS LIKE I WAS A LITTLE LATE.
SORRY! ALL THE CUSTOMERS LEFT EARLY TODAY!
SO I WAS THINKING OF CLOS-ING UP EARLY!
THE GIRLS EVEN WENT OUT FOR KARA-OKE!
OH.
THEN THEY WERE HERE?
SURE THEY WERE!
TH-THEY WERE DRINKING LIKE IT WAS A PARTY NIGHT!
ガラ
THUNK
HEY!
MISTER!!
HUH?!
YOU'RE STILL HERE, YAMA-CHAN?!
Were you in the bathroom?!

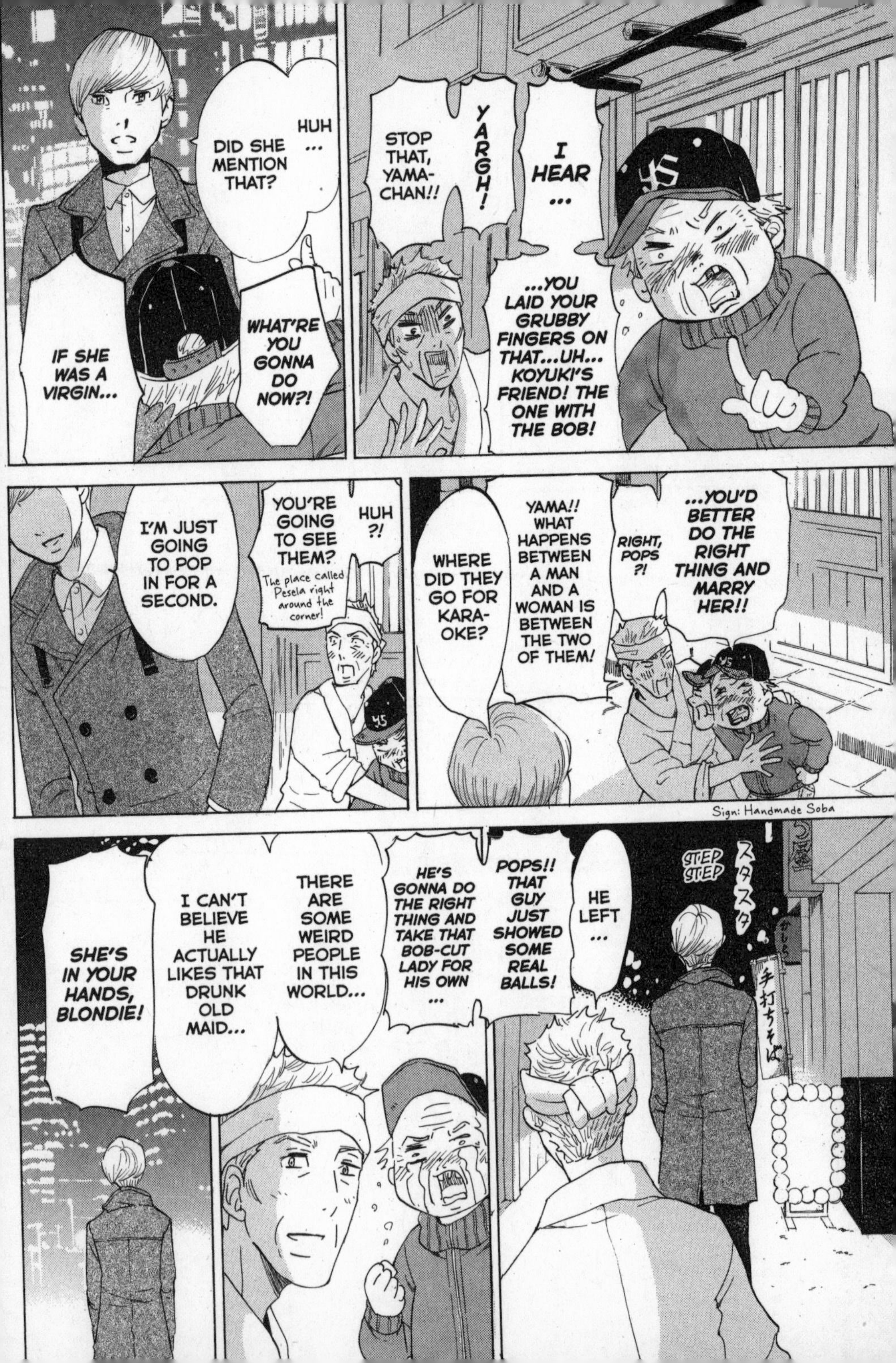
I HEAR ...
...YOU LAID YOUR GRUBBY FINGERS ON THAT...UH... KOYUKI'S FRIEND! THE ONE WITH THE BOB!
YARGH!
STOP THAT, YAMA-CHAN!!
HUH ...
DID SHE MENTION THAT?
WHAT'RE YOU GONNA DO NOW?!
IF SHE WAS A VIRGIN...
...YOU'D BETTER DO THE RIGHT THING AND MARRY HER!!
RIGHT, POPS ?!
YAMA!! WHAT HAPPENS BETWEEN A MAN AND A WOMAN IS BETWEEN THE TWO OF THEM!
WHERE DID THEY GO FOR KARA-OKE?
HUH ?!
YOU'RE GOING TO SEE THEM?
The place called Pesela right around the corner!
I'M JUST GOING TO POP IN FOR A SECOND.
Sign: Handmade Soba
STEP STEP
スタスタ
手打ちそば
HE LEFT ...
POPS!! THAT GUY JUST SHOWED SOME REAL BALLS!
HE'S GONNA DO THE RIGHT THING AND TAKE THAT BOB-CUT LADY FOR HIS OWN ...
THERE ARE SOME WEIRD PEOPLE IN THIS WORLD...
I CAN'T BELIEVE HE ACTUALLY LIKES THAT DRUNK OLD MAID...
SHE'S IN YOUR HANDS, BLONDIE!

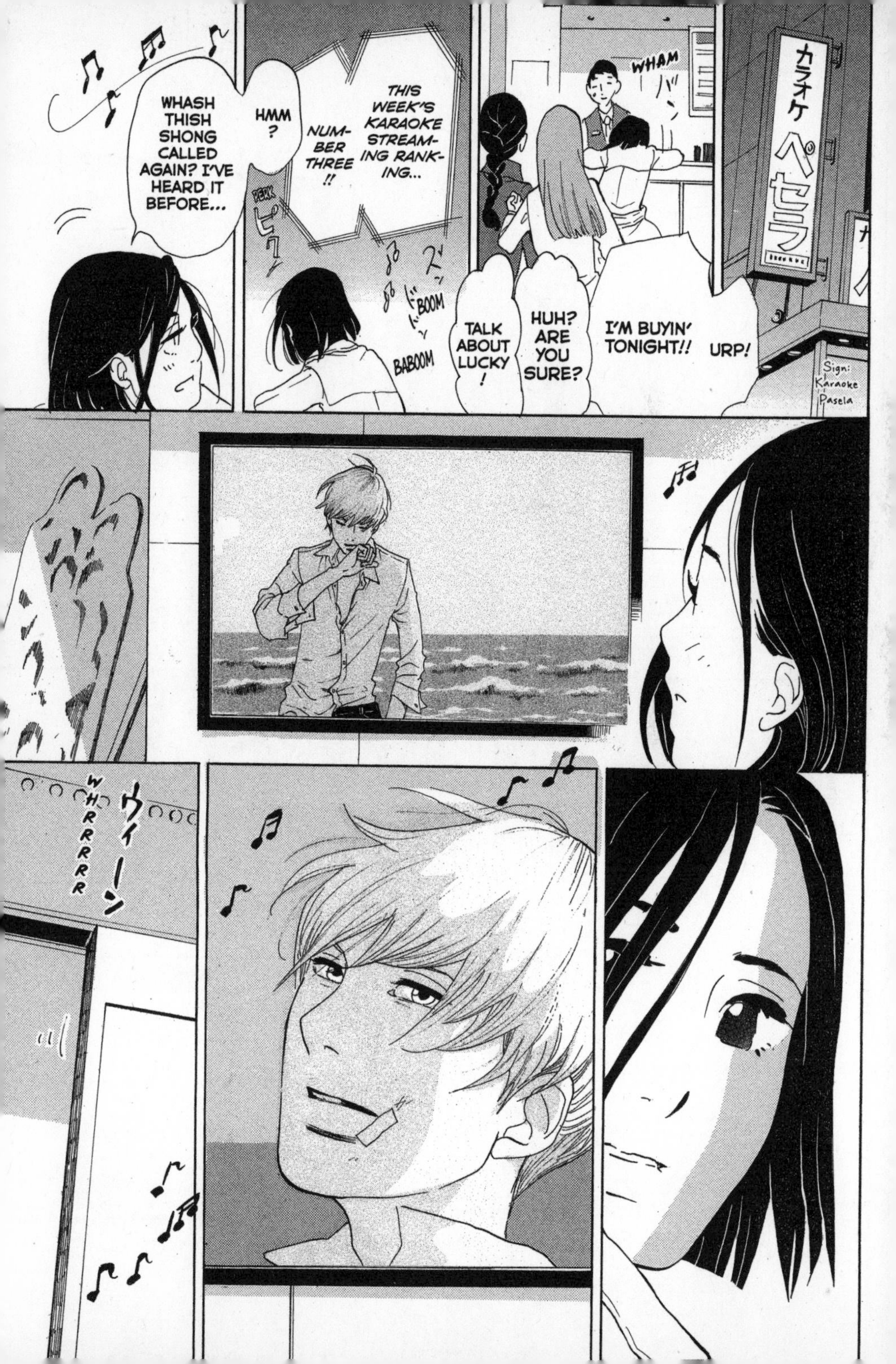
カラオケ ペセラ
Sign: Karaoke Pasela
WHAM
バン
URP!
I'M BUYIN' TONIGHT!!
HUH? ARE YOU SURE?
TALK ABOUT LUCKY!
THIS WEEK'S KARAOKE STREAMING RANKING...
NUMBER THREE!!
BOOM
BABOOM
HMM?
PERK
ピク
WHASH THISH SHONG CALLED AGAIN? I'VE HEARD IT BEFORE...
ウィーン
WHRRRRR

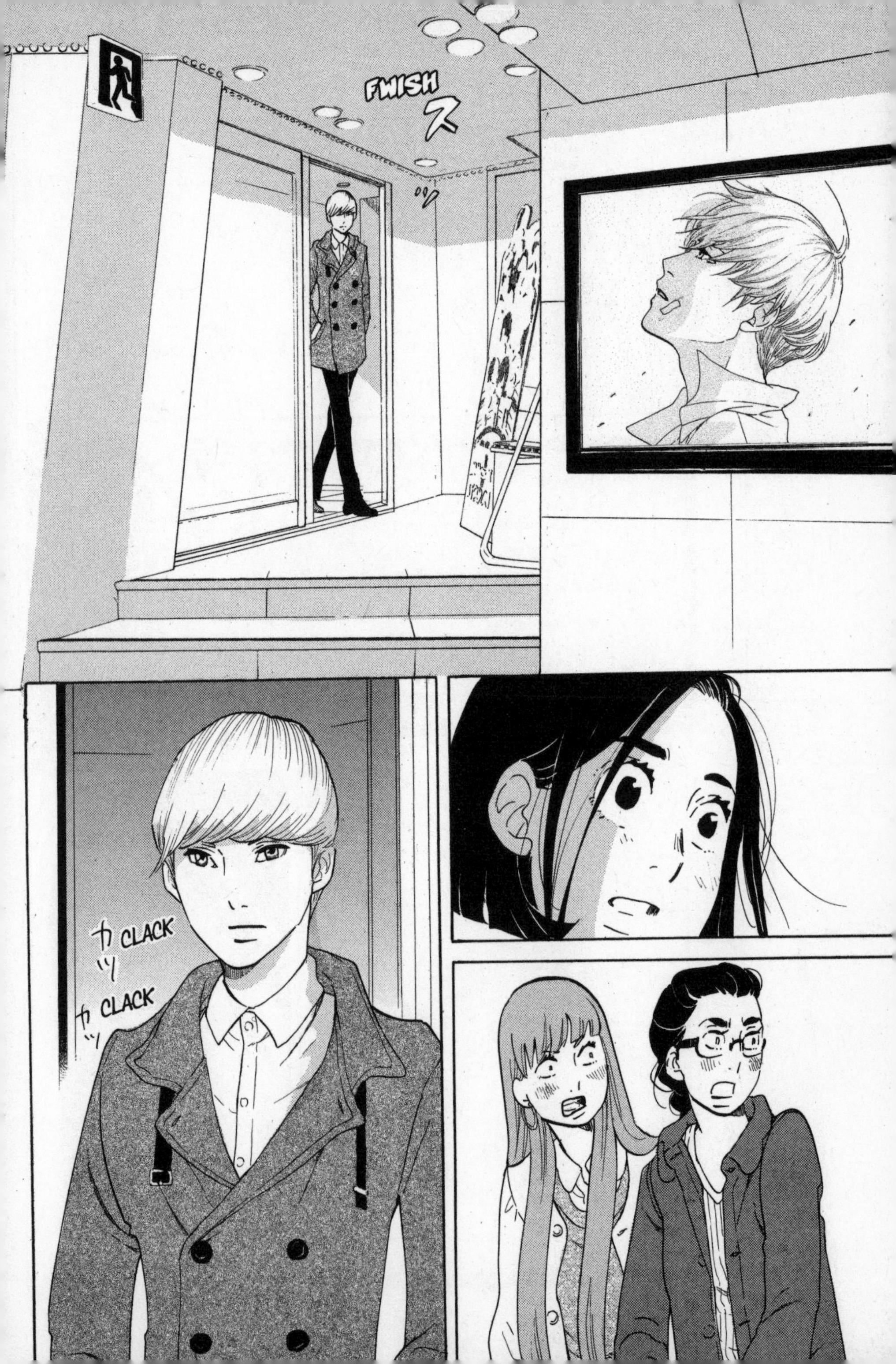
FWISH
ス
ッ
カッ CLACK
カッ CLACK

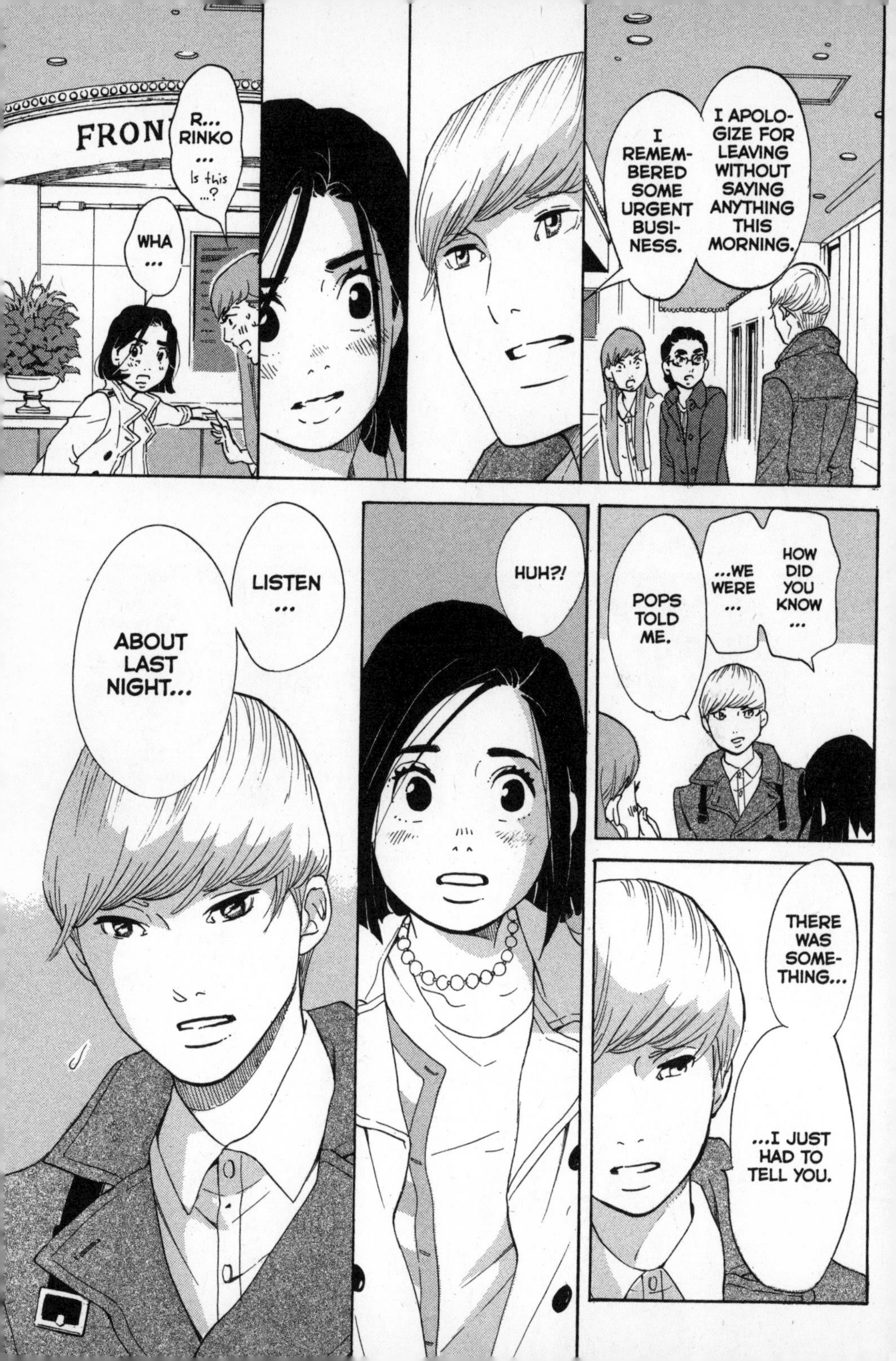
I APOLOGIZE FOR LEAVING WITHOUT SAYING ANYTHING THIS MORNING.
I REMEMBERED SOME URGENT BUSINESS.
FRON
R... RINKO ... Is this ...?
WHA ...
HOW DID YOU KNOW ...
...WE WERE ...
POPS TOLD ME.
THERE WAS SOMETHING...
...I JUST HAD TO TELL YOU.
HUH?!
LISTEN ...
ABOUT LAST NIGHT...

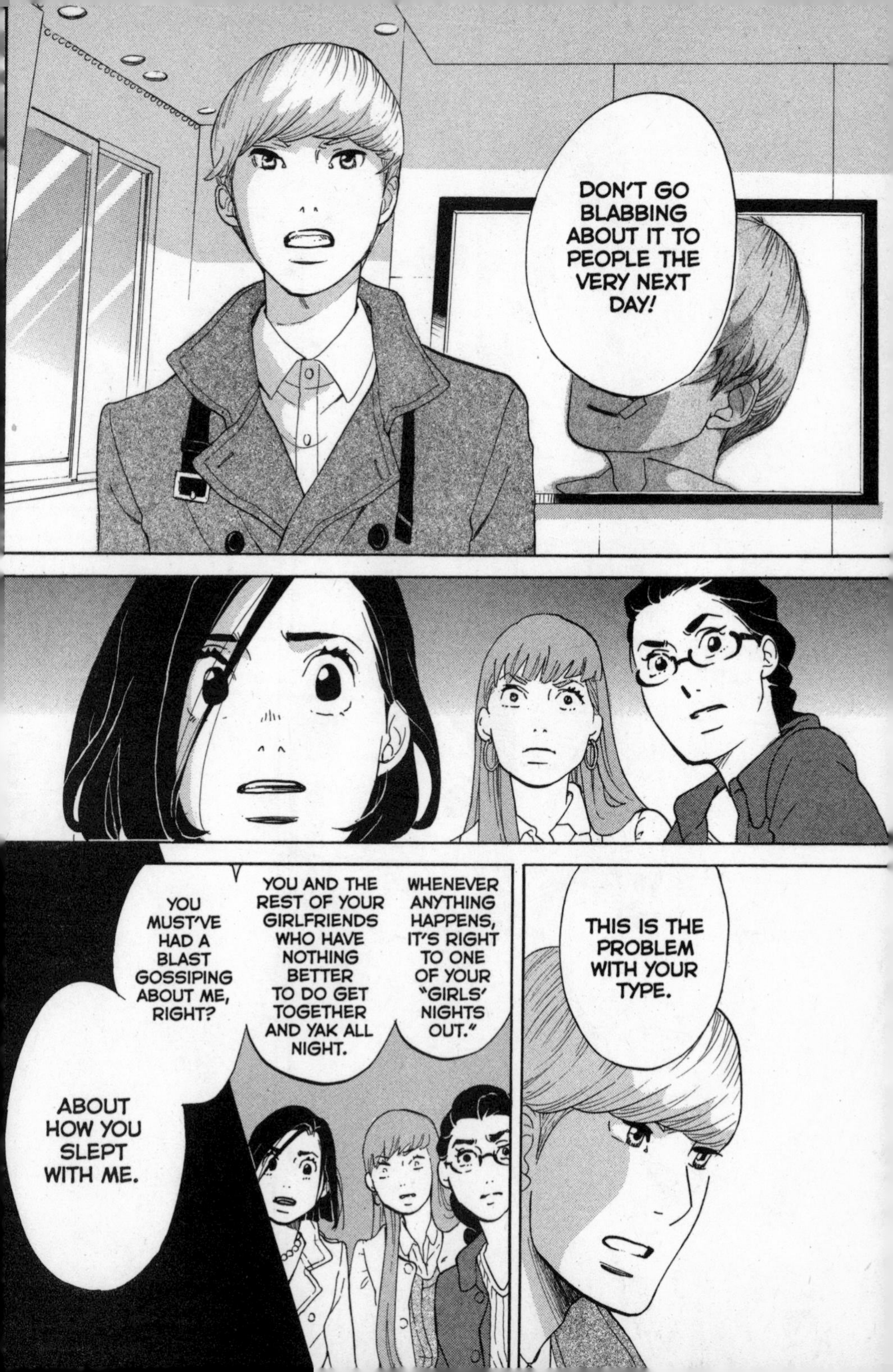
DON'T GO BLABBING ABOUT IT TO PEOPLE THE VERY NEXT DAY!
THIS IS THE PROBLEM WITH YOUR TYPE.
WHENEVER ANYTHING HAPPENS, IT'S RIGHT TO ONE OF YOUR "GIRLS' NIGHTS OUT."
YOU AND THE REST OF YOUR GIRLFRIENDS WHO HAVE NOTHING BETTER TO DO GET TOGETHER AND YAK ALL NIGHT.
YOU MUST'VE HAD A BLAST GOSSIPING ABOUT ME, RIGHT?
ABOUT HOW YOU SLEPT WITH ME.

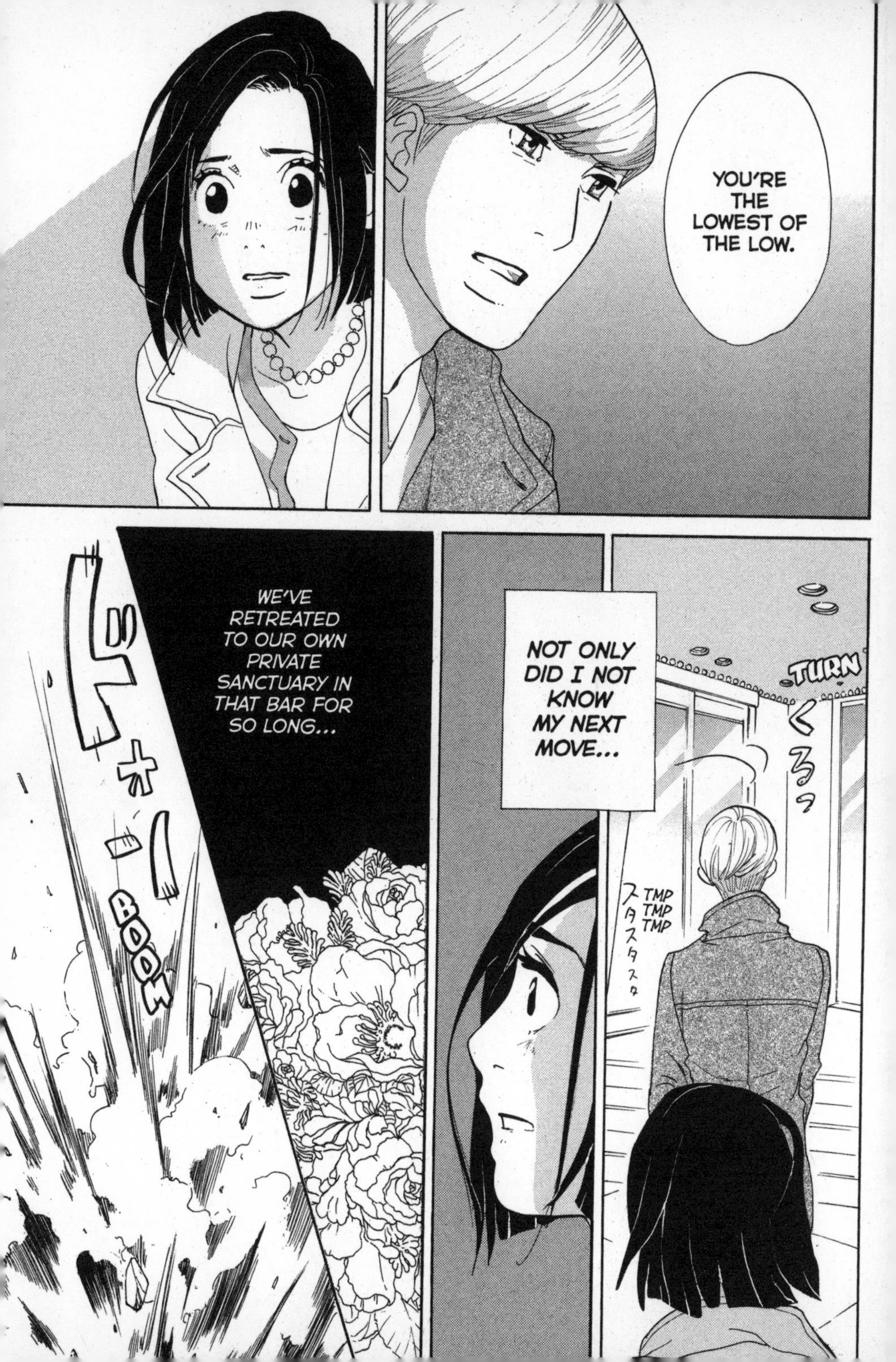
YOU'RE THE LOWEST OF THE LOW.
NOT ONLY DID I NOT KNOW MY NEXT MOVE...
TURN
くるっ
TMP TMP TMP
スタスタ
WE'VE RETREATED TO OUR OWN PRIVATE SANCTUARY IN THAT BAR FOR SO LONG...
BOOM

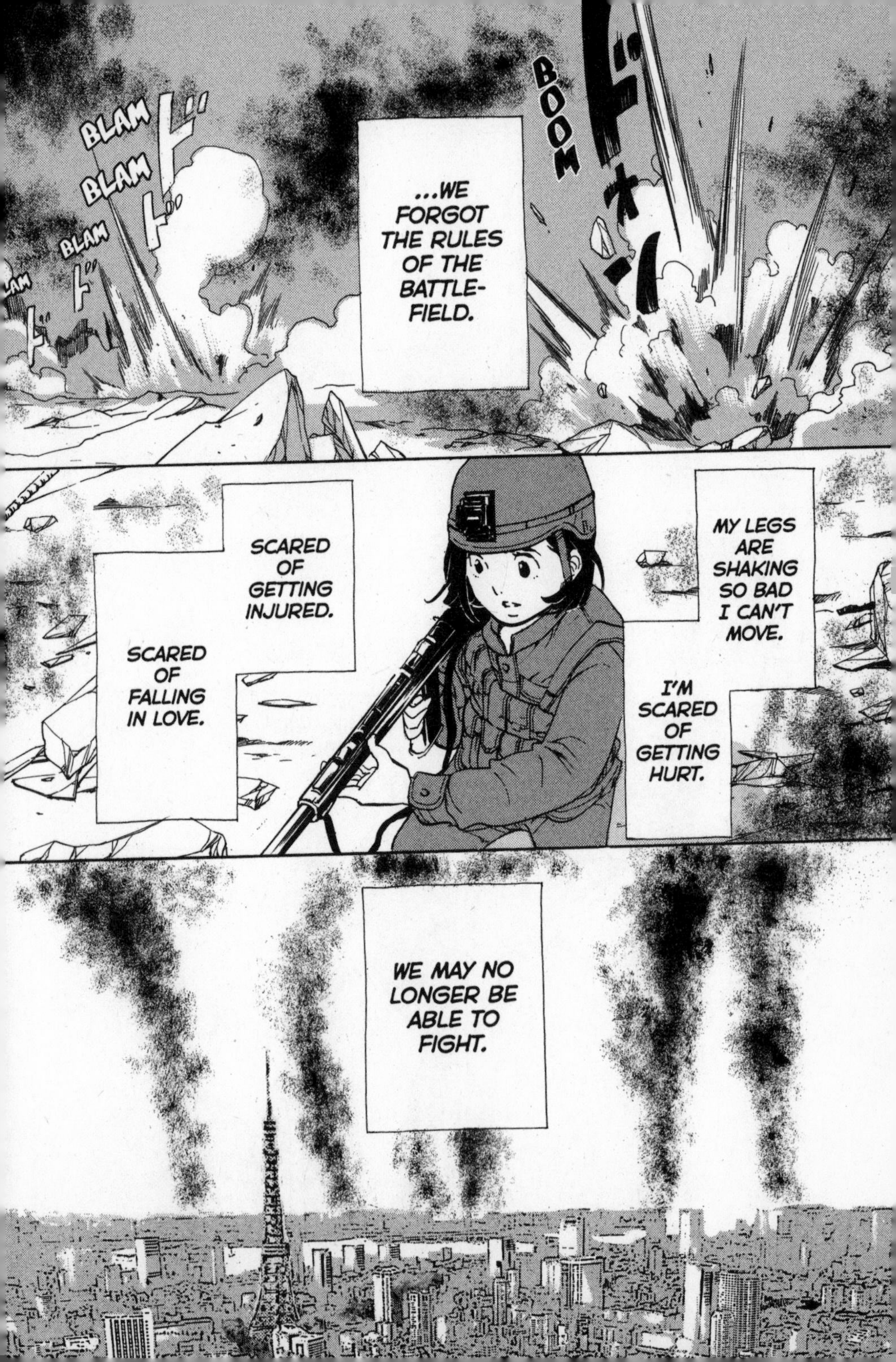
BOOM
...WE FORGOT THE RULES OF THE BATTLE-FIELD.
BLAM
BLAM
BLAM
BLAM
MY LEGS ARE SHAKING SO BAD I CAN'T MOVE.
I'M SCARED OF GETTING HURT.
SCARED OF GETTING INJURED.
SCARED OF FALLING IN LOVE.
WE MAY NO LONGER BE ABLE TO FIGHT.

# ACT 6 CONVEYOR-BELT SUSHI WOMAN

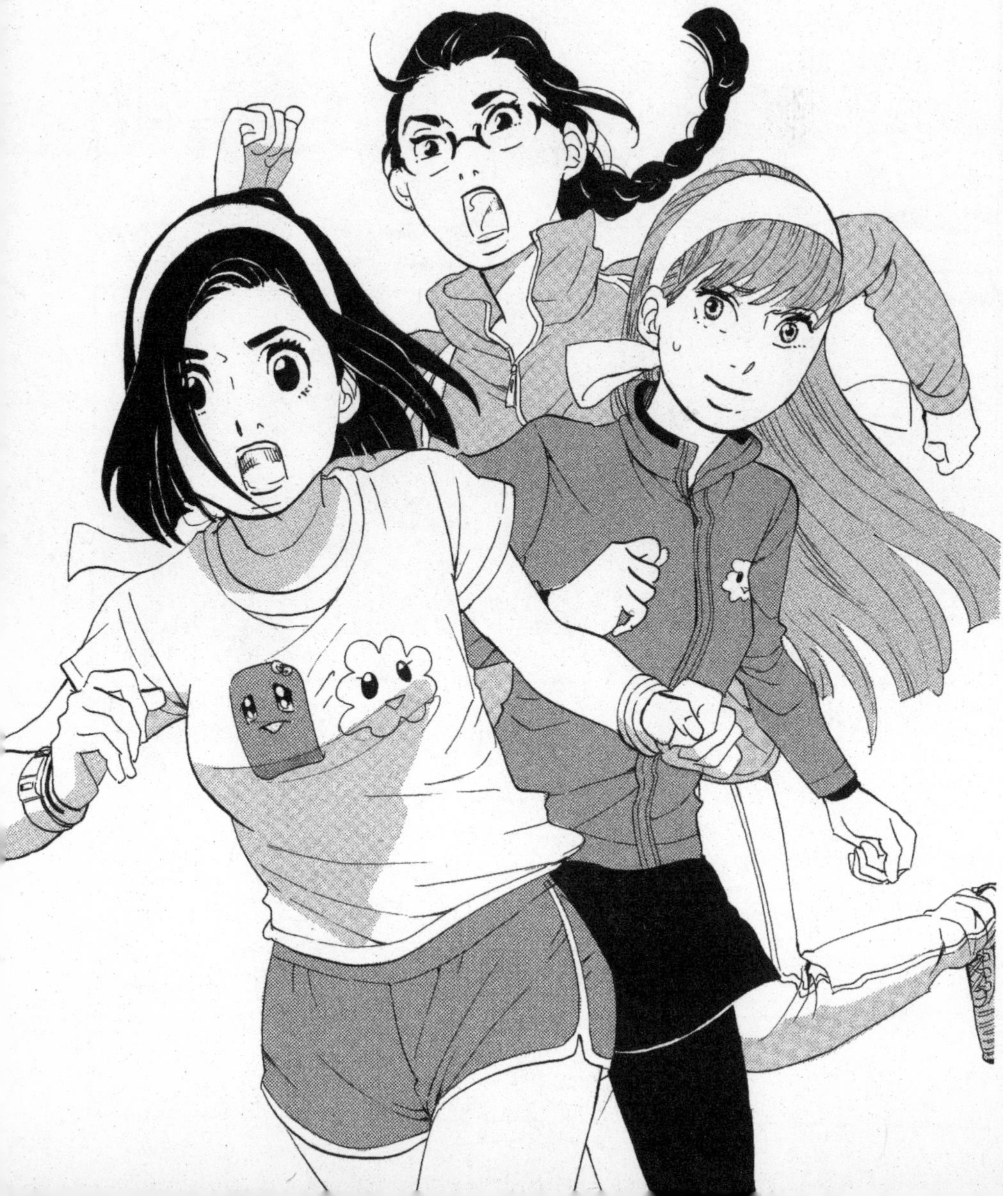

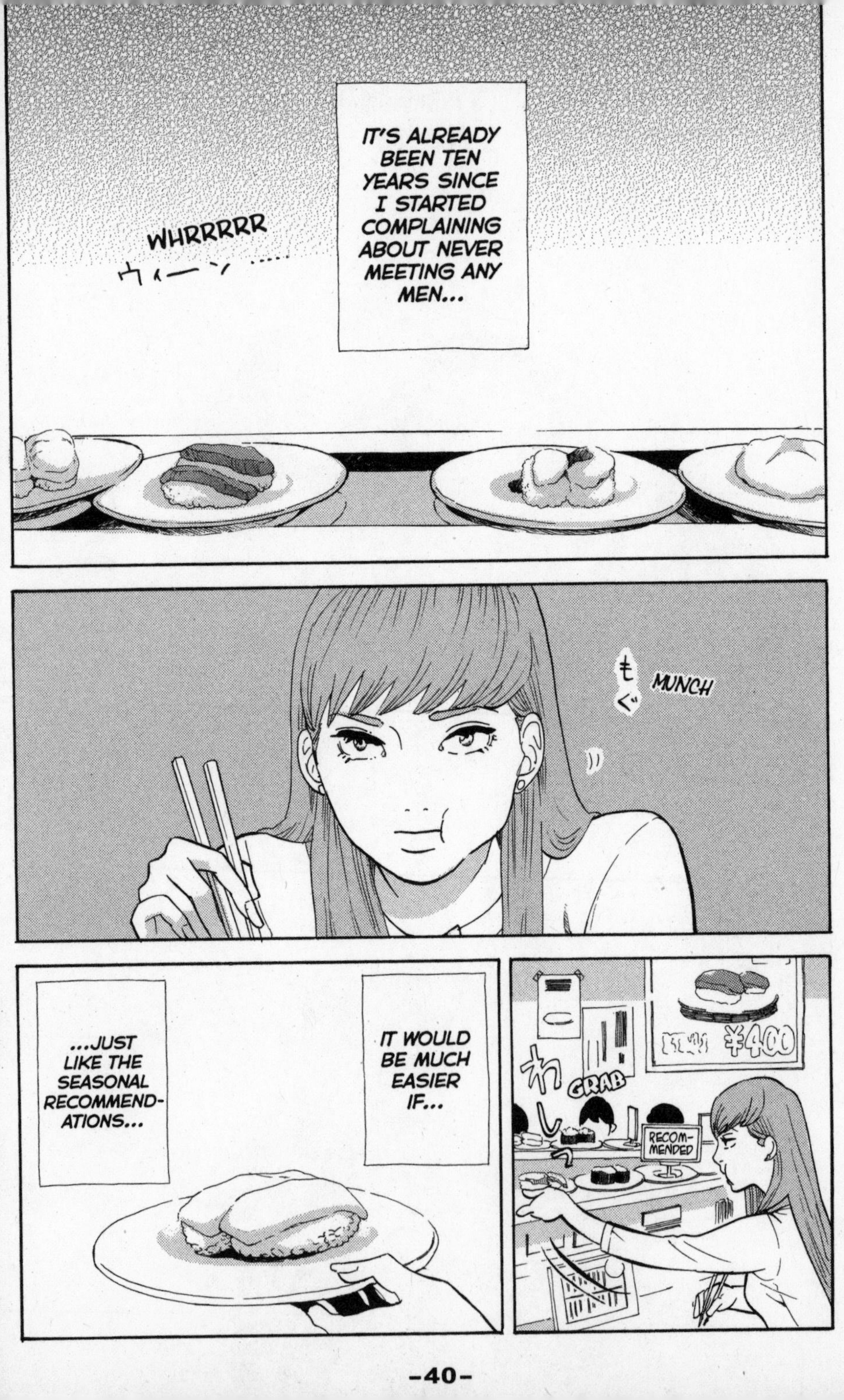

IT'S ALREADY BEEN TEN YEARS SINCE I STARTED COMPLAINING ABOUT NEVER MEETING ANY MEN...
WHRRRRR
ウィーン……
もぐ
MUNCH
¥400
RECOM-MENDED
わし
GRAB
IT WOULD BE MUCH EASIER IF...
...JUST LIKE THE SEASONAL RECOMMEND-ATIONS...

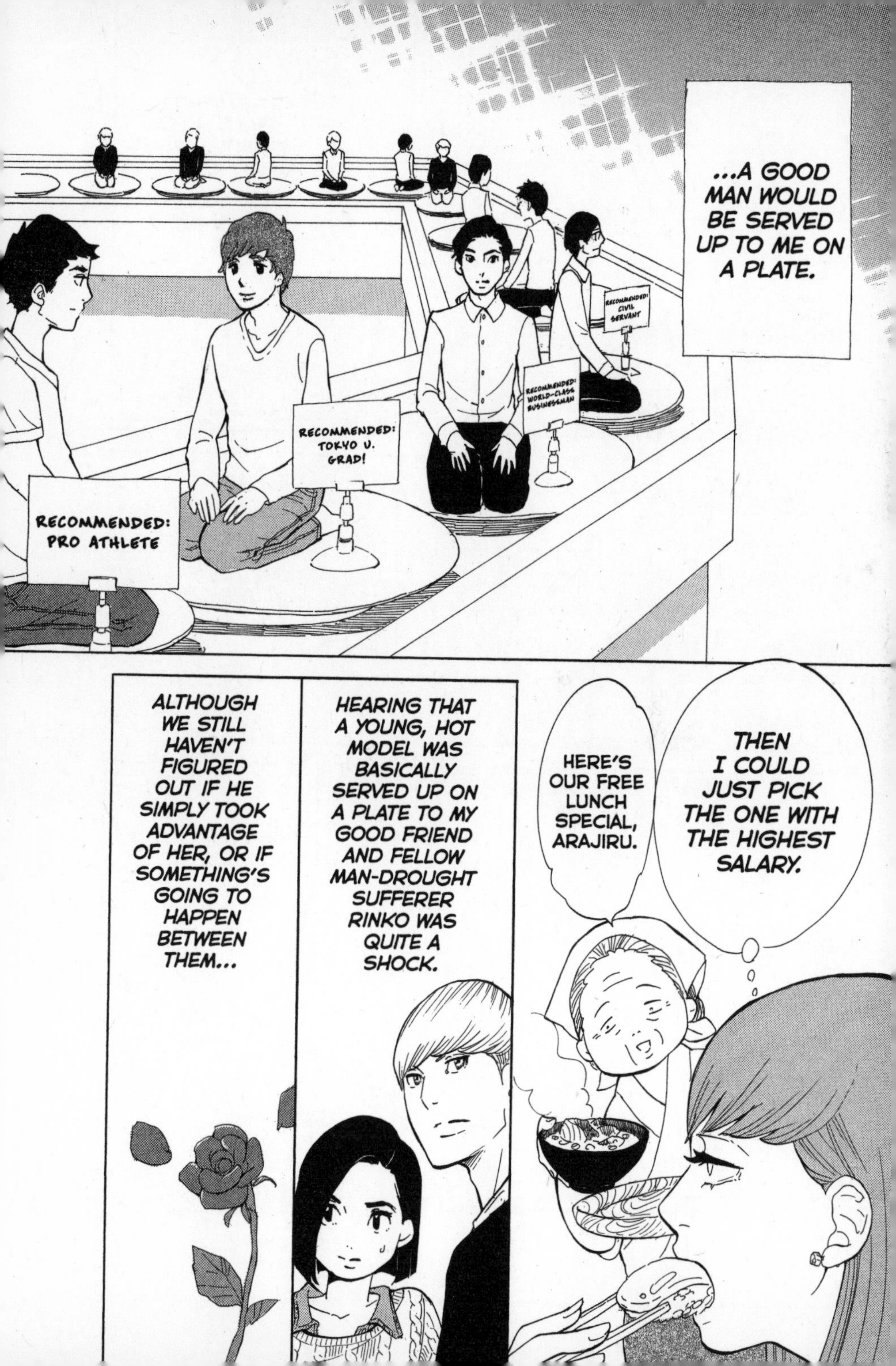
...A GOOD MAN WOULD BE SERVED UP TO ME ON A PLATE.
RECOMMENDED: CIVIL SERVANT
RECOMMENDED: WORLD-CLASS BUSINESSMAN
RECOMMENDED: TOKYO U. GRAD!
RECOMMENDED: PRO ATHLETE
THEN I COULD JUST PICK THE ONE WITH THE HIGHEST SALARY.
HERE'S OUR FREE LUNCH SPECIAL, ARAJIRU.
HEARING THAT A YOUNG, HOT MODEL WAS BASICALLY SERVED UP ON A PLATE TO MY GOOD FRIEND AND FELLOW MAN-DROUGHT SUFFERER RINKO WAS QUITE A SHOCK.
ALTHOUGH WE STILL HAVEN'T FIGURED OUT IF HE SIMPLY TOOK ADVANTAGE OF HER, OR IF SOMETHING'S GOING TO HAPPEN BETWEEN THEM...

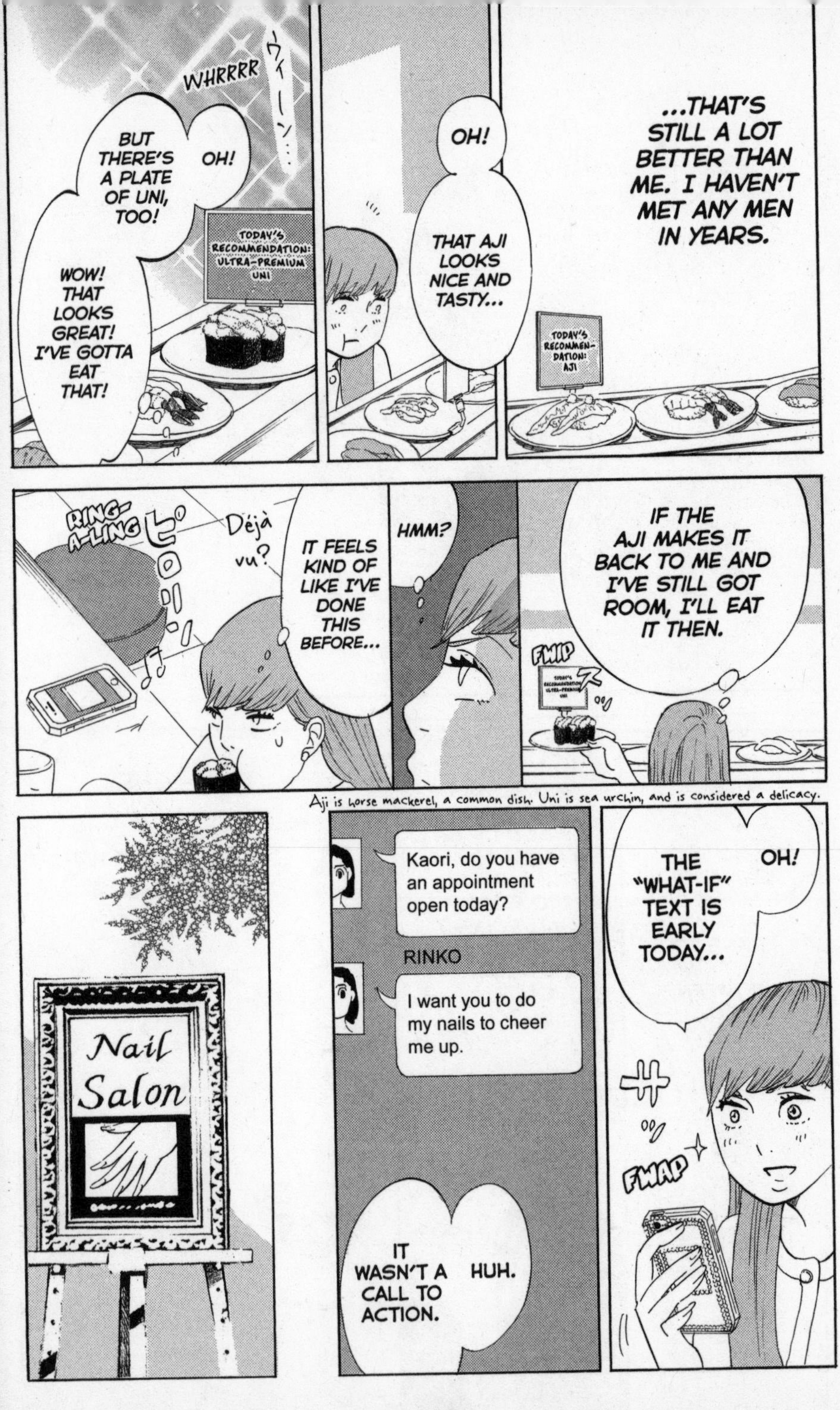
...THAT'S STILL A LOT BETTER THAN ME. I HAVEN'T MET ANY MEN IN YEARS.
TODAY'S RECOMMEN-DATION: AJI
OH!
THAT AJI LOOKS NICE AND TASTY...
WHRRRR
ウィーン…
OH!
BUT THERE'S A PLATE OF UNI, TOO!
TODAY'S RECOMMENDATION: ULTRA-PREMIUM UNI
WOW! THAT LOOKS GREAT! I'VE GOTTA EAT THAT!
IF THE AJI MAKES IT BACK TO ME AND I'VE STILL GOT ROOM, I'LL EAT IT THEN.
FWIP
HMM?
IT FEELS KIND OF LIKE I'VE DONE THIS BEFORE...
RING-A-LING
Déjà vu?
OH!
THE "WHAT-IF" TEXT IS EARLY TODAY...
FWAP
Kaori, do you have an appointment open today?
RINKO
I want you to do my nails to cheer me up.
IT WASN'T A CALL TO ACTION.
HUH.
Nail Salon

Aji is horse mackerel, a common dish. Uni is sea urchin, and is considered a delicacy.

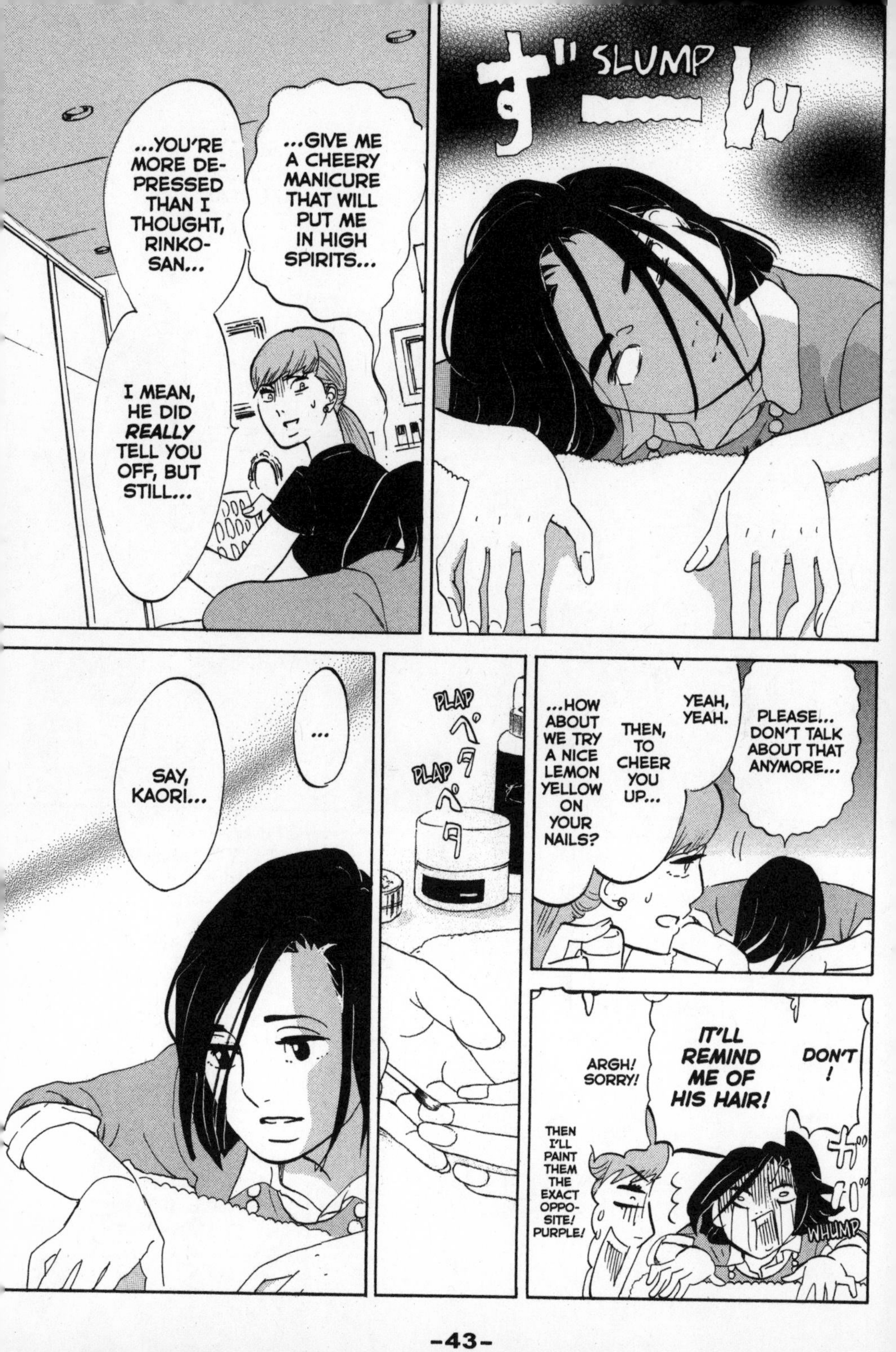
SLUMP
...GIVE ME A CHEERY MANICURE THAT WILL PUT ME IN HIGH SPIRITS...
...YOU'RE MORE DE-PRESSED THAN I THOUGHT, RINKO-SAN...
I MEAN, HE DID *REALLY* TELL YOU OFF, BUT STILL...
PLEASE... DON'T TALK ABOUT THAT ANYMORE...
YEAH, YEAH.
THEN, TO CHEER YOU UP...
...HOW ABOUT WE TRY A NICE LEMON YELLOW ON YOUR NAILS?
DON'T!
IT'LL REMIND ME OF HIS HAIR!
ARGH! SORRY!
THEN I'LL PAINT THEM THE EXACT OPPO-SITE! PURPLE!
WHUMP
PLAP
PLAP
...
SAY, KAORI...

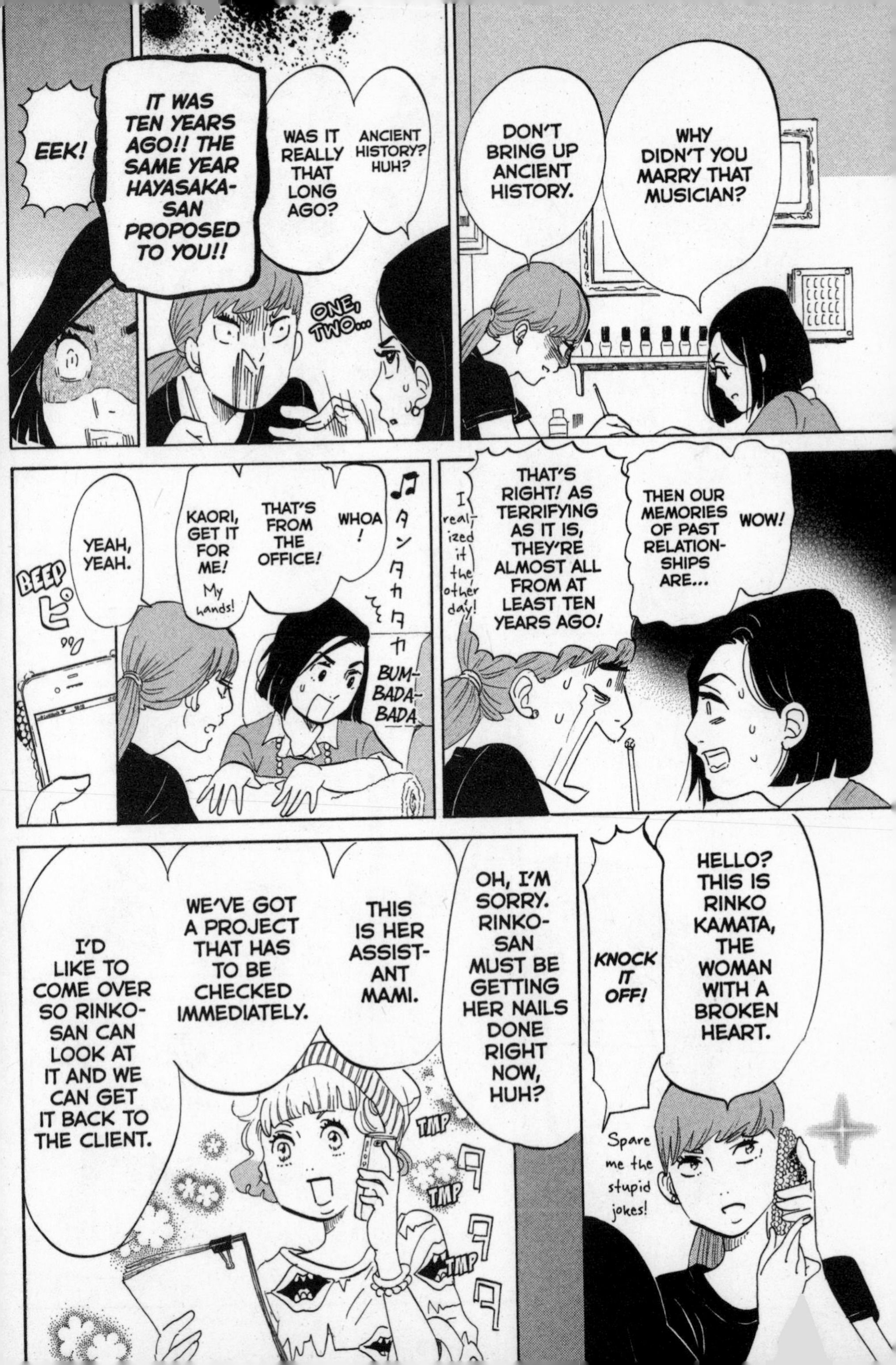

WHY DIDN'T YOU MARRY THAT MUSICIAN?
DON'T BRING UP ANCIENT HISTORY.
ANCIENT HISTORY? HUH?
WAS IT REALLY THAT LONG AGO?
ONE, TWO...
IT WAS TEN YEARS AGO!! THE SAME YEAR HAYASAKA-SAN PROPOSED TO YOU!!
EEK!
WOW!
THEN OUR MEMORIES OF PAST RELATIONSHIPS ARE...
THAT'S RIGHT! AS TERRIFYING AS IT IS, THEY'RE ALMOST ALL FROM AT LEAST TEN YEARS AGO!
I realized it the other day!
タンタカタカ
BUMBADABADA
WHOA!
THAT'S FROM THE OFFICE!
KAORI, GET IT FOR ME!
My hands!
YEAH, YEAH.
BEEP
ピ
HELLO? THIS IS RINKO KAMATA, THE WOMAN WITH A BROKEN HEART.
KNOCK IT OFF!
Spare me the stupid jokes!
OH, I'M SORRY. RINKO-SAN MUST BE GETTING HER NAILS DONE RIGHT NOW, HUH?
THIS IS HER ASSISTANT MAMI.
WE'VE GOT A PROJECT THAT HAS TO BE CHECKED IMMEDIATELY.
I'D LIKE TO COME OVER SO RINKO-SAN CAN LOOK AT IT AND WE CAN GET IT BACK TO THE CLIENT.
TMP
TMP
TMP

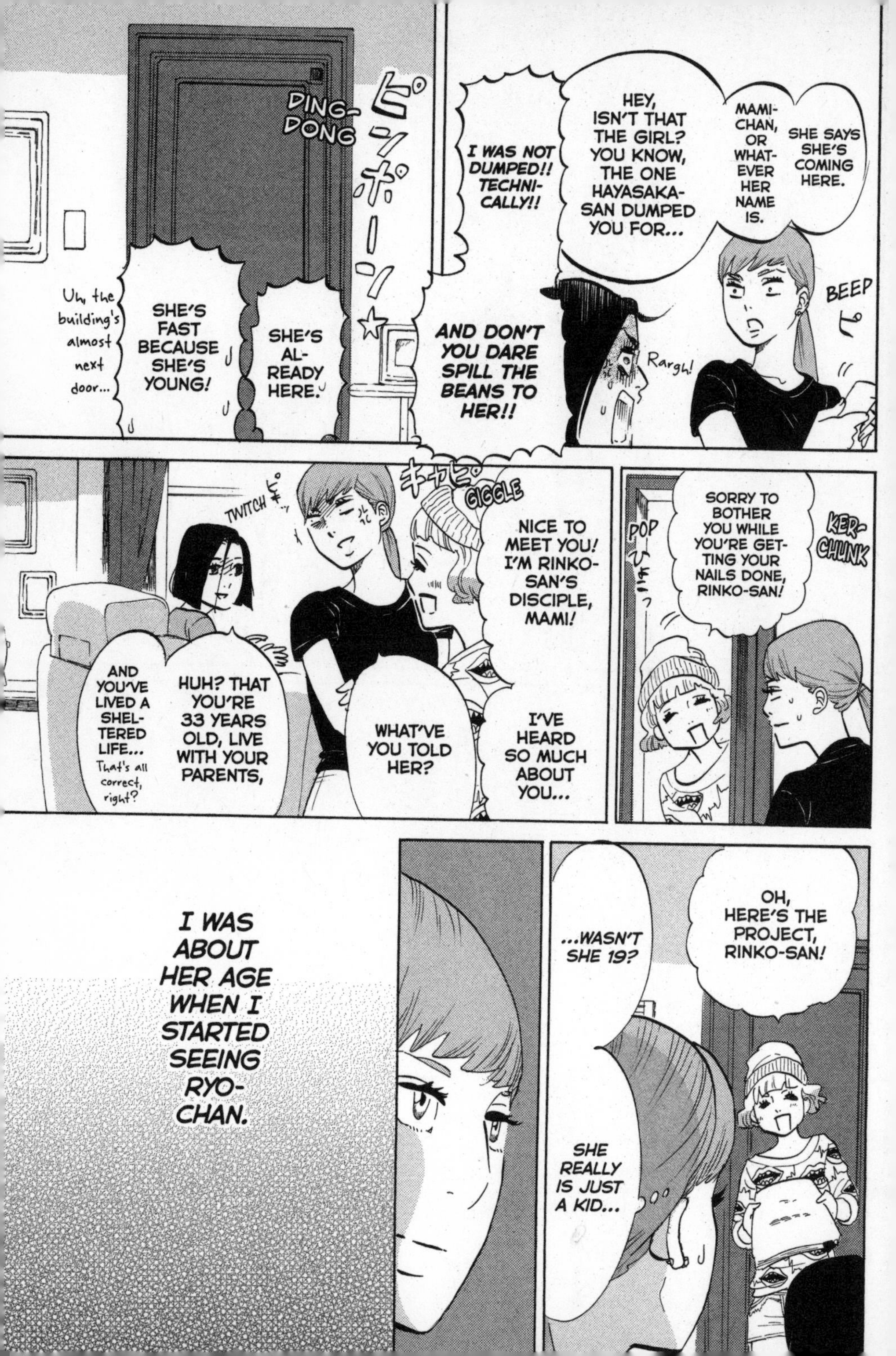
SHE SAYS SHE'S COMING HERE.
MAMI-CHAN, OR WHATEVER HER NAME IS.
BEEP
HEY, ISN'T THAT THE GIRL? YOU KNOW, THE ONE HAYASAKA-SAN DUMPED YOU FOR...
I WAS NOT DUMPED!! TECHNICALLY!!
Rargh!
AND DON'T YOU DARE SPILL THE BEANS TO HER!!
DING-DONG
SHE'S ALREADY HERE.
SHE'S FAST BECAUSE SHE'S YOUNG!
Uh, the building's almost next door...
KER-CHUNK
POP
SORRY TO BOTHER YOU WHILE YOU'RE GETTING YOUR NAILS DONE, RINKO-SAN!
GIGGLE
NICE TO MEET YOU! I'M RINKO-SAN'S DISCIPLE, MAMI!
I'VE HEARD SO MUCH ABOUT YOU...
TWITCH
WHAT'VE YOU TOLD HER?
HUH? THAT YOU'RE 33 YEARS OLD, LIVE WITH YOUR PARENTS,
AND YOU'VE LIVED A SHELTERED LIFE... That's all correct, right?
OH, HERE'S THE PROJECT, RINKO-SAN!
...WASN'T SHE 19?
SHE REALLY IS JUST A KID...
I WAS ABOUT HER AGE WHEN I STARTED SEEING RYO-CHAN.

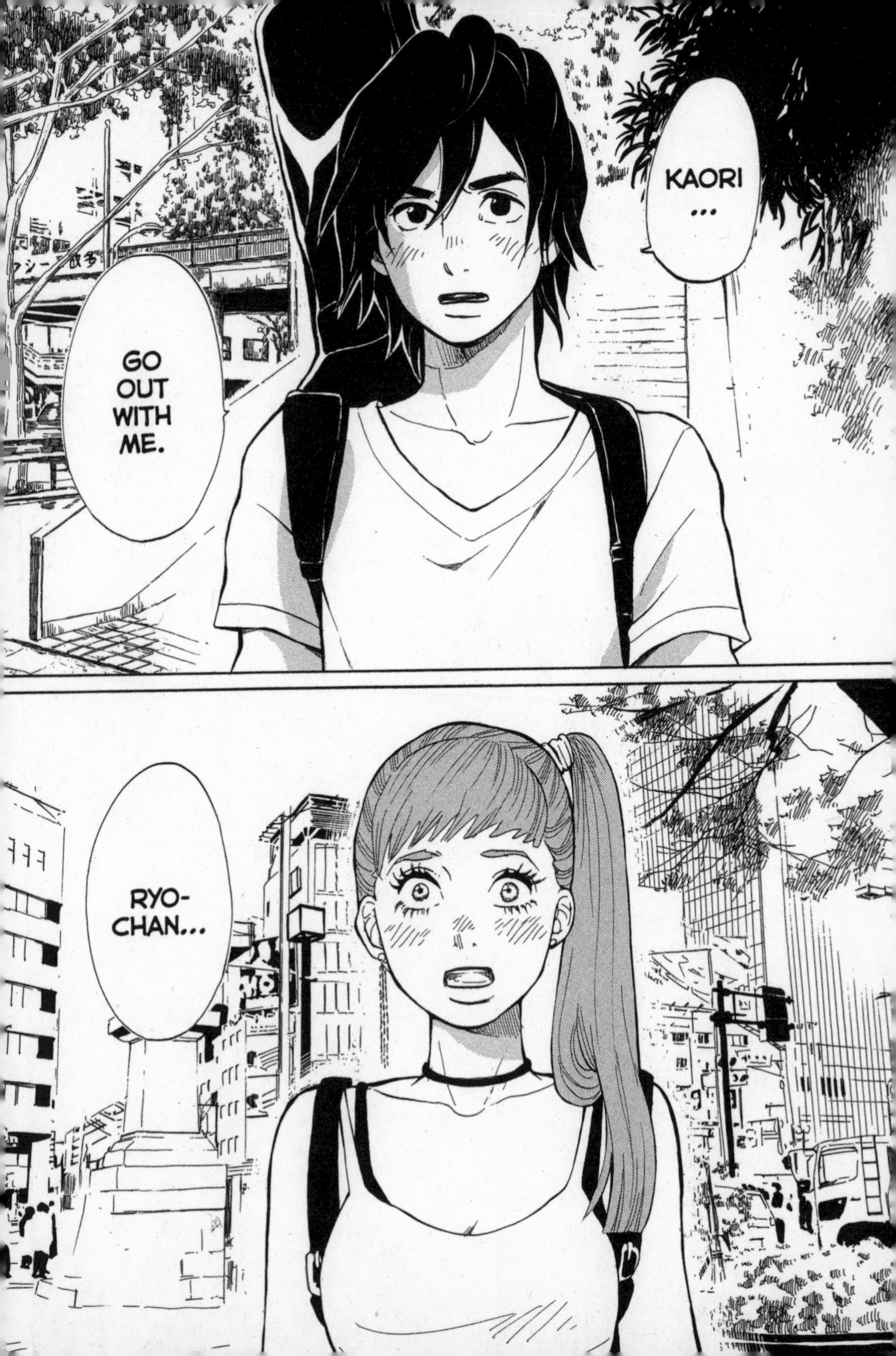
KAORI ...
GO OUT WITH ME.
RYO-CHAN...

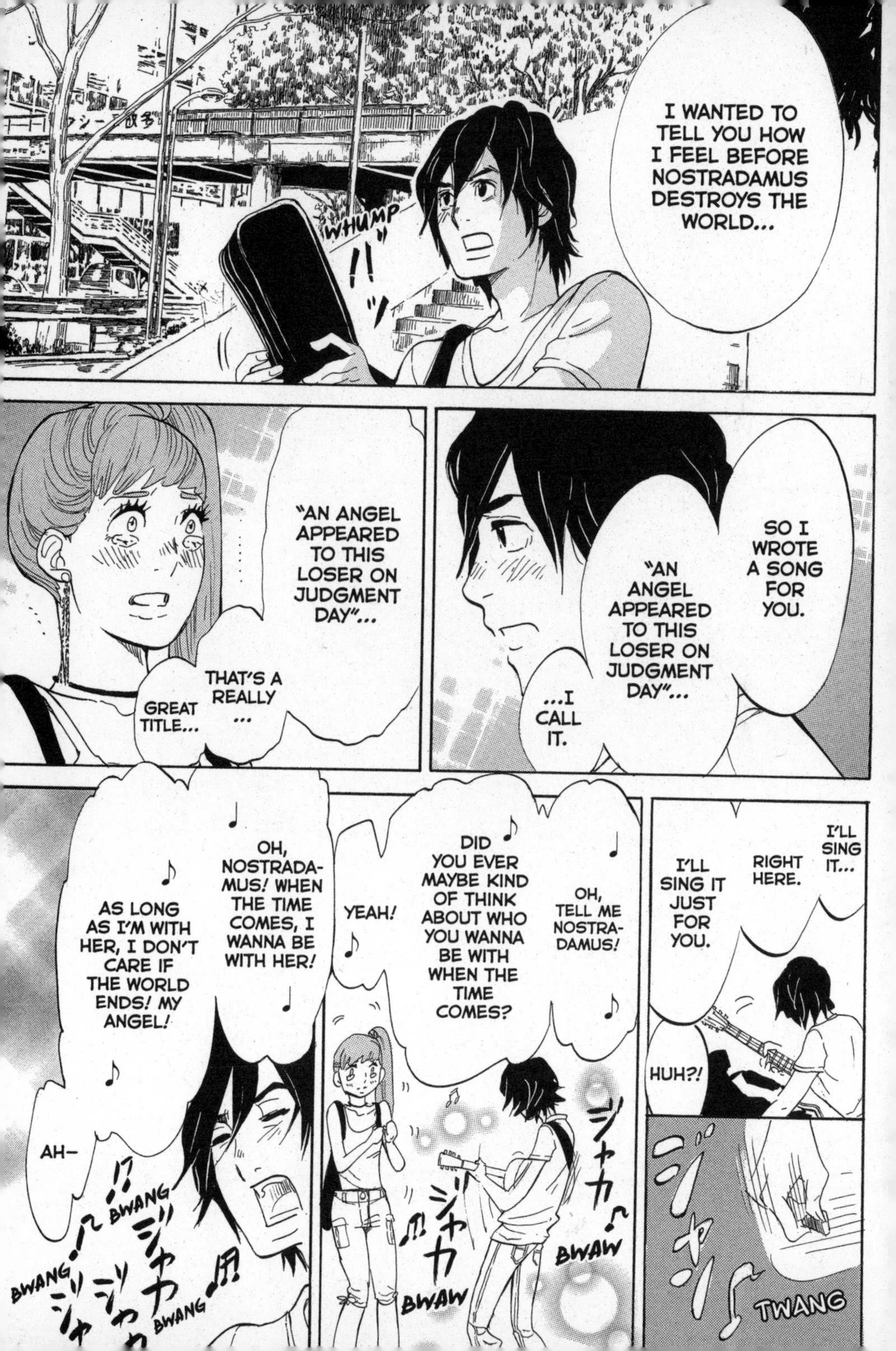
WHUMP
I WANTED TO TELL YOU HOW I FEEL BEFORE NOSTRADAMUS DESTROYS THE WORLD...
SO I WROTE A SONG FOR YOU.
“AN ANGEL APPEARED TO THIS LOSER ON JUDGMENT DAY”...
...I CALL IT.
......
“AN ANGEL APPEARED TO THIS LOSER ON JUDGMENT DAY”...
THAT'S A REALLY...
GREAT TITLE...
I'LL SING IT...
RIGHT HERE.
I'LL SING IT JUST FOR YOU.
HUH?!
TWANG
OH, TELL ME NOSTRADAMUS!
DID YOU EVER MAYBE KIND OF THINK ABOUT WHO YOU WANNA BE WITH WHEN THE TIME COMES?
YEAH!
BWAW
BWAW
OH, NOSTRADAMUS! WHEN THE TIME COMES, I WANNA BE WITH HER!
AS LONG AS I'M WITH HER, I DON'T CARE IF THE WORLD ENDS! MY ANGEL!
AH–
BWANG
BWANG
BWANG

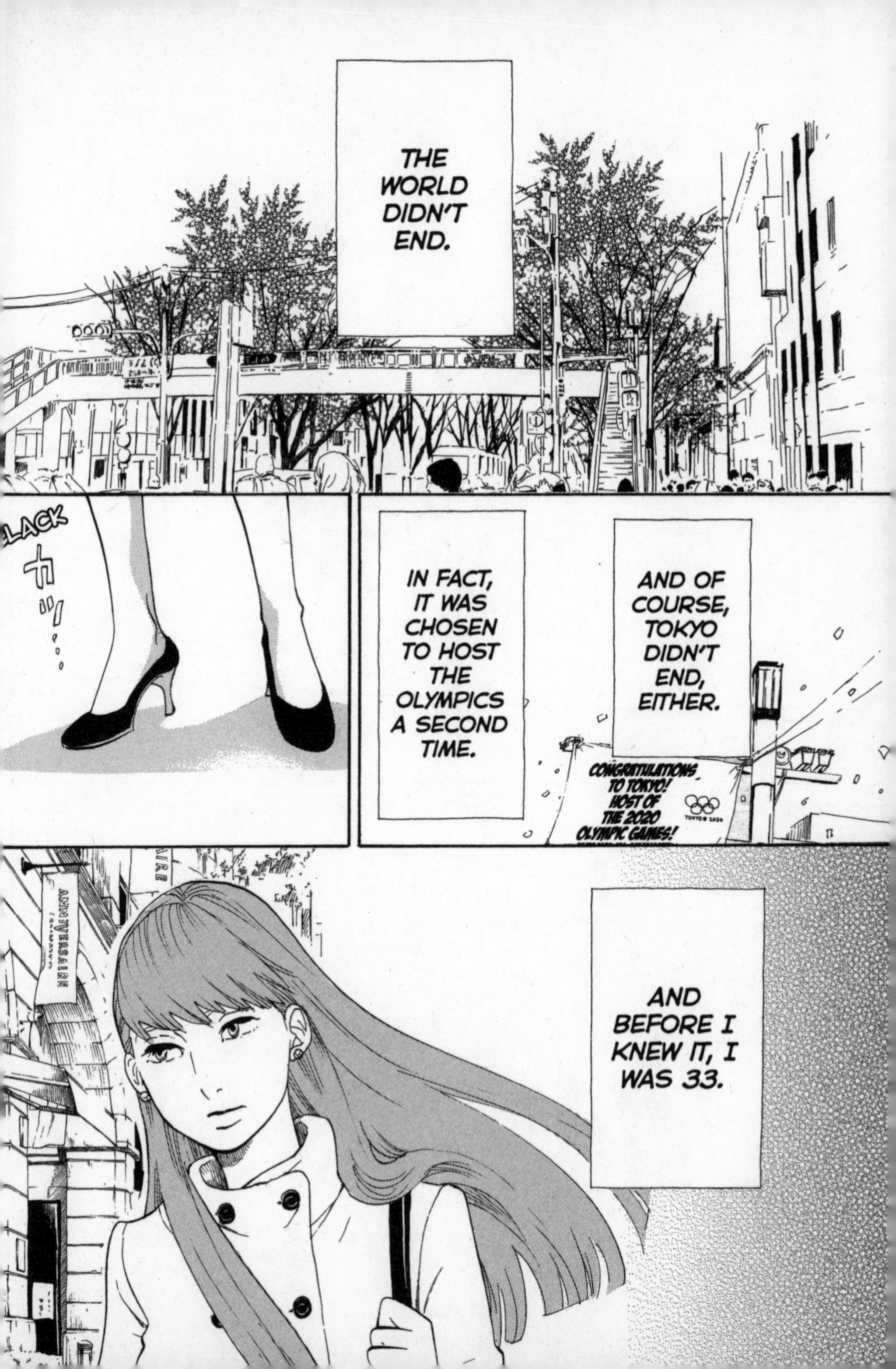
THE WORLD DIDN'T END.
AND OF COURSE, TOKYO DIDN'T END, EITHER.
IN FACT, IT WAS CHOSEN TO HOST THE OLYMPICS A SECOND TIME.
CONGRATULATIONS TO TOKYO! HOST OF THE 2020 OLYMPIC GAMES!
LACK
カッ
AND BEFORE I KNEW IT, I WAS 33.

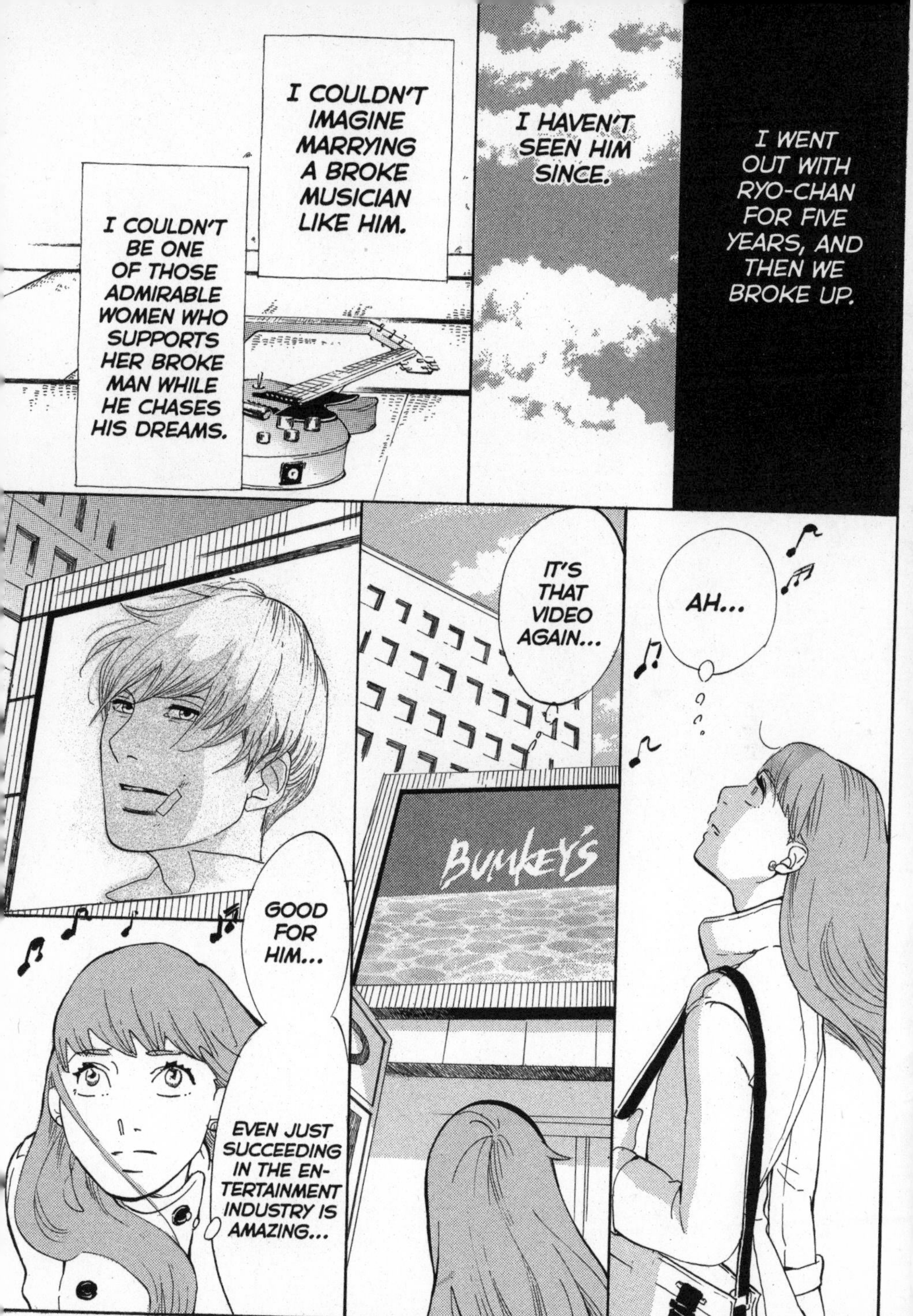
I WENT OUT WITH RYO-CHAN FOR FIVE YEARS, AND THEN WE BROKE UP.
I HAVEN'T SEEN HIM SINCE.
I COULDN'T IMAGINE MARRYING A BROKE MUSICIAN LIKE HIM.
I COULDN'T BE ONE OF THOSE ADMIRABLE WOMEN WHO SUPPORTS HER BROKE MAN WHILE HE CHASES HIS DREAMS.
AH...
IT'S THAT VIDEO AGAIN...
BUMKEY'S
GOOD FOR HIM...
EVEN JUST SUCCEEDING IN THE ENTERTAINMENT INDUSTRY IS AMAZING...

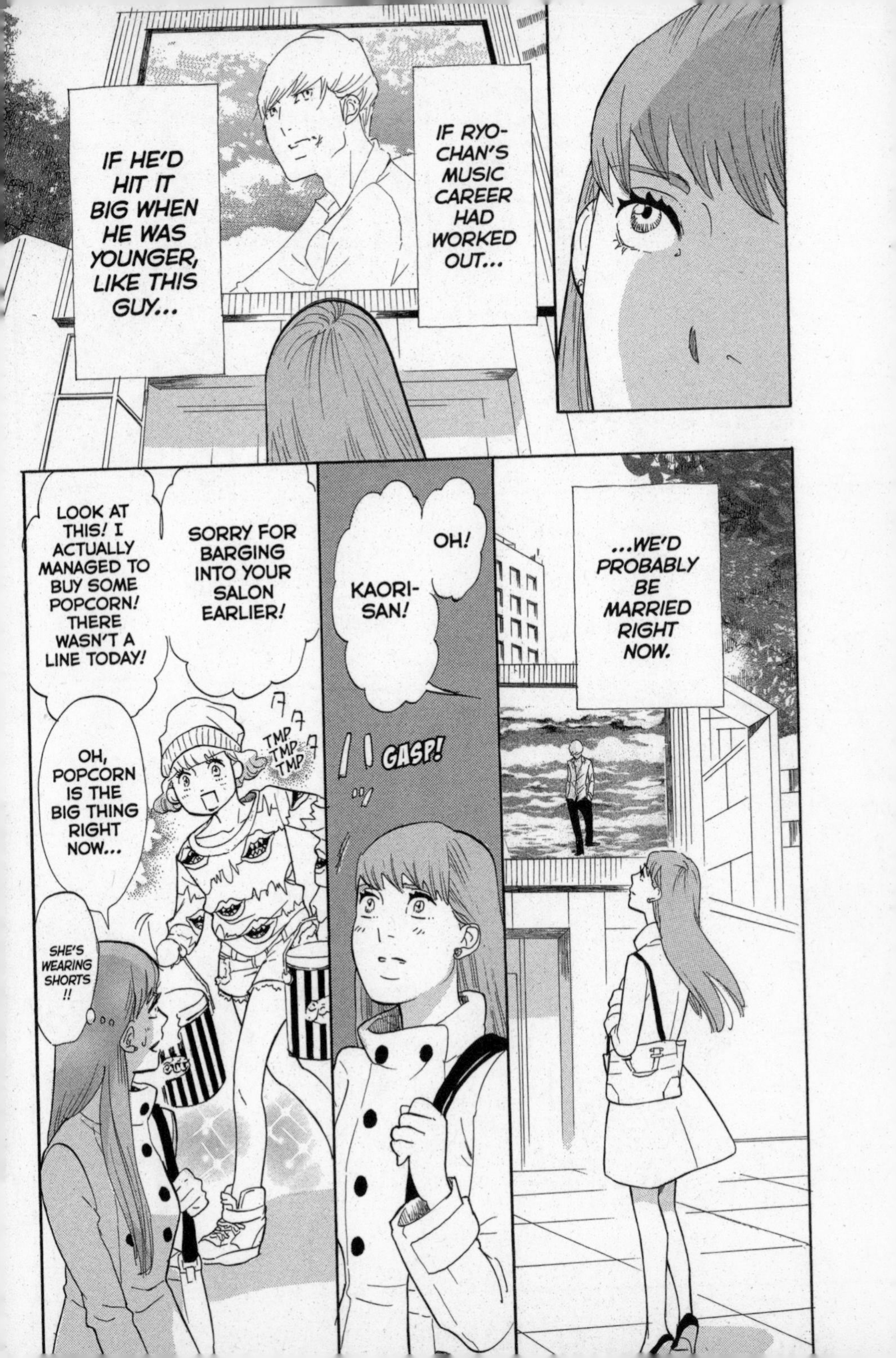
IF RYO-CHAN'S MUSIC CAREER HAD WORKED OUT...
IF HE'D HIT IT BIG WHEN HE WAS YOUNGER, LIKE THIS GUY...
...WE'D PROBABLY BE MARRIED RIGHT NOW.
OH! KAORI-SAN!
GASP!
SORRY FOR BARGING INTO YOUR SALON EARLIER!
LOOK AT THIS! I ACTUALLY MANAGED TO BUY SOME POPCORN! THERE WASN'T A LINE TODAY!
TMP TMP TMP
OH, POPCORN IS THE BIG THING RIGHT NOW...
SHE'S WEARING SHORTS!!

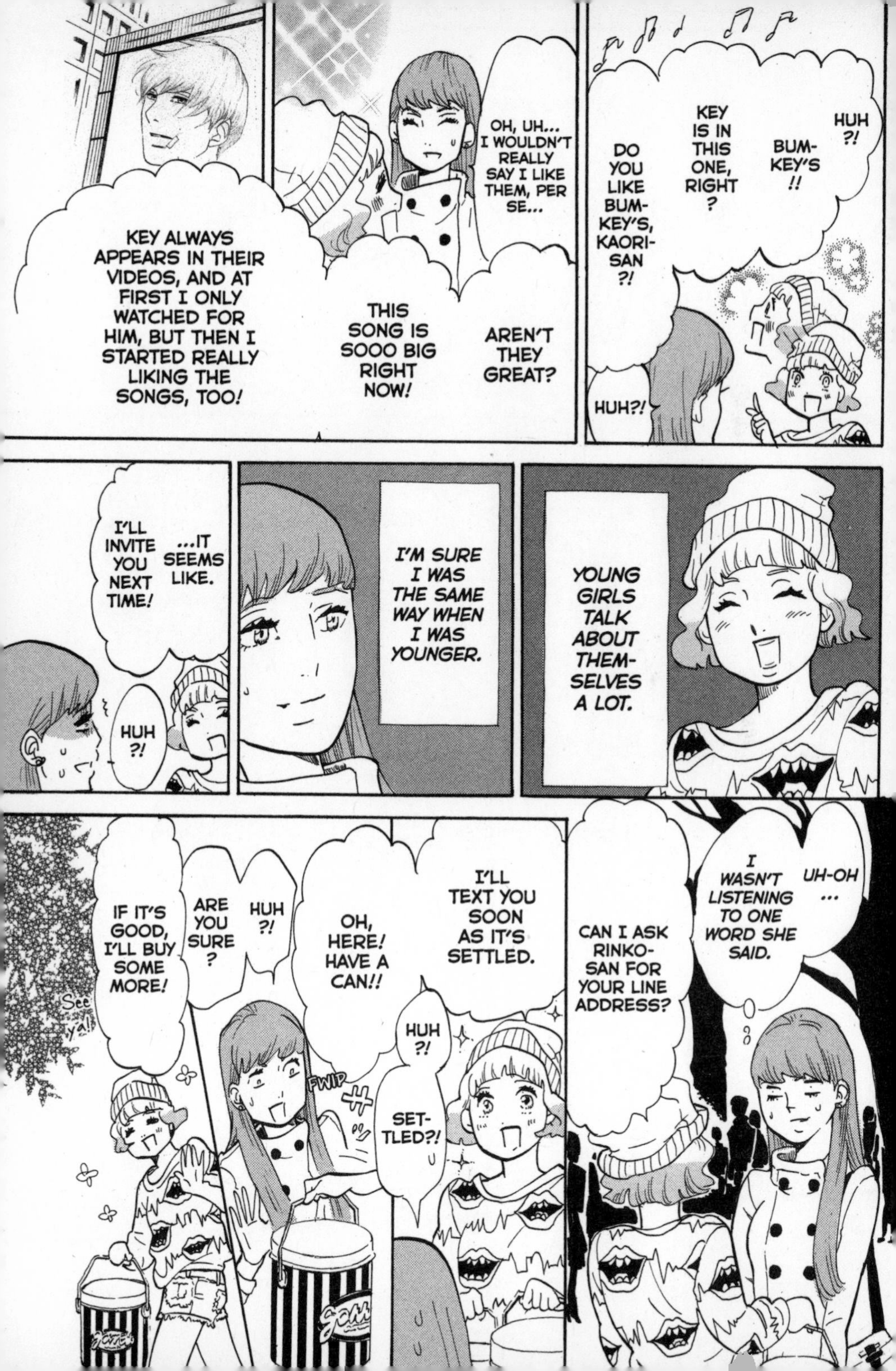
HUH ?!
BUM-KEY'S !!
KEY IS IN THIS ONE, RIGHT ?
DO YOU LIKE BUM-KEY'S, KAORI-SAN ?!
HUH?!
OH, UH... I WOULDN'T REALLY SAY I LIKE THEM, PER SE...
AREN'T THEY GREAT?
THIS SONG IS SOOO BIG RIGHT NOW!
KEY ALWAYS APPEARS IN THEIR VIDEOS, AND AT FIRST I ONLY WATCHED FOR HIM, BUT THEN I STARTED REALLY LIKING THE SONGS, TOO!
YOUNG GIRLS TALK ABOUT THEMSELVES A LOT.
I'M SURE I WAS THE SAME WAY WHEN I WAS YOUNGER.
...IT SEEMS LIKE.
I'LL INVITE YOU NEXT TIME!
HUH ?!
UH-OH ...
I WASN'T LISTENING TO ONE WORD SHE SAID.
CAN I ASK RINKO-SAN FOR YOUR LINE ADDRESS?
I'LL TEXT YOU SOON AS IT'S SETTLED.
HUH ?!
SET-TLED?!
OH, HERE! HAVE A CAN!!
FWIP
HUH ?!
ARE YOU SURE ?
IF IT'S GOOD, I'LL BUY SOME MORE!
See ya!

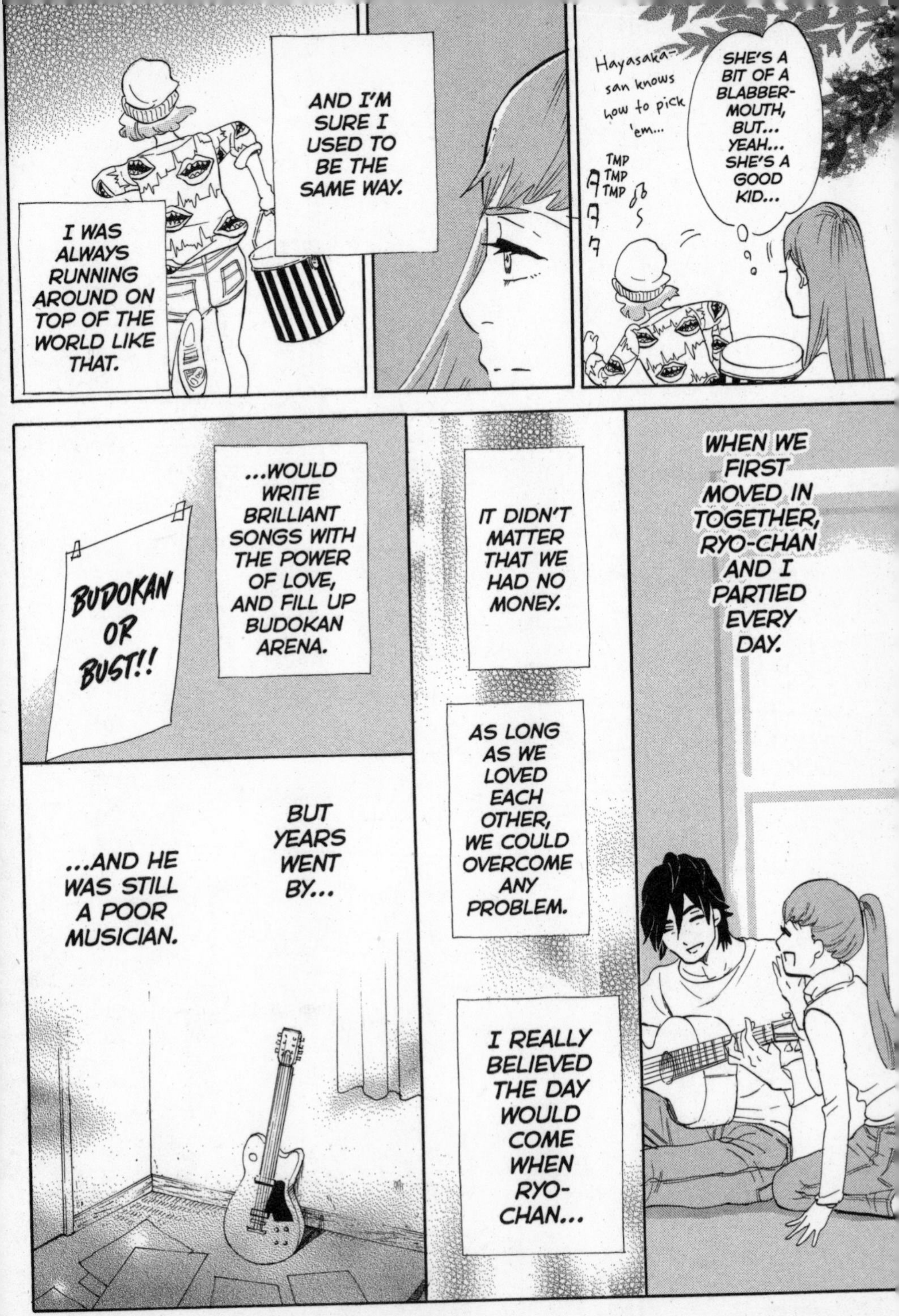

SHE'S A BIT OF A BLABBER-MOUTH, BUT... YEAH... SHE'S A GOOD KID...
Hayasaka-san knows how to pick 'em...
TMP TMP TMP
AND I'M SURE I USED TO BE THE SAME WAY.
I WAS ALWAYS RUNNING AROUND ON TOP OF THE WORLD LIKE THAT.
WHEN WE FIRST MOVED IN TOGETHER, RYO-CHAN AND I PARTIED EVERY DAY.
IT DIDN'T MATTER THAT WE HAD NO MONEY.
AS LONG AS WE LOVED EACH OTHER, WE COULD OVERCOME ANY PROBLEM.
I REALLY BELIEVED THE DAY WOULD COME WHEN RYO-CHAN...
...WOULD WRITE BRILLIANT SONGS WITH THE POWER OF LOVE, AND FILL UP BUDOKAN ARENA.
BUDOKAN OR BUST!!
BUT YEARS WENT BY...
...AND HE WAS STILL A POOR MUSICIAN.

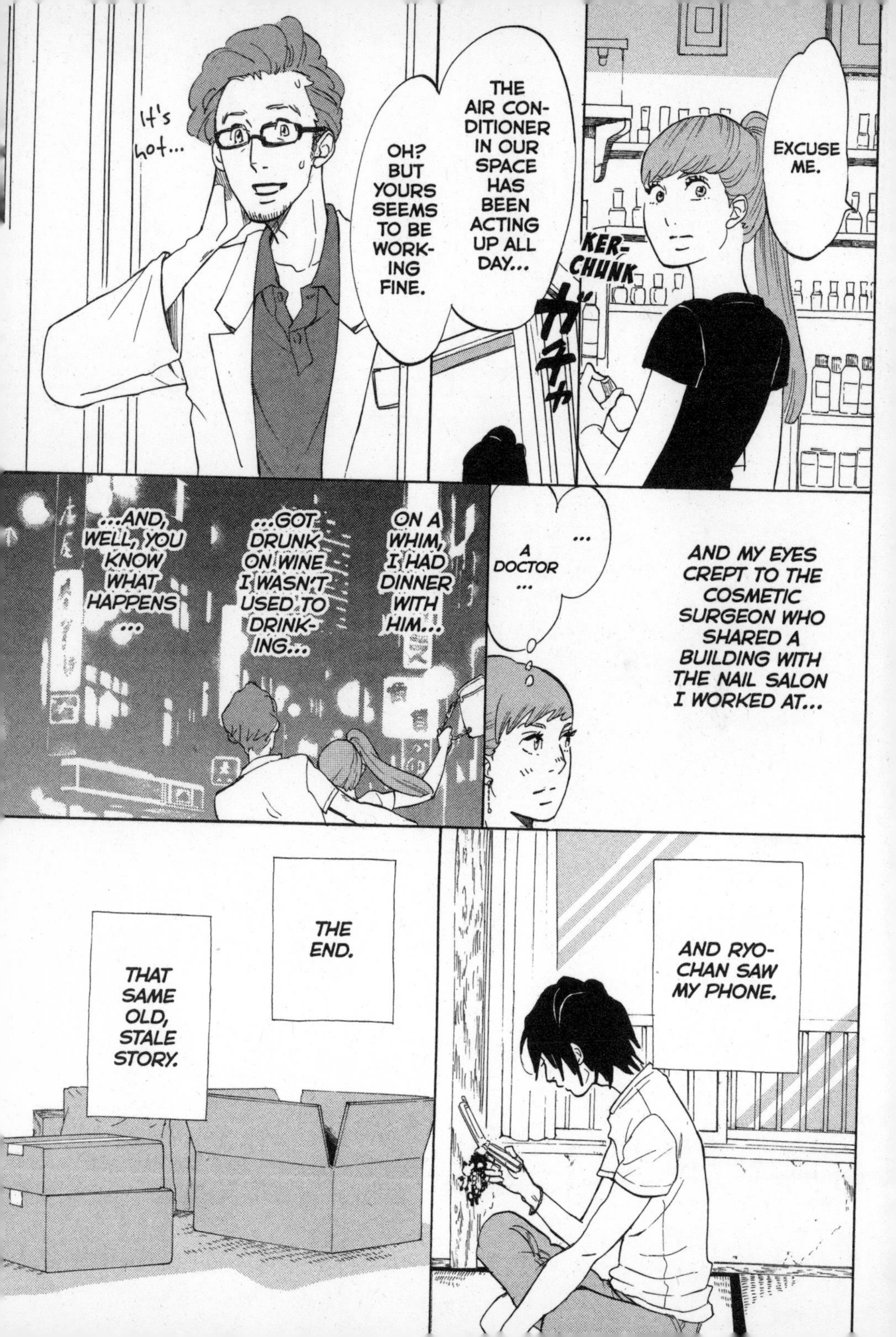
EXCUSE ME.
KER-CHUNK
THE AIR CONDITIONER IN OUR SPACE HAS BEEN ACTING UP ALL DAY...
OH? BUT YOURS SEEMS TO BE WORKING FINE.
It's hot...
AND MY EYES CREPT TO THE COSMETIC SURGEON WHO SHARED A BUILDING WITH THE NAIL SALON I WORKED AT...
...
A DOCTOR ...
ON A WHIM, I HAD DINNER WITH HIM...
...GOT DRUNK ON WINE I WASN'T USED TO DRINKING...
...AND, WELL, YOU KNOW WHAT HAPPENS...
AND RYO-CHAN SAW MY PHONE.
THE END.
THAT SAME OLD, STALE STORY.

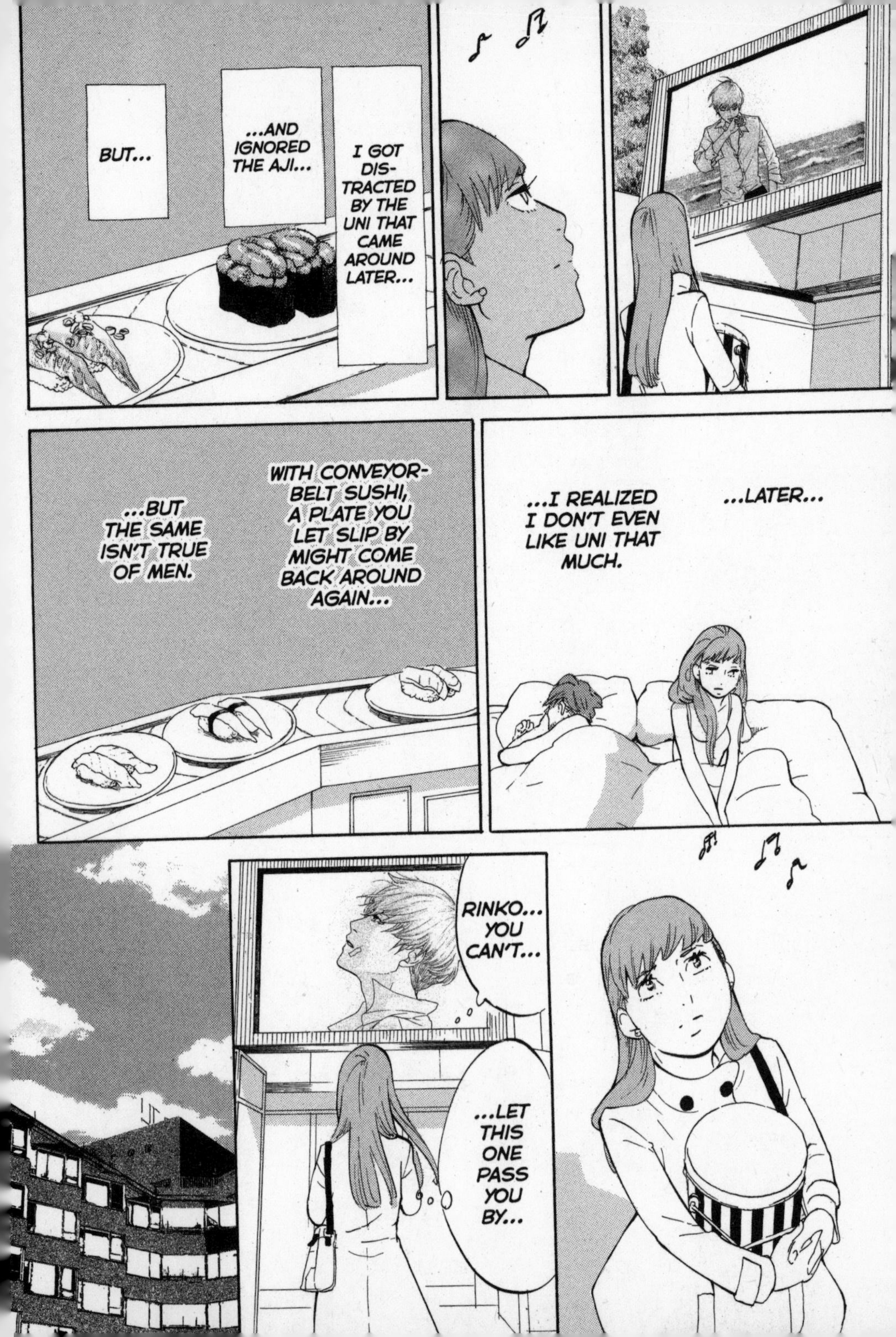
I GOT DIS-TRACTED BY THE UNI THAT CAME AROUND LATER...
...AND IGNORED THE AJI...
BUT...
...LATER...
...I REALIZED I DON'T EVEN LIKE UNI THAT MUCH.
WITH CONVEYOR-BELT SUSHI, A PLATE YOU LET SLIP BY MIGHT COME BACK AROUND AGAIN...
...BUT THE SAME ISN'T TRUE OF MEN.
RINKO... YOU CAN'T...
...LET THIS ONE PASS YOU BY...

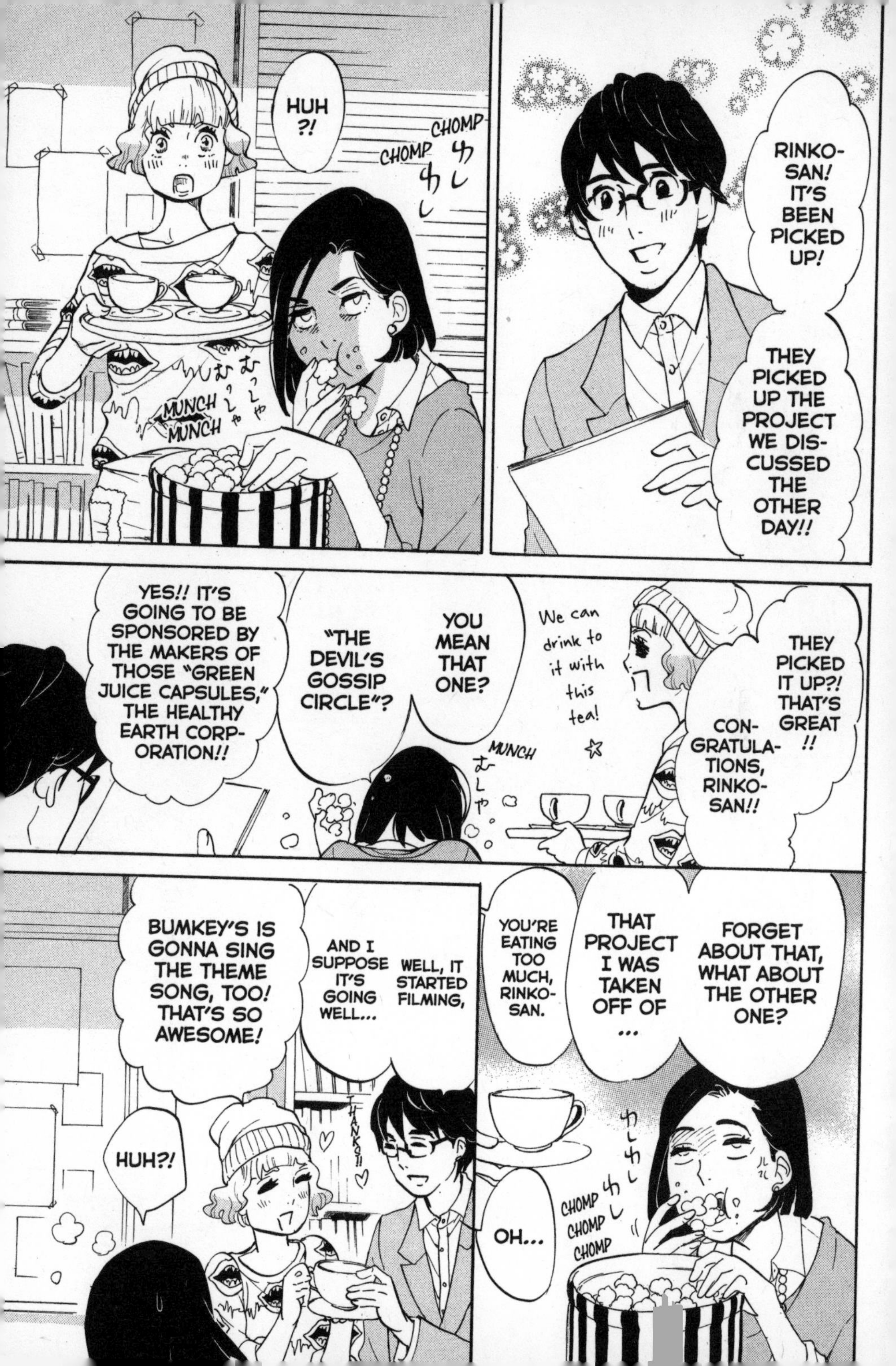
RINKO-SAN! IT'S BEEN PICKED UP!
THEY PICKED UP THE PROJECT WE DISCUSSED THE OTHER DAY!!
HUH?!
CHOMP
CHOMP
MUNCH
MUNCH
THEY PICKED IT UP?! THAT'S GREAT!!
CONGRATULATIONS, RINKO-SAN!!
We can drink to it with this tea! ☆
MUNCH
YOU MEAN THAT ONE?
"THE DEVIL'S GOSSIP CIRCLE"?
YES!! IT'S GOING TO BE SPONSORED BY THE MAKERS OF THOSE "GREEN JUICE CAPSULES," THE HEALTHY EARTH CORPORATION!!
FORGET ABOUT THAT, WHAT ABOUT THE OTHER ONE?
THAT PROJECT I WAS TAKEN OFF OF ...
YOU'RE EATING TOO MUCH, RINKO-SAN.
CHOMP
CHOMP
CHOMP
OH...
WELL, IT STARTED FILMING,
AND I SUPPOSE IT'S GOING WELL...
BUMKEY'S IS GONNA SING THE THEME SONG, TOO! THAT'S SO AWESOME!
THANKS!!
HUH?!

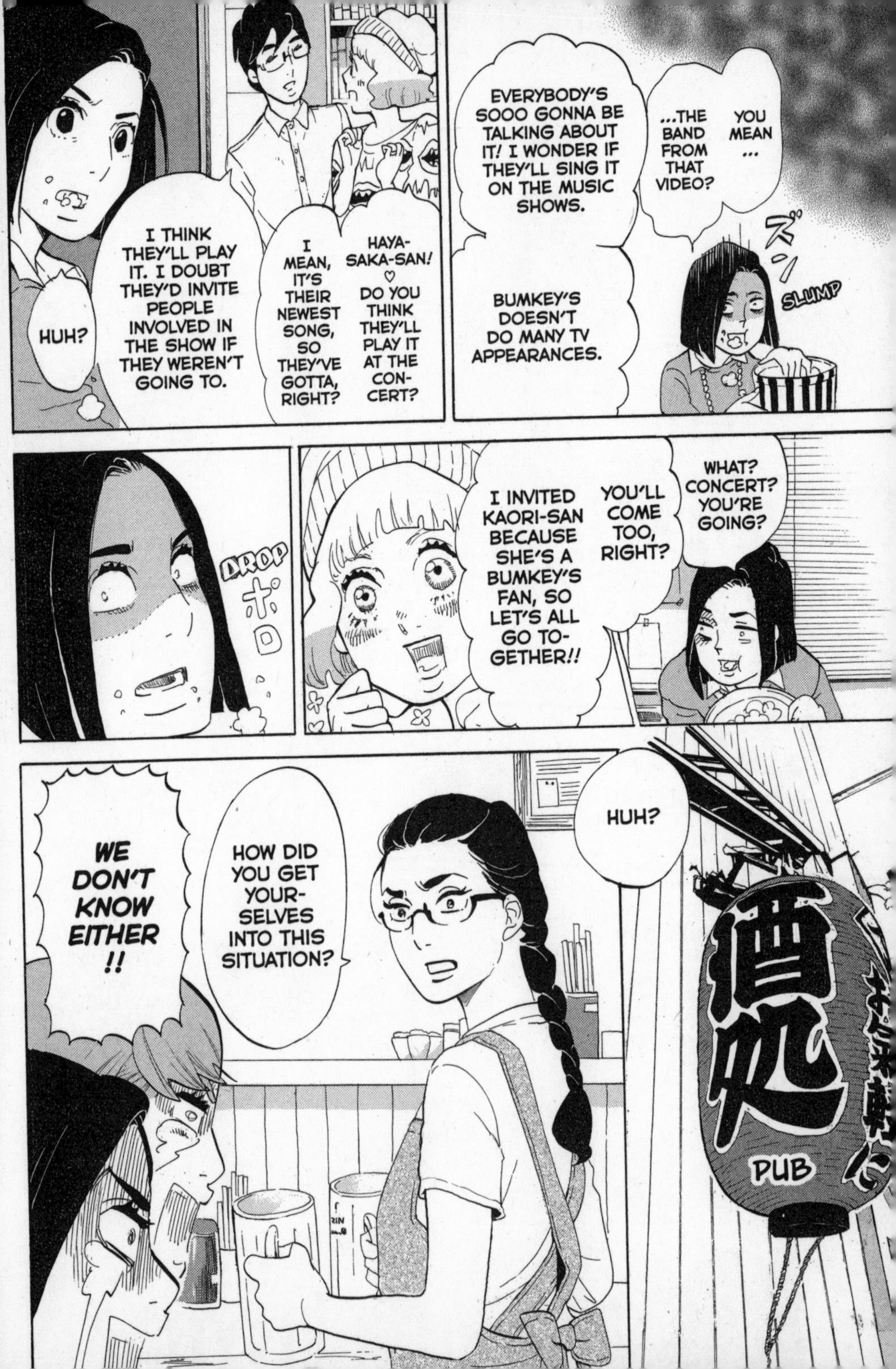
YOU MEAN ...
...THE BAND FROM THAT VIDEO?
EVERYBODY'S SOOO GONNA BE TALKING ABOUT IT! I WONDER IF THEY'LL SING IT ON THE MUSIC SHOWS.
BUMKEY'S DOESN'T DO MANY TV APPEARANCES.
ズン
SLUMP
HAYA-SAKA-SAN! ♡ DO YOU THINK THEY'LL PLAY IT AT THE CON-CERT?
I MEAN, IT'S THEIR NEWEST SONG, SO THEY'VE GOTTA, RIGHT?
I THINK THEY'LL PLAY IT. I DOUBT THEY'D INVITE PEOPLE INVOLVED IN THE SHOW IF THEY WEREN'T GOING TO.
HUH?
WHAT? CONCERT? YOU'RE GOING?
YOU'LL COME TOO, RIGHT?
I INVITED KAORI-SAN BECAUSE SHE'S A BUMKEY'S FAN, SO LET'S ALL GO TO-GETHER!!
DROP
ポロ
酒処
PUB
HUH?
HOW DID YOU GET YOUR-SELVES INTO THIS SITUATION?
WE DON'T KNOW EITHER!!

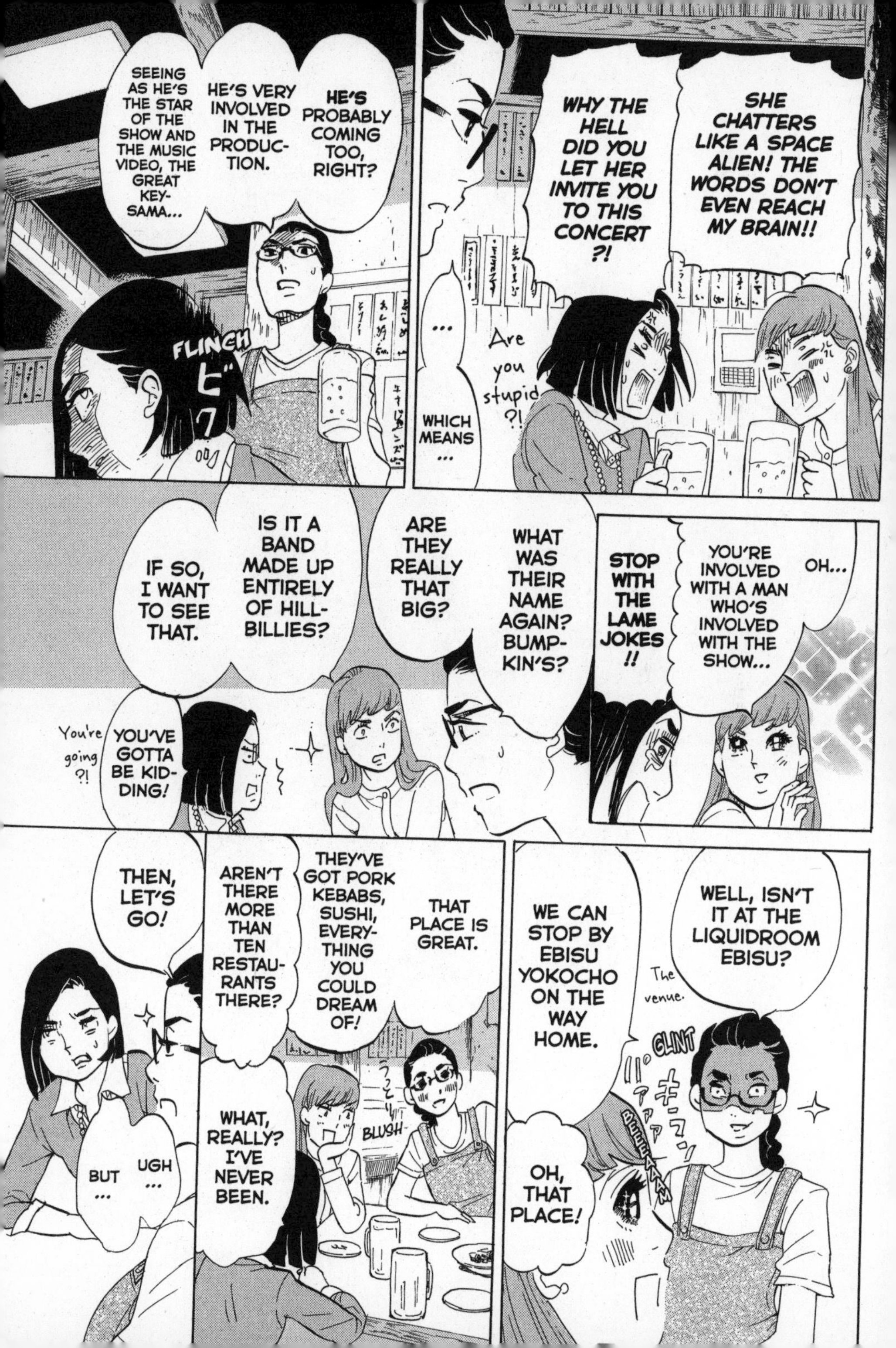
SHE CHATTERS LIKE A SPACE ALIEN! THE WORDS DON'T EVEN REACH MY BRAIN!!
WHY THE HELL DID YOU LET HER INVITE YOU TO THIS CONCERT ?!
Are you stupid ?!
...
WHICH MEANS ...
HE'S PROBABLY COMING TOO, RIGHT?
HE'S VERY INVOLVED IN THE PRODUC-TION.
SEEING AS HE'S THE STAR OF THE SHOW AND THE MUSIC VIDEO, THE GREAT KEY-SAMA...
FLINCH
OH...
YOU'RE INVOLVED WITH A MAN WHO'S INVOLVED WITH THE SHOW...
STOP WITH THE LAME JOKES !!
WHAT WAS THEIR NAME AGAIN? BUMP-KIN'S?
ARE THEY REALLY THAT BIG?
IS IT A BAND MADE UP ENTIRELY OF HILL-BILLIES?
IF SO, I WANT TO SEE THAT.
YOU'VE GOTTA BE KID-DING!
You're going ?!
WELL, ISN'T IT AT THE LIQUIDROOM EBISU?
The venue.
GLINT
WE CAN STOP BY EBISU YOKOCHO ON THE WAY HOME.
OH, THAT PLACE!
THAT PLACE IS GREAT.
THEY'VE GOT PORK KEBABS, SUSHI, EVERY-THING YOU COULD DREAM OF!
AREN'T THERE MORE THAN TEN RESTAU-RANTS THERE?
WHAT, REALLY? I'VE NEVER BEEN.
BLUSH
THEN, LET'S GO!
UGH ...
BUT ...

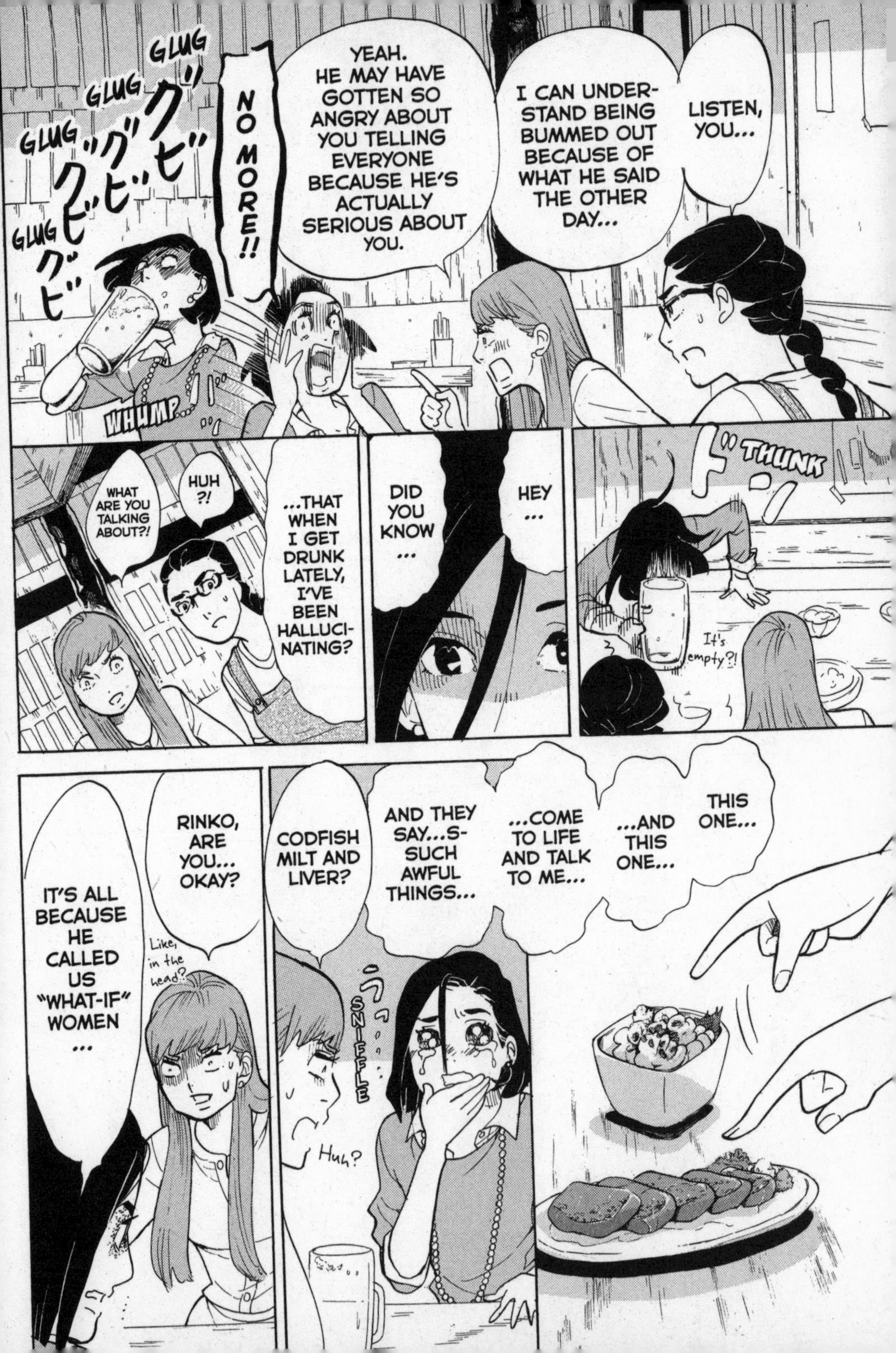
LISTEN, YOU...
I CAN UNDER-STAND BEING BUMMED OUT BECAUSE OF WHAT HE SAID THE OTHER DAY...
YEAH. HE MAY HAVE GOTTEN SO ANGRY ABOUT YOU TELLING EVERYONE BECAUSE HE'S ACTUALLY SERIOUS ABOUT YOU.
NO MORE!!
GLUG
GLUG
GLUG
GLUG
WHUMP
THUNK
It's empty?!
HEY...
DID YOU KNOW...
...THAT WHEN I GET DRUNK LATELY, I'VE BEEN HALLUCI-NATING?
HUH?!
WHAT ARE YOU TALKING ABOUT?!
THIS ONE...
...AND THIS ONE...
...COME TO LIFE AND TALK TO ME...
AND THEY SAY...S-SUCH AWFUL THINGS...
CODFISH MILT AND LIVER?
SNIFFLE
Huh?
RINKO, ARE YOU... OKAY?
Like, in the head?
IT'S ALL BECAUSE HE CALLED US "WHAT-IF" WOMEN...

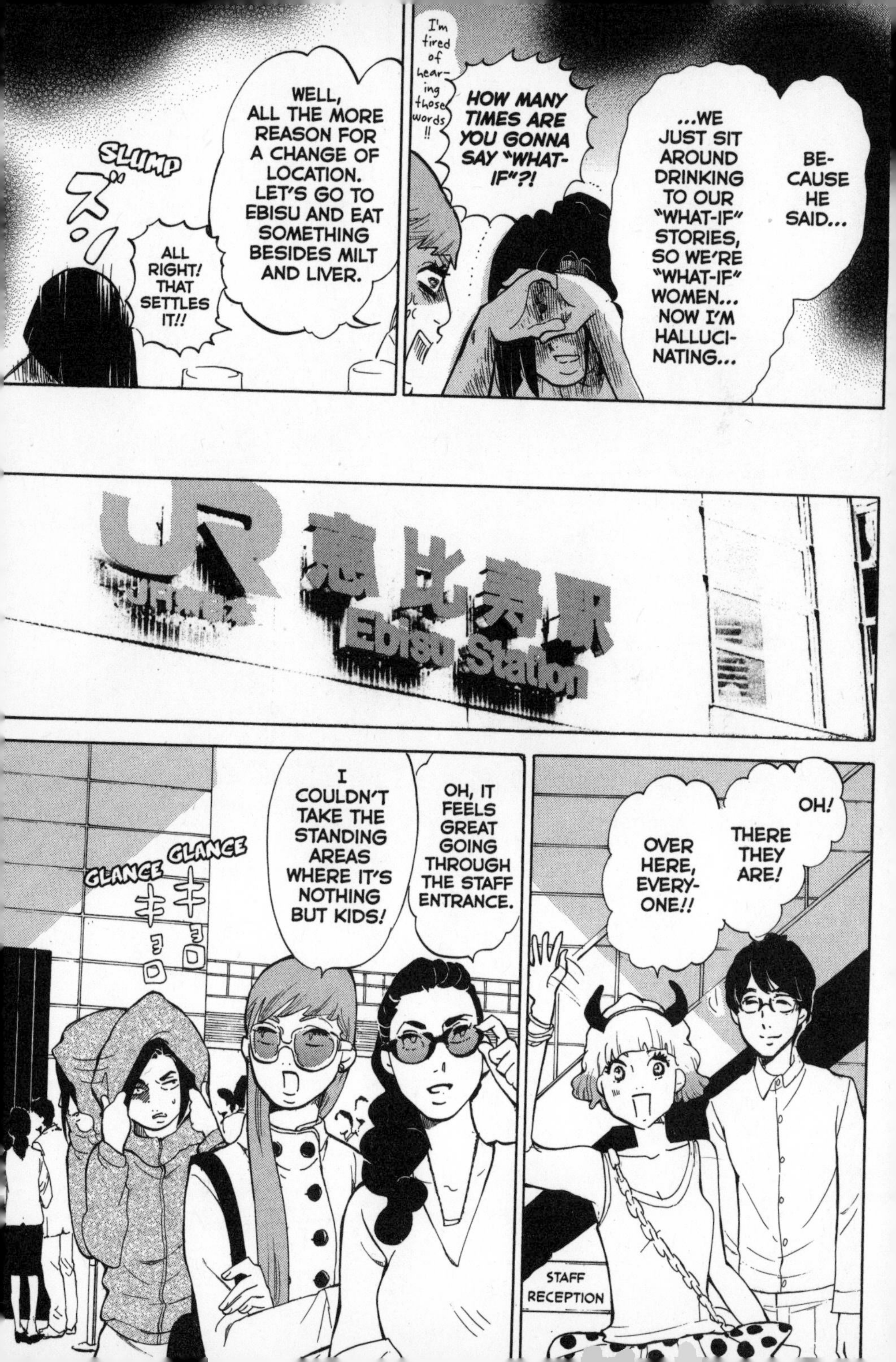
BE-
CAUSE
HE
SAID...
...WE JUST SIT AROUND DRINKING TO OUR "WHAT-IF" STORIES, SO WE'RE "WHAT-IF" WOMEN... NOW I'M HALLUCI-NATING...
HOW MANY TIMES ARE YOU GONNA SAY "WHAT-IF"?!
I'm tired of hear-ing those words!!
WELL, ALL THE MORE REASON FOR A CHANGE OF LOCATION. LET'S GO TO EBISU AND EAT SOMETHING BESIDES MILT AND LIVER.
ALL RIGHT! THAT SETTLES IT!!
SLUMP
ズ
JR
恵比寿駅
Ebisu Station
OH!
THERE THEY ARE!
OVER HERE, EVERY-ONE!!
STAFF RECEPTION
OH, IT FEELS GREAT GOING THROUGH THE STAFF ENTRANCE.
I COULDN'T TAKE THE STANDING AREAS WHERE IT'S NOTHING BUT KIDS!
GLANCE GLANCE
キョロ
キョロ

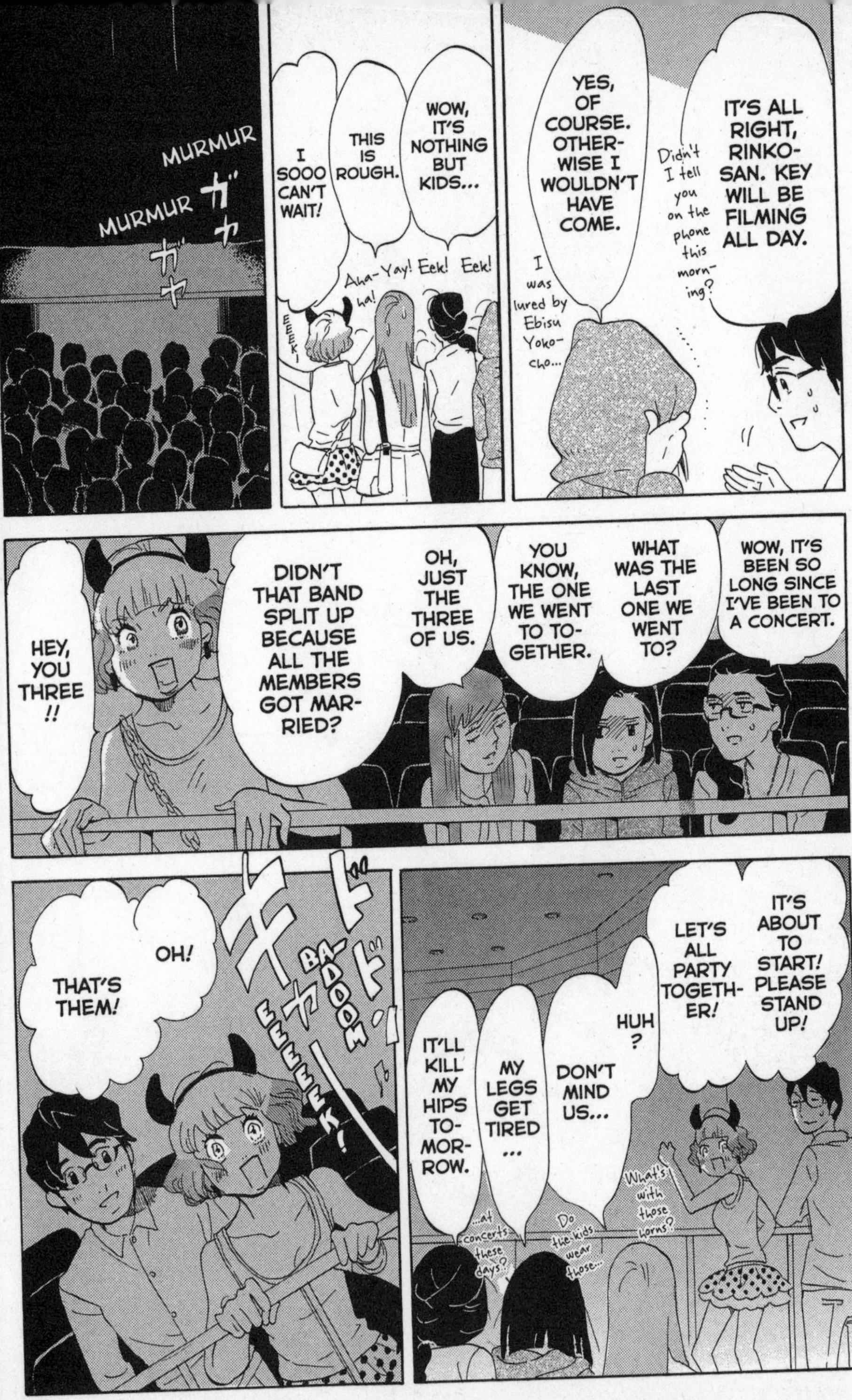
IT'S ALL RIGHT, RINKO-SAN. KEY WILL BE FILMING ALL DAY.
Didn't I tell you on the phone this morning?
YES, OF COURSE. OTHERWISE I WOULDN'T HAVE COME.
I was lured by Ebisu Yokocho...
WOW, IT'S NOTHING BUT KIDS...
THIS IS ROUGH.
I SOOO CAN'T WAIT!
Eek! Eek!
Yay!
Aha-ha!
EEEK!
MURMUR
MURMUR
ガヤ
ガヤ
WOW, IT'S BEEN SO LONG SINCE I'VE BEEN TO A CONCERT.
WHAT WAS THE LAST ONE WE WENT TO?
YOU KNOW, THE ONE WE WENT TO TOGETHER.
OH, JUST THE THREE OF US.
DIDN'T THAT BAND SPLIT UP BECAUSE ALL THE MEMBERS GOT MARRIED?
HEY, YOU THREE!!
IT'S ABOUT TO START! PLEASE STAND UP!
LET'S ALL PARTY TOGETHER!
HUH?
DON'T MIND US...
MY LEGS GET TIRED...
IT'LL KILL MY HIPS TOMORROW.
What's with those horns?
Do the kids wear those...
...at concerts these days?
ドキ
ドキ
BA-DOOM
OH!
THAT'S THEM!
EEEEEEEEK!

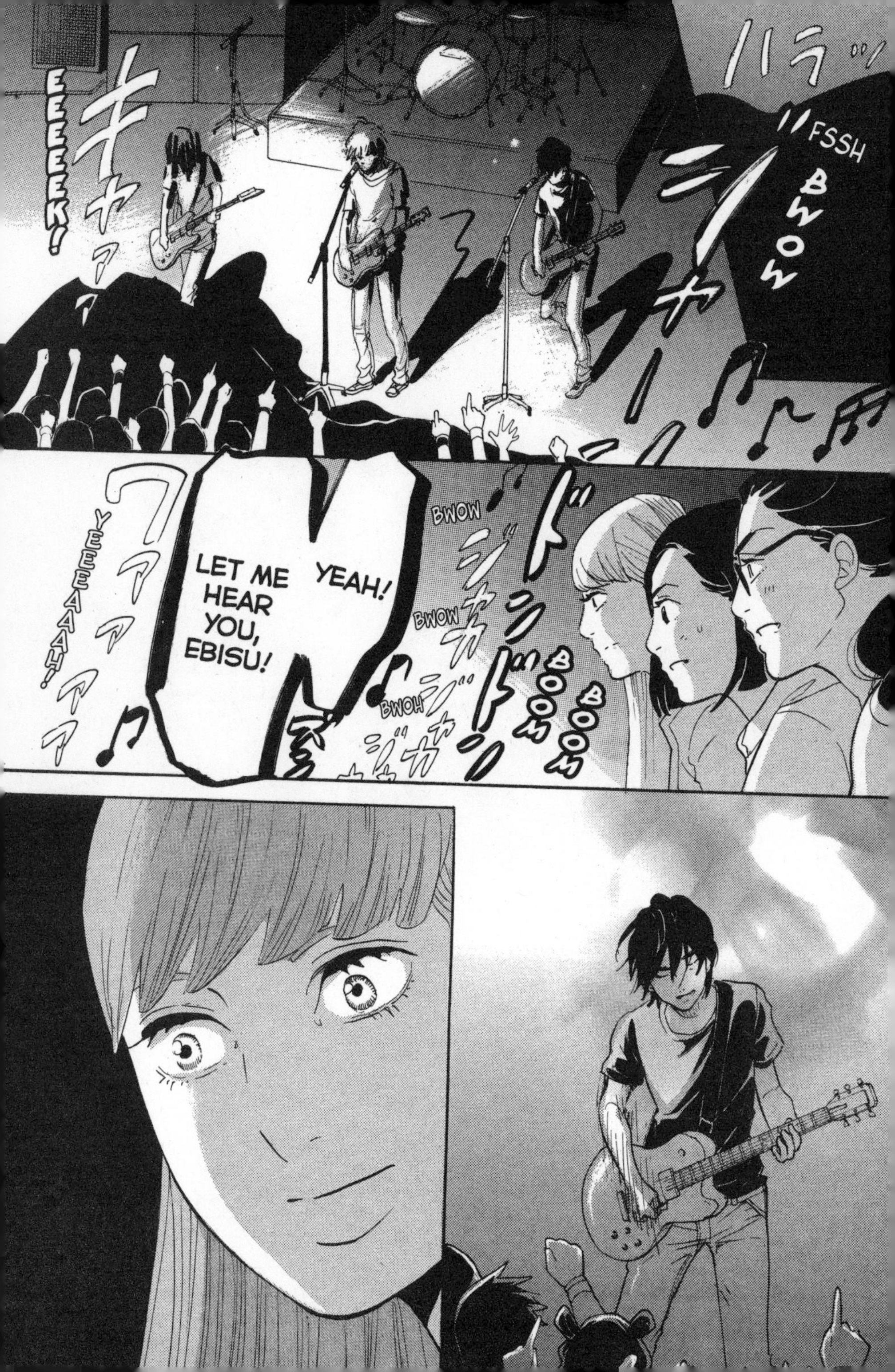
FSSH
BWOW
EEEEEK!
BOOM
BOOM
BWOW
BWOW
BWOH
YEAH!
LET ME HEAR YOU, EBISU!
YEEEAAAH!

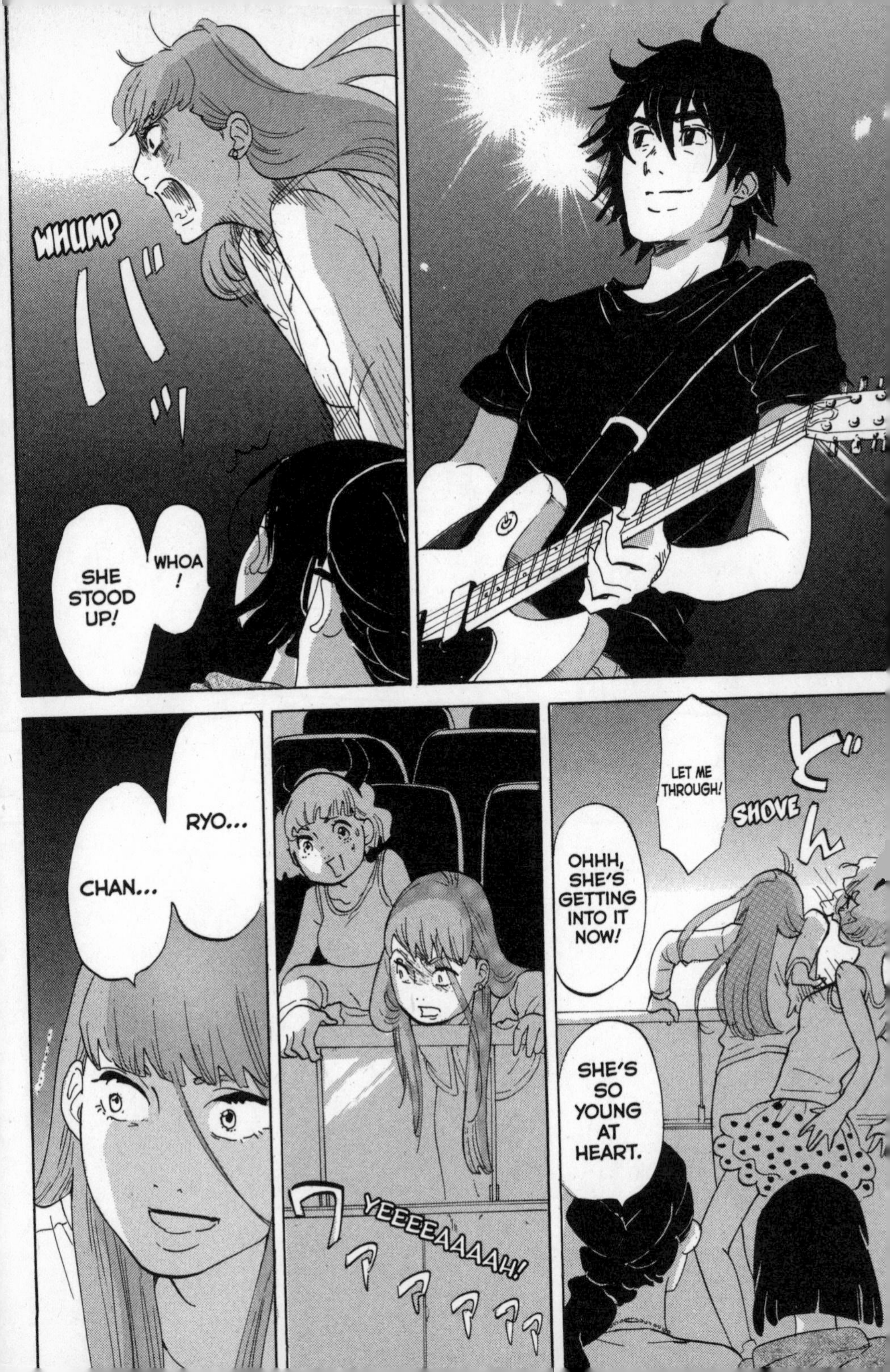
WHUMP
WHOA!
SHE STOOD UP!
LET ME THROUGH!
SHOVE
OHHH, SHE'S GETTING INTO IT NOW!
SHE'S SO YOUNG AT HEART.
YEEEEAAAAAH!
RYO...
CHAN...

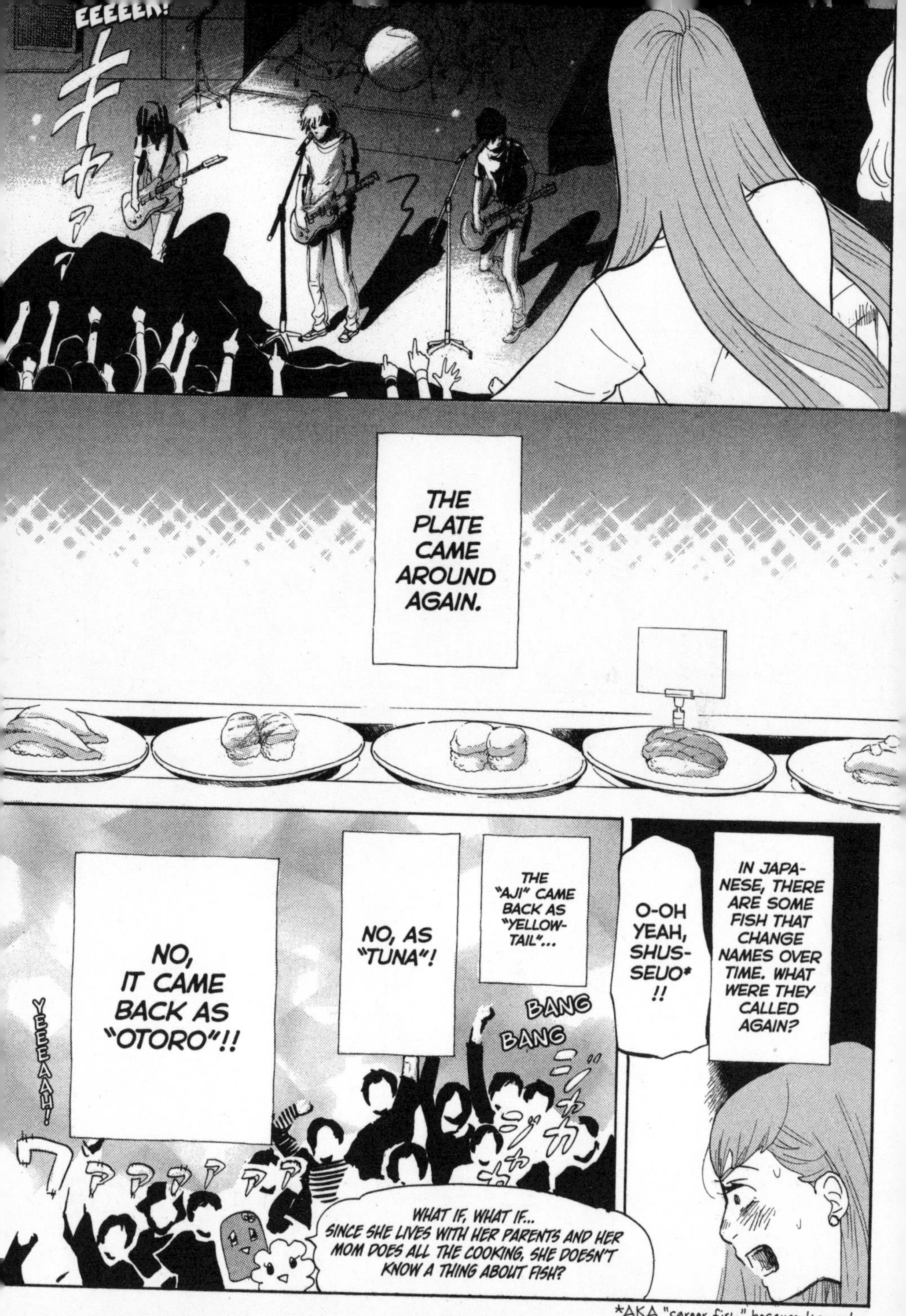
EEEEEN!
THE PLATE CAME AROUND AGAIN.
IN JAPANESE, THERE ARE SOME FISH THAT CHANGE NAMES OVER TIME. WHAT WERE THEY CALLED AGAIN?
O-OH YEAH, SHUSSEUO* !!
THE "AJI" CAME BACK AS "YELLOW-TAIL"...
NO, AS "TUNA"!
NO, IT CAME BACK AS "OTORO"!!
BANG BANG
YEEEAAAH!
WHAT IF, WHAT IF... SINCE SHE LIVES WITH HER PARENTS AND HER MOM DOES ALL THE COOKING, SHE DOESN'T KNOW A THING ABOUT FISH?

*AKA "career fish," because they get "promoted" as they grow.

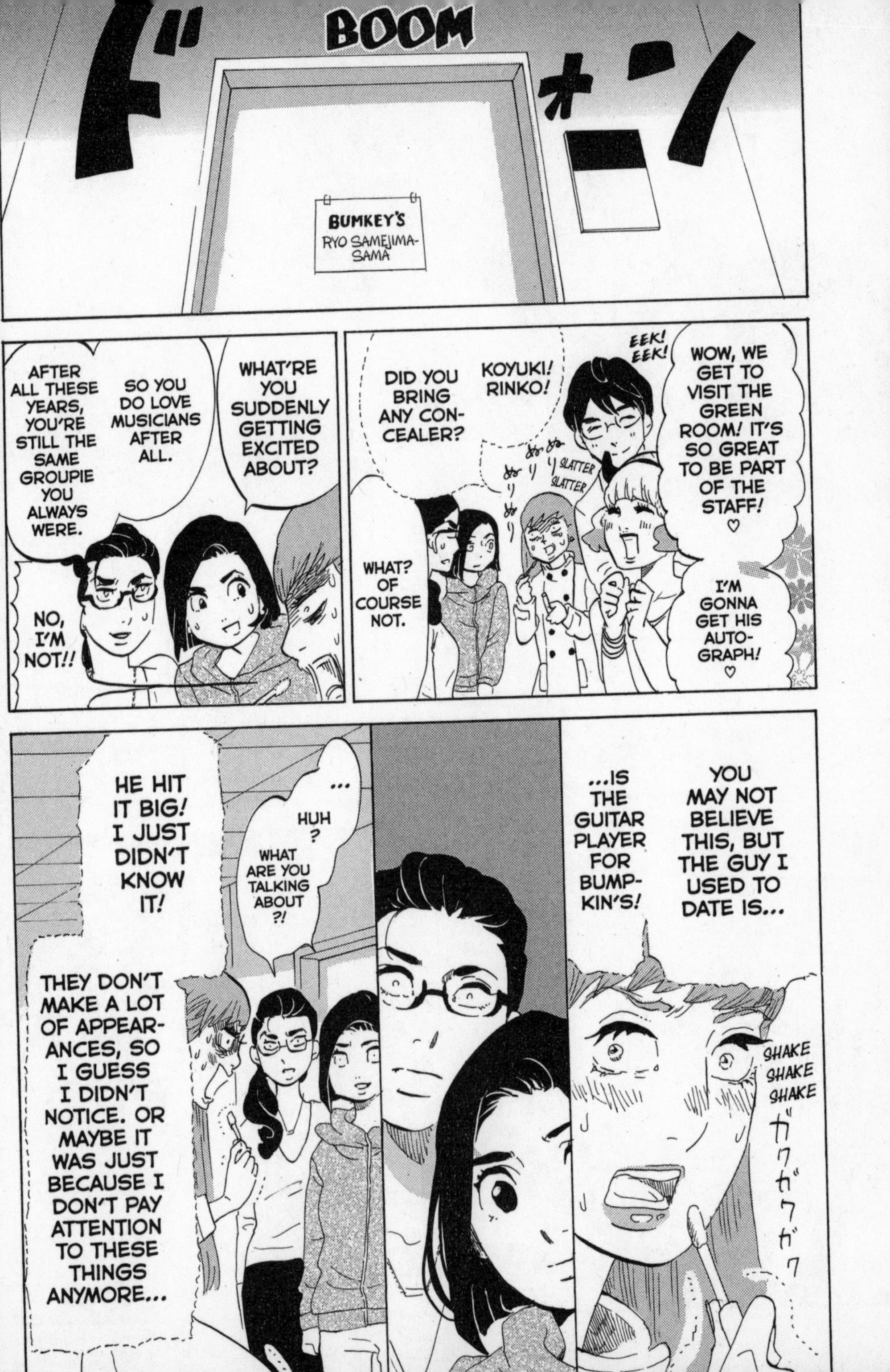
BOOM
BUMKEY'S
RYO SAMEJIMA-SAMA
EEK! EEK!
WOW, WE GET TO VISIT THE GREEN ROOM! IT'S SO GREAT TO BE PART OF THE STAFF! ♡
I'M GONNA GET HIS AUTO-GRAPH! ♡
KOYUKI! RINKO!
SLATTER SLATTER
DID YOU BRING ANY CON-CEALER?
WHAT? OF COURSE NOT.
WHAT'RE YOU SUDDENLY GETTING EXCITED ABOUT?
SO YOU DO LOVE MUSICIANS AFTER ALL.
AFTER ALL THESE YEARS, YOU'RE STILL THE SAME GROUPIE YOU ALWAYS WERE.
NO, I'M NOT!!
YOU MAY NOT BELIEVE THIS, BUT THE GUY I USED TO DATE IS...
...IS THE GUITAR PLAYER FOR BUMP-KIN'S!
SHAKE SHAKE SHAKE
...
HUH?
WHAT ARE YOU TALKING ABOUT?!
HE HIT IT BIG! I JUST DIDN'T KNOW IT!
THEY DON'T MAKE A LOT OF APPEAR-ANCES, SO I GUESS I DIDN'T NOTICE. OR MAYBE IT WAS JUST BECAUSE I DON'T PAY ATTENTION TO THESE THINGS ANYMORE...

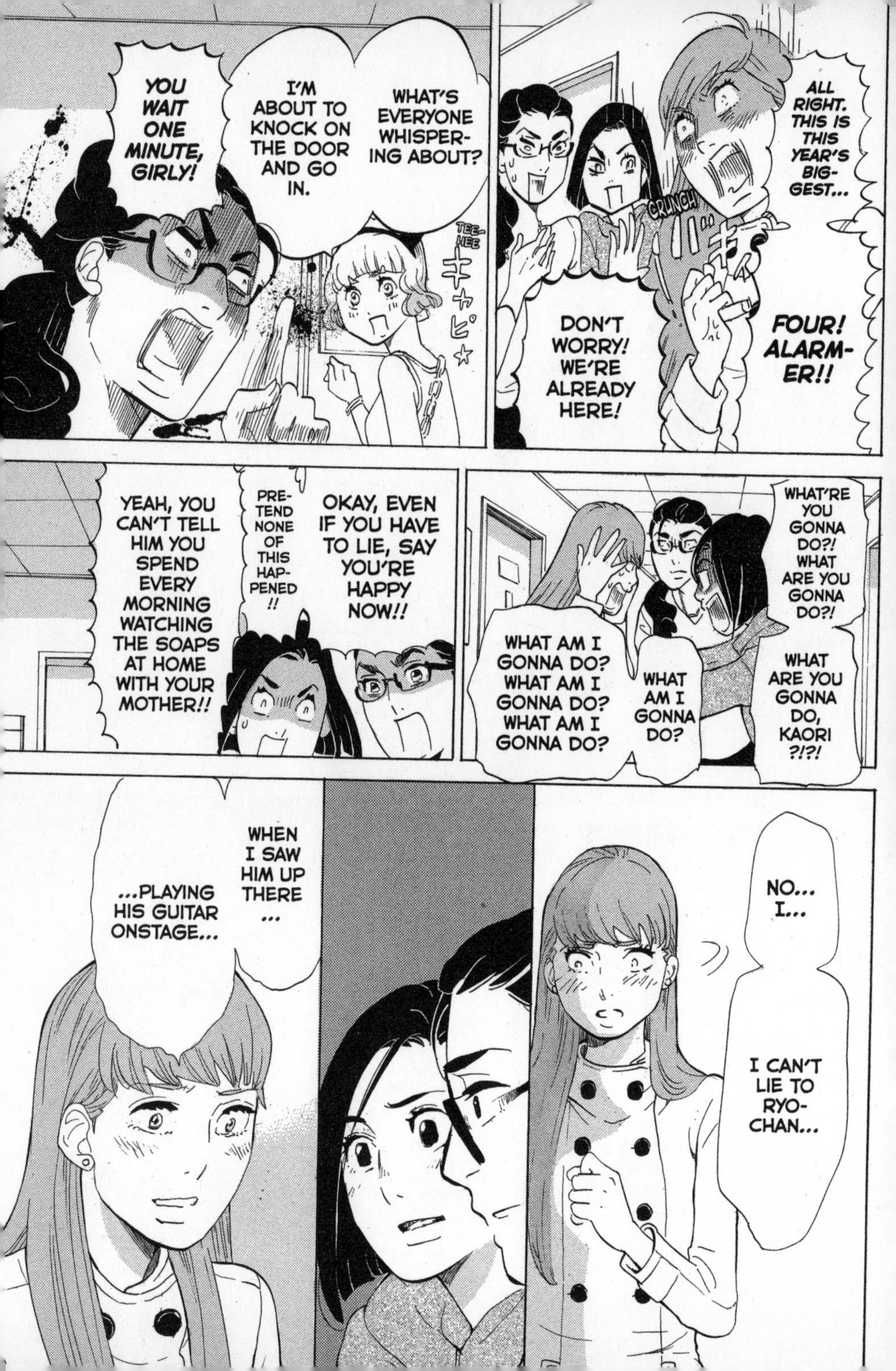
ALL RIGHT. THIS IS THIS YEAR'S BIGGEST...
CRUNCH
FOUR! ALARMER!!
DON'T WORRY! WE'RE ALREADY HERE!
WHAT'S EVERYONE WHISPERING ABOUT?
I'M ABOUT TO KNOCK ON THE DOOR AND GO IN.
TEE-HEE
YOU WAIT ONE MINUTE, GIRLY!
WHAT'RE YOU GONNA DO?! WHAT ARE YOU GONNA DO?!
WHAT ARE YOU GONNA DO, KAORI?!?!
WHAT AM I GONNA DO?
WHAT AM I GONNA DO? WHAT AM I GONNA DO? WHAT AM I GONNA DO?
OKAY, EVEN IF YOU HAVE TO LIE, SAY YOU'RE HAPPY NOW!!
PRETEND NONE OF THIS HAPPENED!!
YEAH, YOU CAN'T TELL HIM YOU SPEND EVERY MORNING WATCHING THE SOAPS AT HOME WITH YOUR MOTHER!!
NO... I...
I CAN'T LIE TO RYO-CHAN...
WHEN I SAW HIM UP THERE...
...PLAYING HIS GUITAR ONSTAGE...

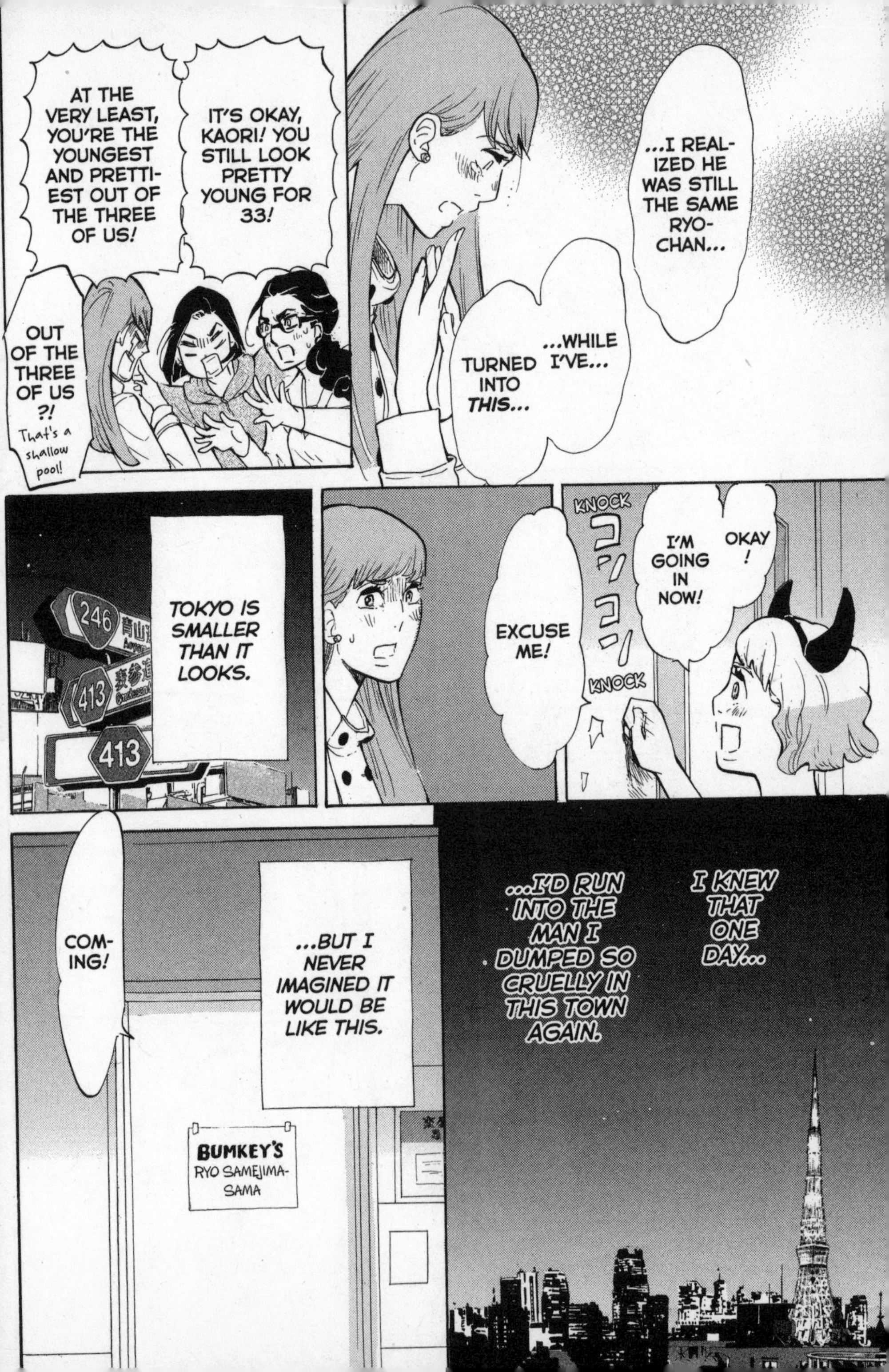
...I REAL-IZED HE WAS STILL THE SAME RYO-CHAN...
...WHILE I'VE... TURNED INTO THIS...
IT'S OKAY, KAORI! YOU STILL LOOK PRETTY YOUNG FOR 33!
AT THE VERY LEAST, YOU'RE THE YOUNGEST AND PRETTI-EST OUT OF THE THREE OF US!
OUT OF THE THREE OF US?!
That's a shallow pool!
KNOCK
KNOCK
I'M GOING IN NOW! OKAY!
EXCUSE ME!
TOKYO IS SMALLER THAN IT LOOKS.
246
413
413
I KNEW THAT ONE DAY...
...I'D RUN INTO THE MAN I DUMPED SO CRUELLY IN THIS TOWN AGAIN.
...BUT I NEVER IMAGINED IT WOULD BE LIKE THIS.
COM-ING!
BUMKEY'S
RYO SAMEJIMA-SAMA

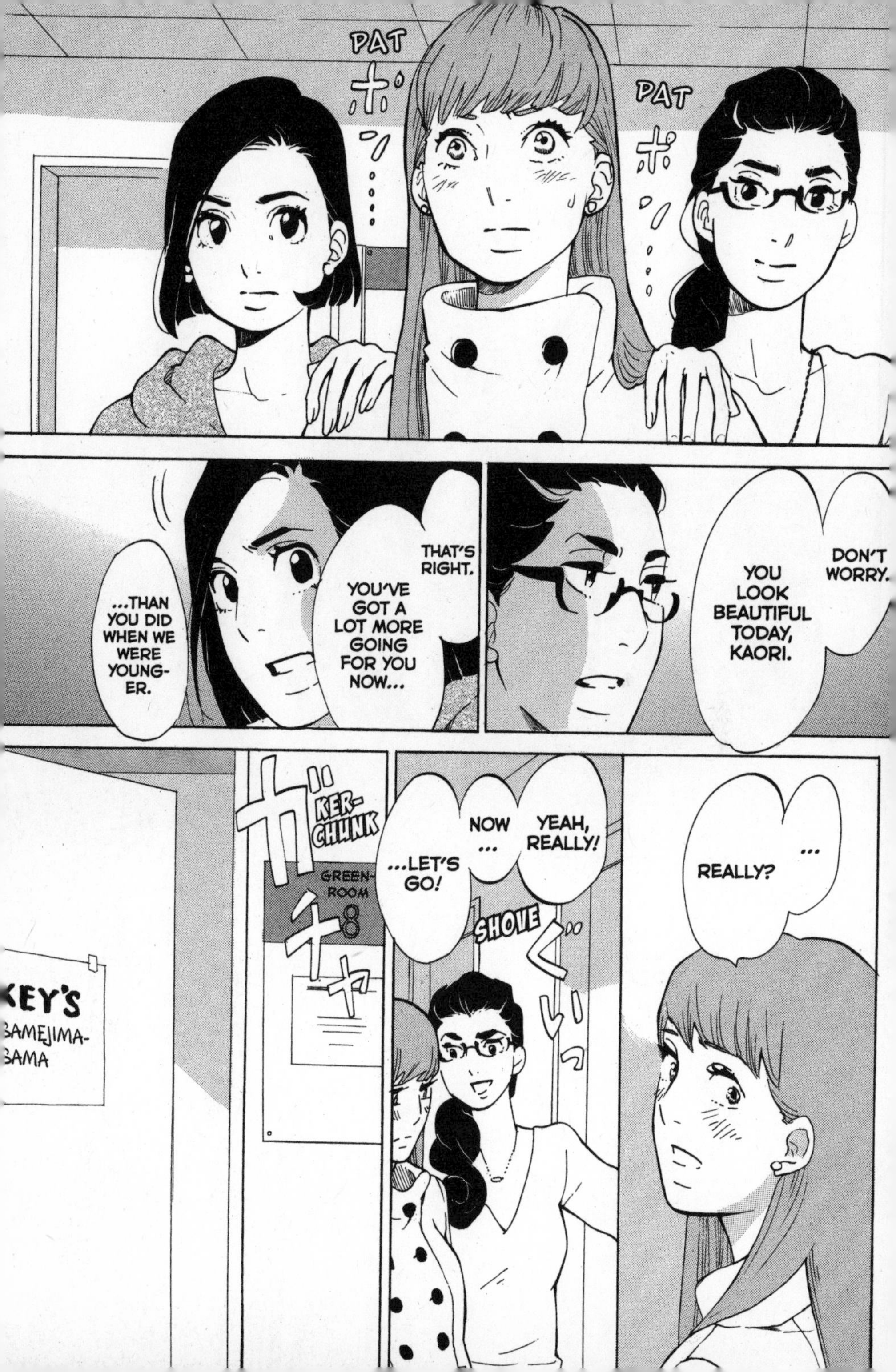
PAT
ポ
PAT
ポ
DON'T WORRY.
YOU LOOK BEAUTIFUL TODAY, KAORI.
THAT'S RIGHT.
YOU'VE GOT A LOT MORE GOING FOR YOU NOW...
...THAN YOU DID WHEN WE WERE YOUNG-ER.
...
REALLY?
YEAH, REALLY!
NOW ...
...LET'S GO!
SHOVE
KER-CHUNK
GREEN-ROOM 8
KEY'S
SAMEJIMA-
SAMA

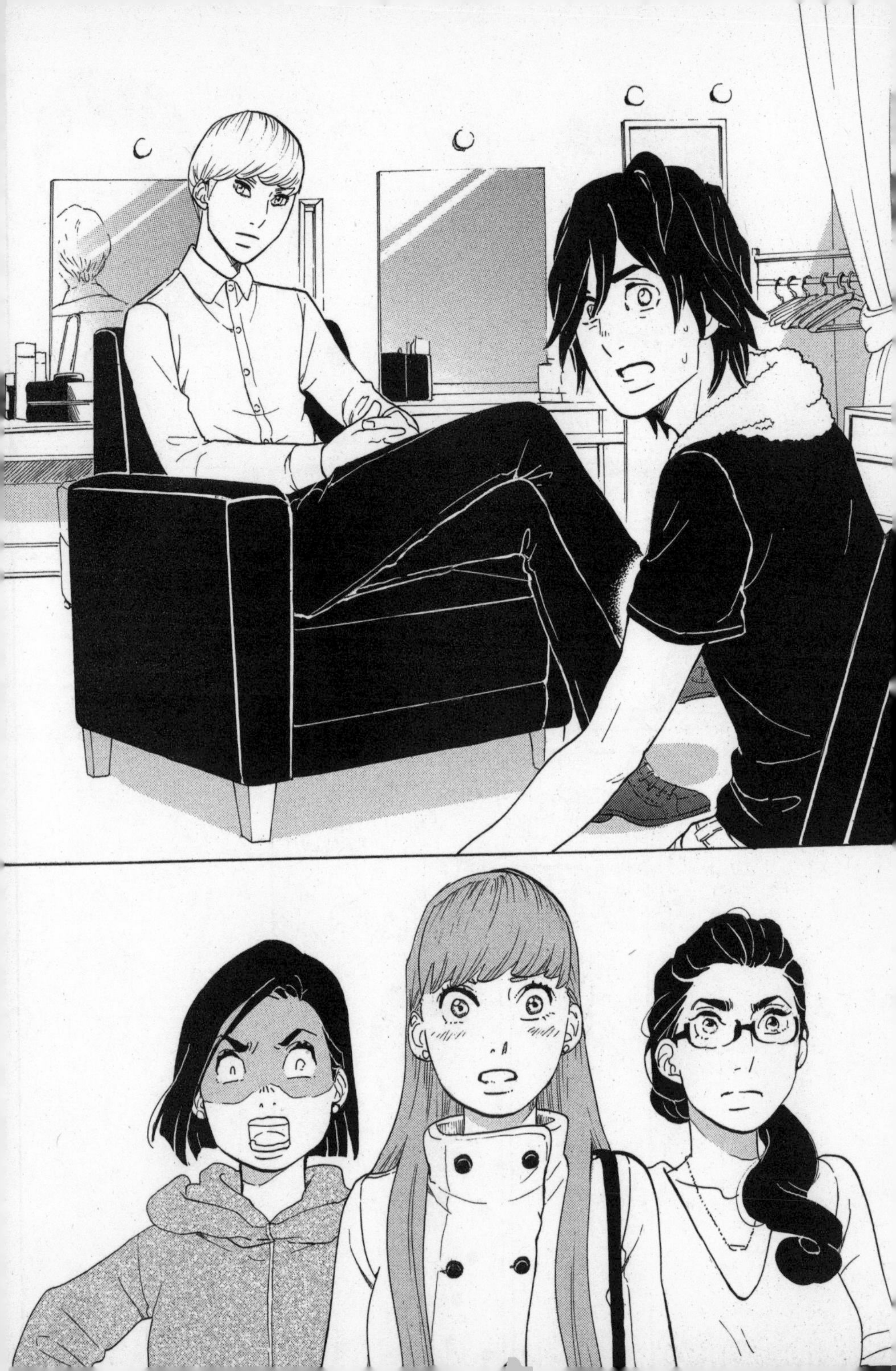

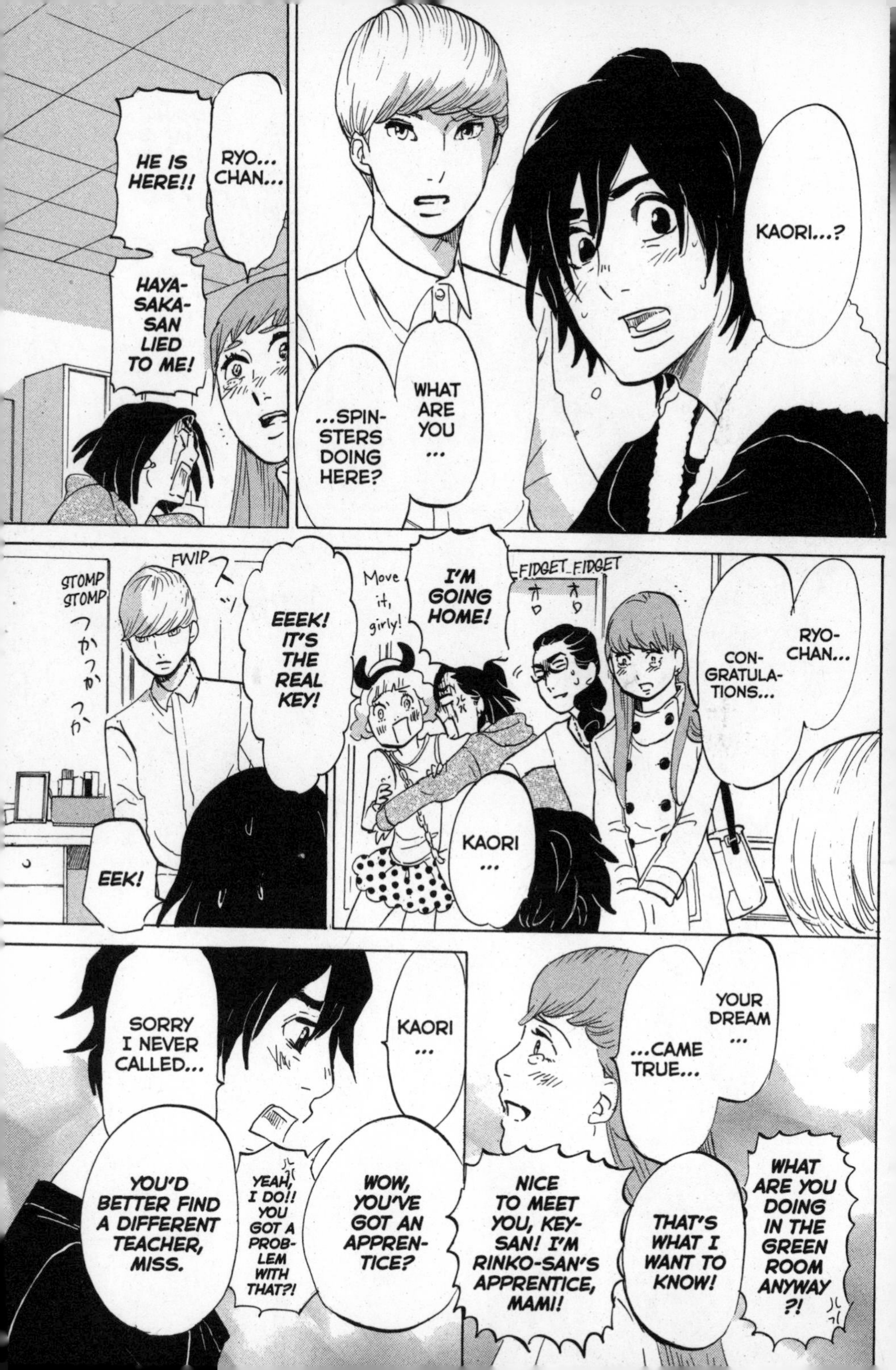
KAORI...?
WHAT ARE YOU ...
...SPIN-STERS DOING HERE?
RYO... CHAN...
HE IS HERE!!
HAYA-SAKA-SAN LIED TO ME!
RYO-CHAN...
CON-GRATULA-TIONS...
KAORI ...
FIDGET FIDGET
オロ オロ
I'M GOING HOME!
Move it, girly!
EEEK! IT'S THE REAL KEY!
FWIP
スッ
STOMP STOMP
つかつかつか
EEK!
YOUR DREAM ...
...CAME TRUE...
WHAT ARE YOU DOING IN THE GREEN ROOM ANYWAY?!
THAT'S WHAT I WANT TO KNOW!
NICE TO MEET YOU, KEY-SAN! I'M RINKO-SAN'S APPRENTICE, MAMI!
WOW, YOU'VE GOT AN APPREN-TICE?
KAORI ...
SORRY I NEVER CALLED...
YEAH, I DO!! YOU GOT A PROB-LEM WITH THAT?!
YOU'D BETTER FIND A DIFFERENT TEACHER, MISS.

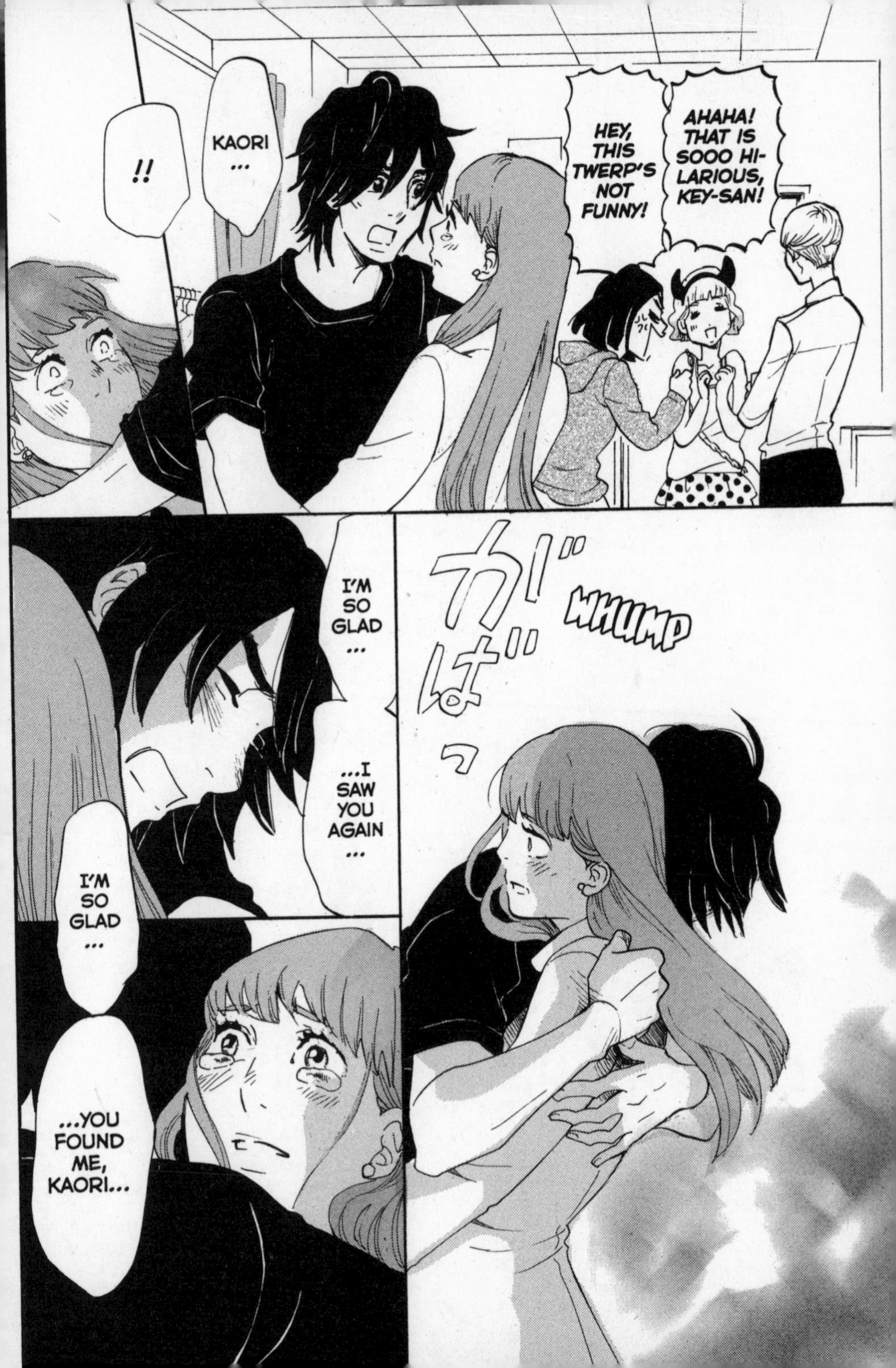
AHAHA! THAT IS SOOO HI-LARIOUS, KEY-SAN!
HEY, THIS TWERP'S NOT FUNNY!
KAORI ...
!!
がばっ
WHUMP
I'M SO GLAD ...
...I SAW YOU AGAIN ...
I'M SO GLAD ...
...YOU FOUND ME, KAORI...

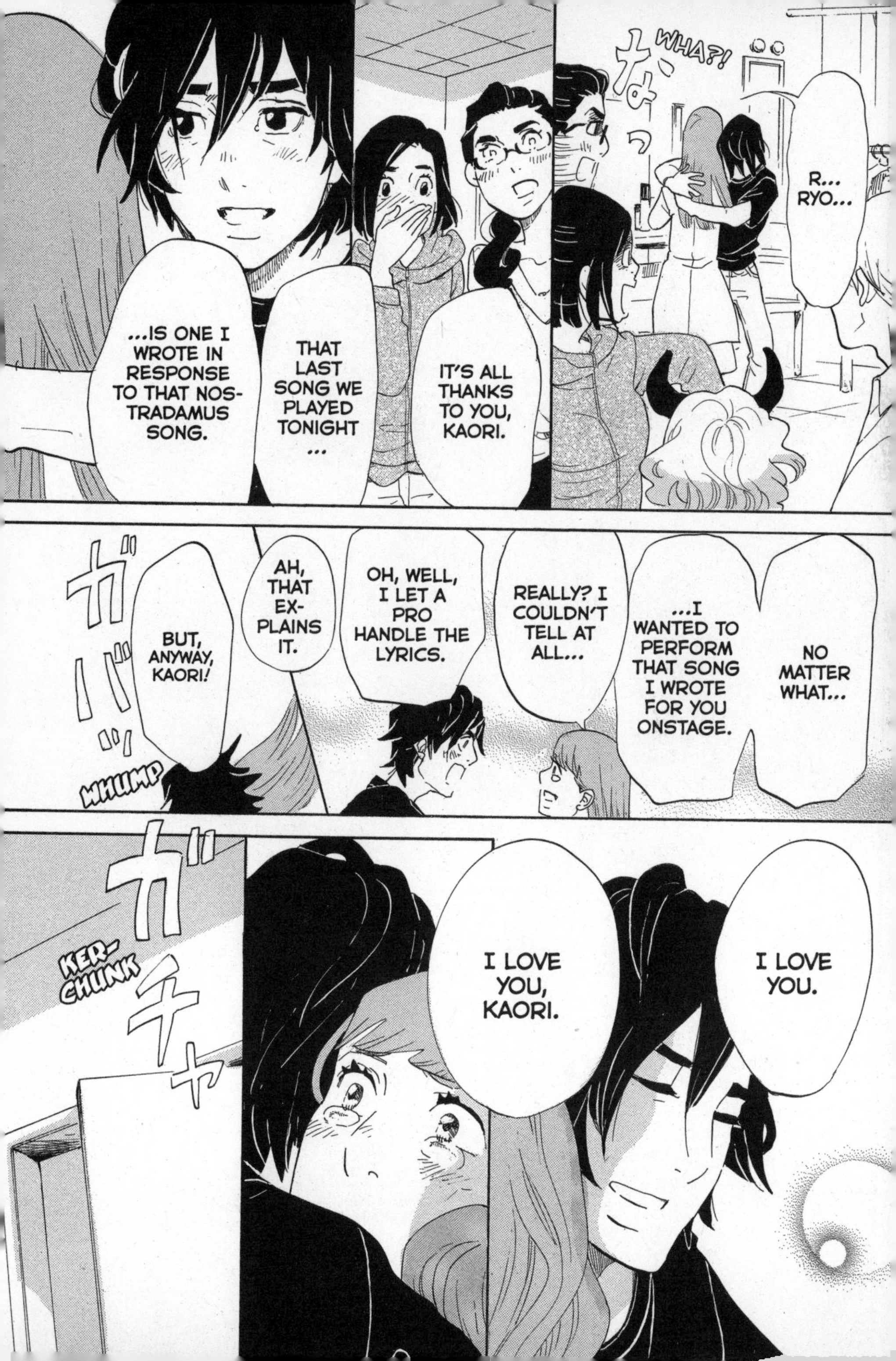
WHA?!
R... RYO...
IT'S ALL THANKS TO YOU, KAORI.
THAT LAST SONG WE PLAYED TONIGHT...
...IS ONE I WROTE IN RESPONSE TO THAT NOS-TRADAMUS SONG.
NO MATTER WHAT...
...I WANTED TO PERFORM THAT SONG I WROTE FOR YOU ONSTAGE.
REALLY? I COULDN'T TELL AT ALL...
OH, WELL, I LET A PRO HANDLE THE LYRICS.
AH, THAT EX-PLAINS IT.
BUT, ANYWAY, KAORI!
WHUMP
I LOVE YOU.
I LOVE YOU, KAORI.
KER-CHUNK

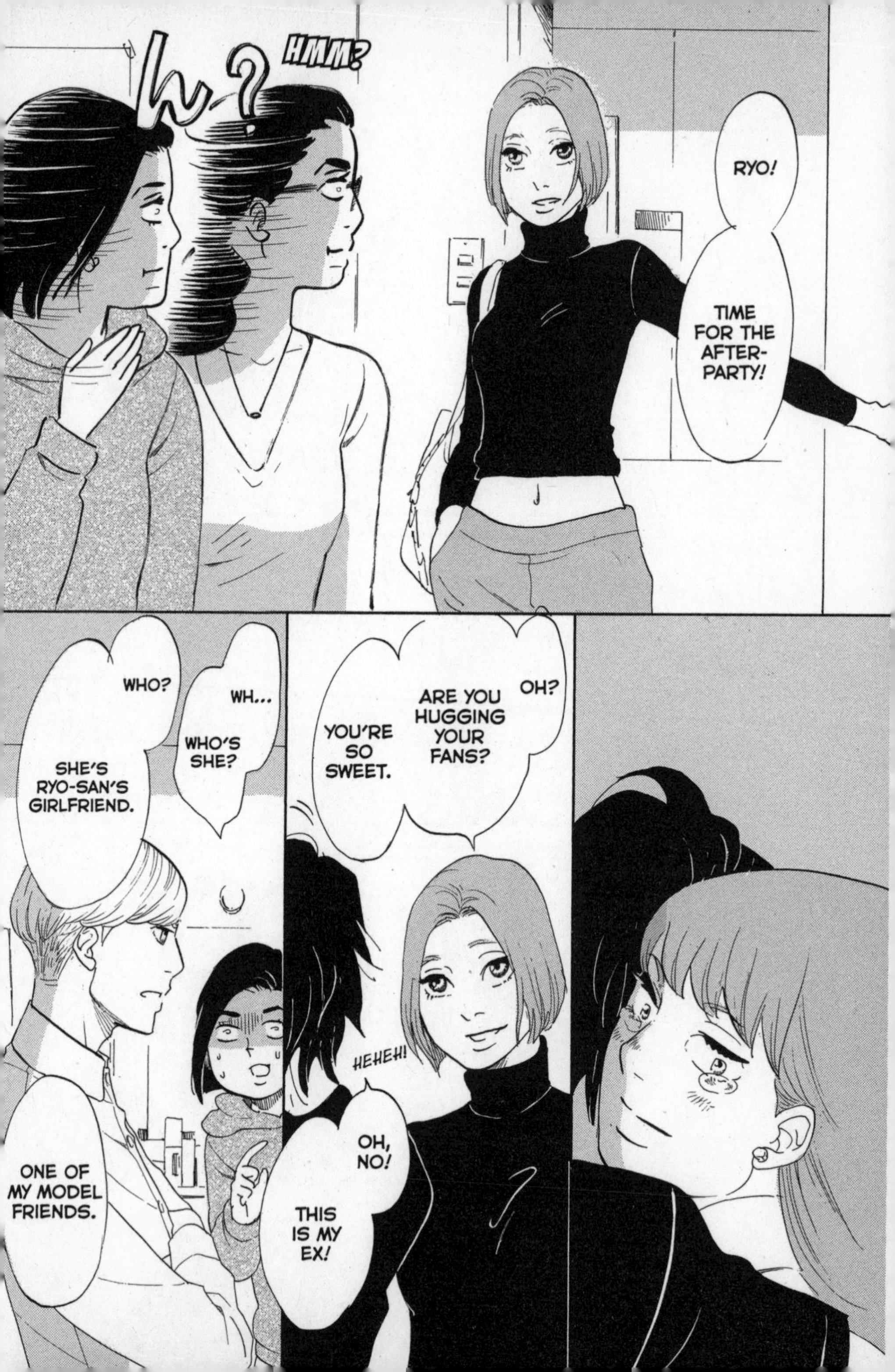
RYO!
TIME FOR THE AFTER-PARTY!
HMM?
ん?
OH? ARE YOU HUGGING YOUR FANS? YOU'RE SO SWEET.
HEHEH!
OH, NO! THIS IS MY EX!
WH... WHO'S SHE?
WHO? SHE'S RYO-SAN'S GIRLFRIEND.
ONE OF MY MODEL FRIENDS.

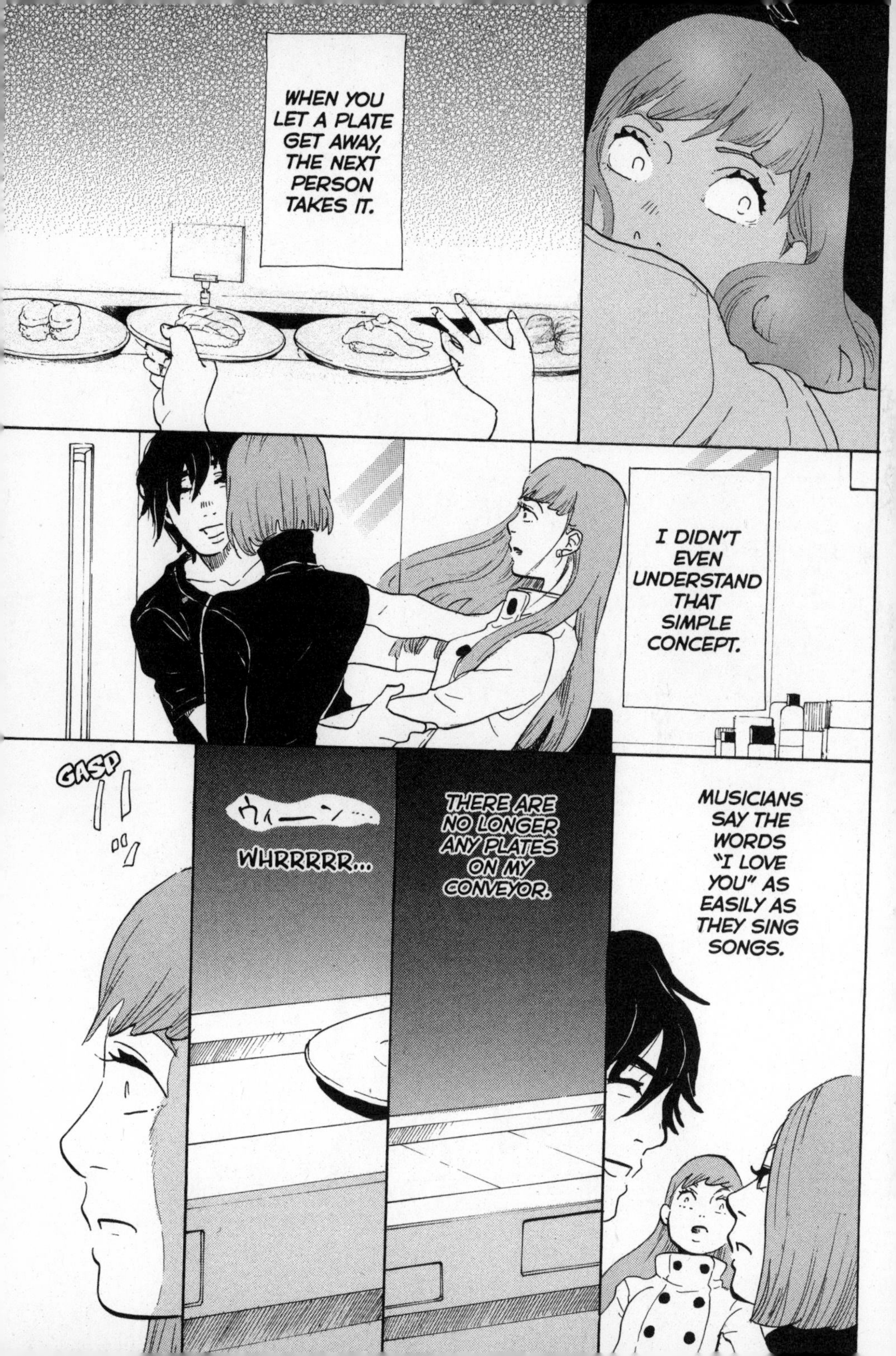
WHEN YOU LET A PLATE GET AWAY, THE NEXT PERSON TAKES IT.
I DIDN'T EVEN UNDERSTAND THAT SIMPLE CONCEPT.
MUSICIANS SAY THE WORDS "I LOVE YOU" AS EASILY AS THEY SING SONGS.
THERE ARE NO LONGER ANY PLATES ON MY CONVEYOR.
ウィーン…
WHRRRRR...
GASP

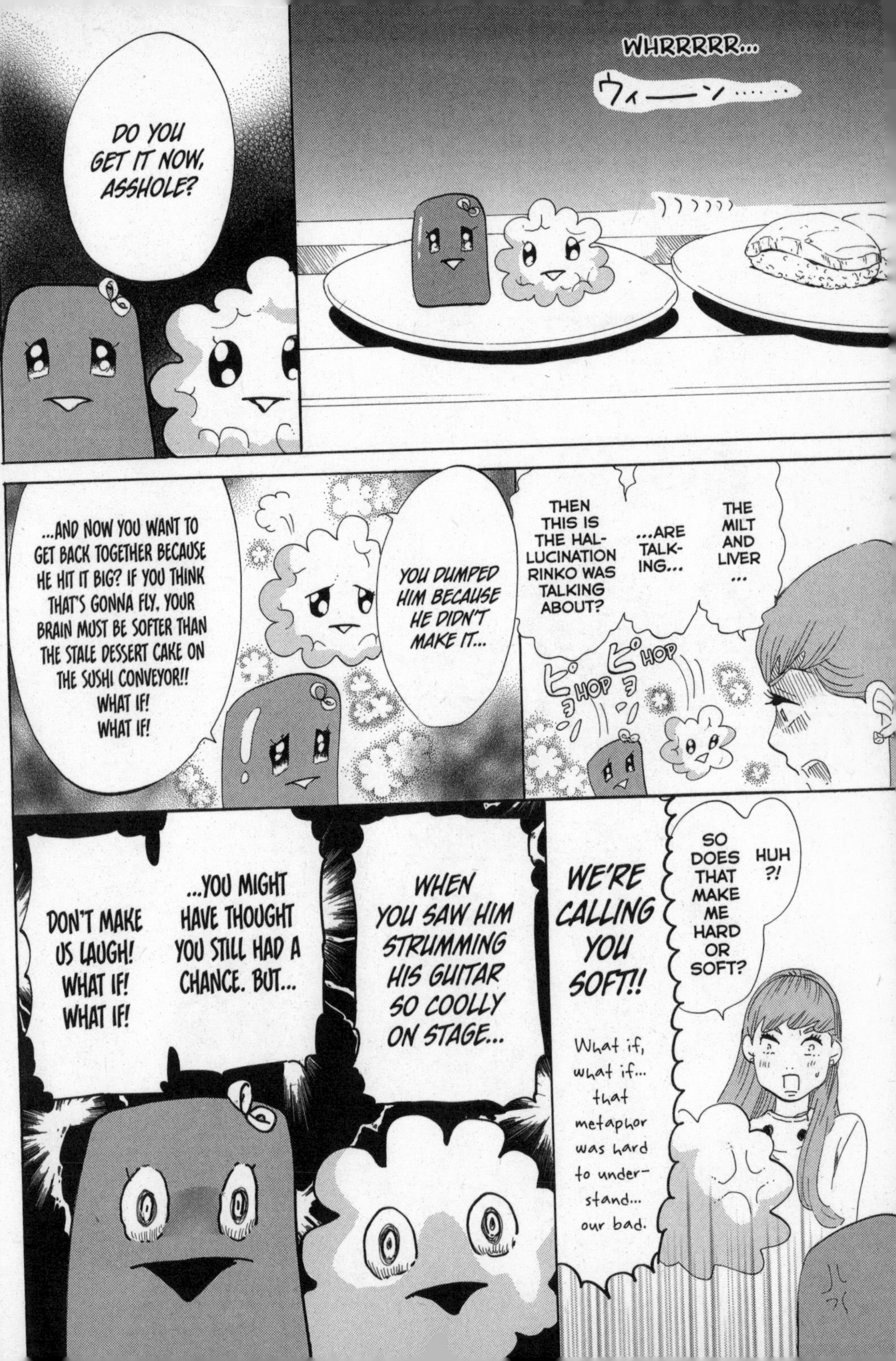
WHRRRRR...
ウィーン……
DO YOU GET IT NOW, ASSHOLE?
THE MILT AND LIVER ...
...ARE TALKING...
THEN THIS IS THE HALLUCINATION RINKO WAS TALKING ABOUT?
ピョ HOP ピョ HOP
YOU DUMPED HIM BECAUSE HE DIDN'T MAKE IT...
...AND NOW YOU WANT TO GET BACK TOGETHER BECAUSE HE HIT IT BIG? IF YOU THINK THAT'S GONNA FLY, YOUR BRAIN MUST BE SOFTER THAN THE STALE DESSERT CAKE ON THE SUSHI CONVEYOR!! WHAT IF! WHAT IF!
HUH ?!
SO DOES THAT MAKE ME HARD OR SOFT?
WE'RE CALLING YOU SOFT!!
What if, what if... that metaphor was hard to understand... our bad.
WHEN YOU SAW HIM STRUMMING HIS GUITAR SO COOLLY ON STAGE...
...YOU MIGHT HAVE THOUGHT YOU STILL HAD A CHANCE. BUT...
DON'T MAKE US LAUGH! WHAT IF! WHAT IF!

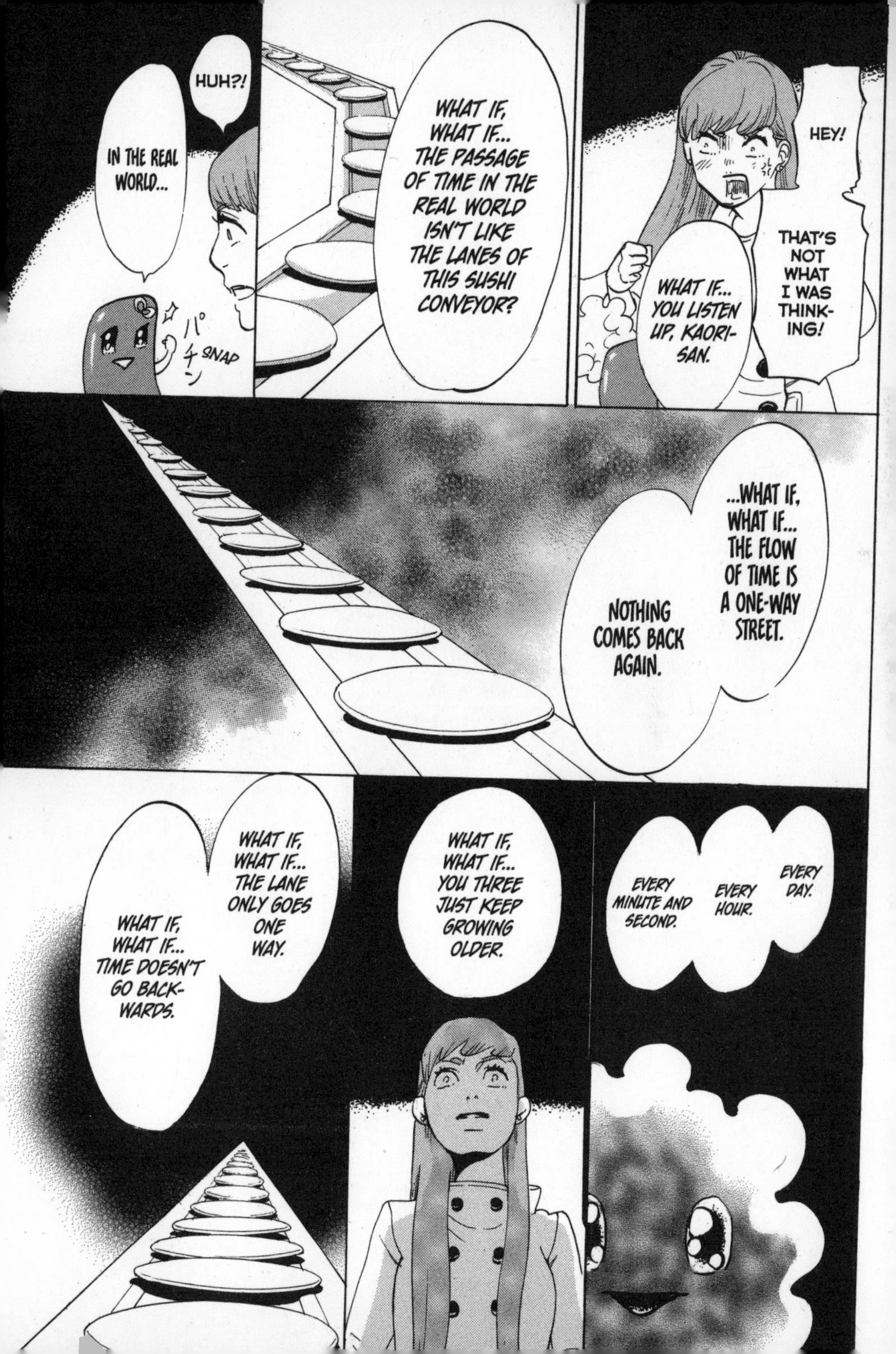
HEY!
THAT'S NOT WHAT I WAS THINK-ING!
WHAT IF... YOU LISTEN UP, KAORI-SAN.
WHAT IF, WHAT IF... THE PASSAGE OF TIME IN THE REAL WORLD ISN'T LIKE THE LANES OF THIS SUSHI CONVEYOR?
HUH?!
IN THE REAL WORLD...
パチン
SNAP
...WHAT IF, WHAT IF... THE FLOW OF TIME IS A ONE-WAY STREET.
NOTHING COMES BACK AGAIN.
EVERY DAY.
EVERY HOUR.
EVERY MINUTE AND SECOND.
WHAT IF, WHAT IF... YOU THREE JUST KEEP GROWING OLDER.
WHAT IF, WHAT IF... THE LANE ONLY GOES ONE WAY.
WHAT IF, WHAT IF... TIME DOESN'T GO BACK-WARDS.

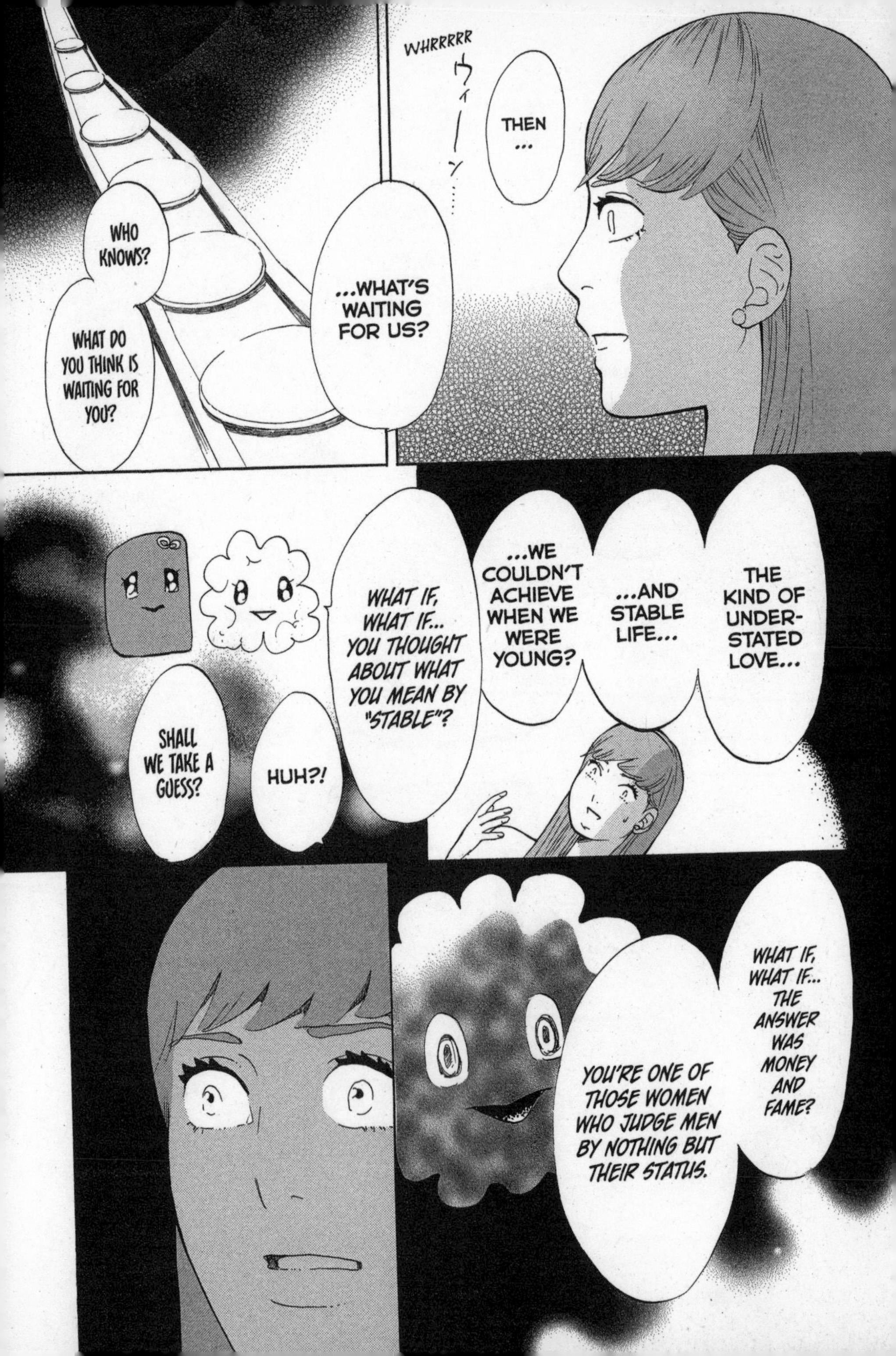
WHRRRRR
ウィーン…
THEN...
...WHAT'S WAITING FOR US?
WHO KNOWS?
WHAT DO YOU THINK IS WAITING FOR YOU?
THE KIND OF UNDER-STATED LOVE...
...AND STABLE LIFE...
...WE COULDN'T ACHIEVE WHEN WE WERE YOUNG?
WHAT IF, WHAT IF... YOU THOUGHT ABOUT WHAT YOU MEAN BY "STABLE"?
HUH?!
SHALL WE TAKE A GUESS?
WHAT IF, WHAT IF... THE ANSWER WAS MONEY AND FAME?
YOU'RE ONE OF THOSE WOMEN WHO JUDGE MEN BY NOTHING BUT THEIR STATUS.

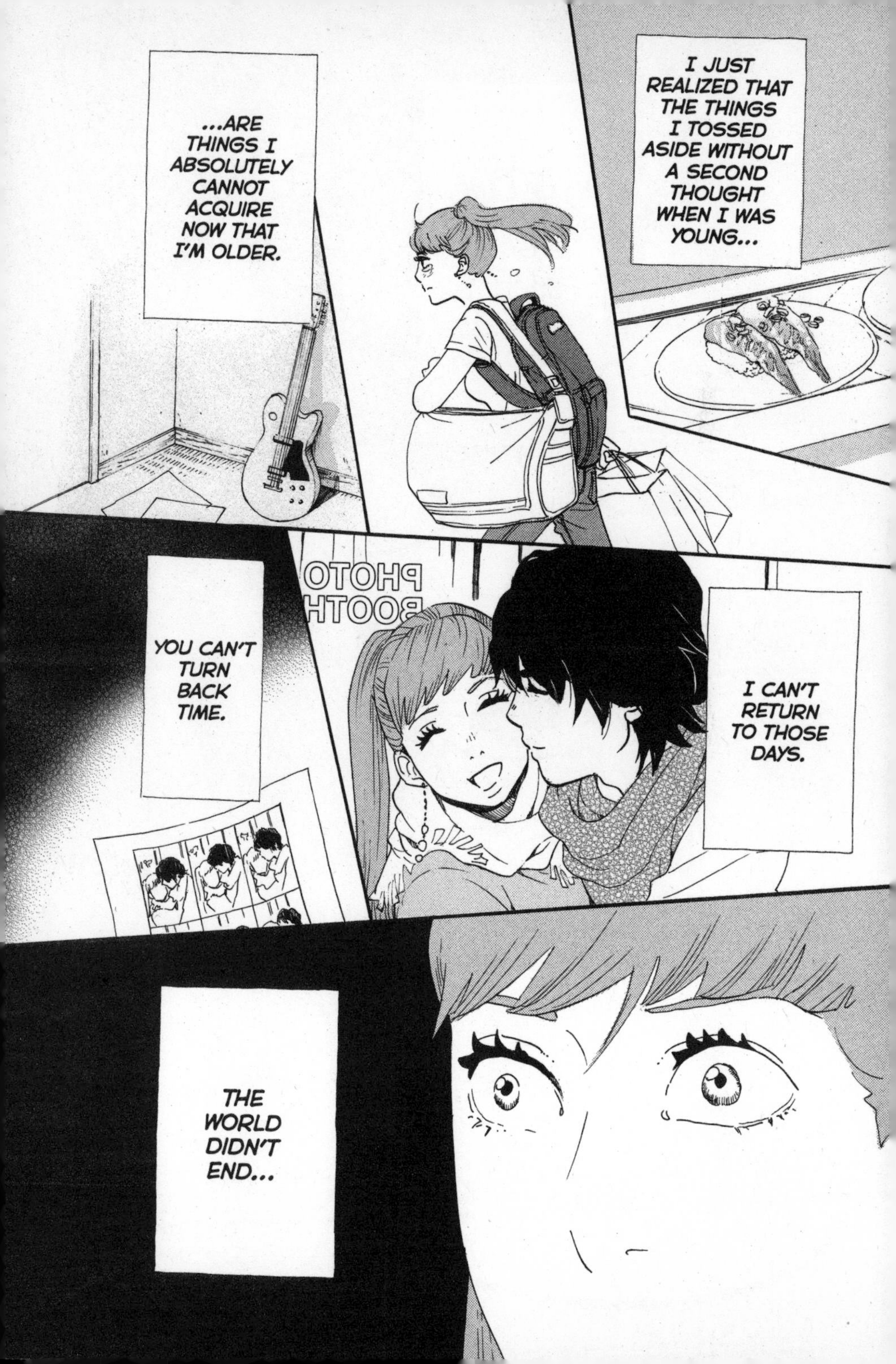
I JUST REALIZED THAT THE THINGS I TOSSED ASIDE WITHOUT A SECOND THOUGHT WHEN I WAS YOUNG...
...ARE THINGS I ABSOLUTELY CANNOT ACQUIRE NOW THAT I'M OLDER.
I CAN'T RETURN TO THOSE DAYS.
PHOTO BOOTH
YOU CAN'T TURN BACK TIME.
THE WORLD DIDN'T END...

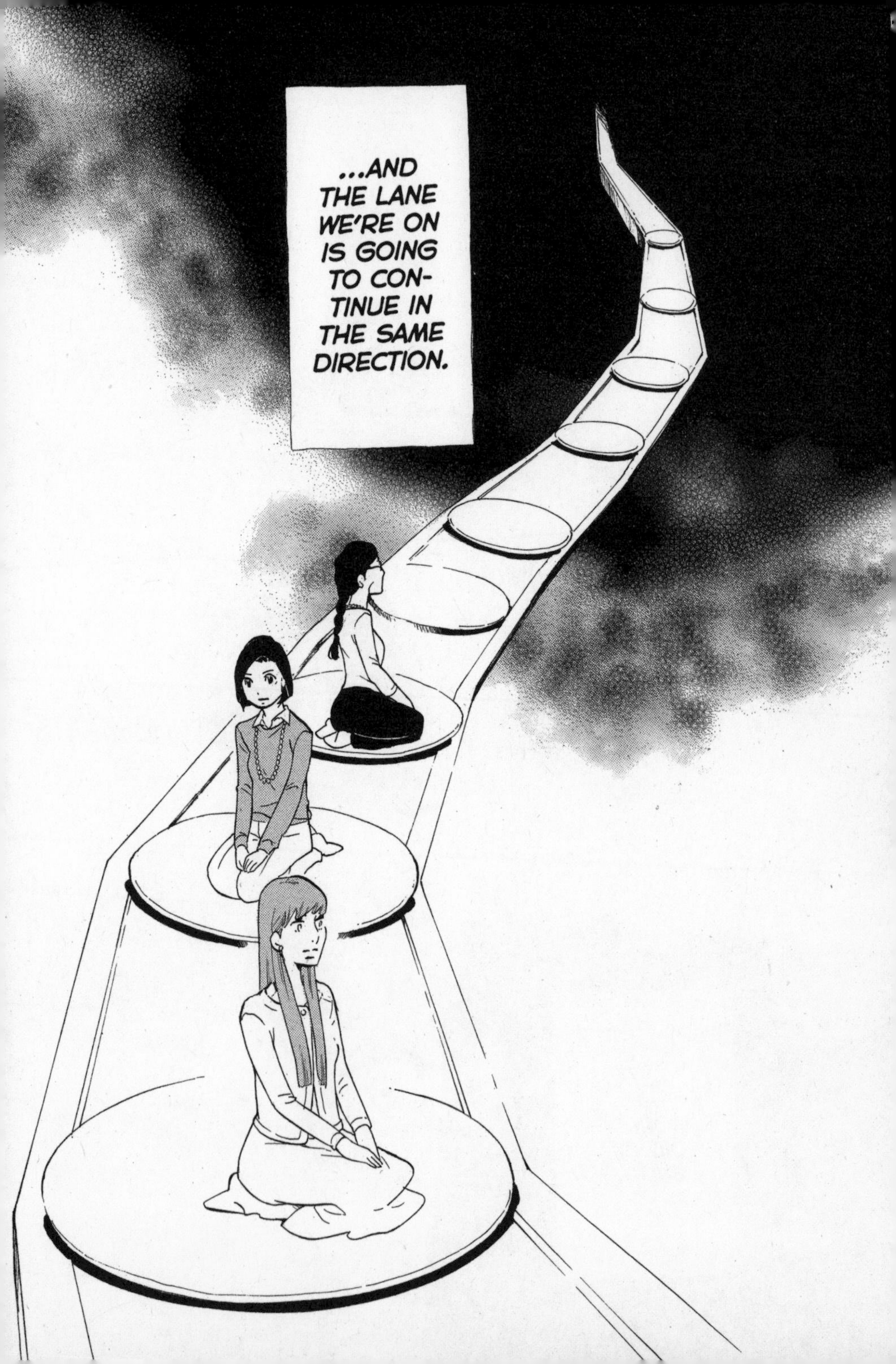
...AND THE LANE WE'RE ON IS GOING TO CON- TINUE IN THE SAME DIRECTION.

# ACT 7 SHIMESABA WOMAN

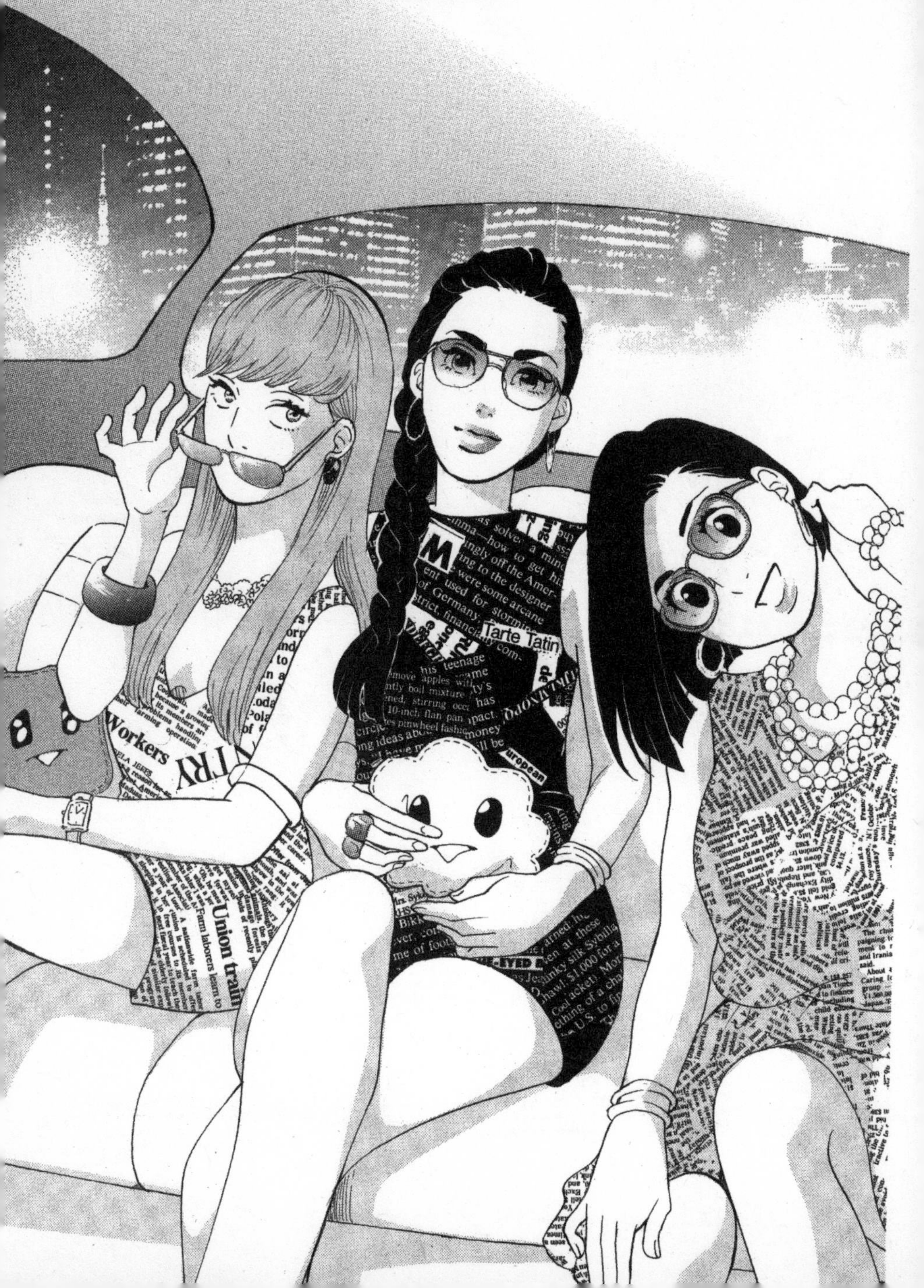

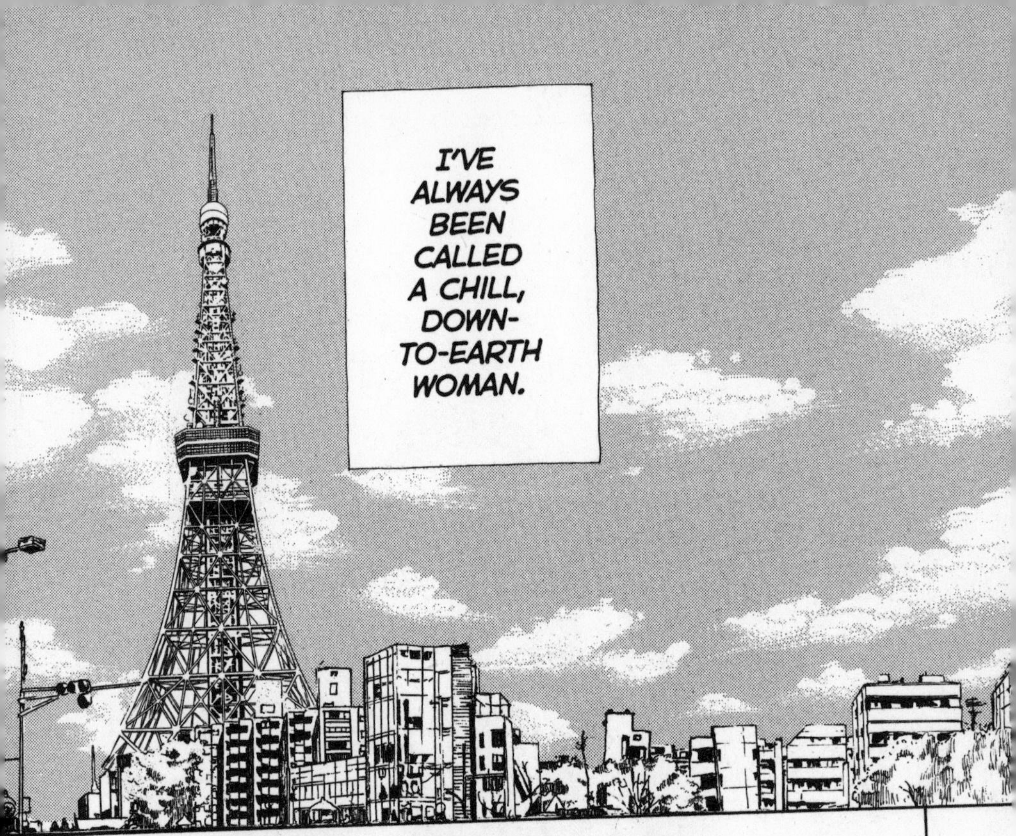
I'VE ALWAYS BEEN CALLED A CHILL, DOWN-TO-EARTH WOMAN.

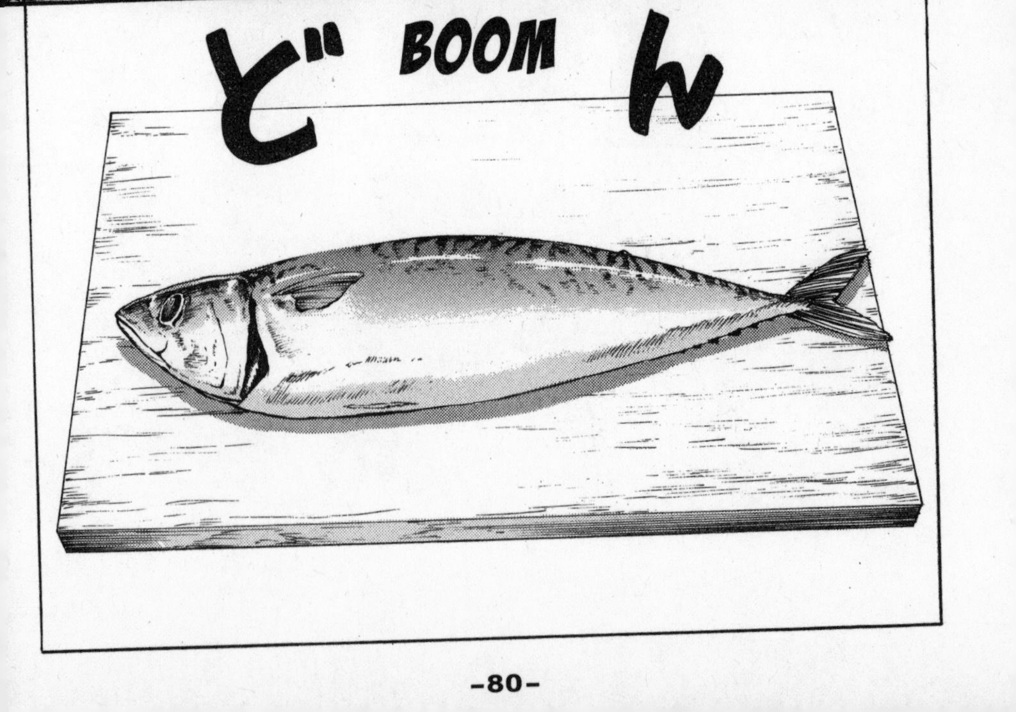
ど BOOM ん

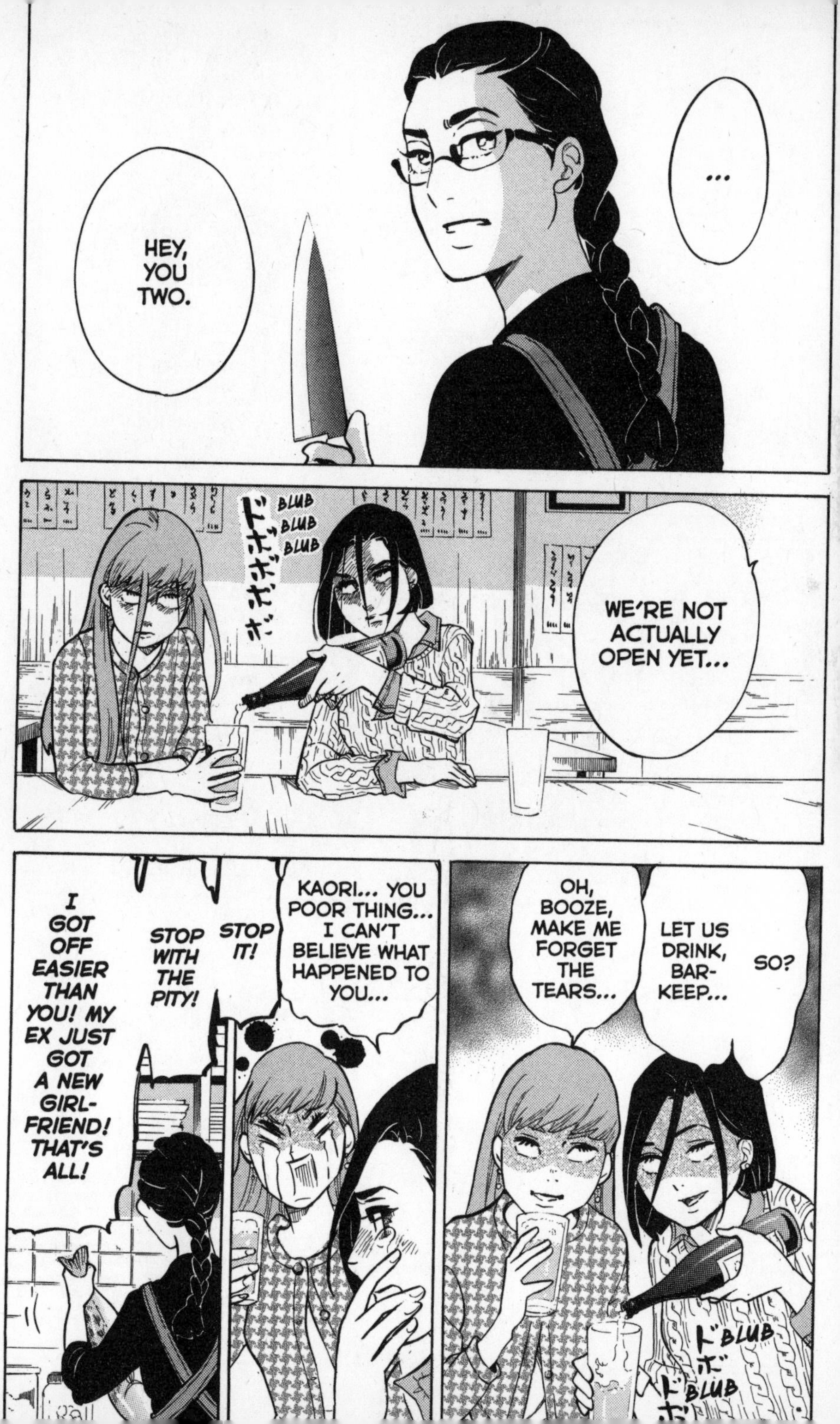
...
HEY, YOU TWO.
WE'RE NOT ACTUALLY OPEN YET...
BLUB BLUB BLUB
SO?
LET US DRINK, BAR-KEEP...
OH, BOOZE, MAKE ME FORGET THE TEARS...
BLUB BLUB
KAORI... YOU POOR THING... I CAN'T BELIEVE WHAT HAPPENED TO YOU...
STOP IT!
STOP WITH THE PITY!
I GOT OFF EASIER THAN YOU! MY EX JUST GOT A NEW GIRL-FRIEND! THAT'S ALL!

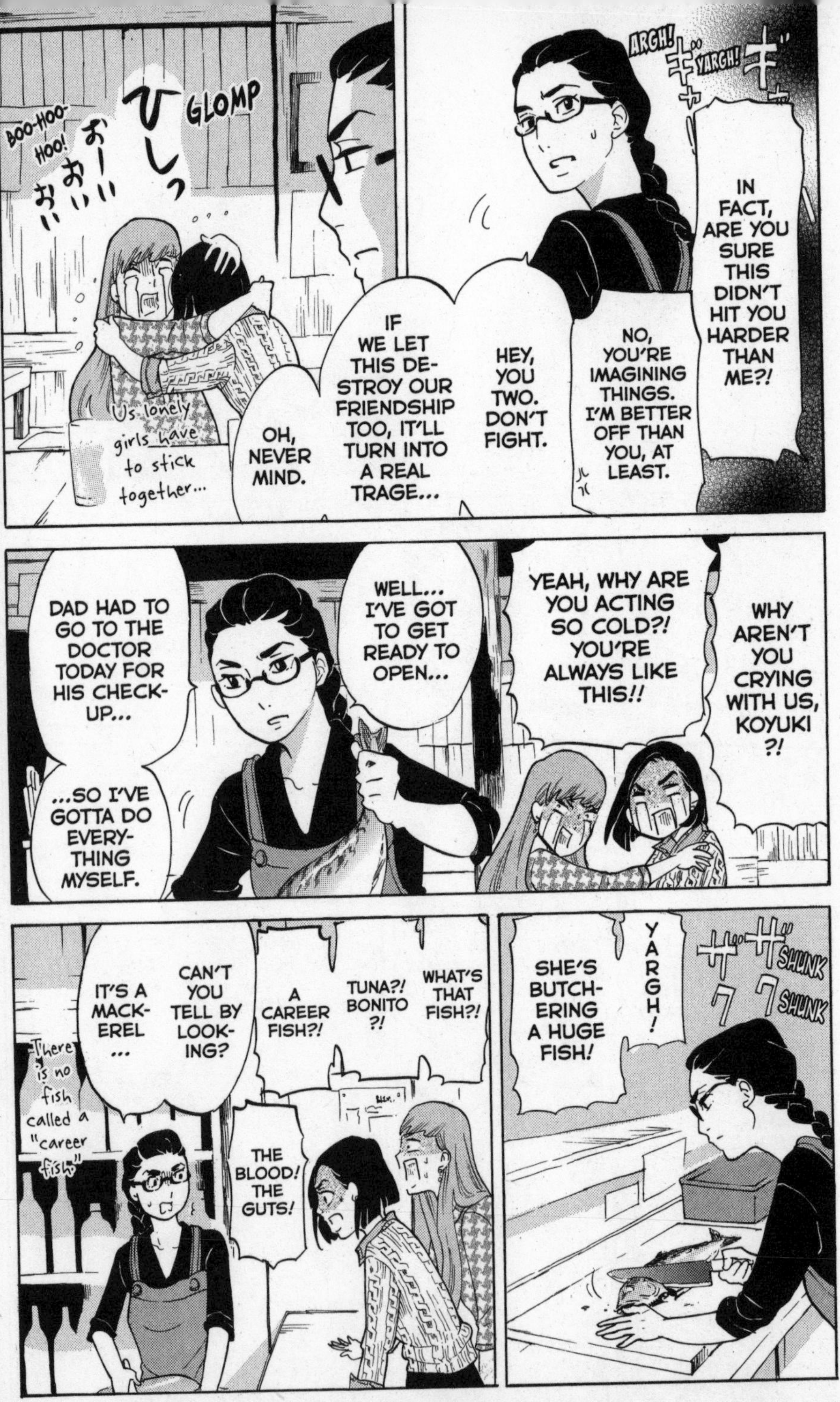
ARGH!
ギャ
YARGH!
ギャ
IN FACT, ARE YOU SURE THIS DIDN'T HIT YOU HARDER THAN ME?!
NO, YOU'RE IMAGINING THINGS. I'M BETTER OFF THAN YOU, AT LEAST.
HEY, YOU TWO. DON'T FIGHT.
IF WE LET THIS DE-STROY OUR FRIENDSHIP TOO, IT'LL TURN INTO A REAL TRAGE...
OH, NEVER MIND.
ひしっ
GLOMP
おーいおいおい
BOO-HOO-HOO!
Us lonely girls have to stick together...
WHY AREN'T YOU CRYING WITH US, KOYUKI?!
YEAH, WHY ARE YOU ACTING SO COLD?! YOU'RE ALWAYS LIKE THIS!!
WELL... I'VE GOT TO GET READY TO OPEN...
DAD HAD TO GO TO THE DOCTOR TODAY FOR HIS CHECK-UP...
...SO I'VE GOTTA DO EVERY-THING MYSELF.
ザク
SHUNK
ザク
SHUNK
YARGH!
SHE'S BUTCH-ERING A HUGE FISH!
WHAT'S THAT FISH?!
TUNA?! BONITO?!
A CAREER FISH?!
CAN'T YOU TELL BY LOOK-ING?
IT'S A MACK-EREL...
THE BLOOD! THE GUTS!
There is no fish called a "career fish."

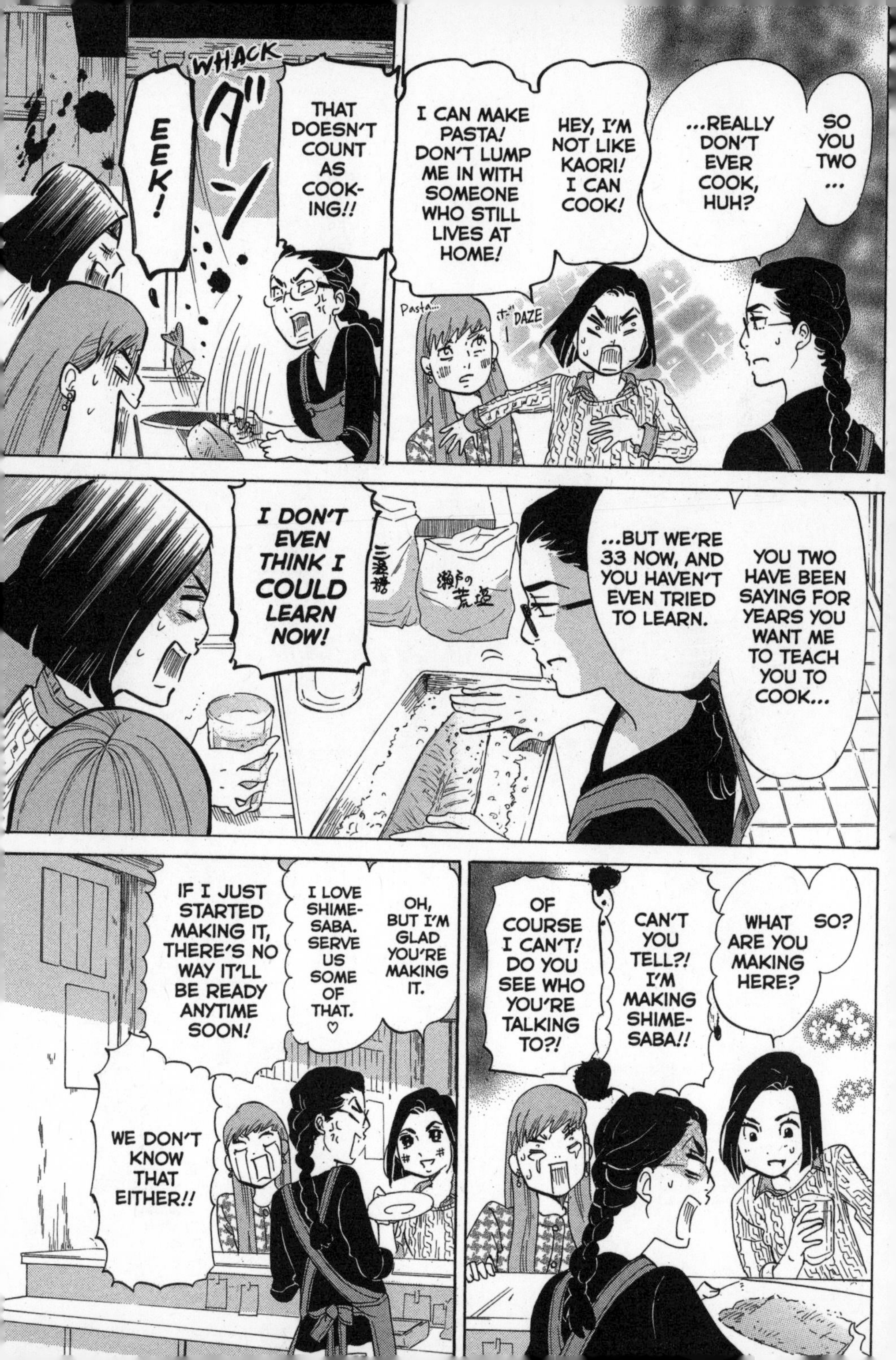
SO YOU TWO ...
...REALLY DON'T EVER COOK, HUH?
HEY, I'M NOT LIKE KAORI! I CAN COOK!
I CAN MAKE PASTA! DON'T LUMP ME IN WITH SOMEONE WHO STILL LIVES AT HOME!
DAZE
Pasta...
WHACK
ダー
THAT DOESN'T COUNT AS COOKING!!
EEK!
YOU TWO HAVE BEEN SAYING FOR YEARS YOU WANT ME TO TEACH YOU TO COOK...
...BUT WE'RE 33 NOW, AND YOU HAVEN'T EVEN TRIED TO LEARN.
瀬戸の荒塩
三温糖
I DON'T EVEN THINK I COULD LEARN NOW!
SO?
WHAT ARE YOU MAKING HERE?
CAN'T YOU TELL?! I'M MAKING SHIME-SABA!!
OF COURSE I CAN'T! DO YOU SEE WHO YOU'RE TALKING TO?!
OH, BUT I'M GLAD YOU'RE MAKING IT.
I LOVE SHIME-SABA. SERVE US SOME OF THAT. ♡
IF I JUST STARTED MAKING IT, THERE'S NO WAY IT'LL BE READY ANYTIME SOON!
WE DON'T KNOW THAT EITHER!!

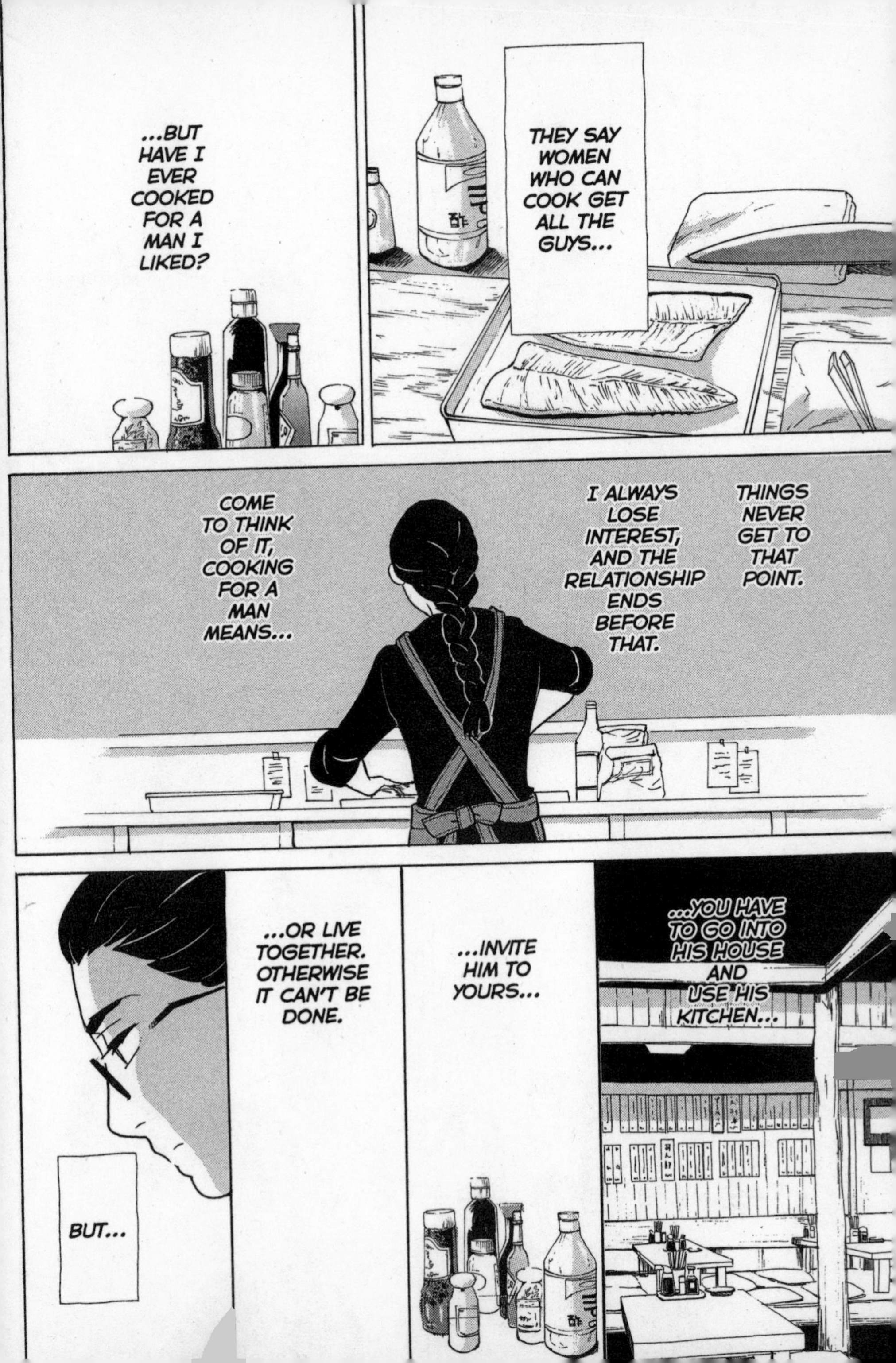
THEY SAY WOMEN WHO CAN COOK GET ALL THE GUYS...
...BUT HAVE I EVER COOKED FOR A MAN I LIKED?
THINGS NEVER GET TO THAT POINT.
I ALWAYS LOSE INTEREST, AND THE RELATIONSHIP ENDS BEFORE THAT.
COME TO THINK OF IT, COOKING FOR A MAN MEANS...
...YOU HAVE TO GO INTO HIS HOUSE AND USE HIS KITCHEN...
...INVITE HIM TO YOURS...
...OR LIVE TOGETHER. OTHERWISE IT CAN'T BE DONE.
BUT...

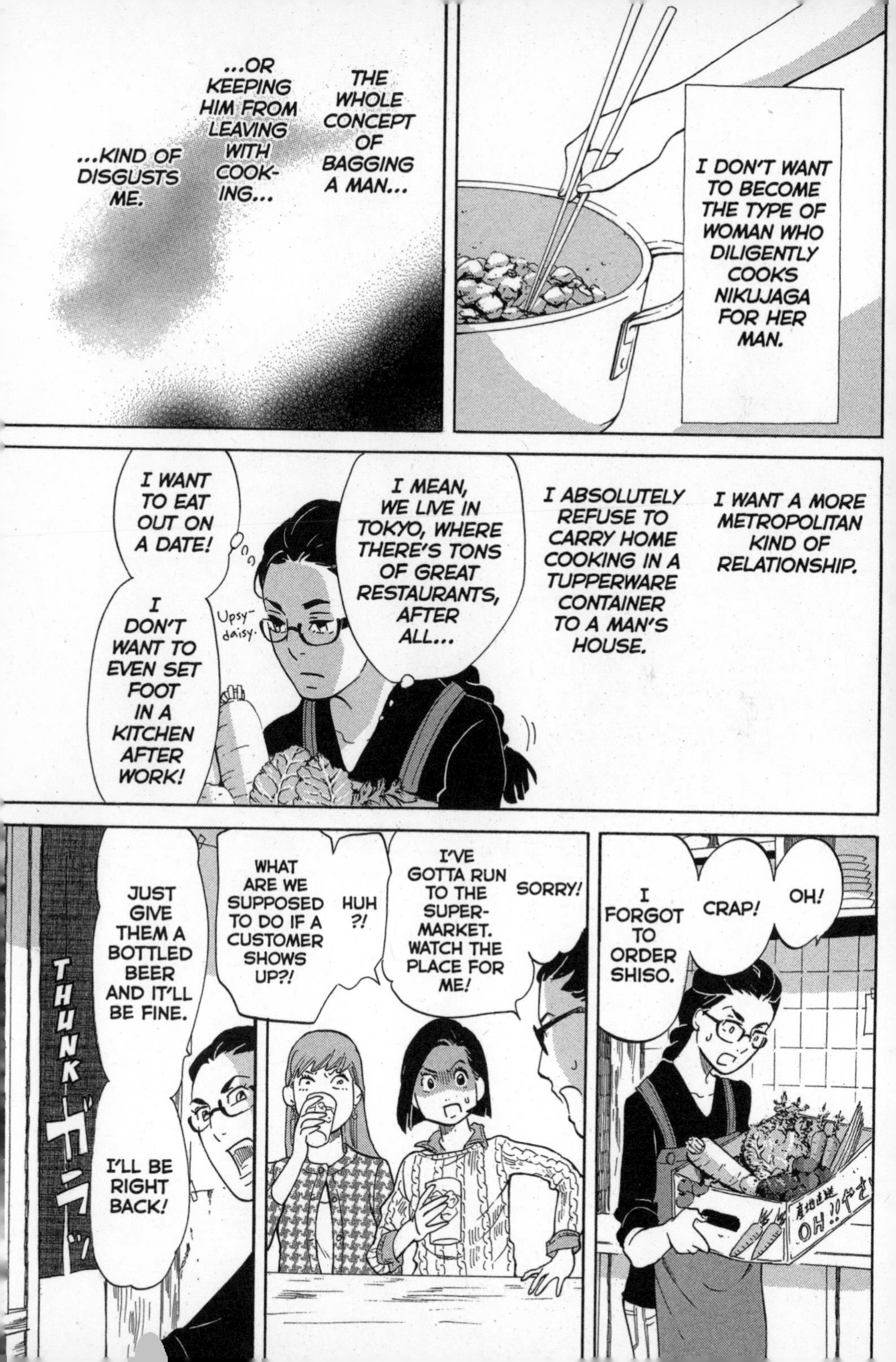
I DON'T WANT TO BECOME THE TYPE OF WOMAN WHO DILIGENTLY COOKS NIKUJAGA FOR HER MAN.
THE WHOLE CONCEPT OF BAGGING A MAN...
...OR KEEPING HIM FROM LEAVING WITH COOKING...
...KIND OF DISGUSTS ME.
I WANT A MORE METROPOLITAN KIND OF RELATIONSHIP.
I ABSOLUTELY REFUSE TO CARRY HOME COOKING IN A TUPPERWARE CONTAINER TO A MAN'S HOUSE.
I MEAN, WE LIVE IN TOKYO, WHERE THERE'S TONS OF GREAT RESTAURANTS, AFTER ALL...
I WANT TO EAT OUT ON A DATE!
Upsy-daisy.
I DON'T WANT TO EVEN SET FOOT IN A KITCHEN AFTER WORK!
OH!
CRAP!
I FORGOT TO ORDER SHISO.
OH!!
SORRY!
I'VE GOTTA RUN TO THE SUPER-MARKET. WATCH THE PLACE FOR ME!
HUH?!
WHAT ARE WE SUPPOSED TO DO IF A CUSTOMER SHOWS UP?!
JUST GIVE THEM A BOTTLED BEER AND IT'LL BE FINE.
I'LL BE RIGHT BACK!
THUNK

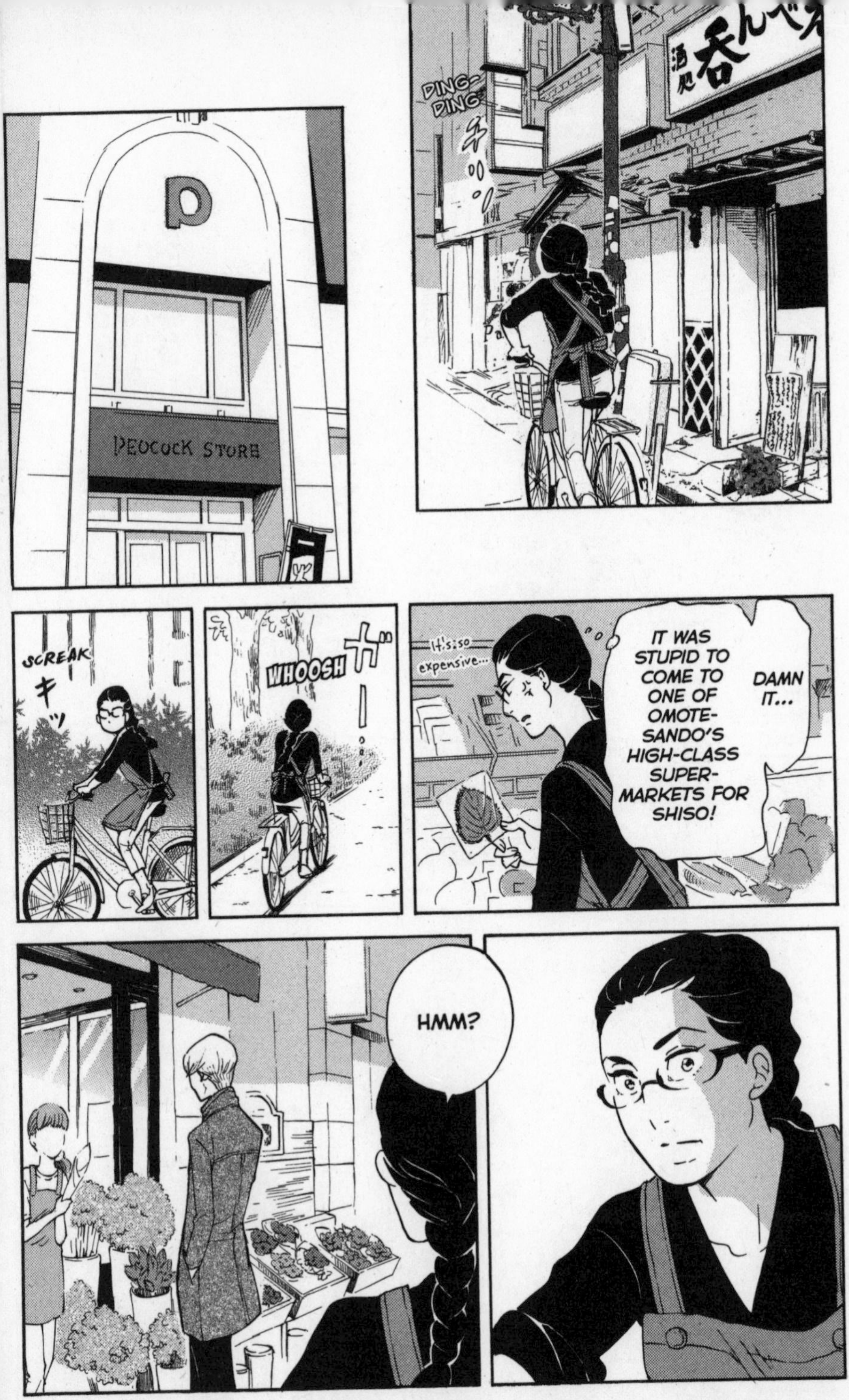
DING-DING
PEOCOCK STORE
DAMN IT...
IT WAS STUPID TO COME TO ONE OF OMOTE-SANDO'S HIGH-CLASS SUPER-MARKETS FOR SHISO!
It's so expensive...
WHOOSH
SCREAK
HMM?

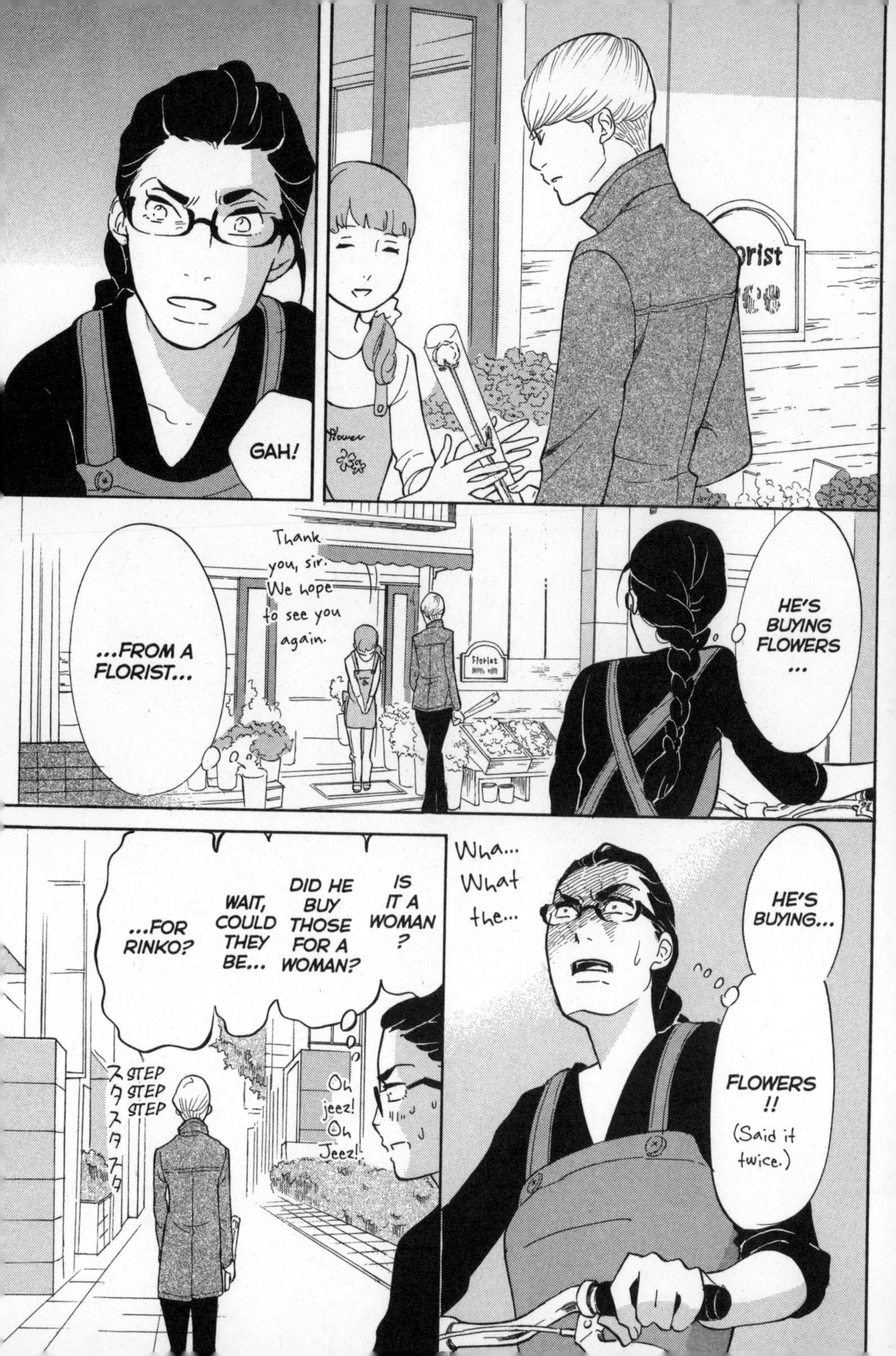
GAH!
HE'S BUYING FLOWERS ...
Thank you, sir. We hope to see you again.
...FROM A FLORIST...
HE'S BUYING...
Wha... What the...
FLOWERS !!
(Said it twice.)
IS IT A WOMAN ?
DID HE BUY THOSE FOR A WOMAN?
WAIT, COULD THEY BE...
...FOR RINKO?
Oh jeez! Oh Jeez!
スタスタスタ STEP STEP STEP

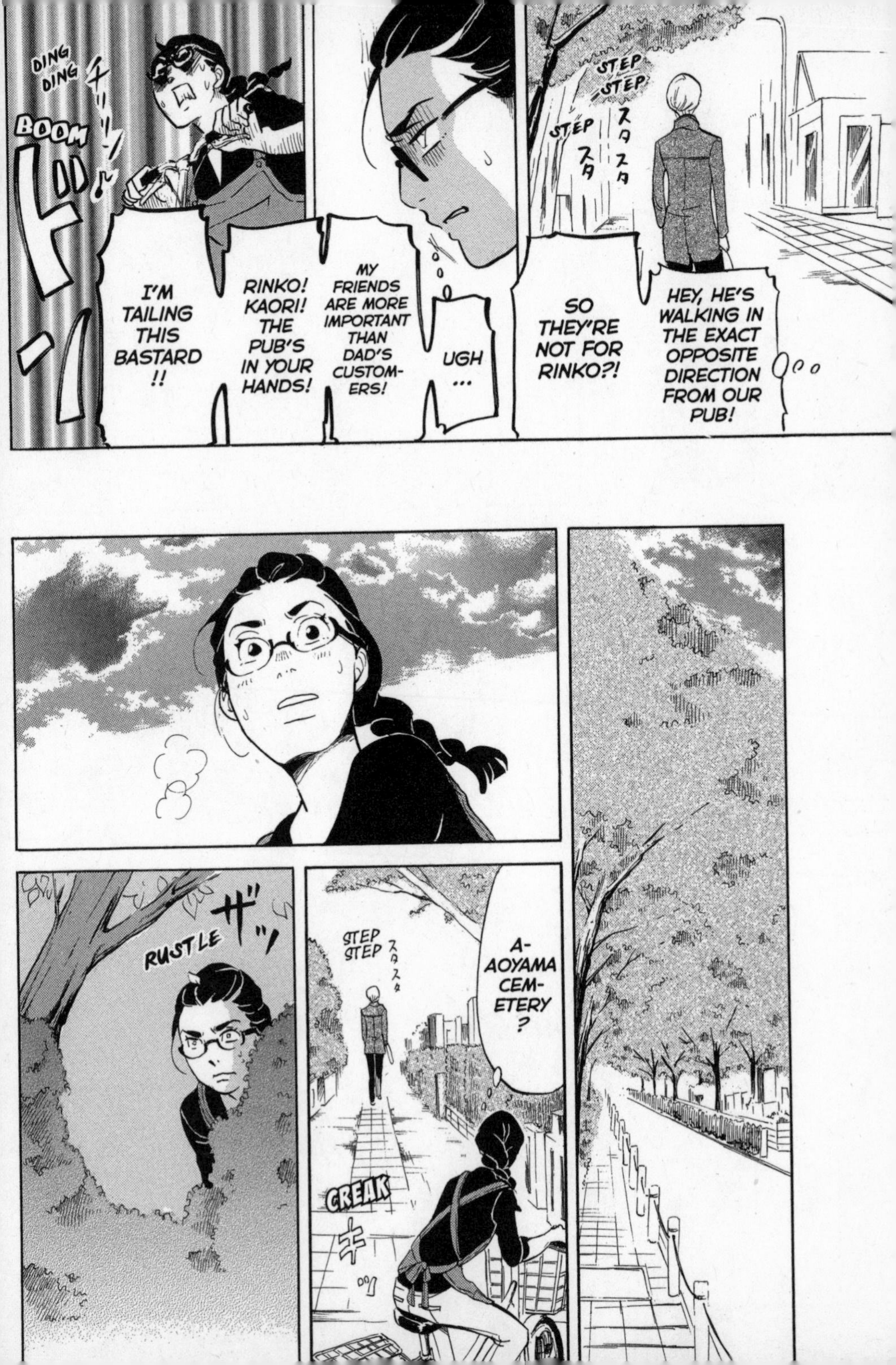
STEP STEP
スタスタ
STEP
スタ
HEY, HE'S WALKING IN THE EXACT OPPOSITE DIRECTION FROM OUR PUB!
SO THEY'RE NOT FOR RINKO?!
UGH ...
MY FRIENDS ARE MORE IMPORTANT THAN DAD'S CUSTOMERS!
RINKO! KAORI! THE PUB'S IN YOUR HANDS!
I'M TAILING THIS BASTARD!!
DING DING
チリーン
BOOM
ドーン
A-AOYAMA CEMETERY?
STEP STEP
スタスタ
CREAK
キッ
RUSTLE
ザッ

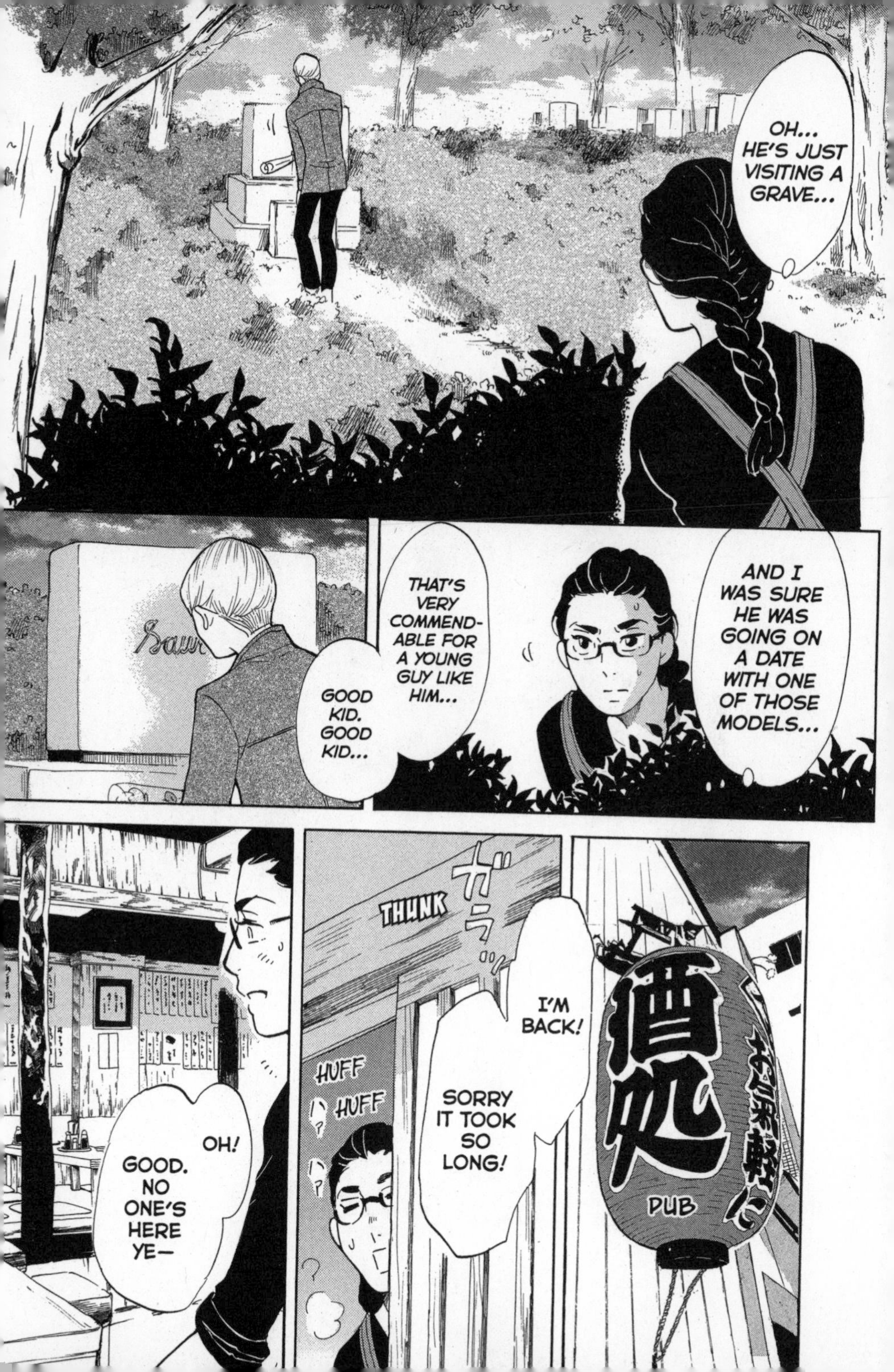
OH... HE'S JUST VISITING A GRAVE...
AND I WAS SURE HE WAS GOING ON A DATE WITH ONE OF THOSE MODELS...
THAT'S VERY COMMENDABLE FOR A YOUNG GUY LIKE HIM...
GOOD KID. GOOD KID...
酒処
PUB
THUNK
ガラッ
I'M BACK!
SORRY IT TOOK SO LONG!
HUFF HUFF
ハァ ハァ
OH!
GOOD. NO ONE'S HERE YE—

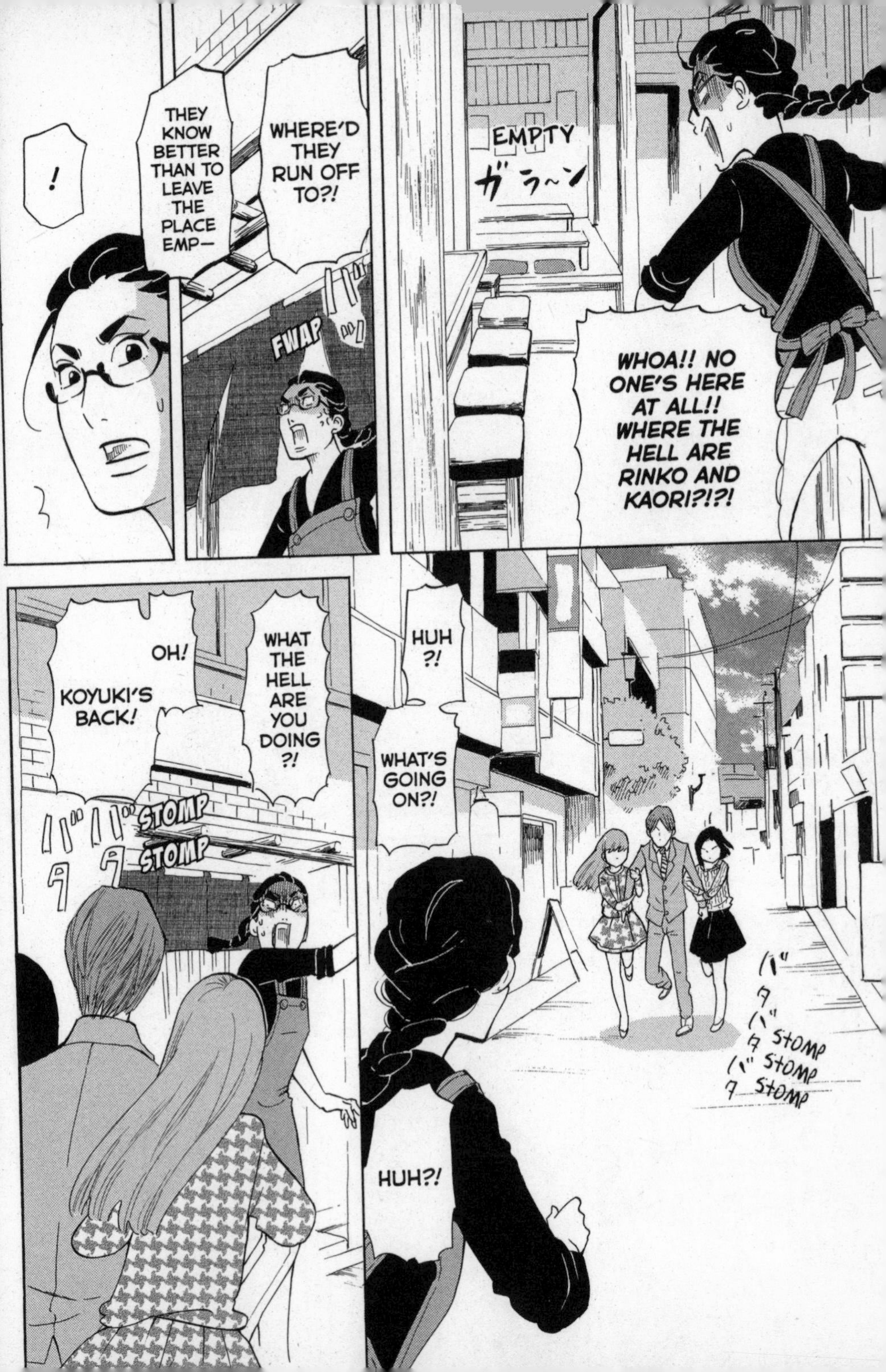
EMPTY
ガラ～ン
WHOA!! NO ONE'S HERE AT ALL!! WHERE THE HELL ARE RINKO AND KAORI?!?!
WHERE'D THEY RUN OFF TO?!
FWAP
バッ
THEY KNOW BETTER THAN TO LEAVE THE PLACE EMP—
!
HUH ?!
WHAT'S GOING ON?!
バタバタバタ
STOMP STOMP STOMP
HUH?!
WHAT THE HELL ARE YOU DOING ?!
OH!
KOYUKI'S BACK!
STOMP
STOMP

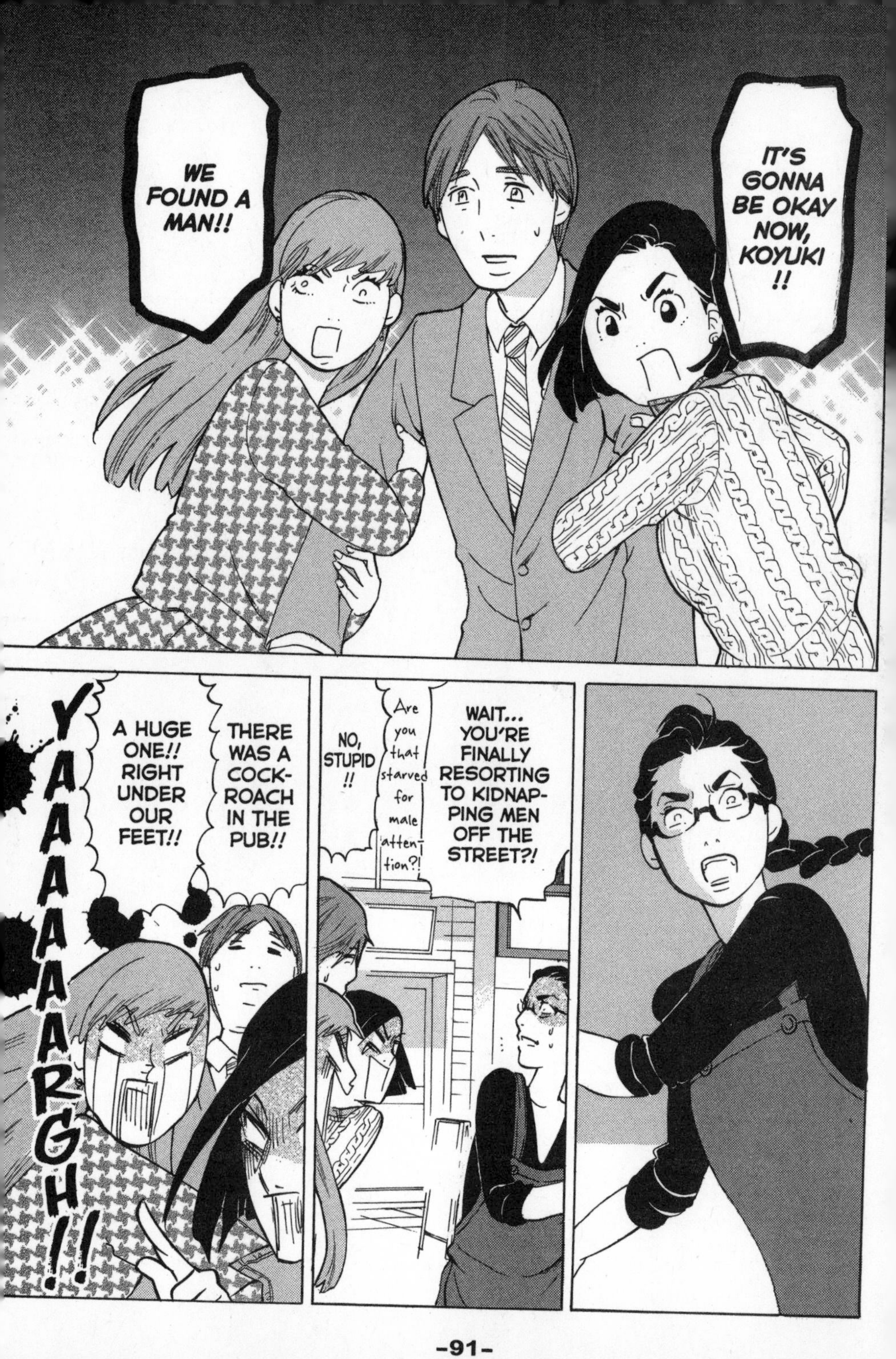
IT'S GONNA BE OKAY NOW, KOYUKI!!
WE FOUND A MAN!!
WAIT... YOU'RE FINALLY RESORTING TO KIDNAPPING MEN OFF THE STREET?!
Are you that starved for male attention?!
NO, STUPID!!
THERE WAS A COCKROACH IN THE PUB!!
A HUGE ONE!! RIGHT UNDER OUR FEET!!
YAAAAAARGH!!

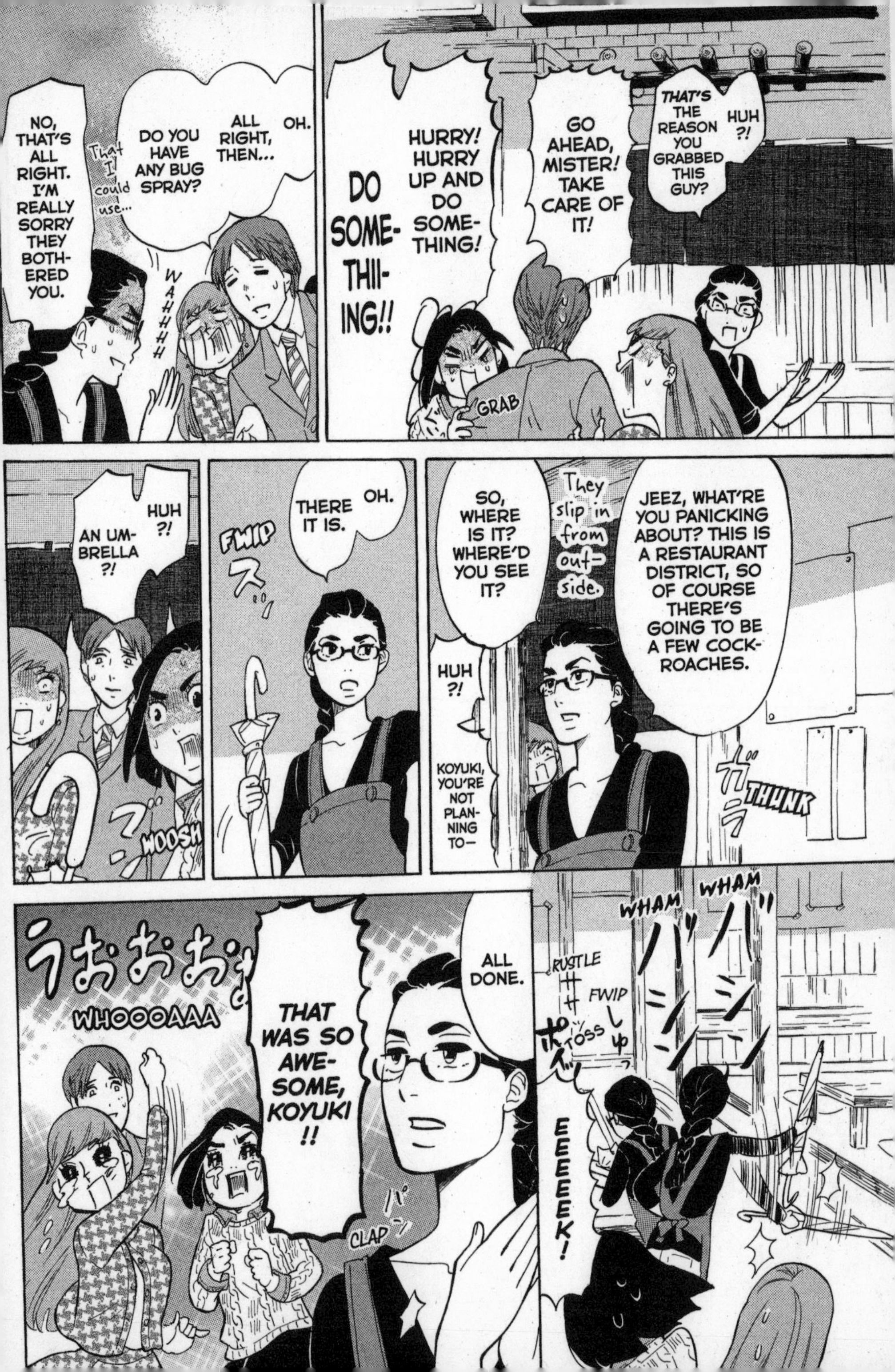

HUH ?!
THAT'S THE REASON YOU GRABBED THIS GUY?
GO AHEAD, MISTER! TAKE CARE OF IT!
HURRY! HURRY UP AND DO SOME-THING!
DO SOME-THIII-ING!!
GRAB
OH.
ALL RIGHT, THEN...
DO YOU HAVE ANY BUG SPRAY?
That I could use...
NO, THAT'S ALL RIGHT. I'M REALLY SORRY THEY BOTH-ERED YOU.
WAHHHH
JEEZ, WHAT'RE YOU PANICKING ABOUT? THIS IS A RESTAURANT DISTRICT, SO OF COURSE THERE'S GOING TO BE A FEW COCK-ROACHES.
They slip in from out-side.
SO, WHERE IS IT? WHERE'D YOU SEE IT?
HUH ?!
KOYUKI, YOU'RE NOT PLAN-NING TO—
THUNK
OH.
THERE IT IS.
FWIP
HUH ?!
AN UM-BRELLA ?!
WOOSH
WHAM
WHAM
RUSTLE
FWIP
TOSS
EEEEEEK!
ALL DONE.
THAT WAS SO AWE-SOME, KOYUKI !!
うおおおぉ
WHOOOAAA
CLAP

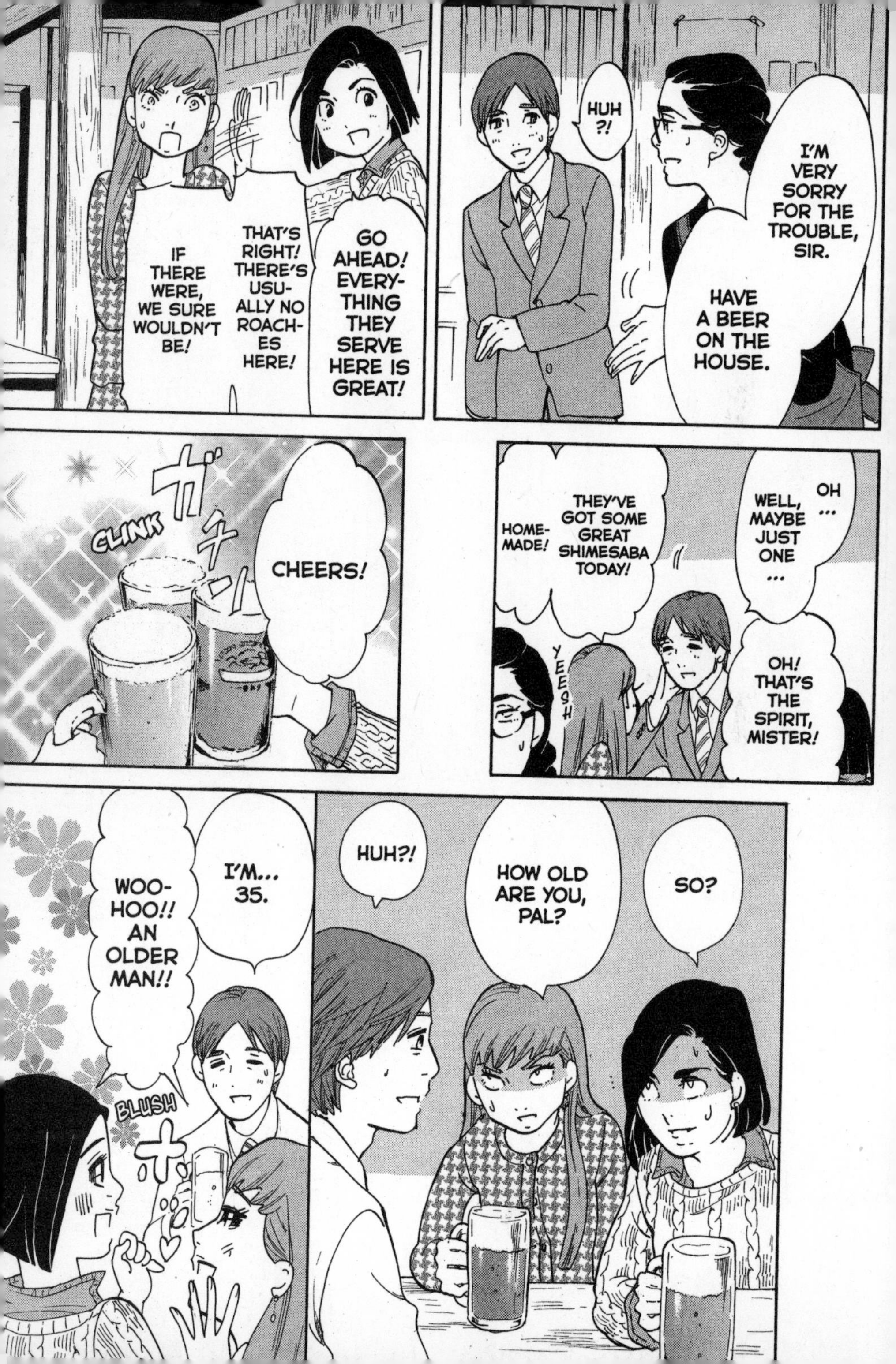
I'M VERY SORRY FOR THE TROUBLE, SIR.
HAVE A BEER ON THE HOUSE.
HUH ?!
GO AHEAD! EVERYTHING THEY SERVE HERE IS GREAT!
THAT'S RIGHT! THERE'S USUALLY NO ROACHES HERE!
IF THERE WERE, WE SURE WOULDN'T BE!
OH ...
WELL, MAYBE JUST ONE ...
OH! THAT'S THE SPIRIT, MISTER!
THEY'VE GOT SOME GREAT SHIMESABA TODAY!
HOME-MADE!
YEESH
CHEERS!
ガチ
CLINK
SO?
HOW OLD ARE YOU, PAL?
HUH?!
I'M... 35.
WOO-HOO!! AN OLDER MAN!!
BLUSH

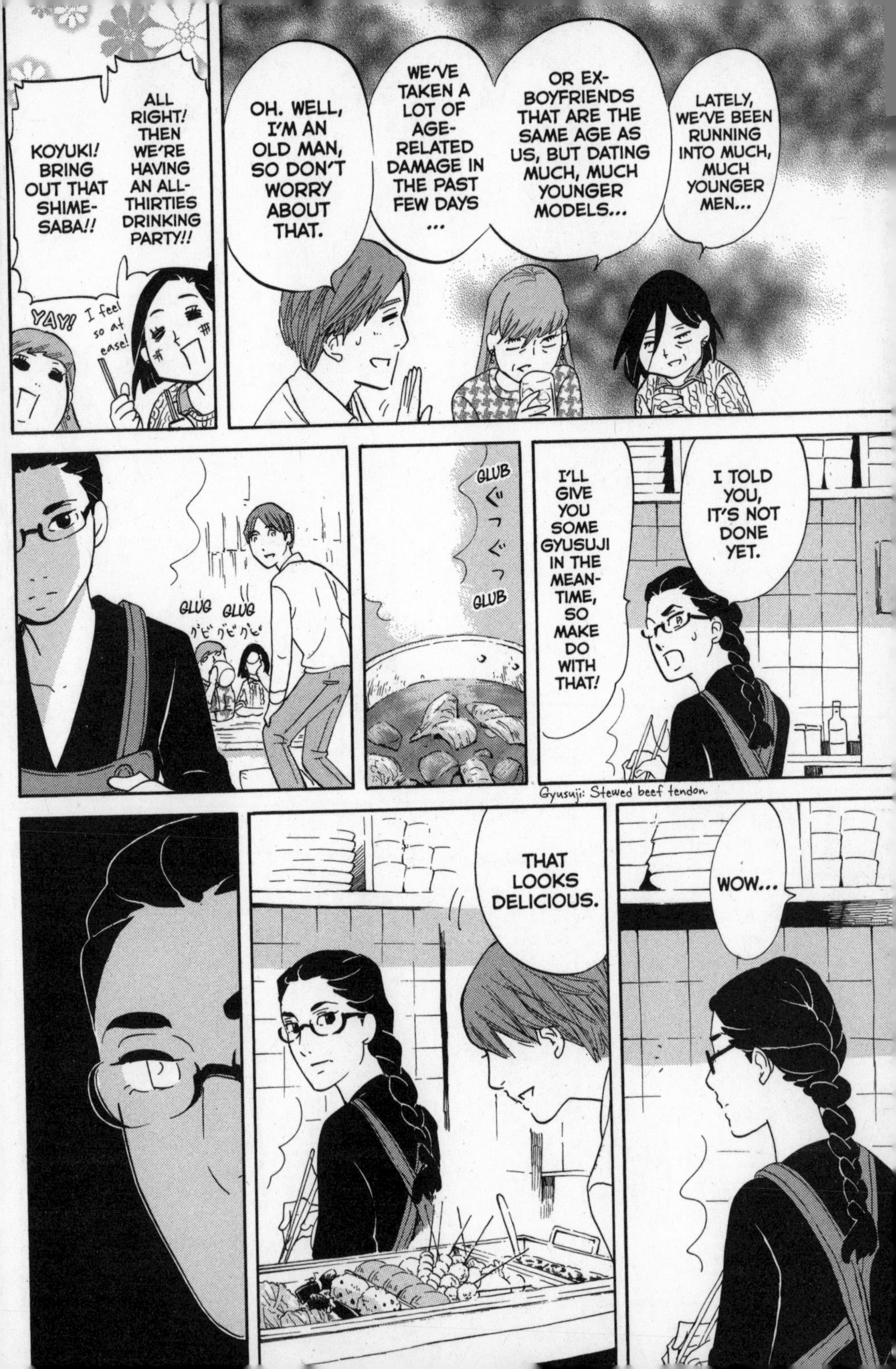
LATELY, WE'VE BEEN RUNNING INTO MUCH, MUCH YOUNGER MEN...
OR EX-BOYFRIENDS THAT ARE THE SAME AGE AS US, BUT DATING MUCH, MUCH YOUNGER MODELS...
WE'VE TAKEN A LOT OF AGE-RELATED DAMAGE IN THE PAST FEW DAYS ...
OH. WELL, I'M AN OLD MAN, SO DON'T WORRY ABOUT THAT.
ALL RIGHT! THEN WE'RE HAVING AN ALL-THIRTIES DRINKING PARTY!!
KOYUKI! BRING OUT THAT SHIME-SABA!!
I feel so at ease!
YAY!
I TOLD YOU, IT'S NOT DONE YET.
I'LL GIVE YOU SOME GYUSUJI IN THE MEAN-TIME, SO MAKE DO WITH THAT!
GLUB ぐつぐつ GLUB
GLUG GLUG グビグビ
WOW...
THAT LOOKS DELICIOUS.

Gyusuji: Stewed beef tendon.

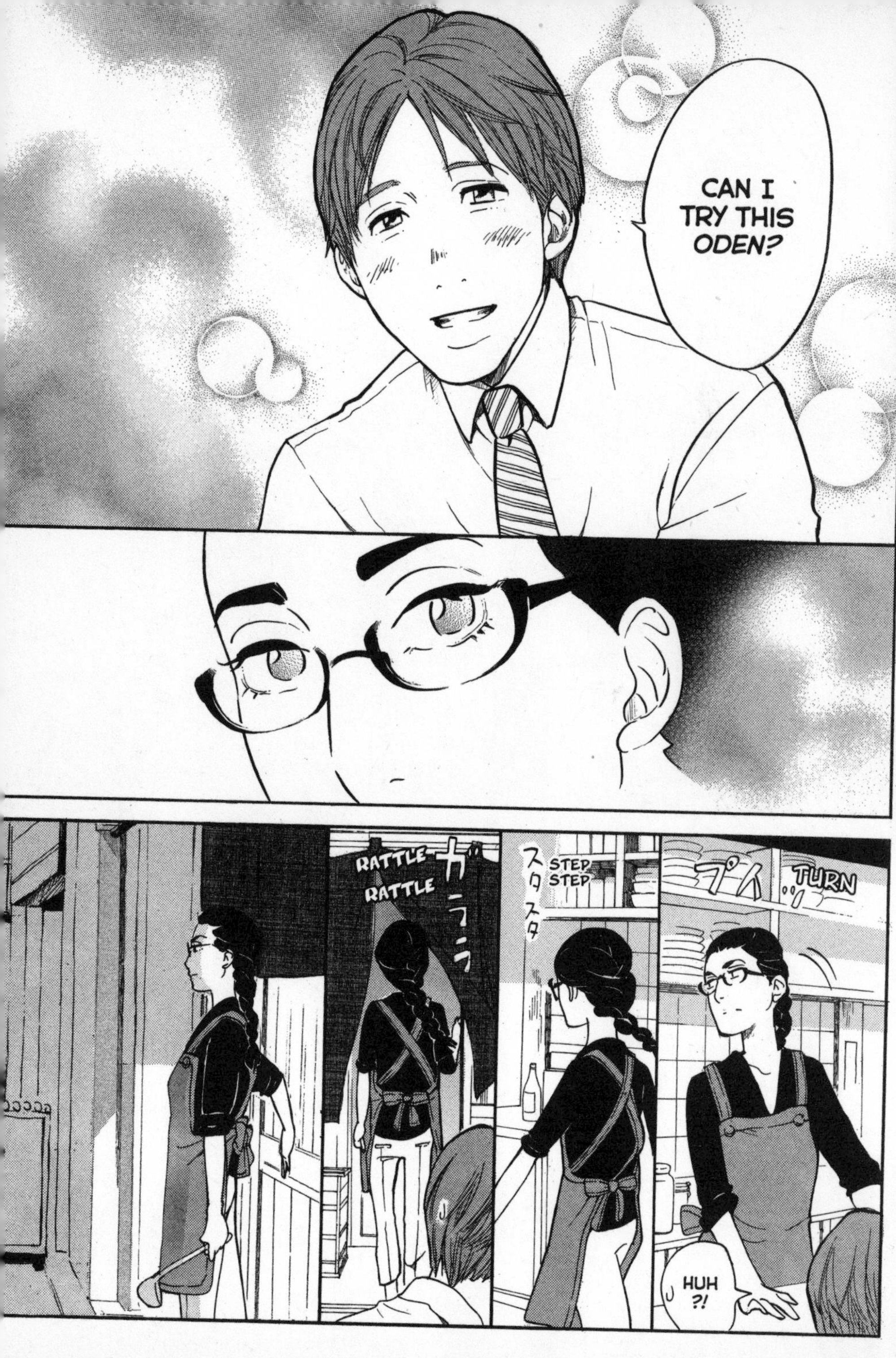

CAN I TRY THIS ODEN?
TURN
プイ
HUH ?!
STEP STEP
スタスタ
RATTLE RATTLE
ガララ

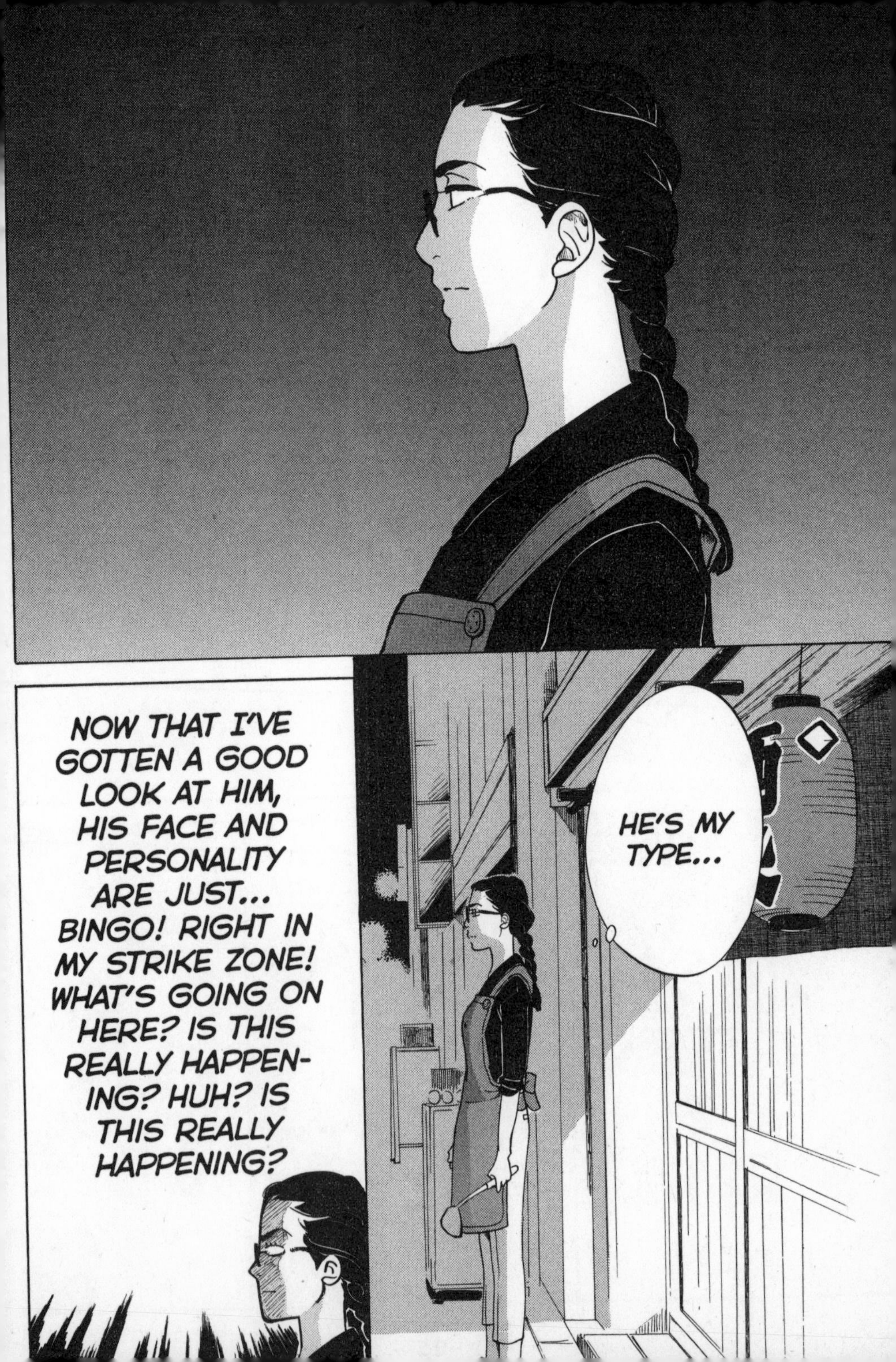
HE'S MY TYPE...
NOW THAT I'VE GOTTEN A GOOD LOOK AT HIM, HIS FACE AND PERSONALITY ARE JUST... BINGO! RIGHT IN MY STRIKE ZONE! WHAT'S GOING ON HERE? IS THIS REALLY HAPPEN-ING? HUH? IS THIS REALLY HAPPENING?

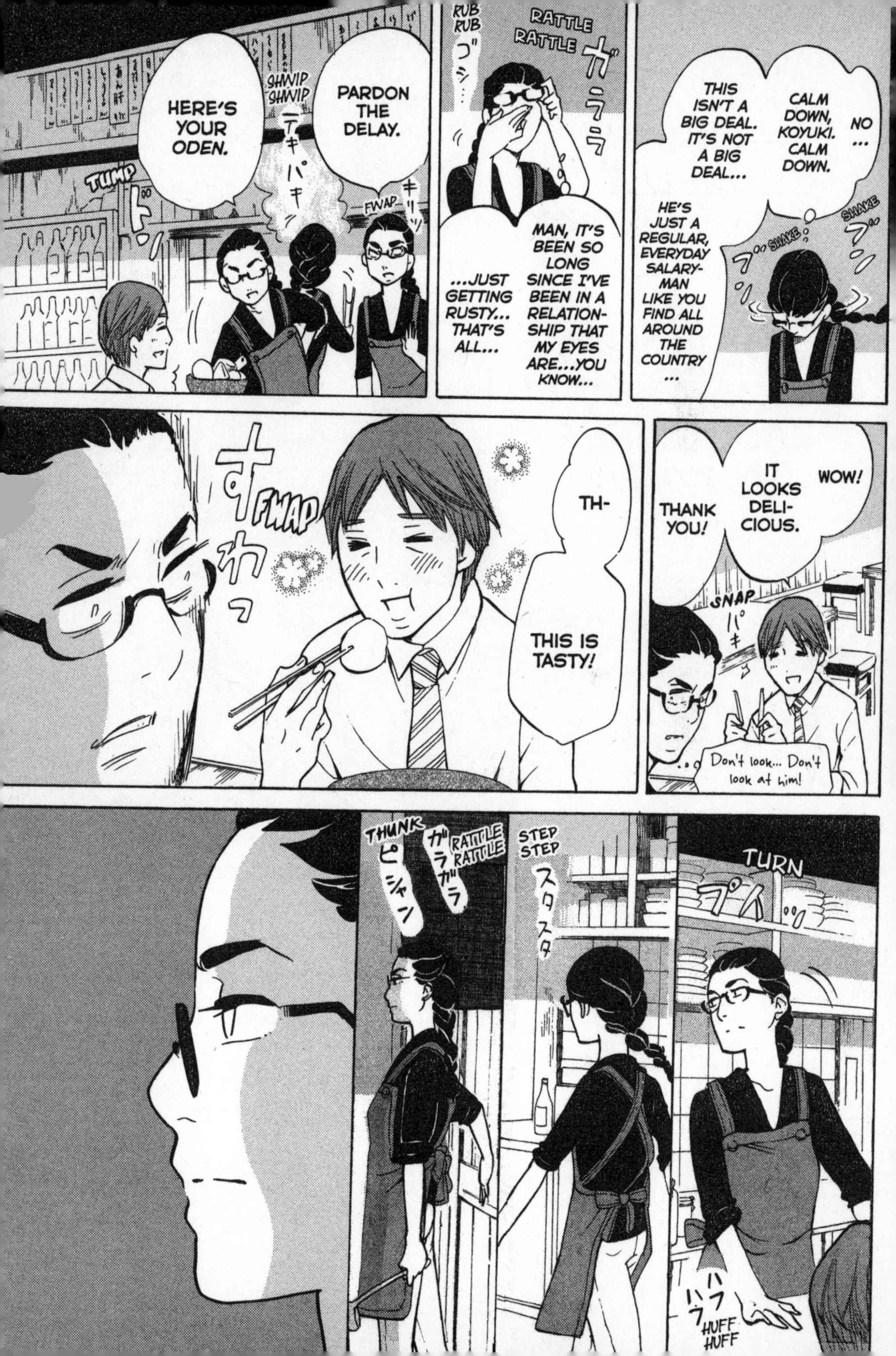
NO ...
CALM DOWN, KOYUKI. CALM DOWN.
THIS ISN'T A BIG DEAL. IT'S NOT A BIG DEAL...
HE'S JUST A REGULAR, EVERYDAY SALARYMAN LIKE YOU FIND ALL AROUND THE COUNTRY ...
SHAKE SHAKE
RATTLE RATTLE
ガラララ
RUB RUB
ゴシ…
MAN, IT'S BEEN SO LONG SINCE I'VE BEEN IN A RELATIONSHIP THAT MY EYES ARE...YOU KNOW...
...JUST GETTING RUSTY... THAT'S ALL...
FWAP
キリッ
PARDON THE DELAY.
SHWIP SHWIP
テキパキ
HERE'S YOUR ODEN.
TUMP
ドン
WOW!
IT LOOKS DELICIOUS.
THANK YOU!
SNAP
パキ
Don't look... Don't look at him!
TH-
THIS IS TASTY!
FWAP
すわっ
TURN
プイ
HUFF HUFF
ハフハフ
STEP STEP
スタスタ
RATTLE RATTLE
ガラガラ
THUNK
ピシャン

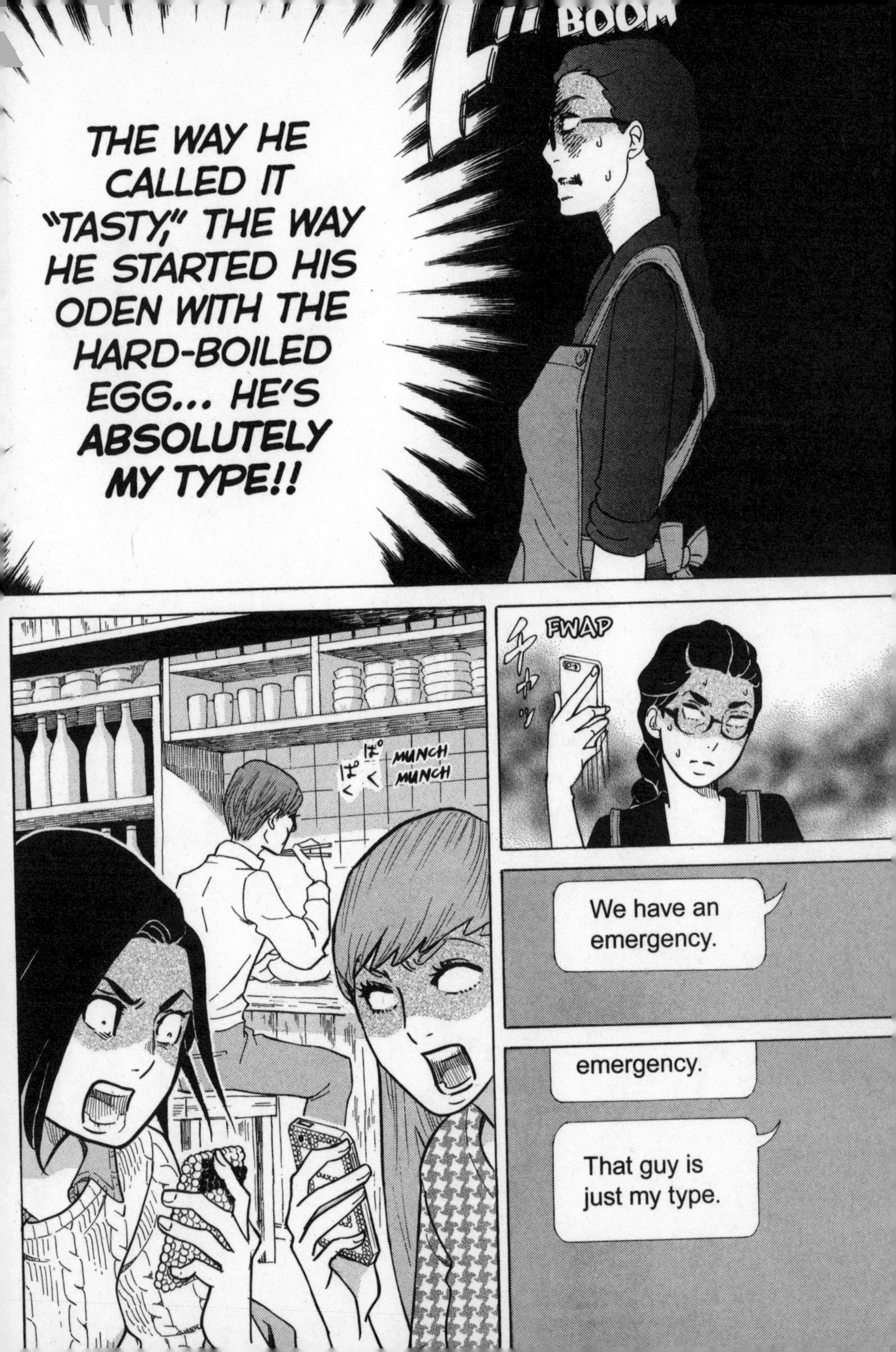
BOOM
THE WAY HE CALLED IT "TASTY," THE WAY HE STARTED HIS ODEN WITH THE HARD-BOILED EGG... HE'S ABSOLUTELY MY TYPE!!
FWAP
We have an emergency.
emergency.
That guy is just my type.
MUNCH MUNCH

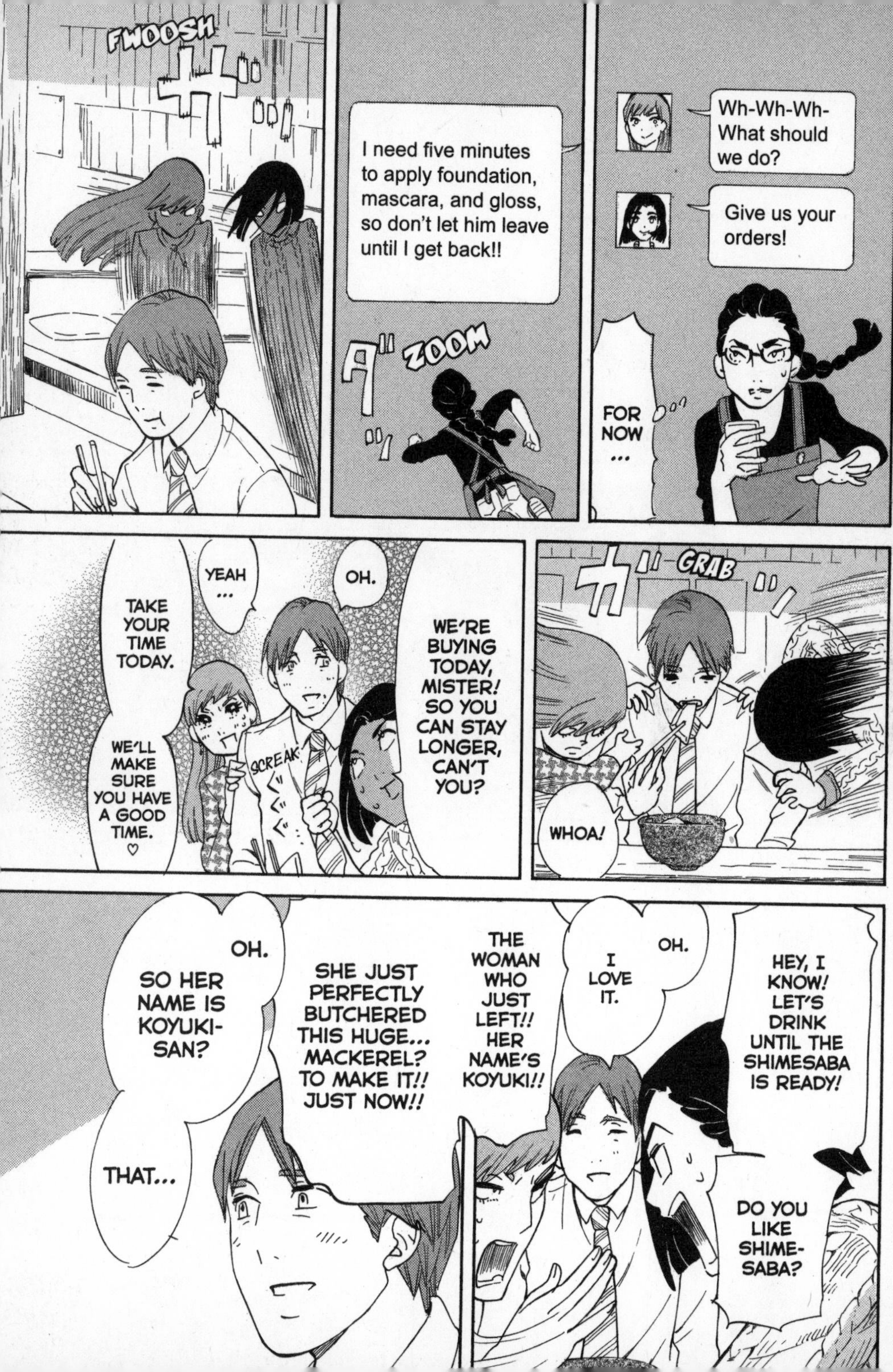
Wh-Wh-Wh- What should we do?
Give us your orders!
FOR NOW ...
I need five minutes to apply foundation, mascara, and gloss, so don't let him leave until I get back!!
ZOOM
FWOOSH
GRAB
WHOA!
WE'RE BUYING TODAY, MISTER! SO YOU CAN STAY LONGER, CAN'T YOU?
OH.
YEAH ...
TAKE YOUR TIME TODAY.
WE'LL MAKE SURE YOU HAVE A GOOD TIME. ♡
SCREAK
HEY, I KNOW! LET'S DRINK UNTIL THE SHIMESABA IS READY!
DO YOU LIKE SHIME-SABA?
OH.
I LOVE IT.
THE WOMAN WHO JUST LEFT!! HER NAME'S KOYUKI!!
SHE JUST PERFECTLY BUTCHERED THIS HUGE... MACKEREL? TO MAKE IT!! JUST NOW!!
OH.
SO HER NAME IS KOYUKI-SAN?
THAT...

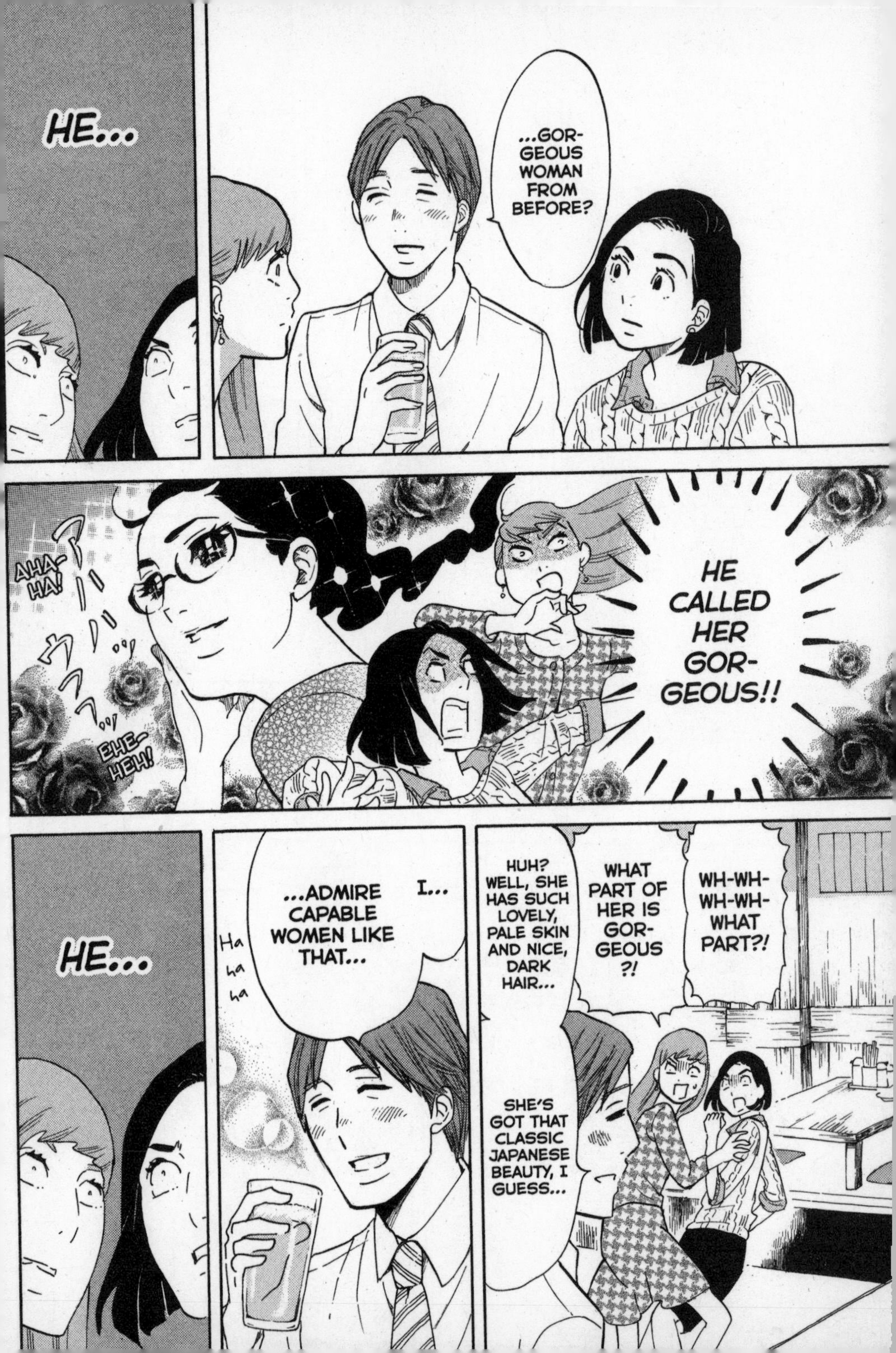
...GOR-GEOUS WOMAN FROM BEFORE?
HE...
HE CALLED HER GOR-GEOUS!!
AHA-HA!
EHE-HEH!
WH-WH-WH-WH-WHAT PART?!
WHAT PART OF HER IS GOR-GEOUS?!
HUH? WELL, SHE HAS SUCH LOVELY, PALE SKIN AND NICE, DARK HAIR...
SHE'S GOT THAT CLASSIC JAPANESE BEAUTY, I GUESS...
I...
...ADMIRE CAPABLE WOMEN LIKE THAT...
Ha ha ha
HE...

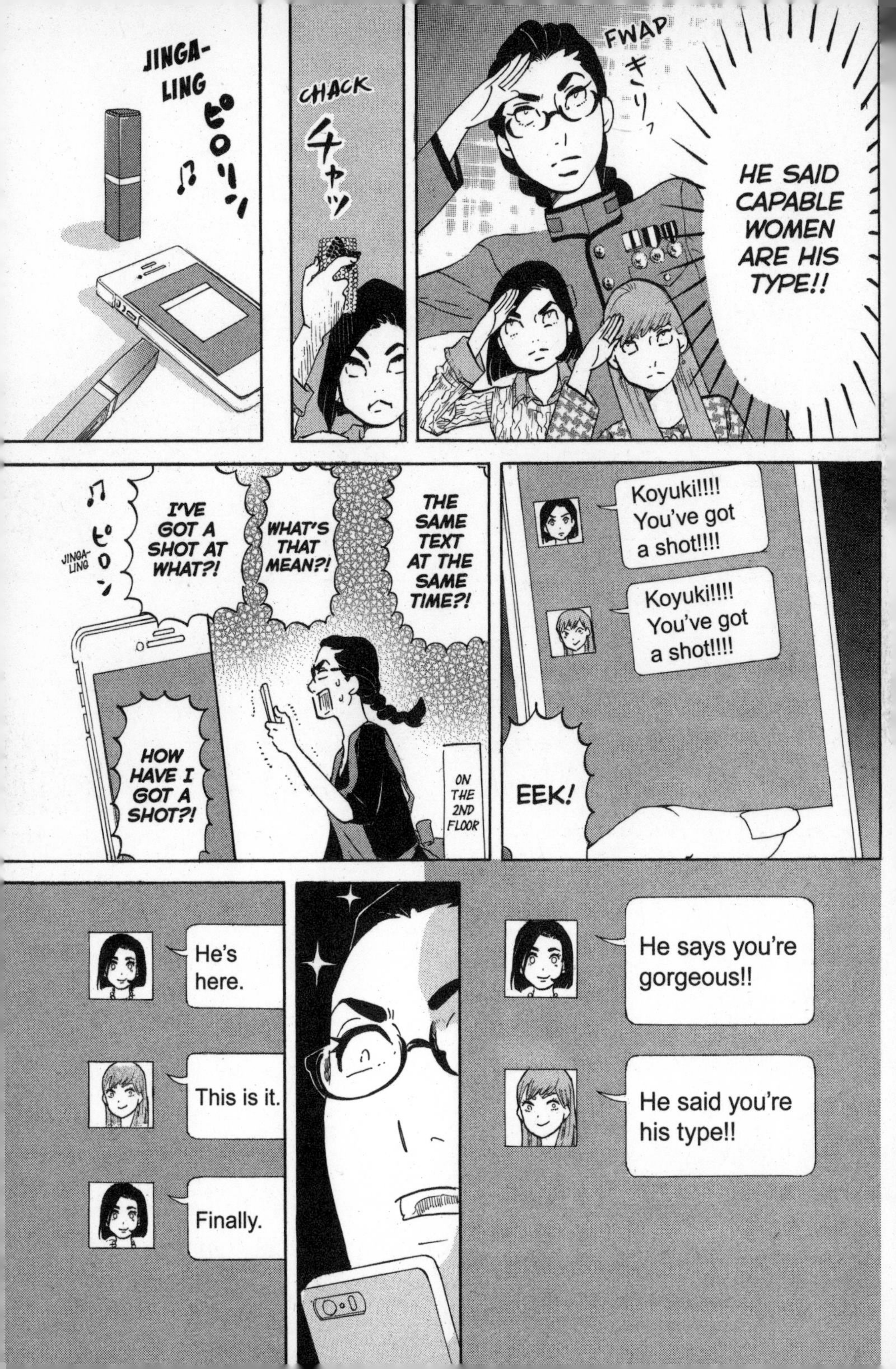
FWAP
キリッ
HE SAID CAPABLE WOMEN ARE HIS TYPE!!
CHACK
チャッ
JINGA-LING
THE SAME TEXT AT THE SAME TIME?!
WHAT'S THAT MEAN?!
I'VE GOT A SHOT AT WHAT?!
JINGA-LING
ピロン
HOW HAVE I GOT A SHOT?!
ON THE 2ND FLOOR
Koyuki!!!! You've got a shot!!!!
Koyuki!!!! You've got a shot!!!!
EEK!
He says you're gorgeous!!
He said you're his type!!
He's here.
This is it.
Finally.

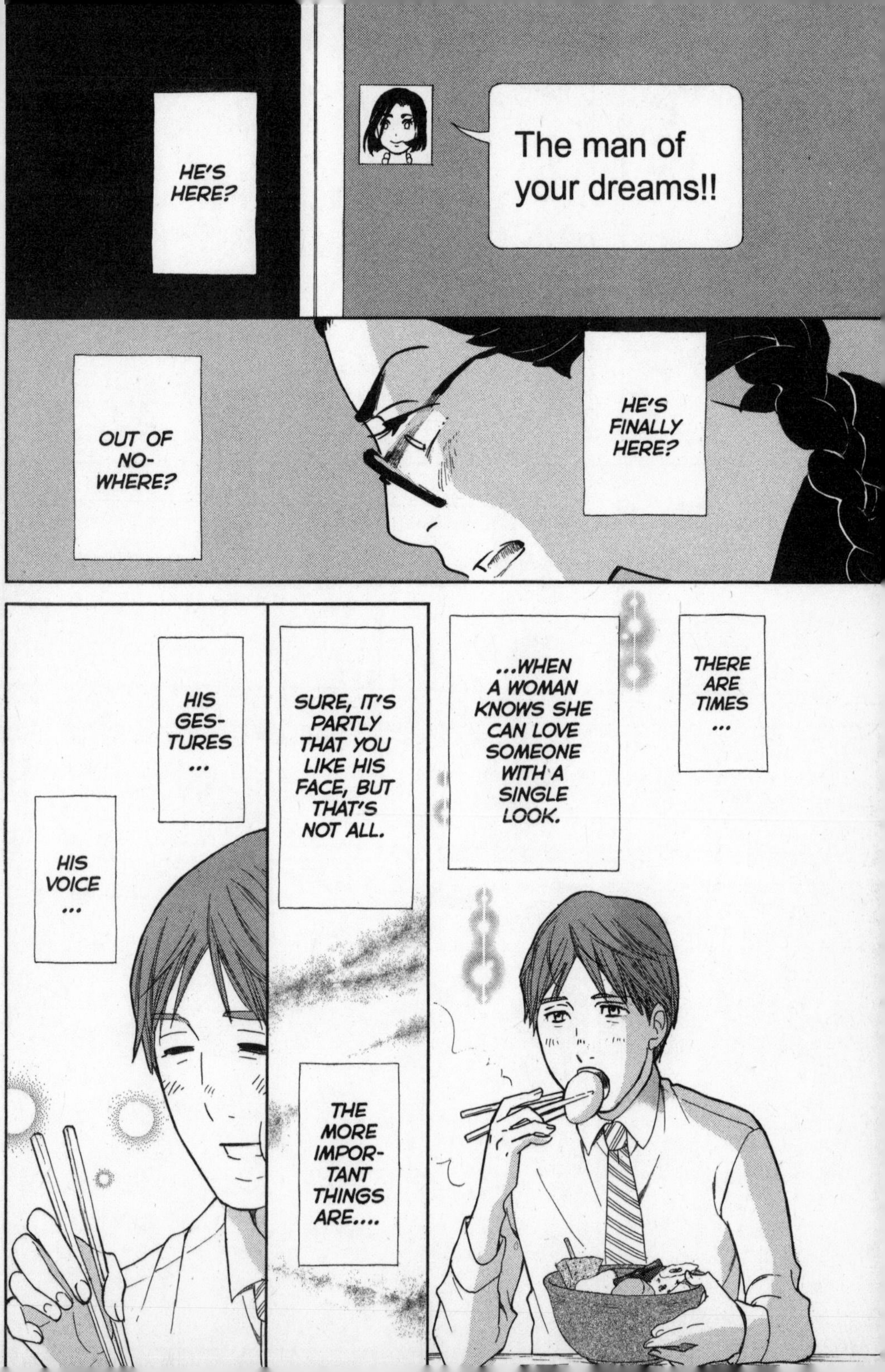
The man of your dreams!!
HE'S HERE?
HE'S FINALLY HERE?
OUT OF NO-WHERE?
THERE ARE TIMES...
...WHEN A WOMAN KNOWS SHE CAN LOVE SOMEONE WITH A SINGLE LOOK.
SURE, IT'S PARTLY THAT YOU LIKE HIS FACE, BUT THAT'S NOT ALL.
THE MORE IMPOR-TANT THINGS ARE....
HIS GES-TURES...
HIS VOICE...

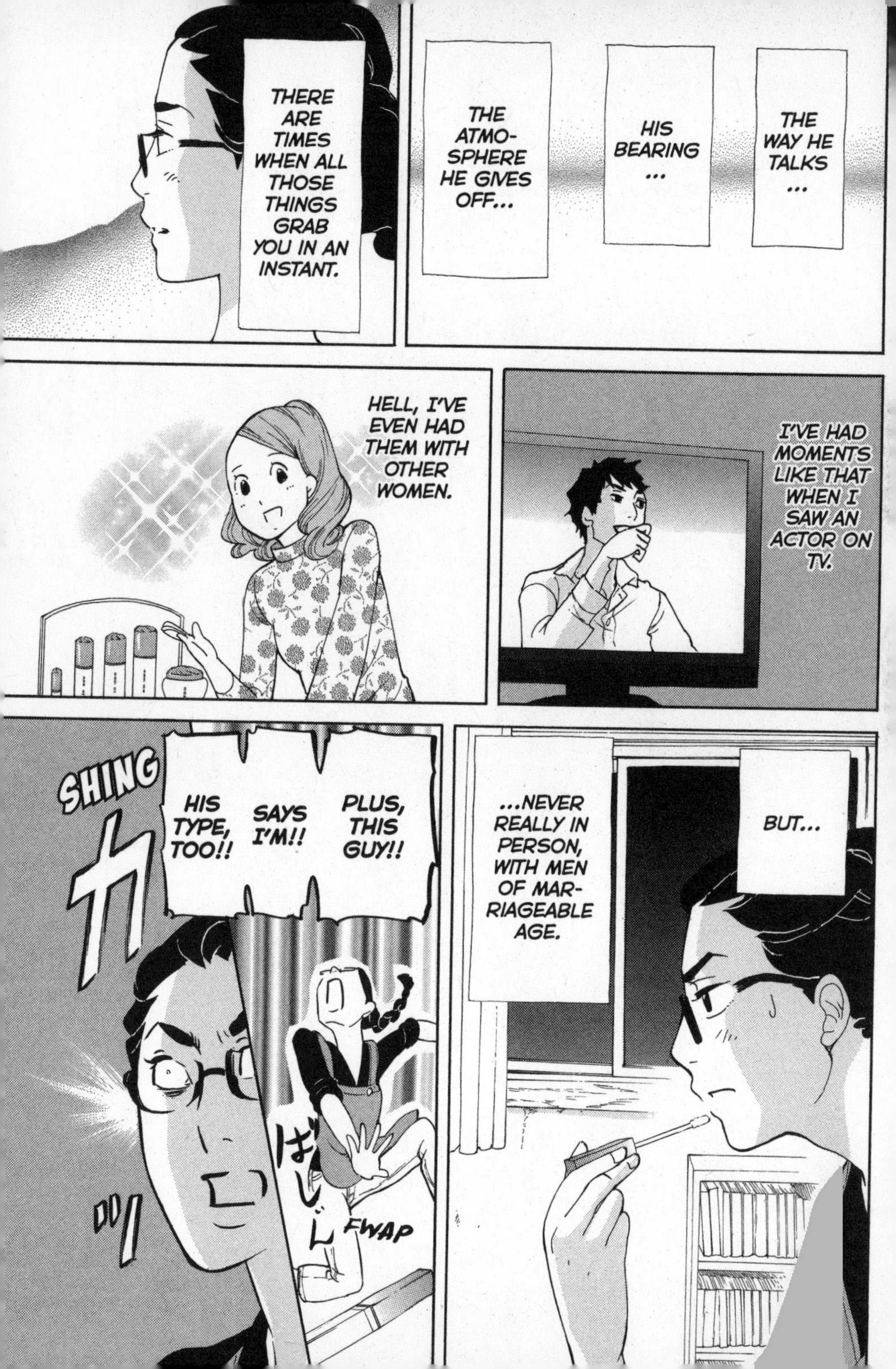
THE WAY HE TALKS...
HIS BEARING...
THE ATMOSPHERE HE GIVES OFF...
THERE ARE TIMES WHEN ALL THOSE THINGS GRAB YOU IN AN INSTANT.
I'VE HAD MOMENTS LIKE THAT WHEN I SAW AN ACTOR ON TV.
HELL, I'VE EVEN HAD THEM WITH OTHER WOMEN.
BUT...
...NEVER REALLY IN PERSON, WITH MEN OF MARRIAGEABLE AGE.
PLUS, THIS GUY!!
SAYS I'M!!
HIS TYPE, TOO!!
SHING
FWAP

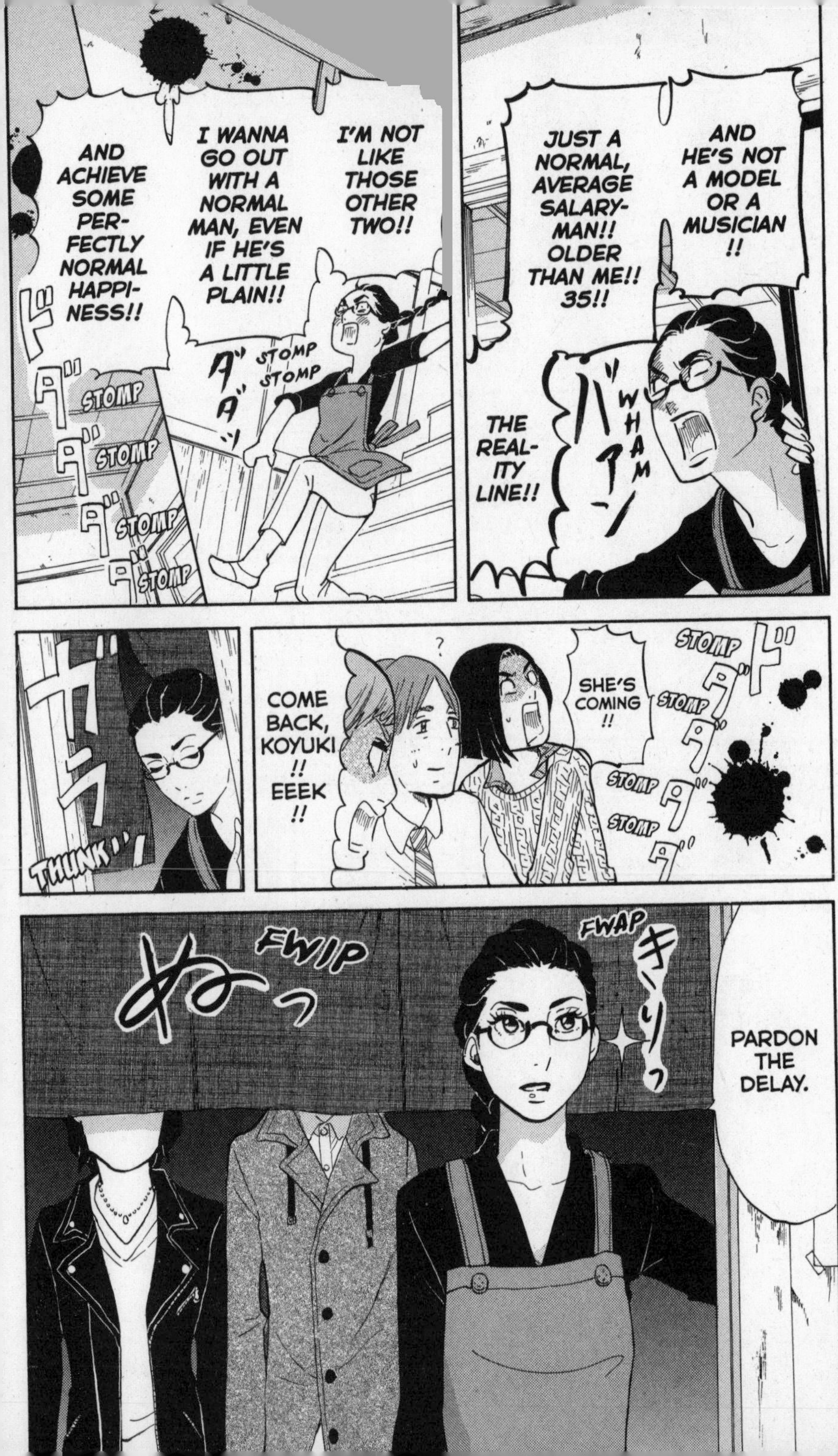
AND HE'S NOT A MODEL OR A MUSICIAN!!
JUST A NORMAL, AVERAGE SALARYMAN!! OLDER THAN ME!! 35!!
WHAM
THE REALITY LINE!!
I'M NOT LIKE THOSE OTHER TWO!!
I WANNA GO OUT WITH A NORMAL MAN, EVEN IF HE'S A LITTLE PLAIN!!
AND ACHIEVE SOME PERFECTLY NORMAL HAPPINESS!!
STOMP STOMP
STOMP
STOMP
STOMP
STOMP
STOMP
STOMP
STOMP
STOMP
SHE'S COMING!!
?
COME BACK, KOYUKI!!
EEEK!!
THUNK
FWAP
PARDON THE DELAY.
FWIP

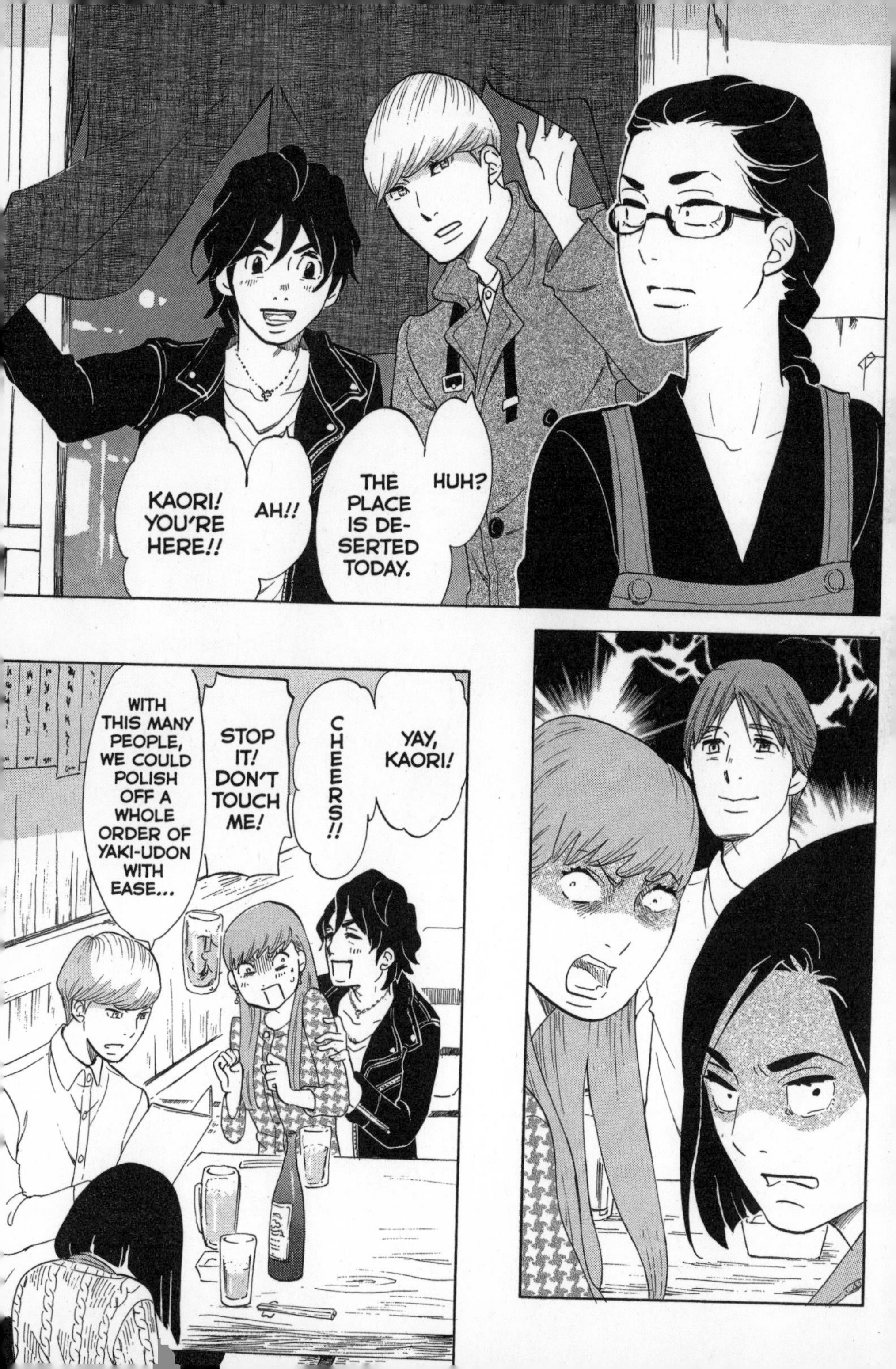
HUH?
THE PLACE IS DESERTED TODAY.
AH!!
KAORI! YOU'RE HERE!!
YAY, KAORI!
CHEERS!!
STOP IT! DON'T TOUCH ME!
WITH THIS MANY PEOPLE, WE COULD POLISH OFF A WHOLE ORDER OF YAKI-UDON WITH EASE...

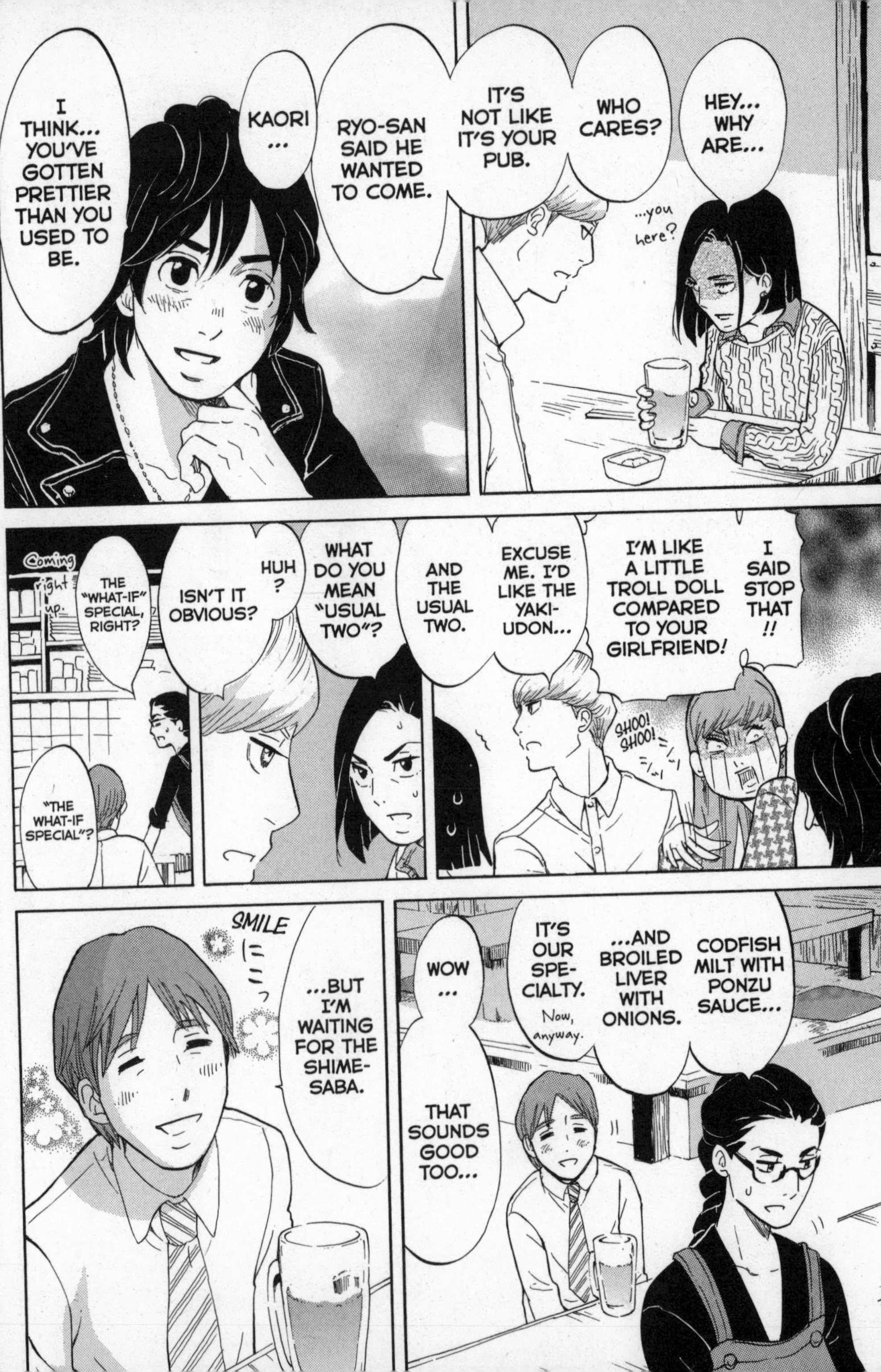
HEY... WHY ARE...
...you here?
WHO CARES?
IT'S NOT LIKE IT'S YOUR PUB.
RYO-SAN SAID HE WANTED TO COME.
KAORI...
I THINK... YOU'VE GOTTEN PRETTIER THAN YOU USED TO BE.
I SAID STOP THAT!!
I'M LIKE A LITTLE TROLL DOLL COMPARED TO YOUR GIRLFRIEND!
SHOO! SHOO!
EXCUSE ME. I'D LIKE THE YAKI-UDON...
AND THE USUAL TWO.
WHAT DO YOU MEAN "USUAL TWO"?
HUH?
ISN'T IT OBVIOUS?
THE "WHAT-IF" SPECIAL, RIGHT?
Coming right up.
"THE WHAT-IF SPECIAL"?
CODFISH MILT WITH PONZU SAUCE...
...AND BROILED LIVER WITH ONIONS.
IT'S OUR SPECIALTY.
Now, anyway.
WOW...
THAT SOUNDS GOOD TOO...
...BUT I'M WAITING FOR THE SHIME-SABA.
SMILE

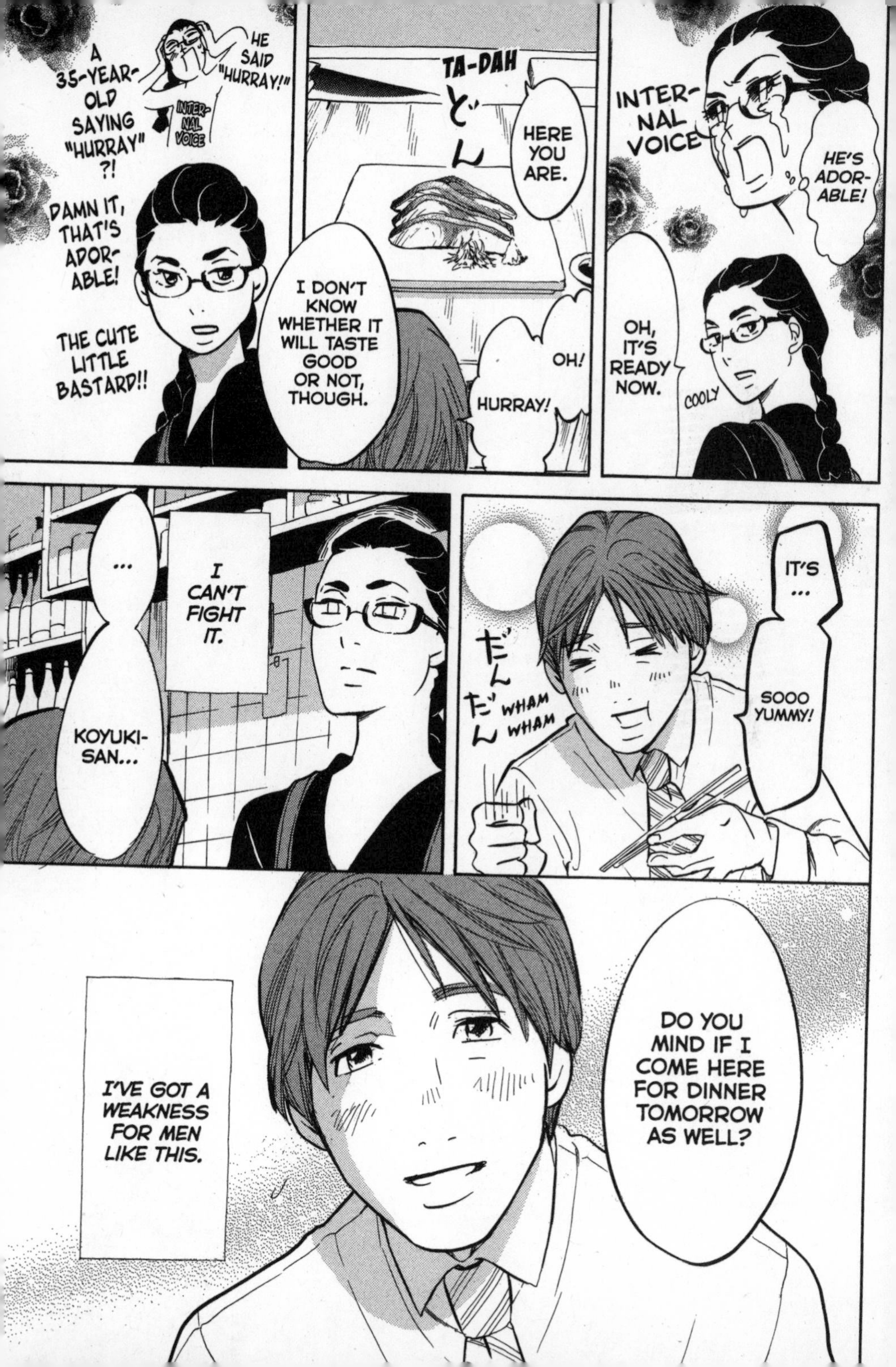
INTER-NAL VOICE
HE'S ADOR-ABLE!
OH, IT'S READY NOW.
COOLY
HERE YOU ARE.
TA-DAH どん
OH!
HURRAY!
I DON'T KNOW WHETHER IT WILL TASTE GOOD OR NOT, THOUGH.
HE SAID "HURRAY!"
INTER-NAL VOICE
A 35-YEAR-OLD SAYING "HURRAY"?!
DAMN IT, THAT'S ADOR-ABLE!
THE CUTE LITTLE BASTARD!!
IT'S... SOOO YUMMY!
だんだん WHAM WHAM
... KOYUKI-SAN...
I CAN'T FIGHT IT.
DO YOU MIND IF I COME HERE FOR DINNER TOMORROW AS WELL?
I'VE GOT A WEAKNESS FOR MEN LIKE THIS.

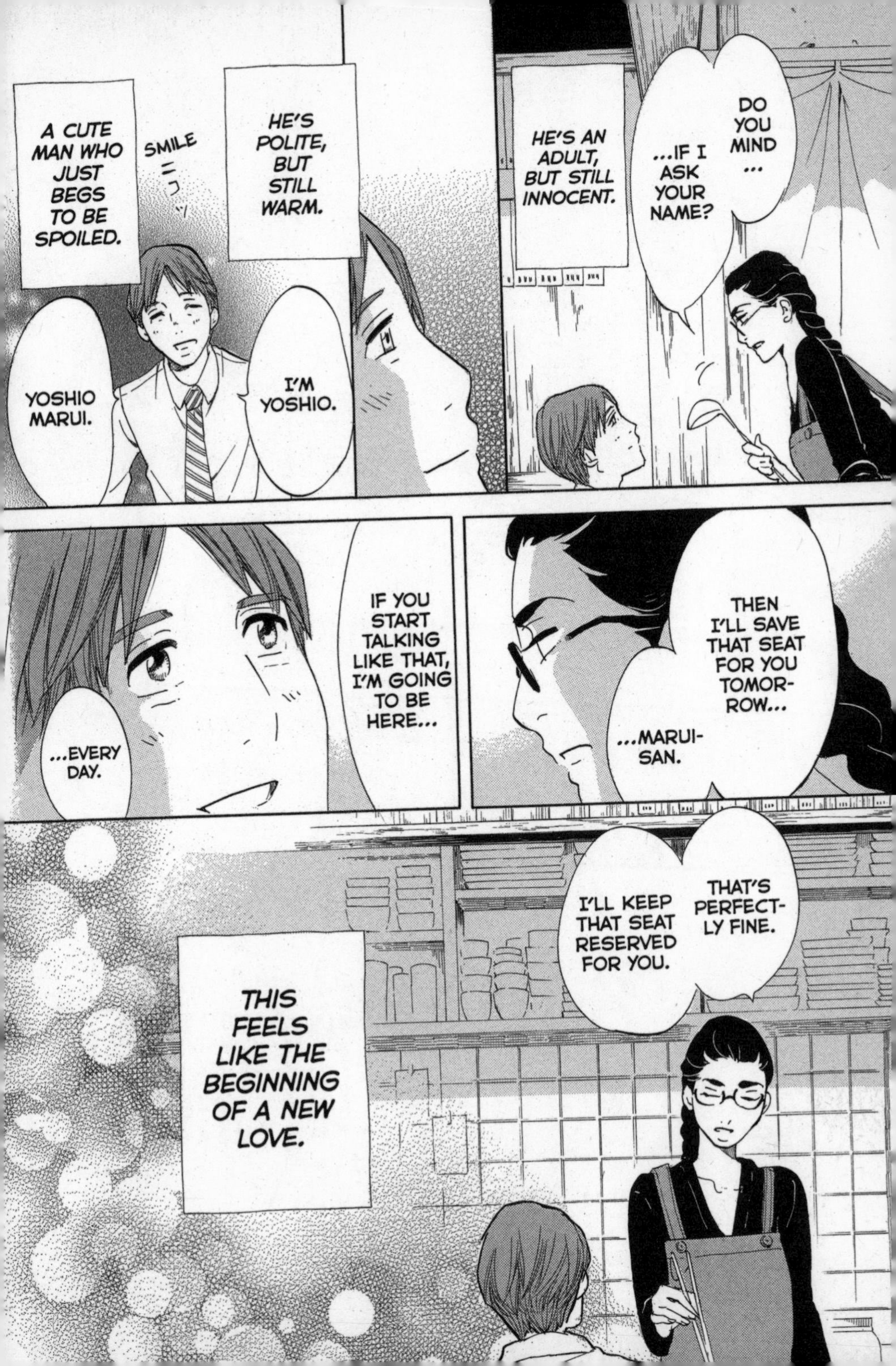
DO YOU MIND...
...IF I ASK YOUR NAME?
HE'S AN ADULT, BUT STILL INNOCENT.
HE'S POLITE, BUT STILL WARM.
I'M YOSHIO.
A CUTE MAN WHO JUST BEGS TO BE SPOILED.
SMILE
ニコッ
YOSHIO MARUI.
THEN I'LL SAVE THAT SEAT FOR YOU TOMOR-ROW...
...MARUI-SAN.
IF YOU START TALKING LIKE THAT, I'M GOING TO BE HERE...
...EVERY DAY.
THAT'S PERFECT-LY FINE.
I'LL KEEP THAT SEAT RESERVED FOR YOU.
THIS FEELS LIKE THE BEGINNING OF A NEW LOVE.

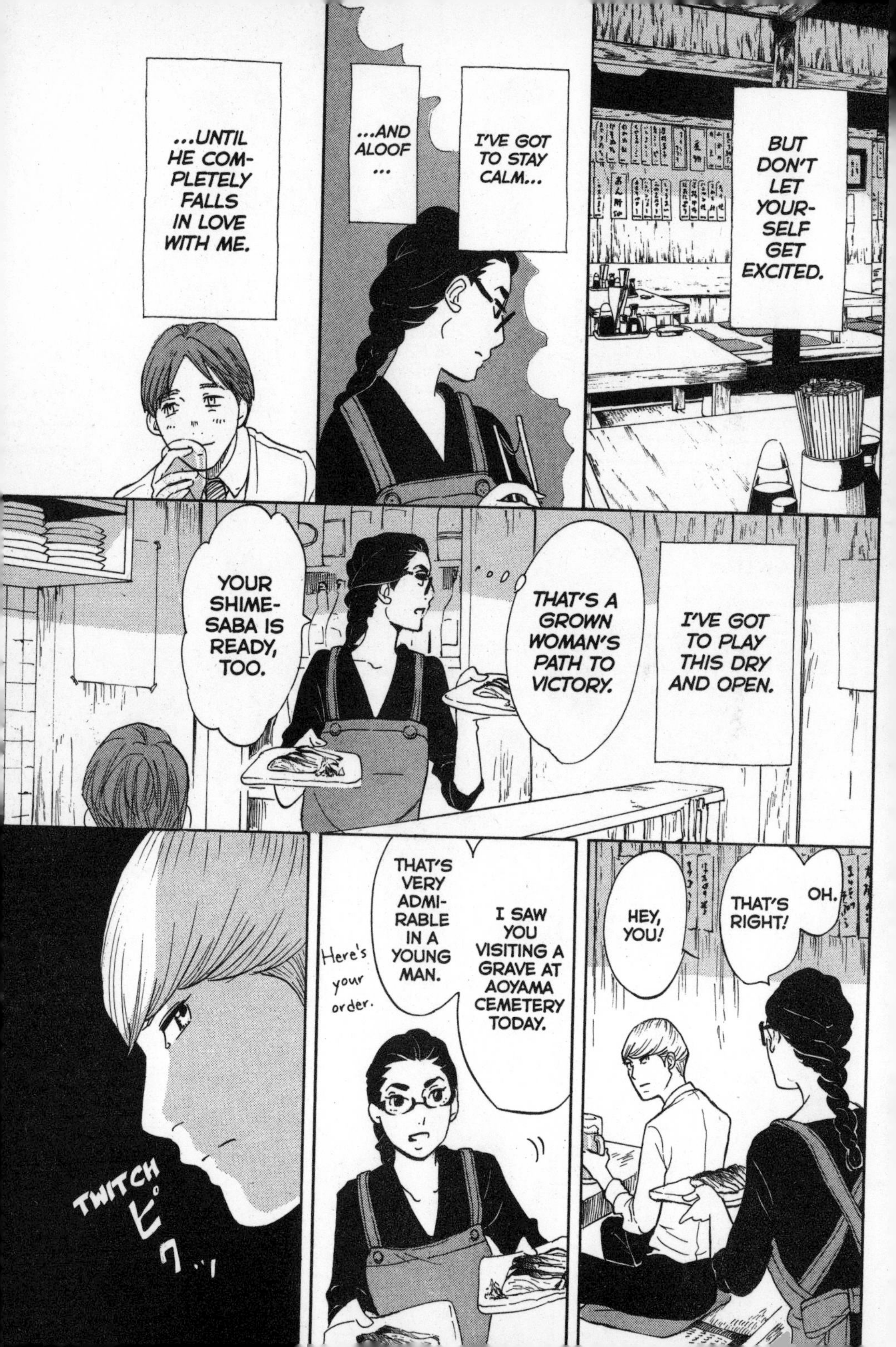
BUT DON'T LET YOURSELF GET EXCITED.
I'VE GOT TO STAY CALM...
...AND ALOOF...
...UNTIL HE COMPLETELY FALLS IN LOVE WITH ME.
I'VE GOT TO PLAY THIS DRY AND OPEN.
THAT'S A GROWN WOMAN'S PATH TO VICTORY.
YOUR SHIME-SABA IS READY, TOO.
OH.
THAT'S RIGHT!
HEY, YOU!
I SAW YOU VISITING A GRAVE AT AOYAMA CEMETERY TODAY.
THAT'S VERY ADMIRABLE IN A YOUNG MAN.
Here's your order.
TWITCH
ピク

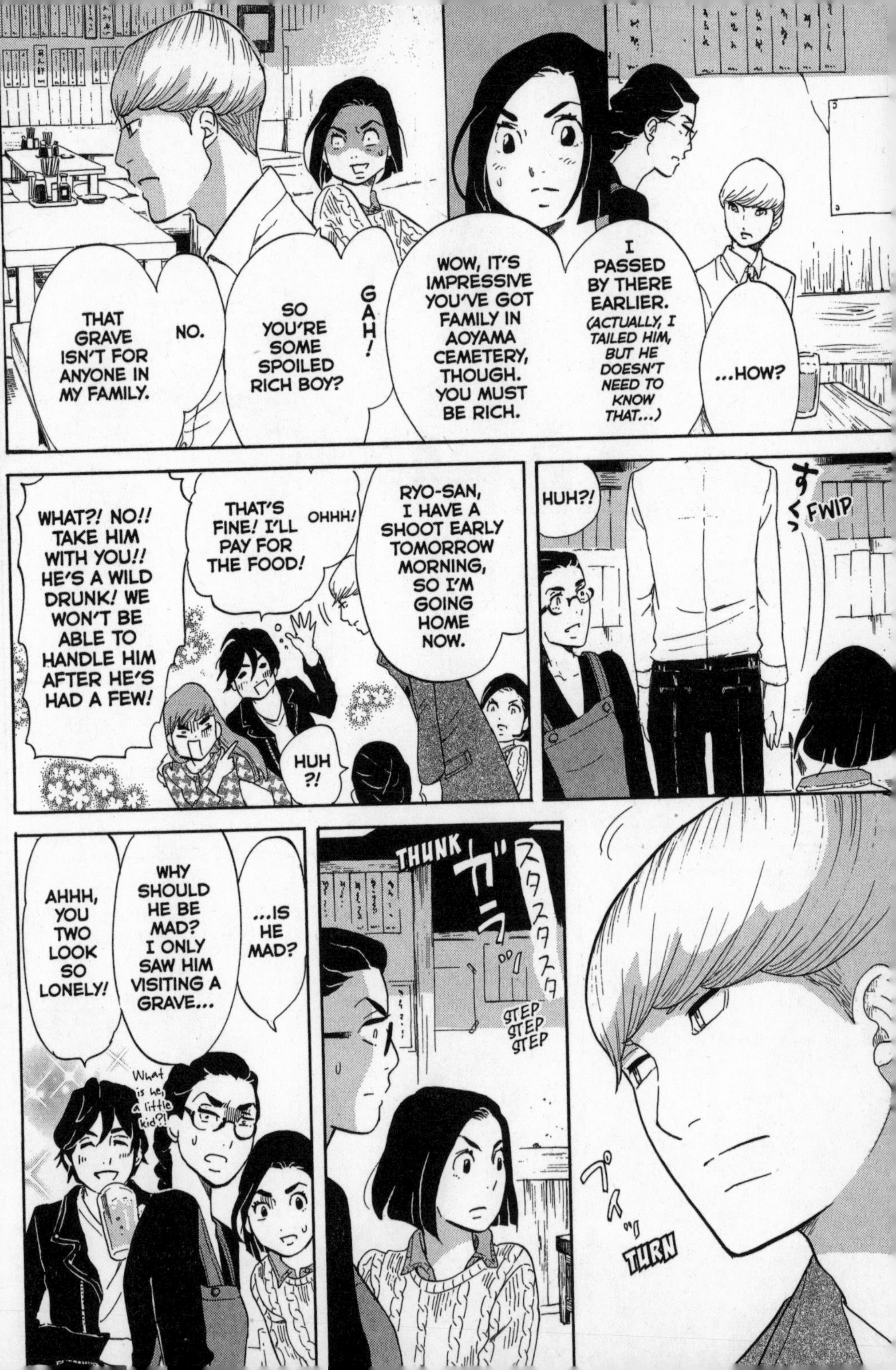
...HOW?
I PASSED BY THERE EARLIER. (ACTUALLY, I TAILED HIM, BUT HE DOESN'T NEED TO KNOW THAT...)
WOW, IT'S IMPRESSIVE YOU'VE GOT FAMILY IN AOYAMA CEMETERY, THOUGH. YOU MUST BE RICH.
GAH!
SO YOU'RE SOME SPOILED RICH BOY?
NO.
THAT GRAVE ISN'T FOR ANYONE IN MY FAMILY.
すくっ
FWIP
HUH?!
RYO-SAN, I HAVE A SHOOT EARLY TOMORROW MORNING, SO I'M GOING HOME NOW.
OHHH!
THAT'S FINE! I'LL PAY FOR THE FOOD!
HUH?!
WHAT?! NO!! TAKE HIM WITH YOU!! HE'S A WILD DRUNK! WE WON'T BE ABLE TO HANDLE HIM AFTER HE'S HAD A FEW!
プイッ
TURN
スタスタスタ
STEP STEP STEP
ガラッ
THUNK
...IS HE MAD?
WHY SHOULD HE BE MAD? I ONLY SAW HIM VISITING A GRAVE...
AHHH, YOU TWO LOOK SO LONELY!
What is he, a little kid?!

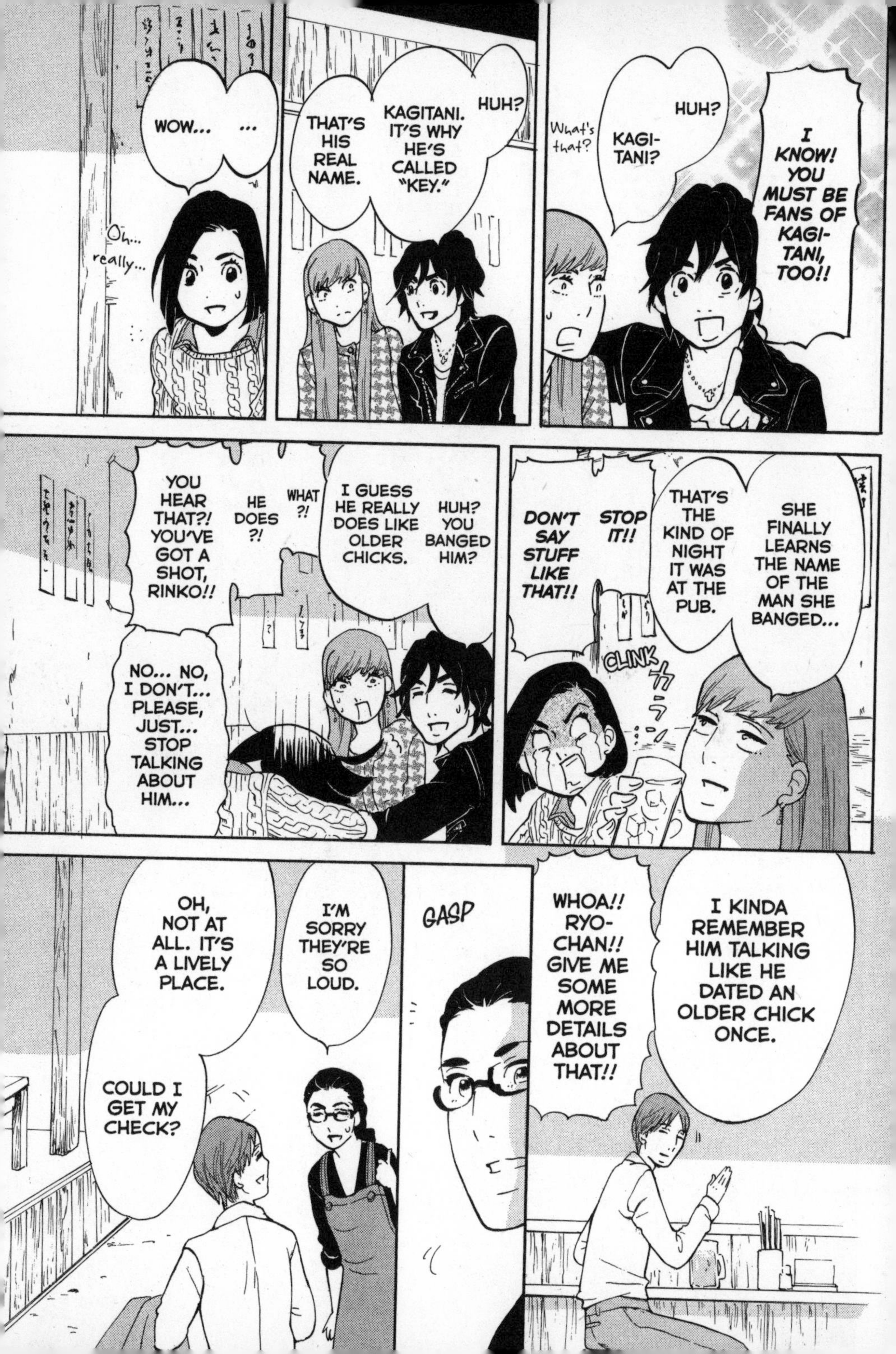
I KNOW! YOU MUST BE FANS OF KAGITANI, TOO!!
HUH? KAGI-TANI?
What's that?
HUH?
KAGITANI. IT'S WHY HE'S CALLED "KEY."
THAT'S HIS REAL NAME.
WOW... ...
Oh... really...
SHE FINALLY LEARNS THE NAME OF THE MAN SHE BANGED...
THAT'S THE KIND OF NIGHT IT WAS AT THE PUB.
STOP IT!!
DON'T SAY STUFF LIKE THAT!!
CLINK
HUH? YOU BANGED HIM?
I GUESS HE REALLY DOES LIKE OLDER CHICKS.
WHAT?!
HE DOES?!
YOU HEAR THAT?! YOU'VE GOT A SHOT, RINKO!!
NO... NO, I DON'T... PLEASE, JUST... STOP TALKING ABOUT HIM...
I KINDA REMEMBER HIM TALKING LIKE HE DATED AN OLDER CHICK ONCE.
WHOA!! RYO-CHAN!! GIVE ME SOME MORE DETAILS ABOUT THAT!!
GASP
I'M SORRY THEY'RE SO LOUD.
OH, NOT AT ALL. IT'S A LIVELY PLACE.
COULD I GET MY CHECK?

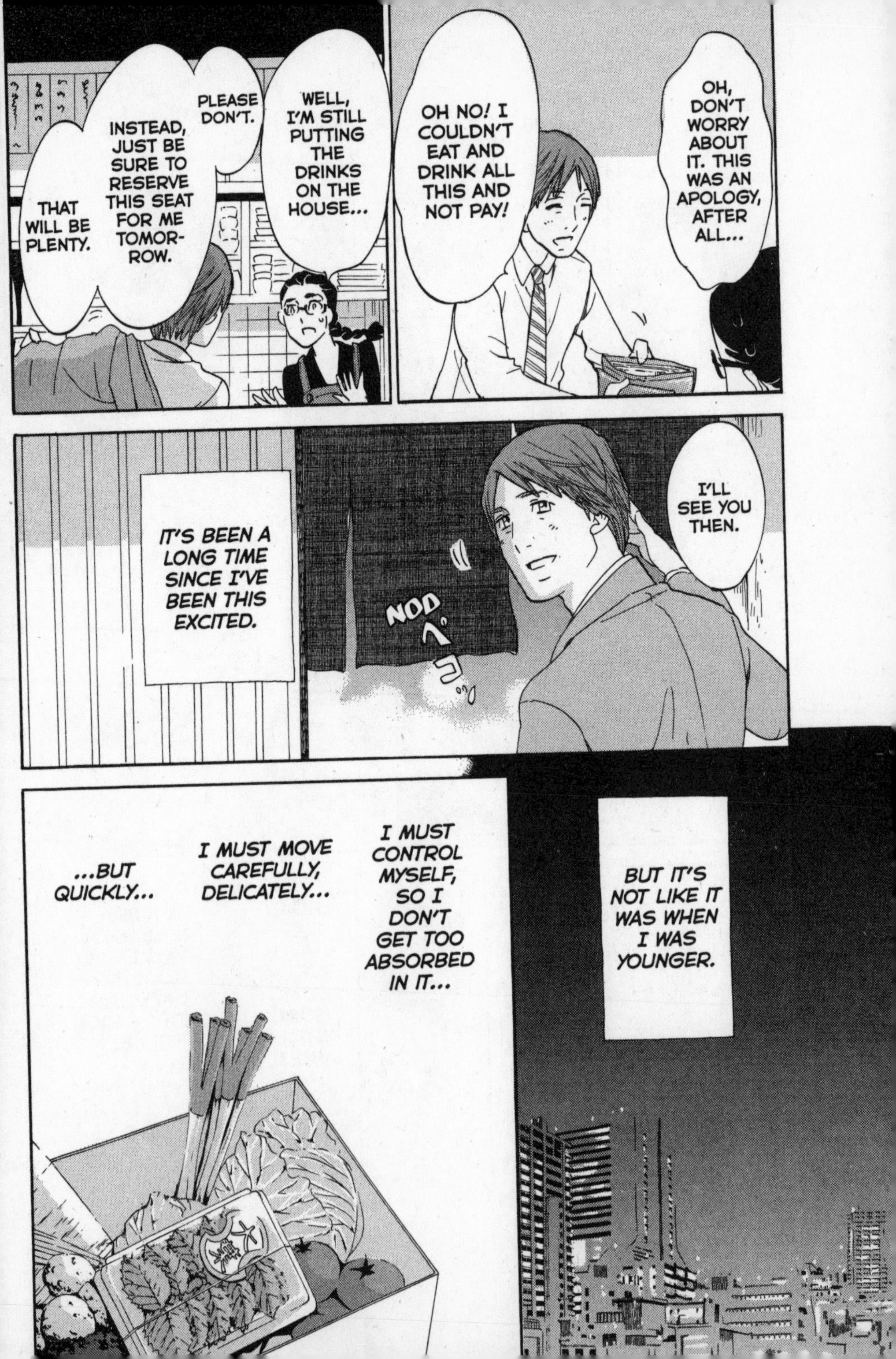
OH, DON'T WORRY ABOUT IT. THIS WAS AN APOLOGY, AFTER ALL...
OH NO! I COULDN'T EAT AND DRINK ALL THIS AND NOT PAY!
WELL, I'M STILL PUTTING THE DRINKS ON THE HOUSE...
PLEASE DON'T.
INSTEAD, JUST BE SURE TO RESERVE THIS SEAT FOR ME TOMORROW.
THAT WILL BE PLENTY.
I'LL SEE YOU THEN.
NOD
IT'S BEEN A LONG TIME SINCE I'VE BEEN THIS EXCITED.
BUT IT'S NOT LIKE IT WAS WHEN I WAS YOUNGER.
I MUST CONTROL MYSELF, SO I DON'T GET TOO ABSORBED IN IT...
I MUST MOVE CAREFULLY, DELICATELY...
...BUT QUICKLY...

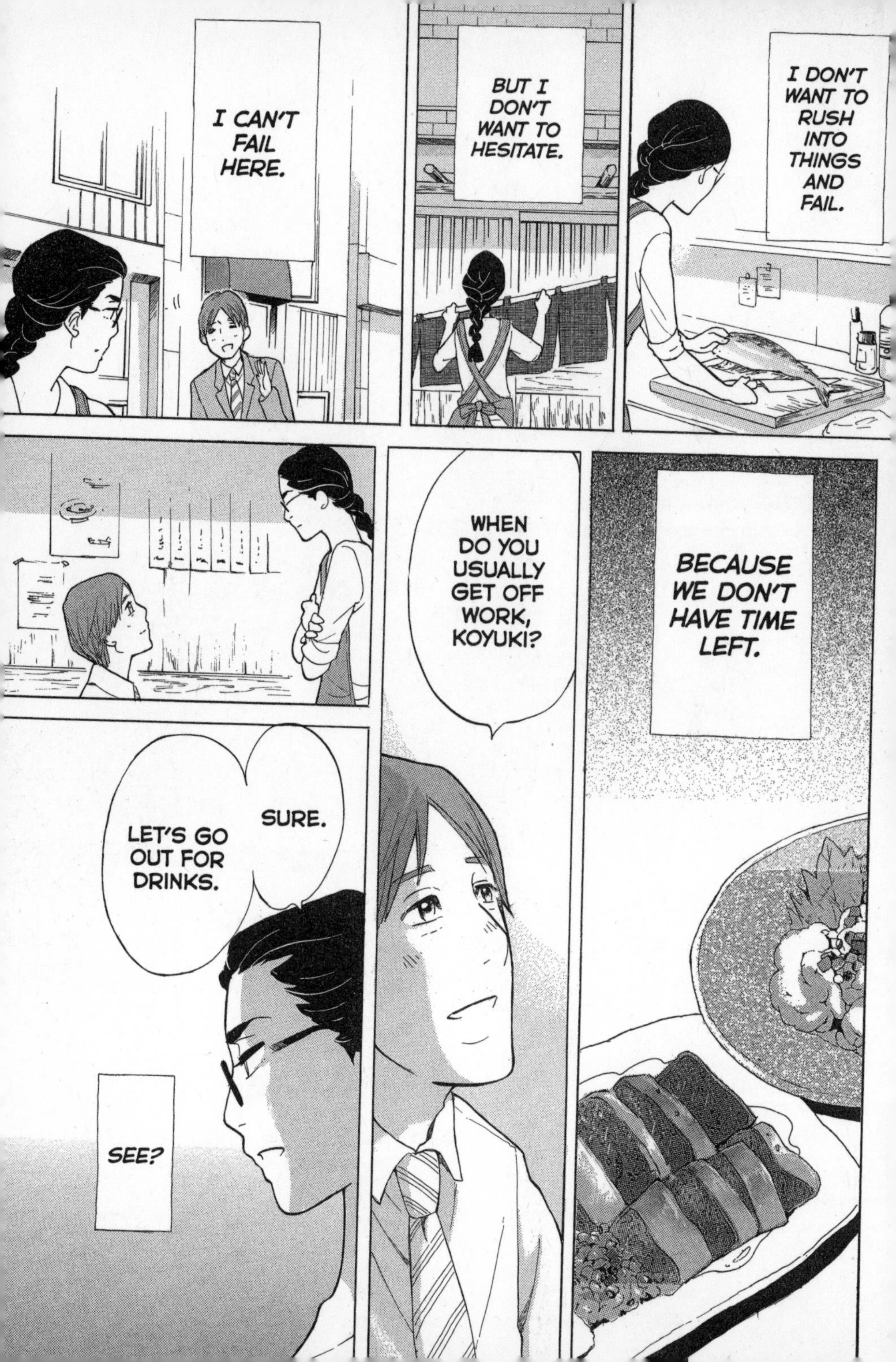
I DON'T WANT TO RUSH INTO THINGS AND FAIL.
BUT I DON'T WANT TO HESITATE.
I CAN'T FAIL HERE.
BECAUSE WE DON'T HAVE TIME LEFT.
WHEN DO YOU USUALLY GET OFF WORK, KOYUKI?
SURE.
LET'S GO OUT FOR DRINKS.
SEE?

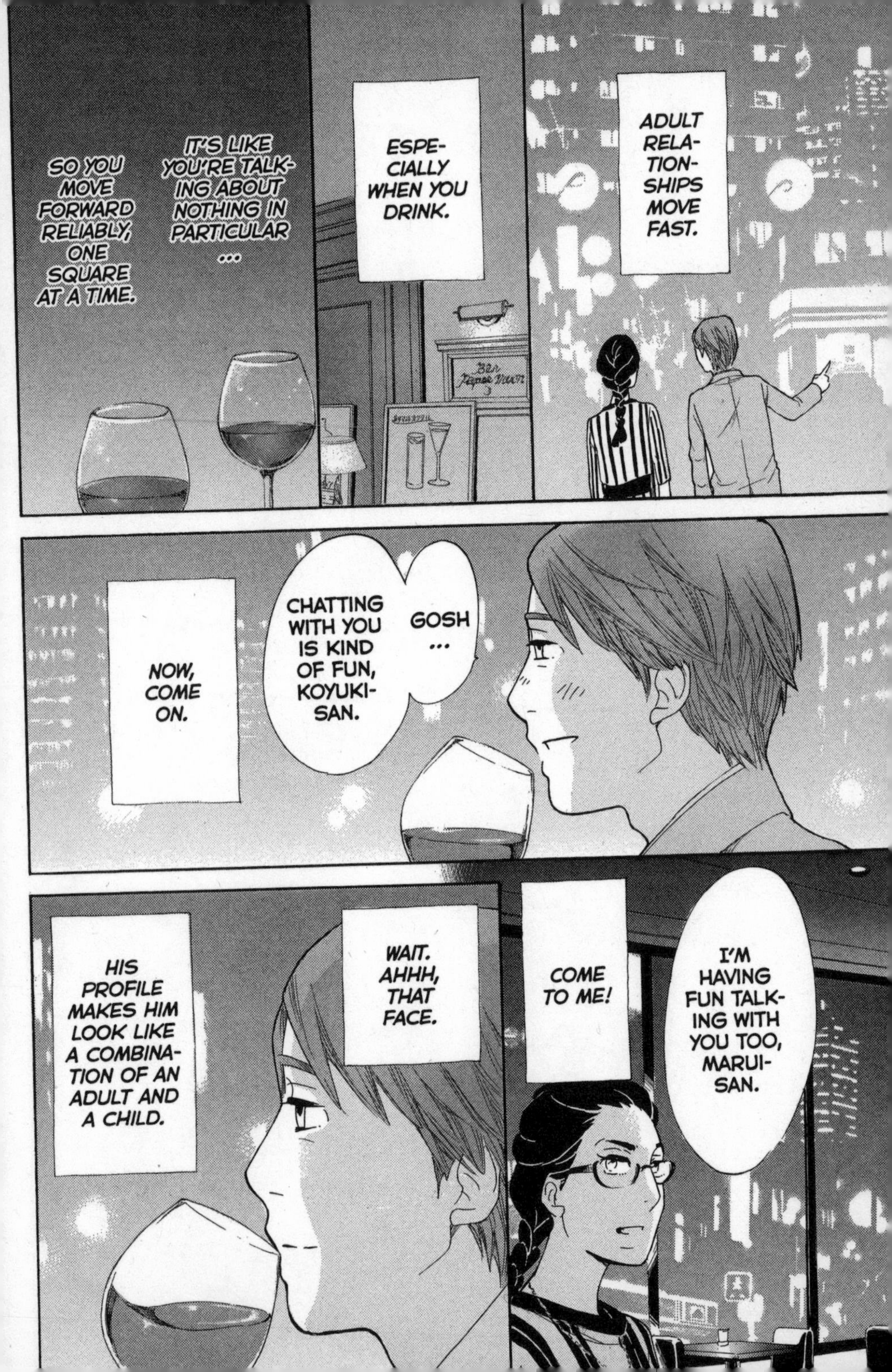
ADULT RELATIONSHIPS MOVE FAST.
ESPECIALLY WHEN YOU DRINK.
IT'S LIKE YOU'RE TALKING ABOUT NOTHING IN PARTICULAR...
SO YOU MOVE FORWARD RELIABLY, ONE SQUARE AT A TIME.
GOSH...
CHATTING WITH YOU IS KIND OF FUN, KOYUKI-SAN.
NOW, COME ON.
I'M HAVING FUN TALKING WITH YOU TOO, MARUI-SAN.
COME TO ME!
WAIT. AHHH, THAT FACE.
HIS PROFILE MAKES HIM LOOK LIKE A COMBINATION OF AN ADULT AND A CHILD.

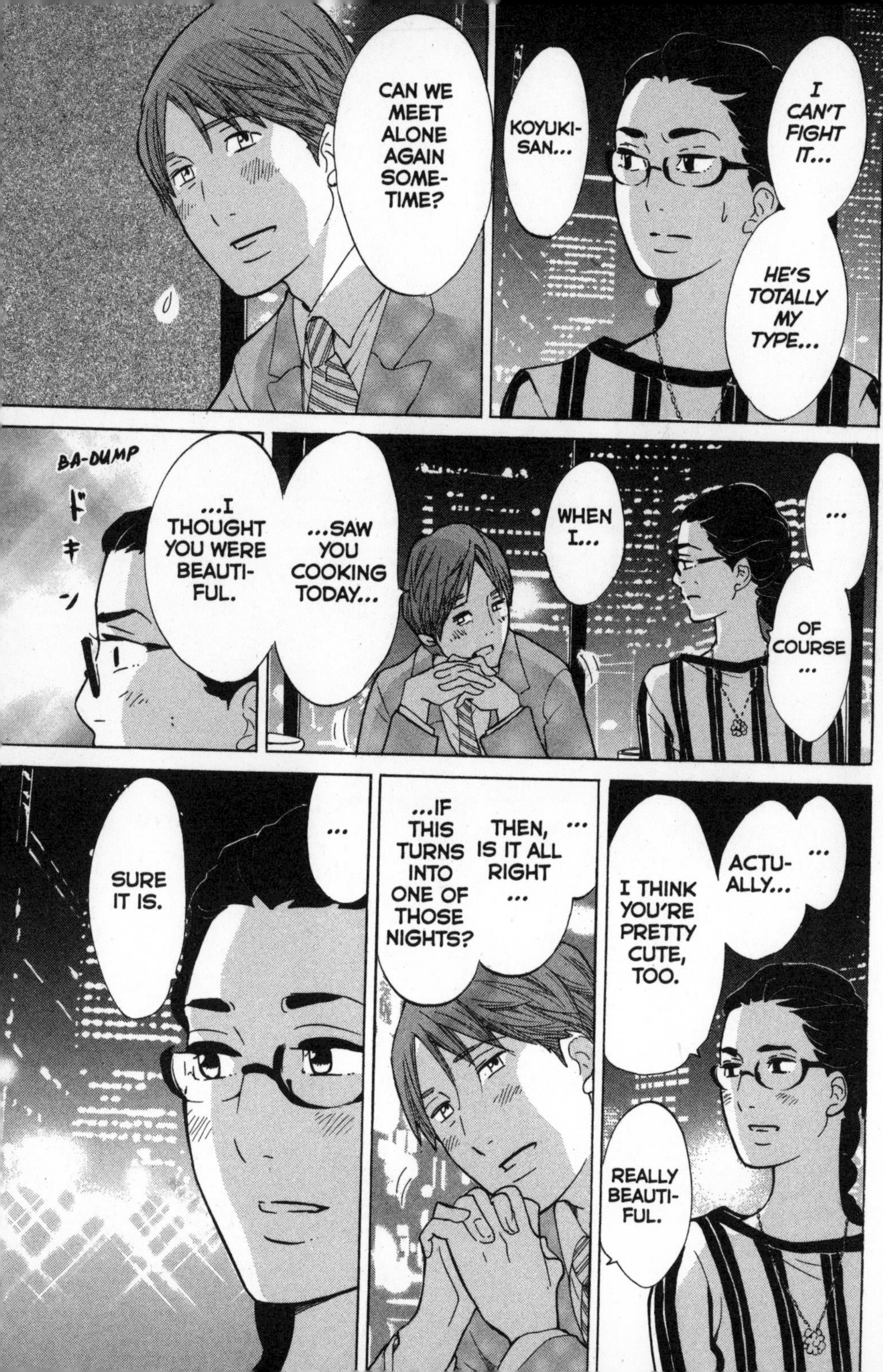
I CAN'T FIGHT IT...
HE'S TOTALLY MY TYPE...
KOYUKI-SAN...
CAN WE MEET ALONE AGAIN SOMETIME?
...
OF COURSE...
WHEN I...
...SAW YOU COOKING TODAY...
...I THOUGHT YOU WERE BEAUTIFUL.
BA-DUMP
ドキン
...
ACTUALLY...
I THINK YOU'RE PRETTY CUTE, TOO.
REALLY BEAUTIFUL.
...
THEN, IS IT ALL RIGHT...
...IF THIS TURNS INTO ONE OF THOSE NIGHTS?
...
SURE IT IS.

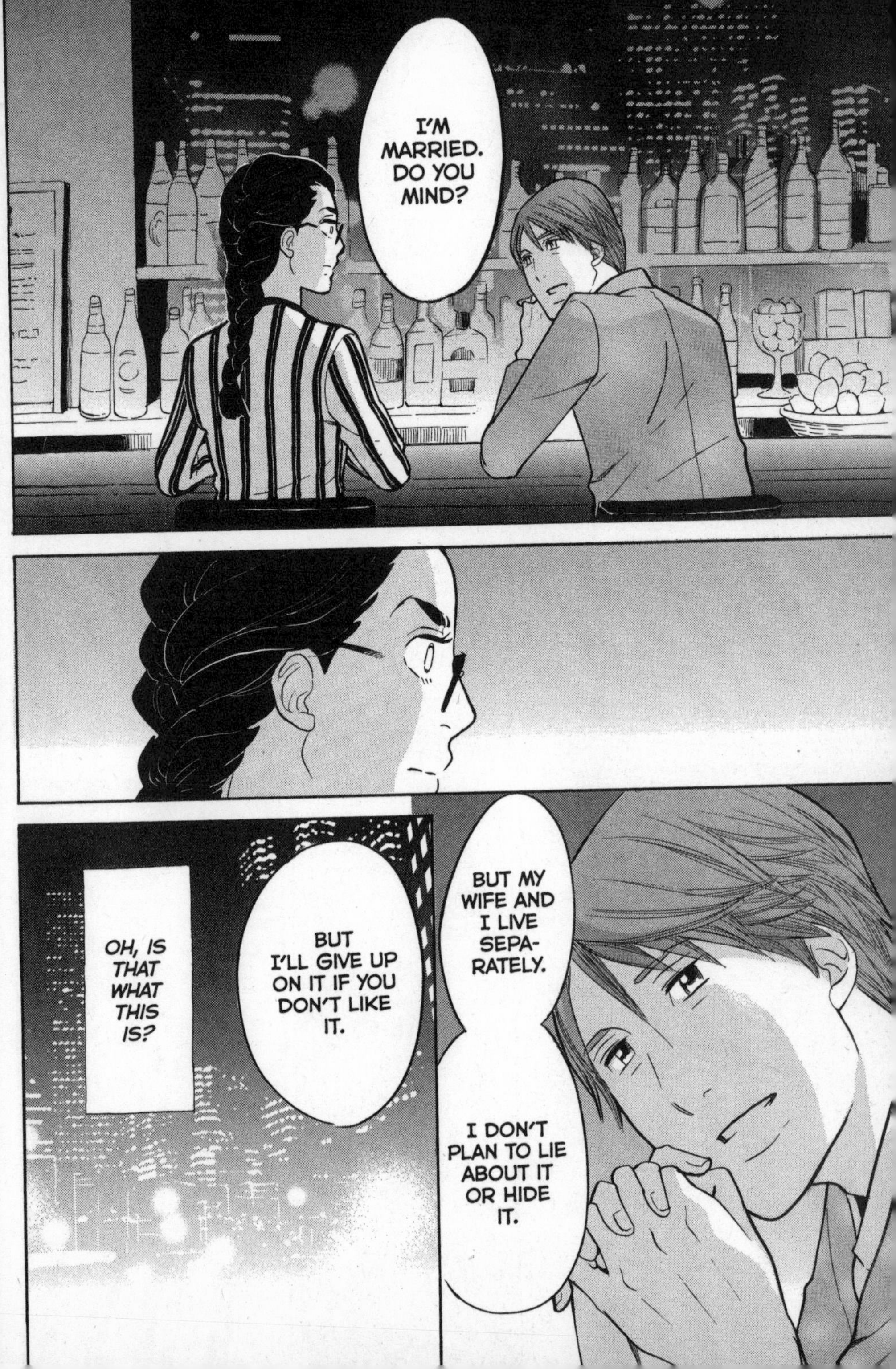
I'M MARRIED. DO YOU MIND?
BUT MY WIFE AND I LIVE SEPA-RATELY.
I DON'T PLAN TO LIE ABOUT IT OR HIDE IT.
BUT I'LL GIVE UP ON IT IF YOU DON'T LIKE IT.
OH, IS THAT WHAT THIS IS?

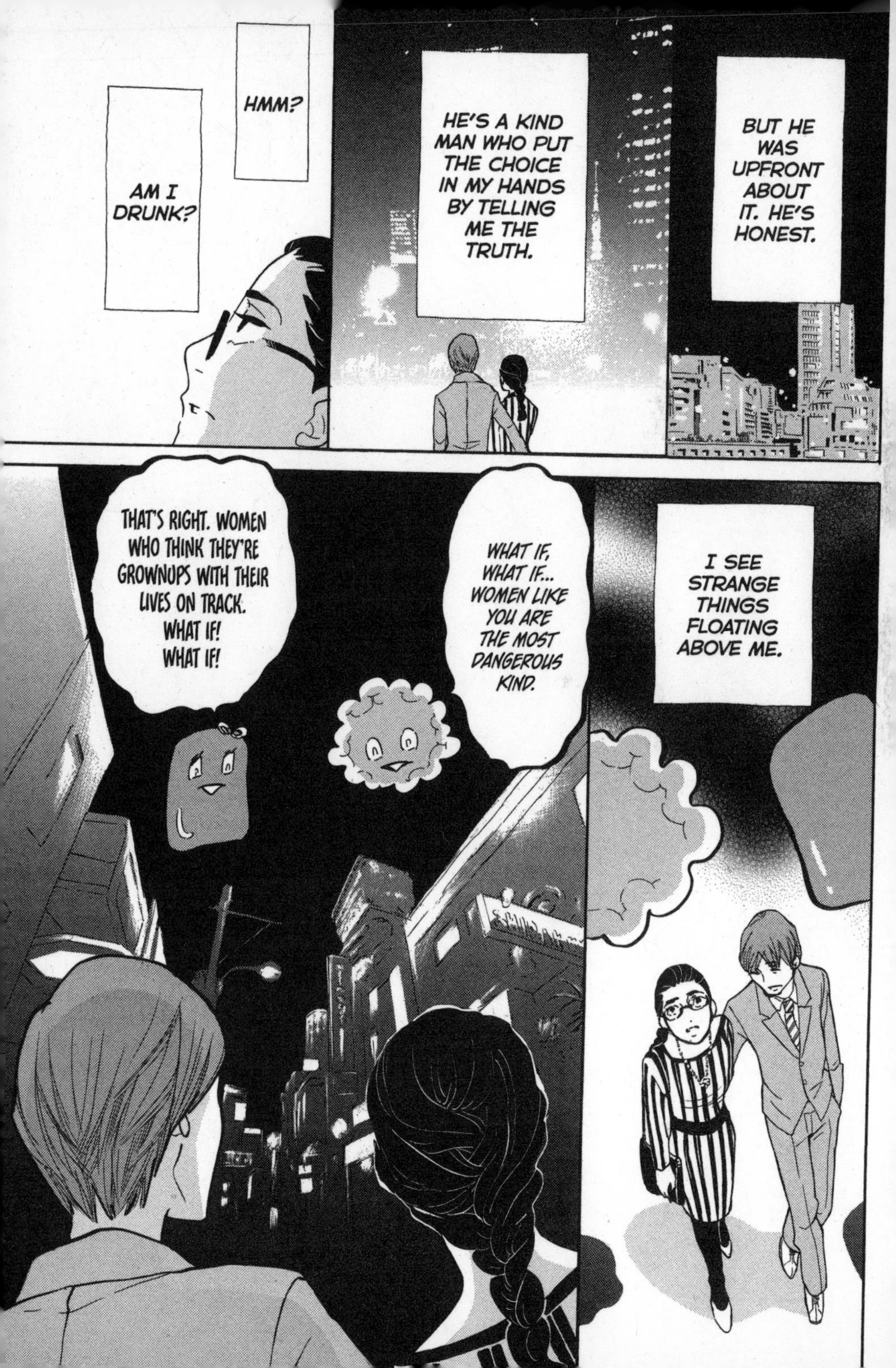
BUT HE WAS UPFRONT ABOUT IT. HE'S HONEST.
HE'S A KIND MAN WHO PUT THE CHOICE IN MY HANDS BY TELLING ME THE TRUTH.
HMM?
AM I DRUNK?
I SEE STRANGE THINGS FLOATING ABOVE ME.
WHAT IF, WHAT IF... WOMEN LIKE YOU ARE THE MOST DANGEROUS KIND.
THAT'S RIGHT. WOMEN WHO THINK THEY'RE GROWNUPS WITH THEIR LIVES ON TRACK. WHAT IF! WHAT IF!

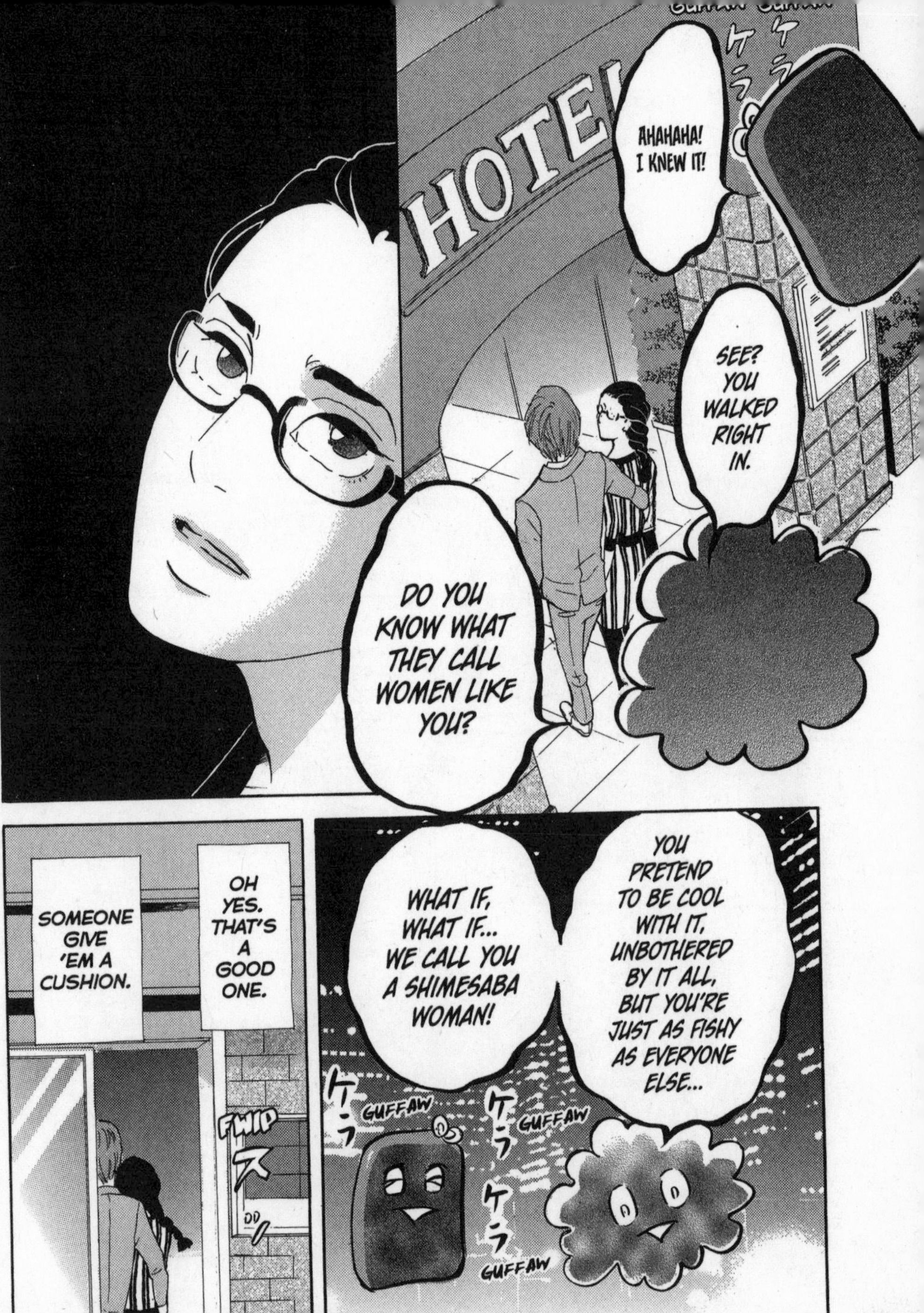
ケラケラ
AHAHAHA! I KNEW IT!
SEE? YOU WALKED RIGHT IN.
DO YOU KNOW WHAT THEY CALL WOMEN LIKE YOU?
YOU PRETEND TO BE COOL WITH IT, UNBOTHERED BY IT ALL, BUT YOU'RE JUST AS FISHY AS EVERYONE ELSE...
WHAT IF, WHAT IF... WE CALL YOU A SHIMESABA WOMAN!
ケラ GUFFAW
ケラ GUFFAW
ケラ GUFFAW
OH YES. THAT'S A GOOD ONE.
SOMEONE GIVE 'EM A CUSHION.
FWIP ス

# ACT 8 PUNCH-DRUNK WOMEN

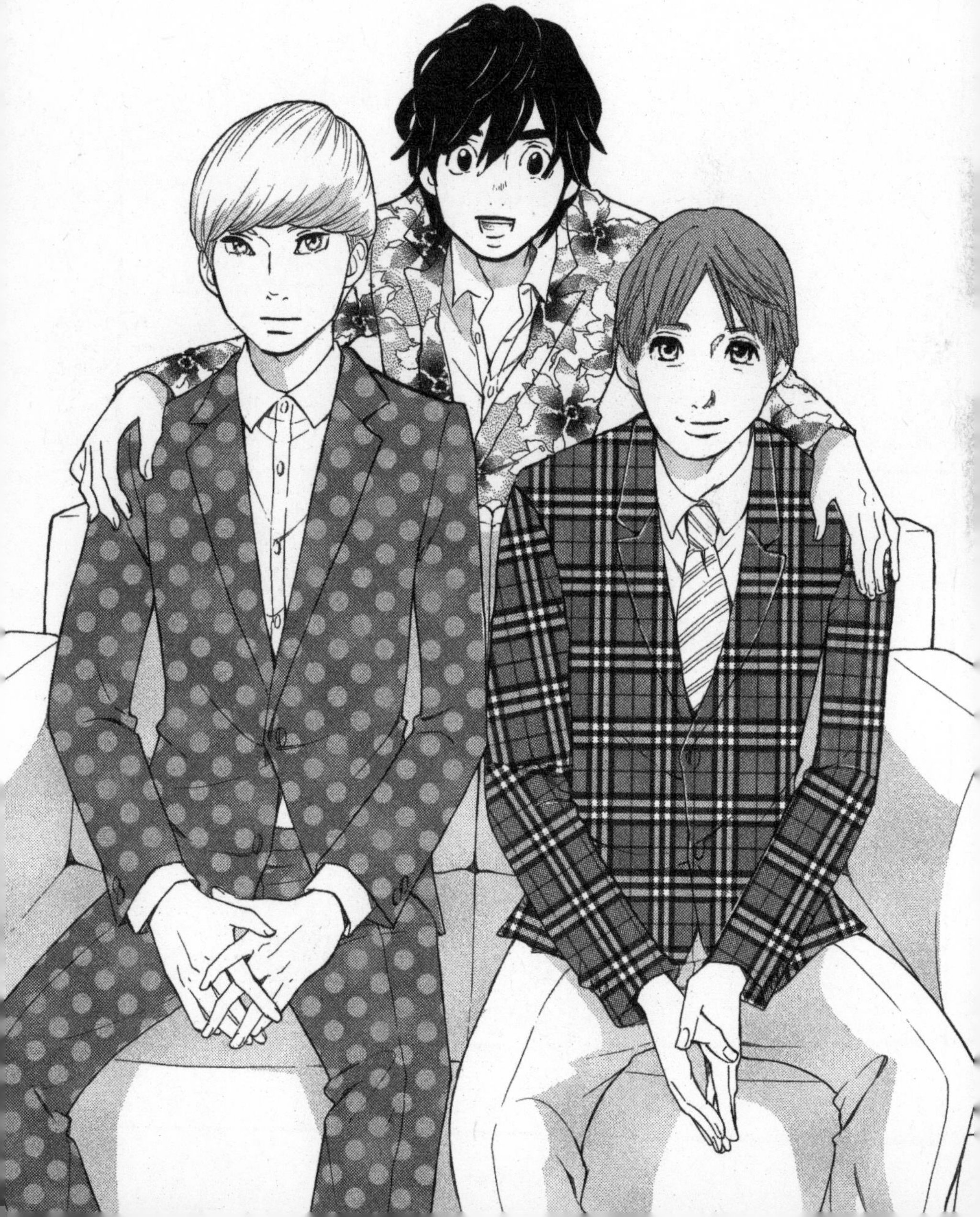

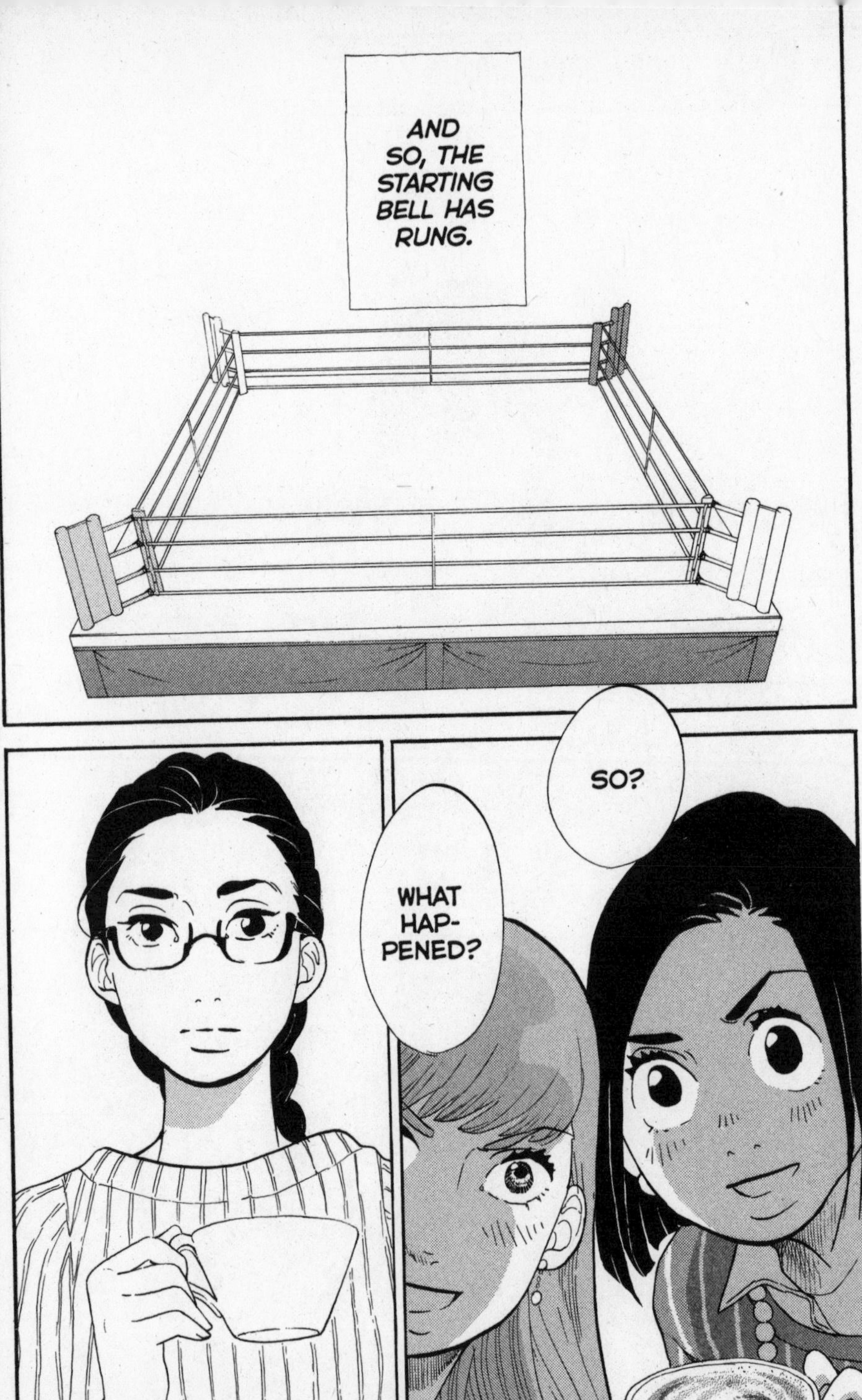
AND SO, THE STARTING BELL HAS RUNG.
SO?
WHAT HAPPENED?

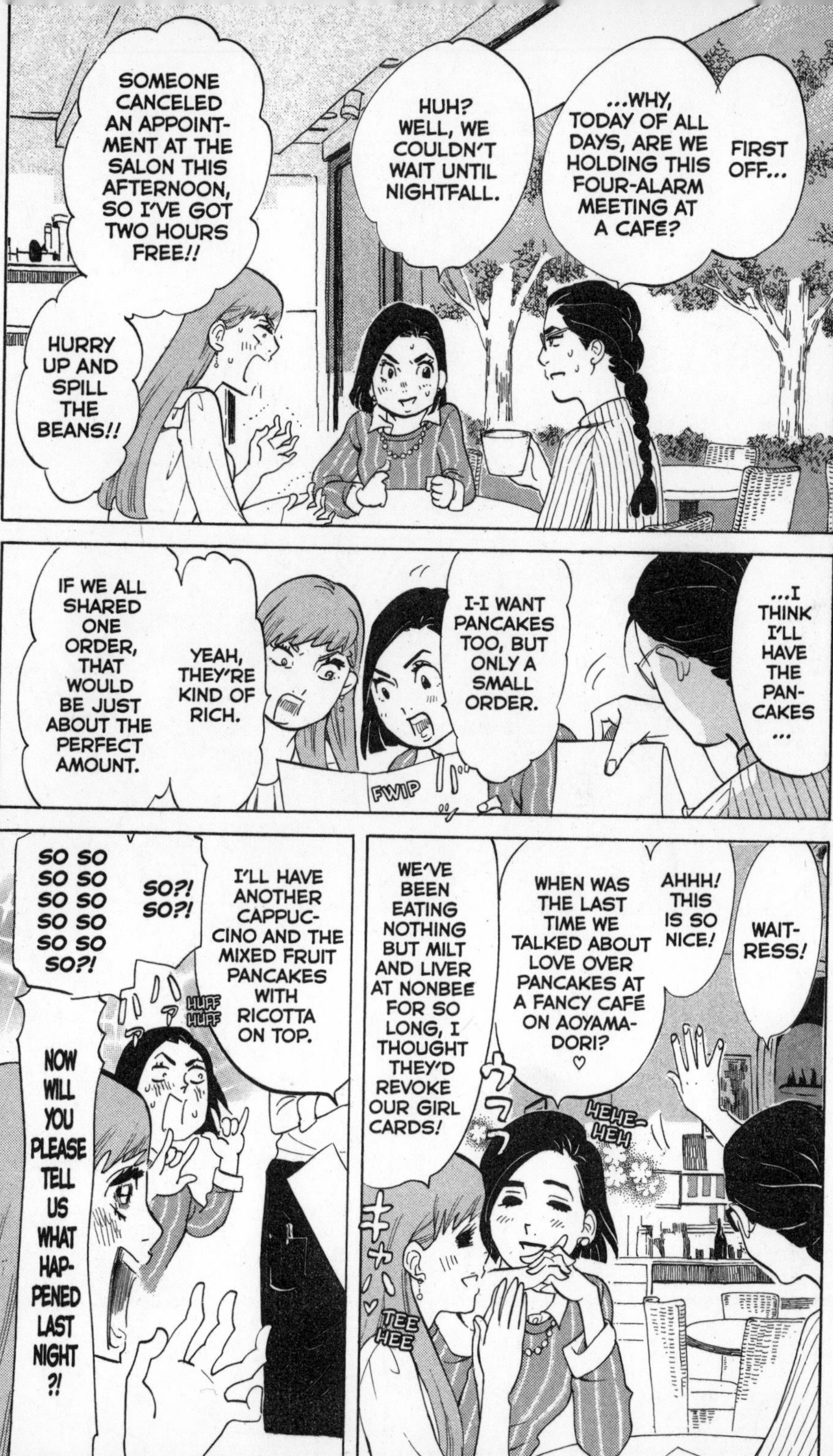
FIRST OFF...
...WHY, TODAY OF ALL DAYS, ARE WE HOLDING THIS FOUR-ALARM MEETING AT A CAFE?
HUH? WELL, WE COULDN'T WAIT UNTIL NIGHTFALL.
SOMEONE CANCELED AN APPOINTMENT AT THE SALON THIS AFTERNOON, SO I'VE GOT TWO HOURS FREE!!
HURRY UP AND SPILL THE BEANS!!
...I THINK I'LL HAVE THE PANCAKES...
I-I WANT PANCAKES TOO, BUT ONLY A SMALL ORDER.
YEAH, THEY'RE KIND OF RICH.
IF WE ALL SHARED ONE ORDER, THAT WOULD BE JUST ABOUT THE PERFECT AMOUNT.
FWIP
WAITRESS!
AHHH! THIS IS SO NICE!
WHEN WAS THE LAST TIME WE TALKED ABOUT LOVE OVER PANCAKES AT A FANCY CAFE ON AOYAMA-DORI? ♡
WE'VE BEEN EATING NOTHING BUT MILT AND LIVER AT NONBEE FOR SO LONG, I THOUGHT THEY'D REVOKE OUR GIRL CARDS!
HEHE-HEH
TEE HEE
I'LL HAVE ANOTHER CAPPUCCINO AND THE MIXED FRUIT PANCAKES WITH RICOTTA ON TOP.
SO?! SO?!
SO SO SO SO SO SO SO SO SO SO SO?!
HUFF HUFF
NOW WILL YOU PLEASE TELL US WHAT HAPPENED LAST NIGHT?!

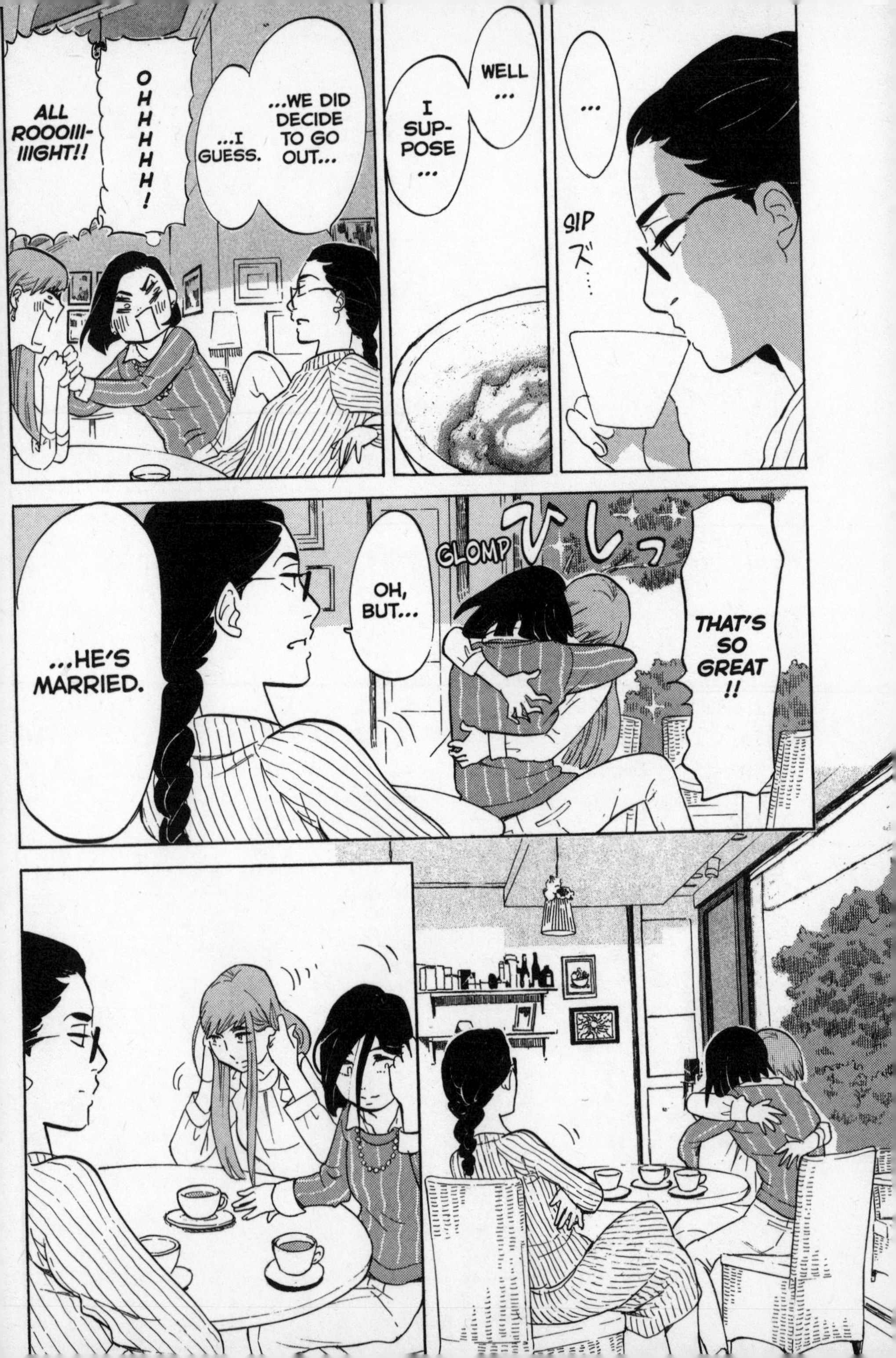
...
SIP
ズ...
WELL ...
I SUPPOSE ...
...WE DID DECIDE TO GO OUT...
...I GUESS.
OHHHHHH!
ALL ROOOIII-IIIGHT!!
THAT'S SO GREAT!!
GLOMP
ひしっ
OH, BUT...
...HE'S MARRIED.

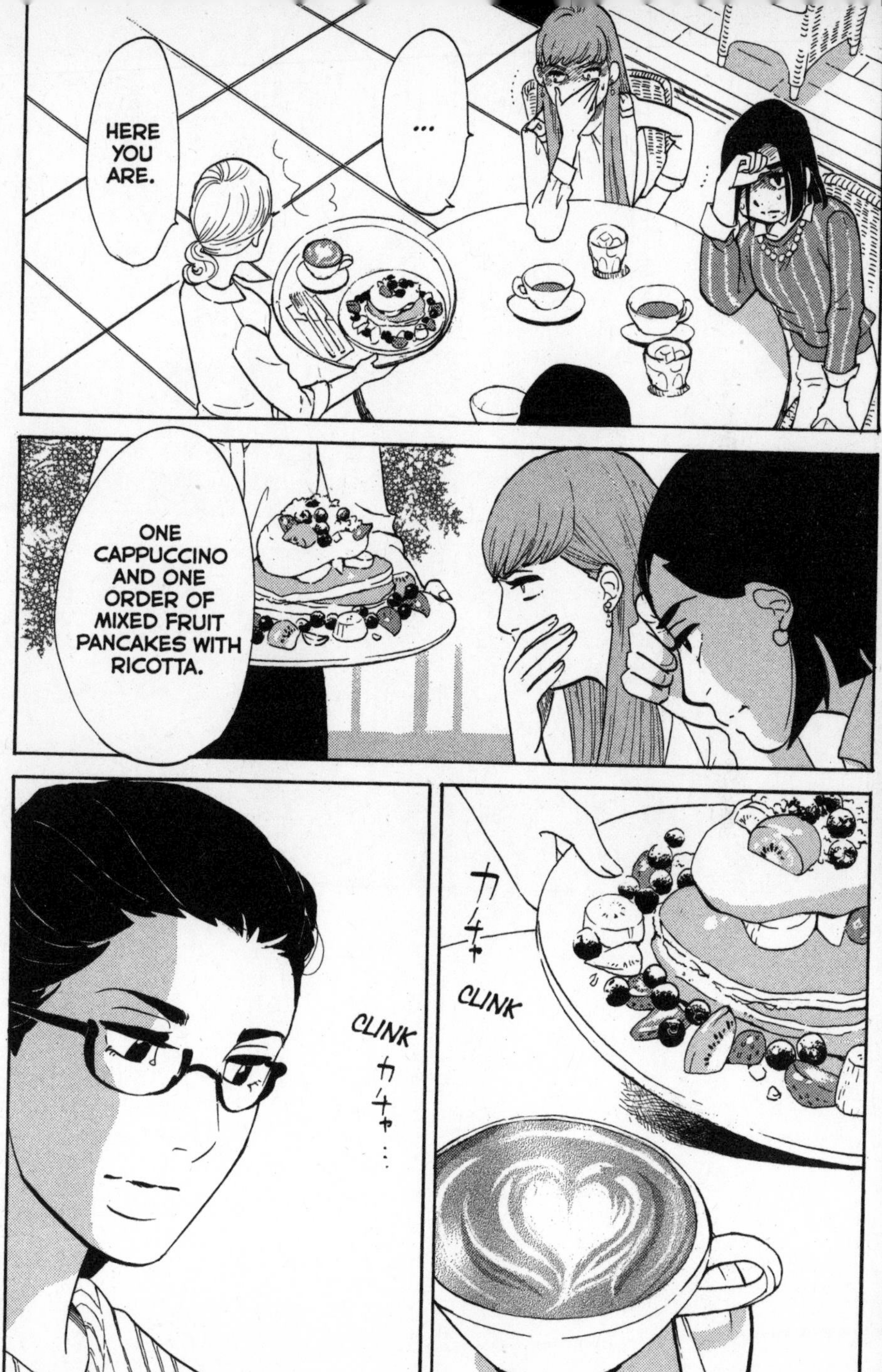
...
HERE YOU ARE.
ONE CAPPUCCINO AND ONE ORDER OF MIXED FRUIT PANCAKES WITH RICOTTA.
カチャ
CLINK
CLINK
カチャ...

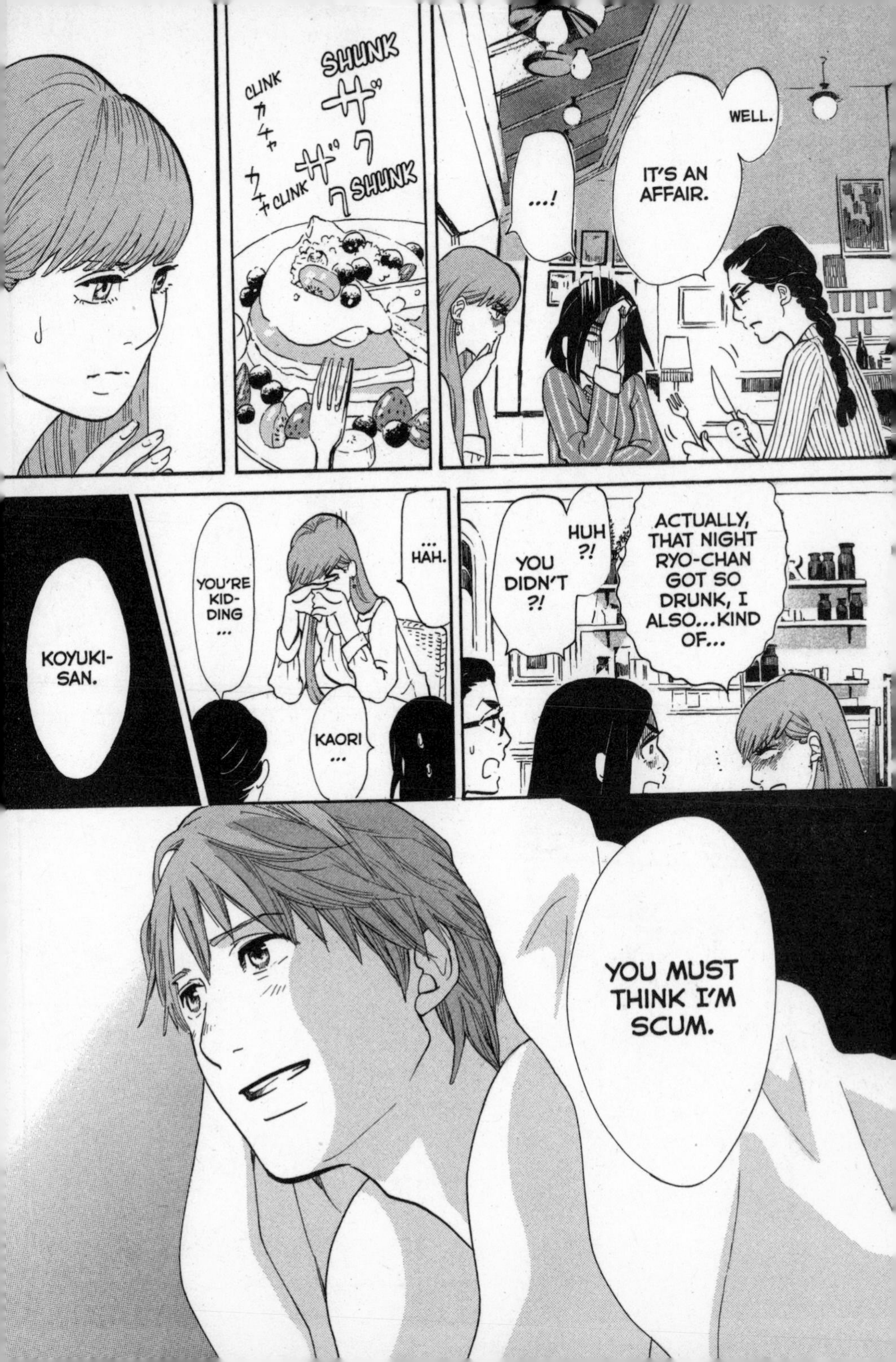
WELL.
IT'S AN AFFAIR.
...!
SHUNK ザク
CLINK カチャ
ザク SHUNK
カチャ CLINK
ACTUALLY, THAT NIGHT RYO-CHAN GOT SO DRUNK, I ALSO...KIND OF...
HUH?!
YOU DIDN'T?!
...HAH.
YOU'RE KIDDING...
KAORI...
KOYUKI-SAN.
YOU MUST THINK I'M SCUM.

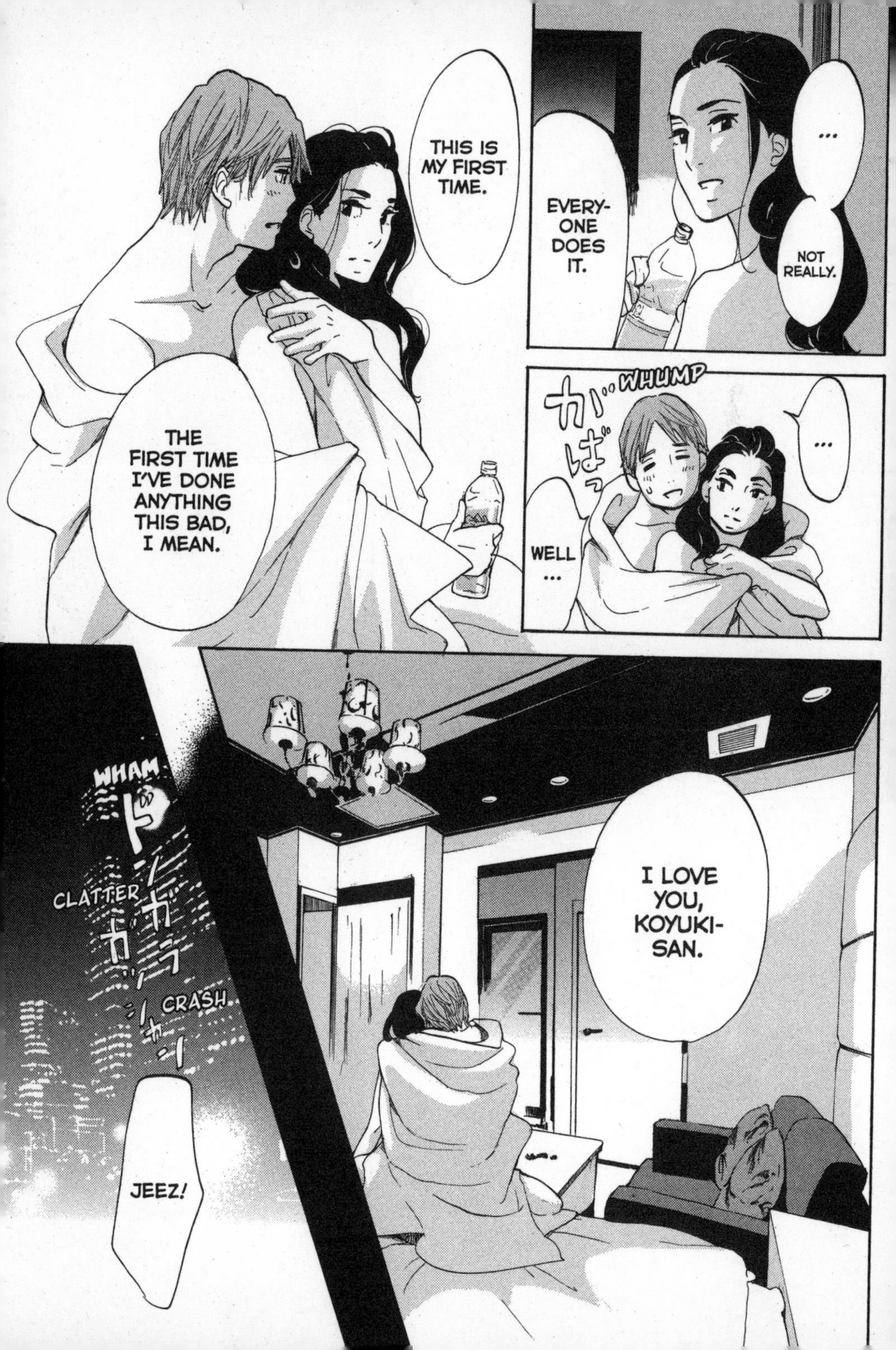
...
NOT REALLY.
EVERY-ONE DOES IT.
WHUMP
...
WELL ...
THIS IS MY FIRST TIME.
THE FIRST TIME I'VE DONE ANYTHING THIS BAD, I MEAN.
I LOVE YOU, KOYUKI-SAN.
WHAM
CLATTER
CRASH
JEEZ!

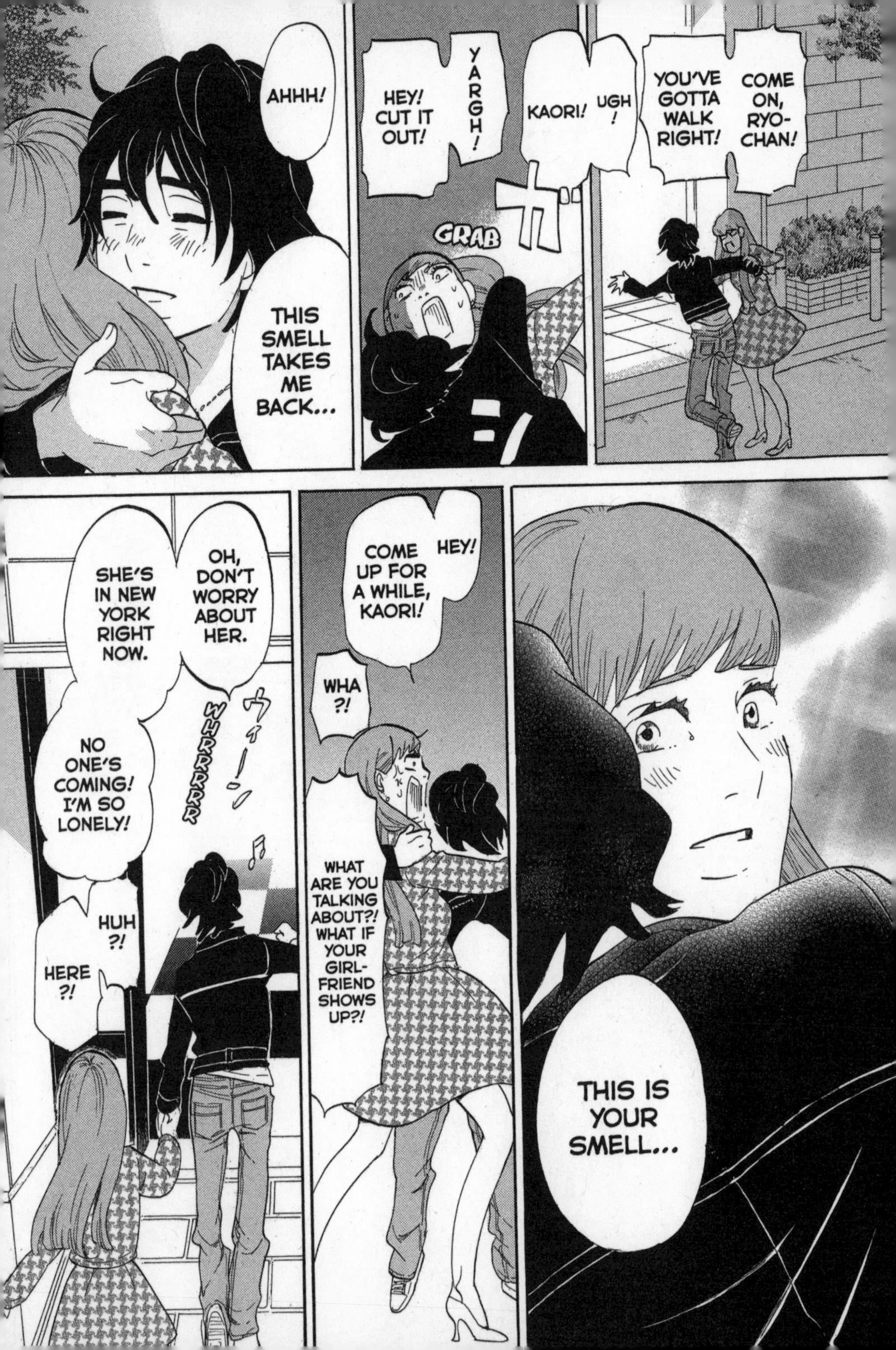
COME ON, RYO-CHAN!
YOU'VE GOTTA WALK RIGHT!
UGH!
KAORI!
YARGH!
HEY! CUT IT OUT!
GRAB
AHHH!
THIS SMELL TAKES ME BACK...
THIS IS YOUR SMELL...
HEY!
COME UP FOR A WHILE, KAORI!
WHA?!
WHAT ARE YOU TALKING ABOUT?! WHAT IF YOUR GIRLFRIEND SHOWS UP?!
OH, DON'T WORRY ABOUT HER.
SHE'S IN NEW YORK RIGHT NOW.
WHRRRRR
NO ONE'S COMING! I'M SO LONELY!
HUH?!
HERE?!

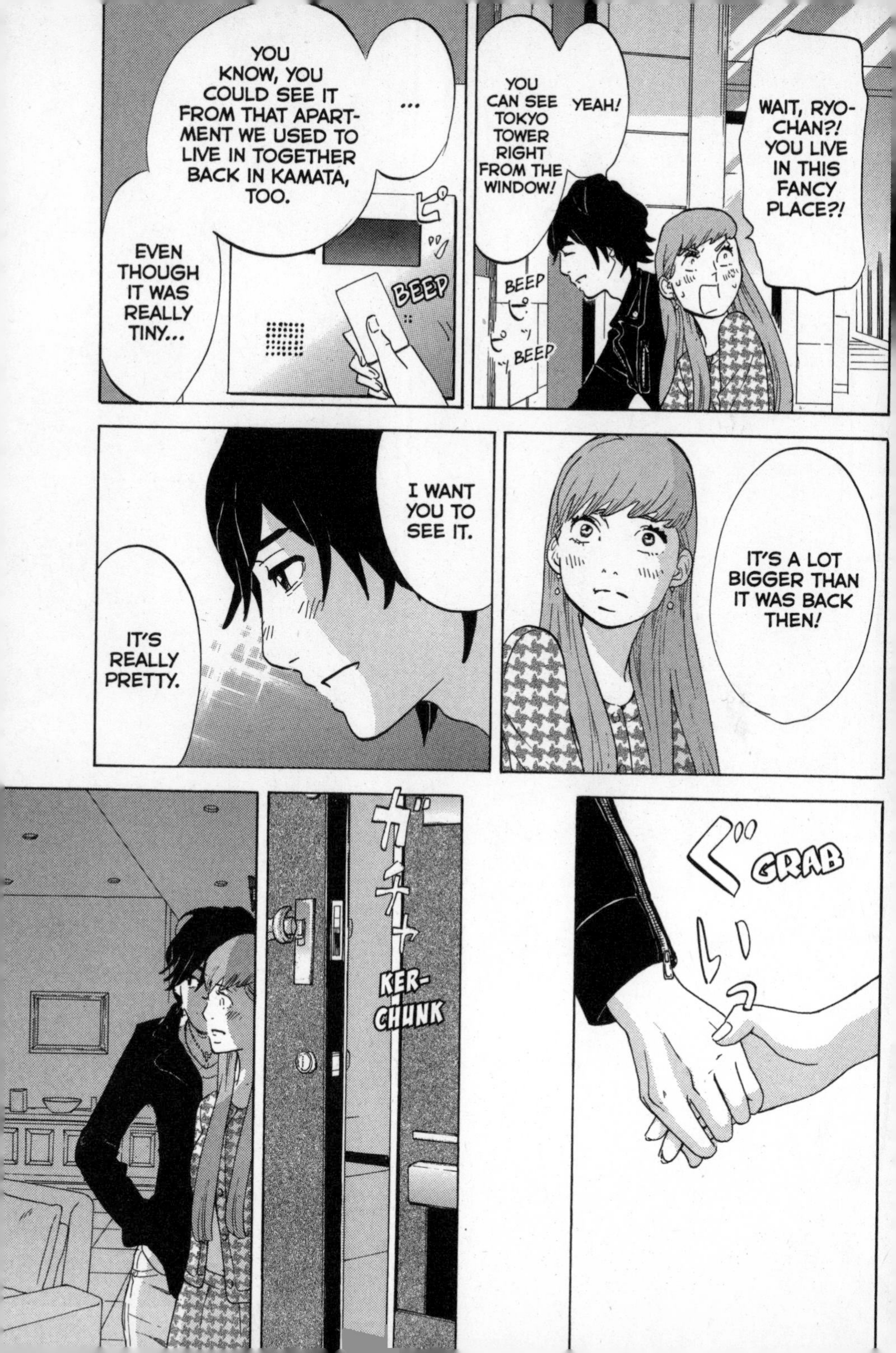
WAIT, RYO-CHAN?! YOU LIVE IN THIS FANCY PLACE?!
YEAH!
YOU CAN SEE TOKYO TOWER RIGHT FROM THE WINDOW!
BEEP
BEEP
BEEP
...
YOU KNOW, YOU COULD SEE IT FROM THAT APARTMENT WE USED TO LIVE IN TOGETHER BACK IN KAMATA, TOO.
BEEP
EVEN THOUGH IT WAS REALLY TINY...
IT'S A LOT BIGGER THAN IT WAS BACK THEN!
I WANT YOU TO SEE IT.
IT'S REALLY PRETTY.
GRAB
KER-CHUNK

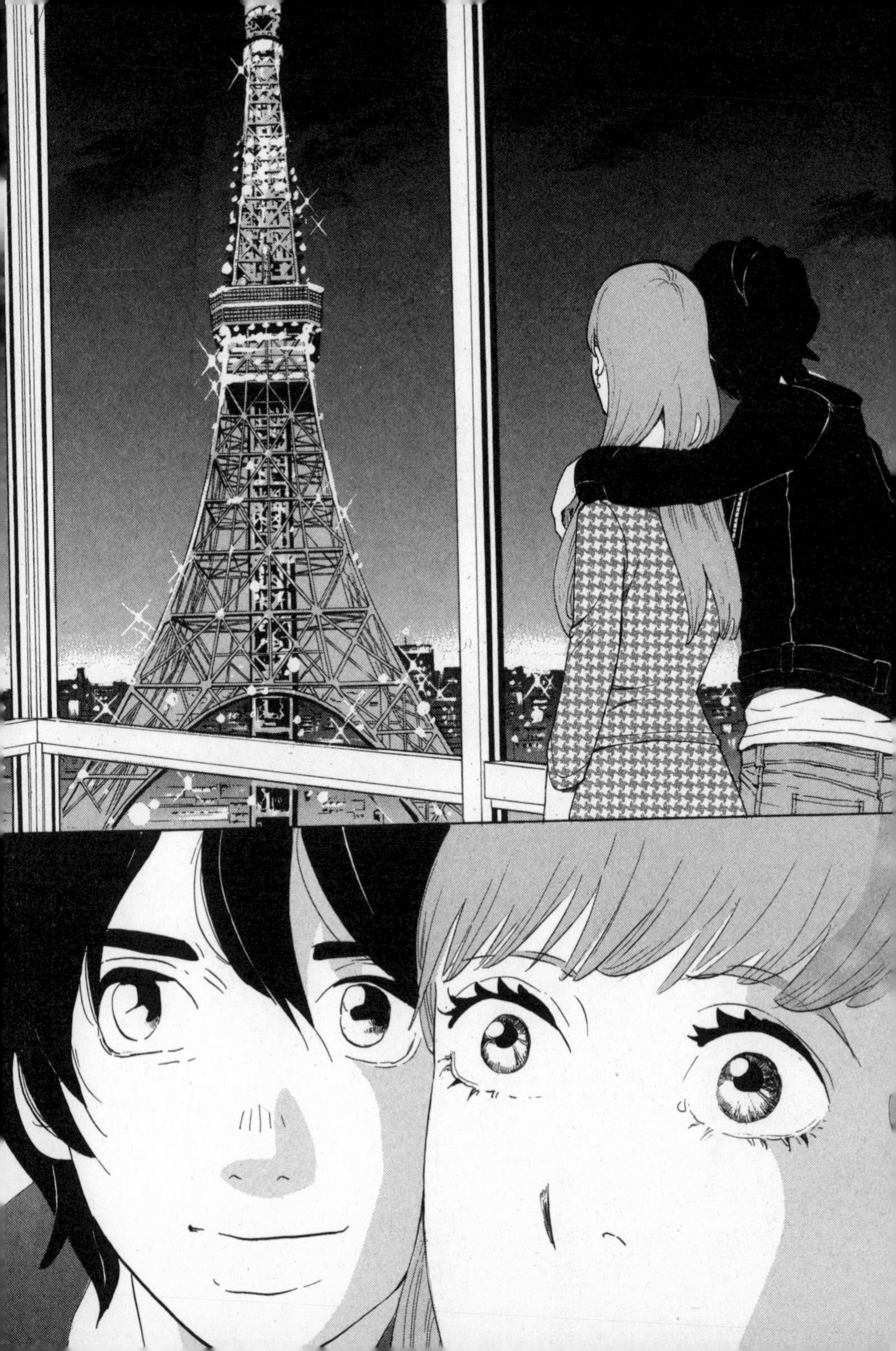

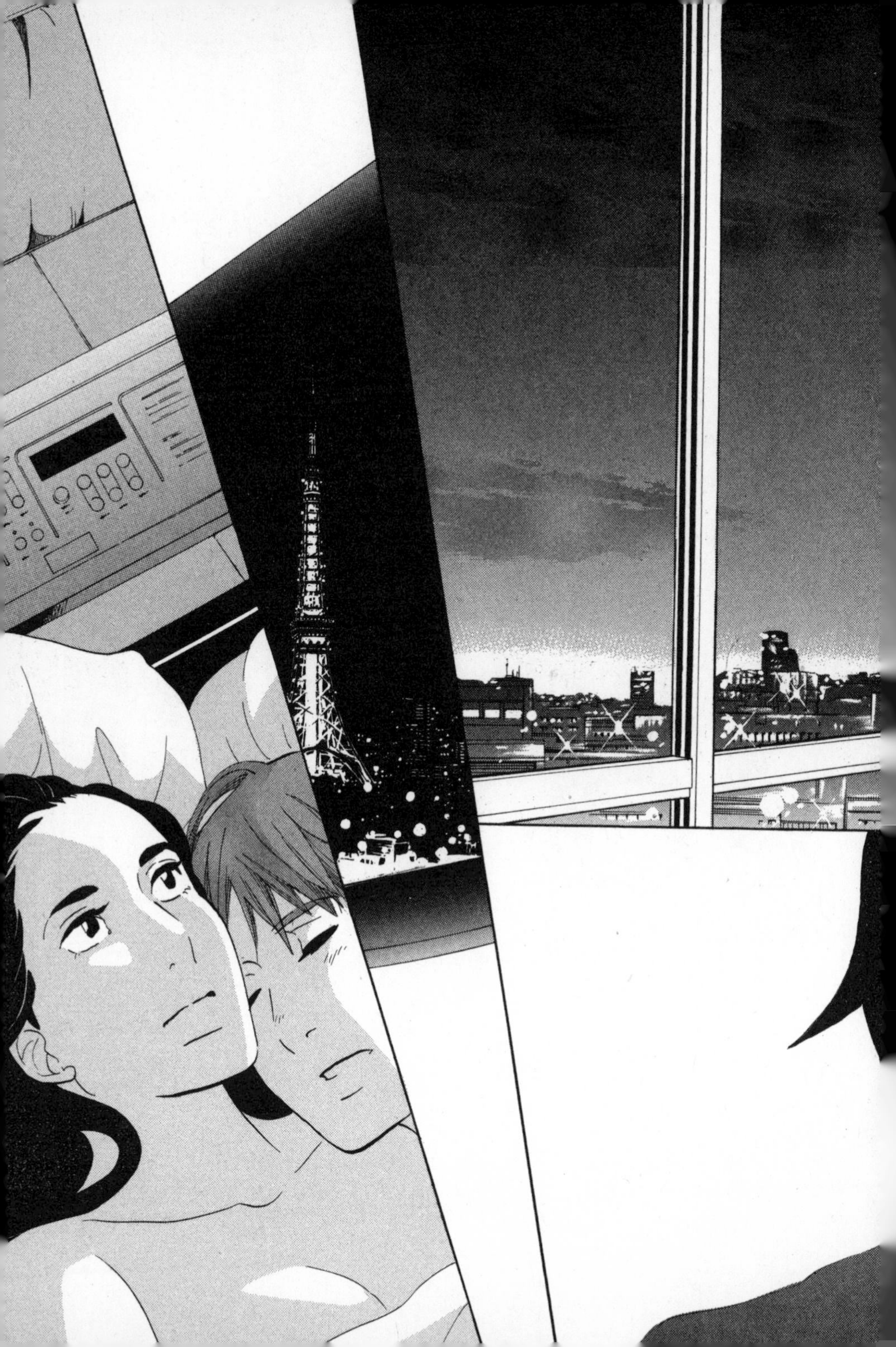

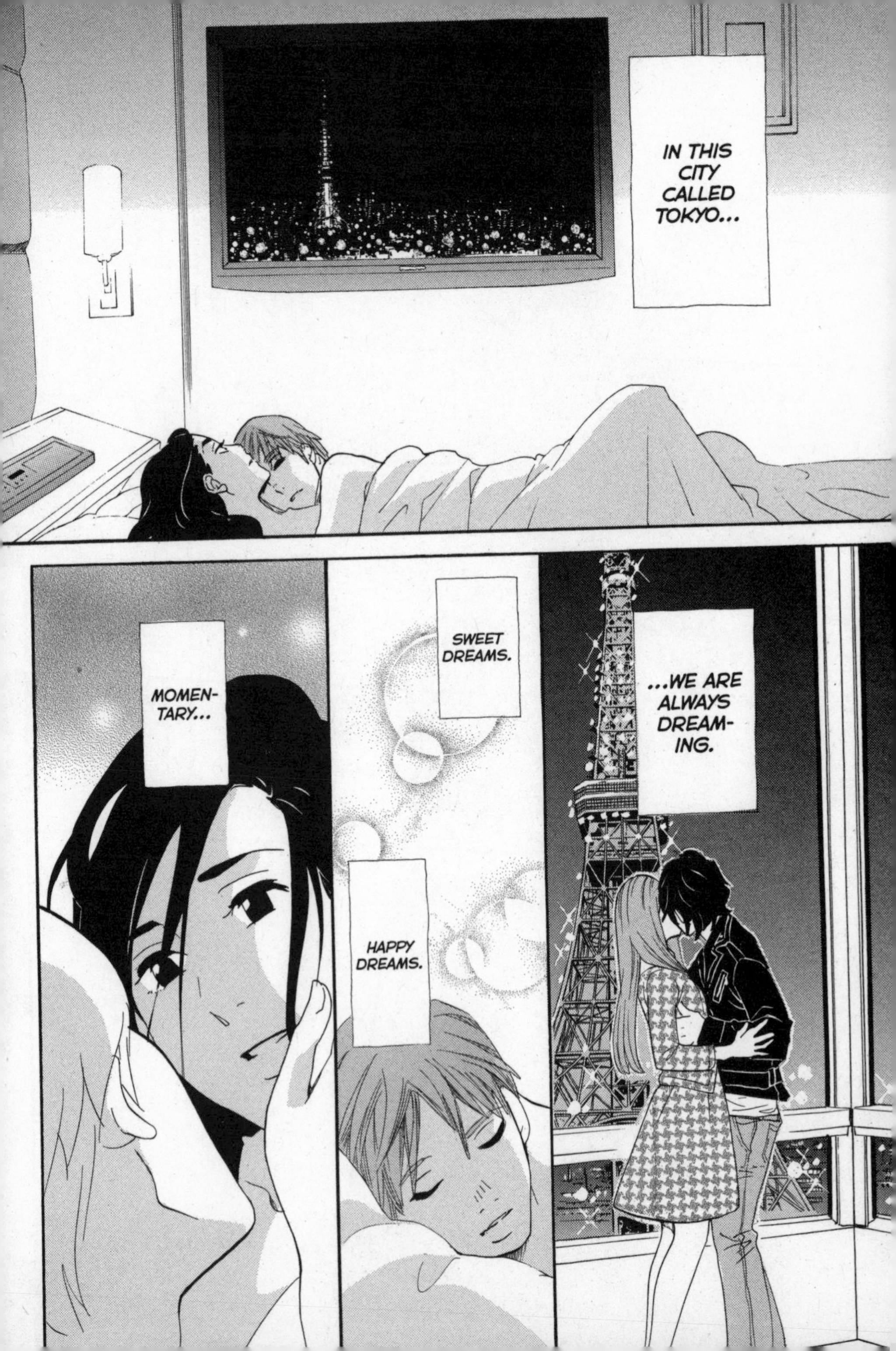
IN THIS CITY CALLED TOKYO...
...WE ARE ALWAYS DREAMING.
SWEET DREAMS.
HAPPY DREAMS.
MOMENTARY...

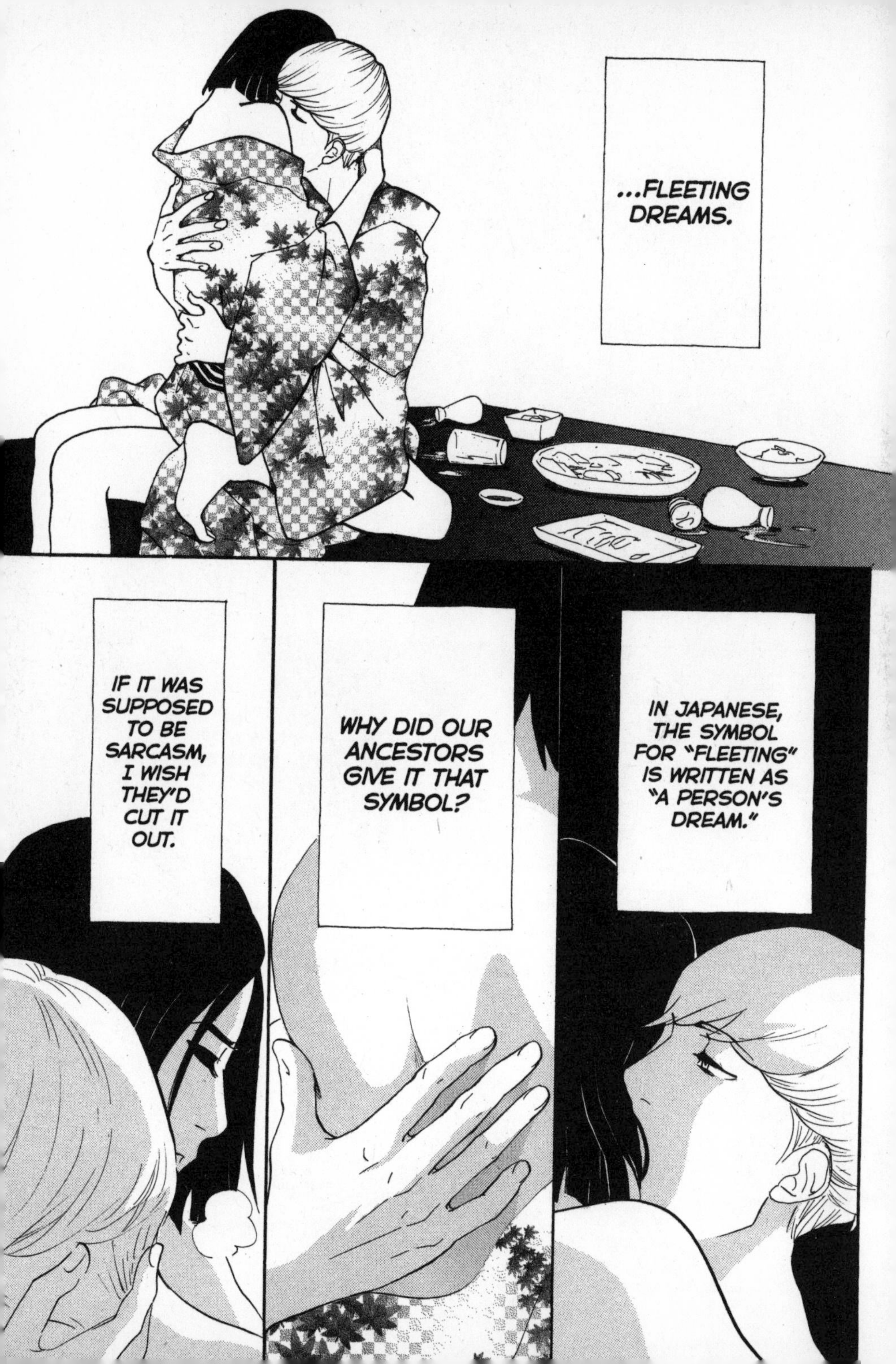
...FLEETING DREAMS.
IN JAPANESE, THE SYMBOL FOR "FLEETING" IS WRITTEN AS "A PERSON'S DREAM."
WHY DID OUR ANCESTORS GIVE IT THAT SYMBOL?
IF IT WAS SUPPOSED TO BE SARCASM, I WISH THEY'D CUT IT OUT.

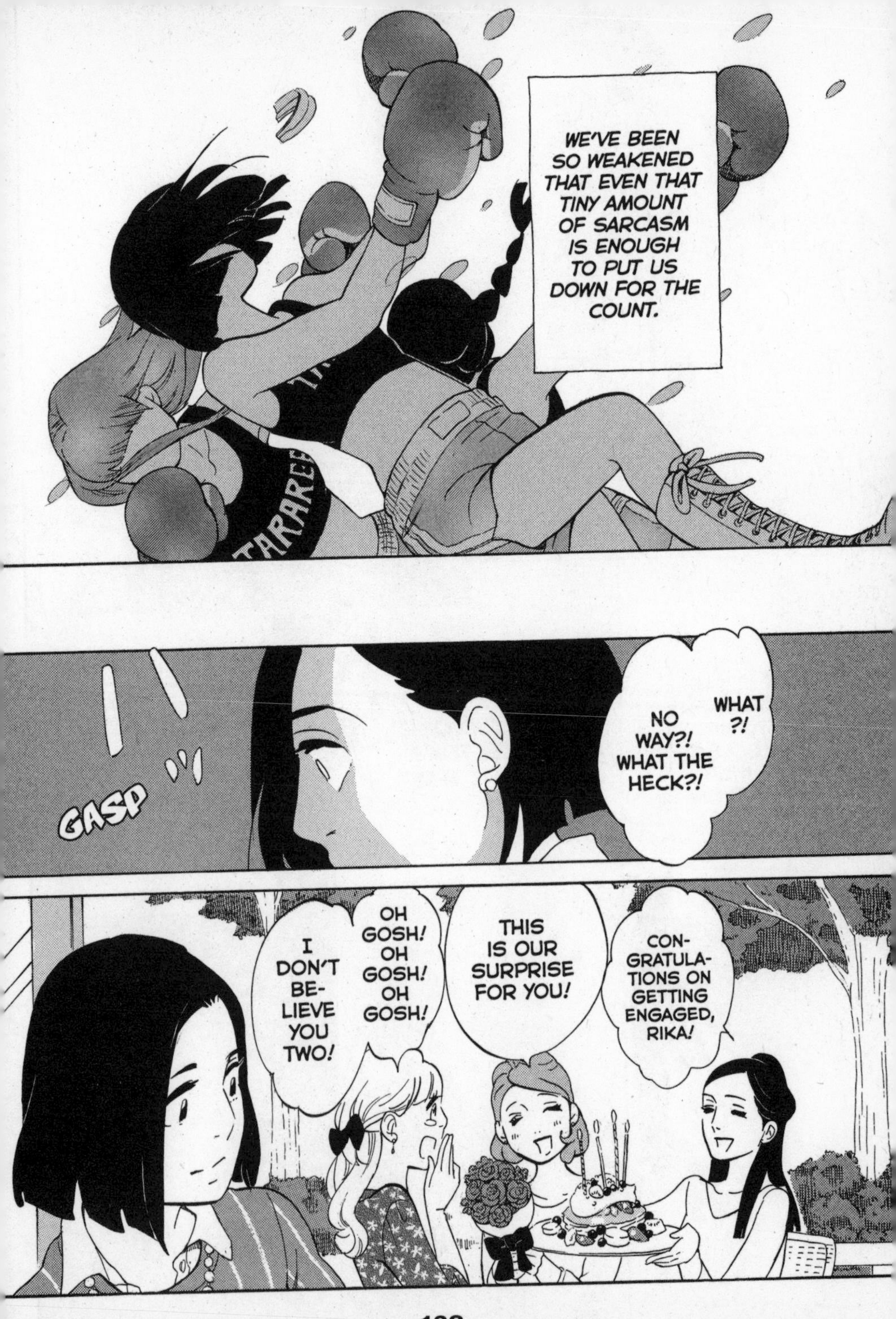
WE'VE BEEN SO WEAKENED THAT EVEN THAT TINY AMOUNT OF SARCASM IS ENOUGH TO PUT US DOWN FOR THE COUNT.
TARAREE
WHAT?!
NO WAY?! WHAT THE HECK?!
GASP
CON-GRATULA-TIONS ON GETTING ENGAGED, RIKA!
THIS IS OUR SURPRISE FOR YOU!
OH GOSH! OH GOSH! OH GOSH!
I DON'T BE-LIEVE YOU TWO!

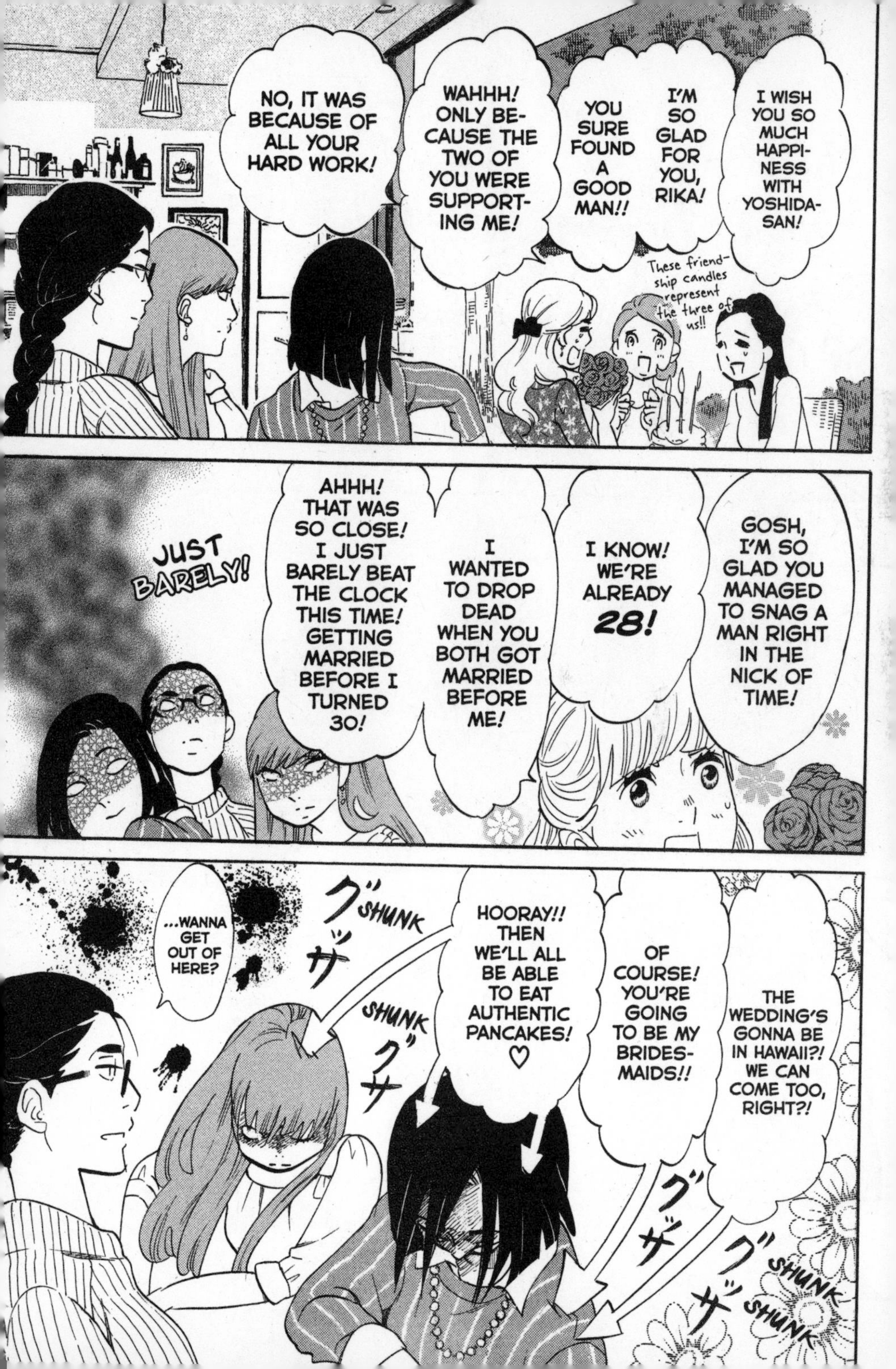
I WISH YOU SO MUCH HAPPINESS WITH YOSHIDA-SAN!
I'M SO GLAD FOR YOU, RIKA!
YOU SURE FOUND A GOOD MAN!!
These friendship candles represent the three of us!!
WAHHH! ONLY BECAUSE THE TWO OF YOU WERE SUPPORTING ME!
NO, IT WAS BECAUSE OF ALL YOUR HARD WORK!
GOSH, I'M SO GLAD YOU MANAGED TO SNAG A MAN RIGHT IN THE NICK OF TIME!
I KNOW! WE'RE ALREADY 28!
I WANTED TO DROP DEAD WHEN YOU BOTH GOT MARRIED BEFORE ME!
AHHH! THAT WAS SO CLOSE! I JUST BARELY BEAT THE CLOCK THIS TIME! GETTING MARRIED BEFORE I TURNED 30!
JUST BARELY!
THE WEDDING'S GONNA BE IN HAWAII?! WE CAN COME TOO, RIGHT?!
OF COURSE! YOU'RE GOING TO BE MY BRIDESMAIDS!!
SHUNK SHUNK
HOORAY!! THEN WE'LL ALL BE ABLE TO EAT AUTHENTIC PANCAKES! ♡
SHUNK
SHUNK
...WANNA GET OUT OF HERE?

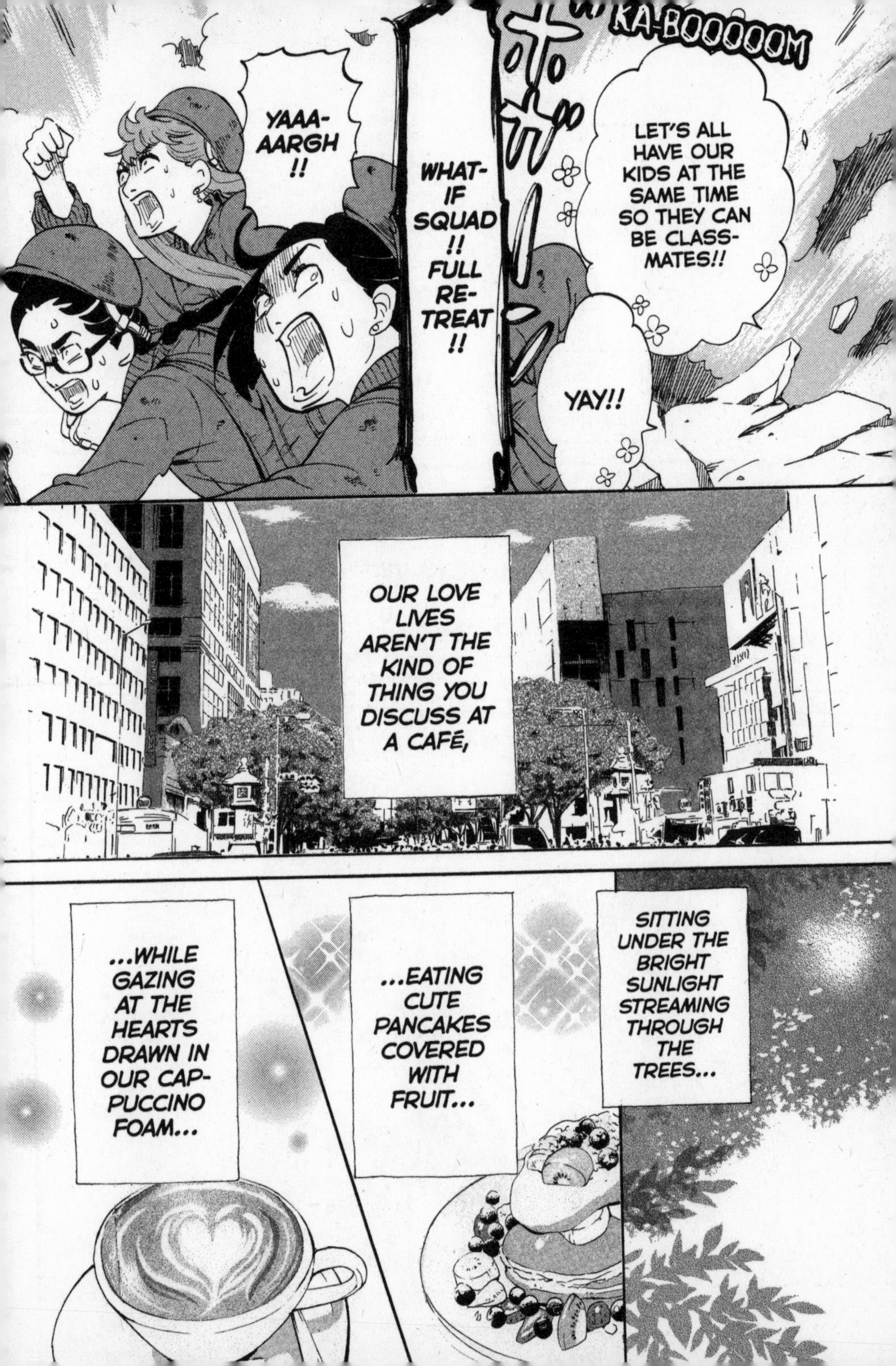
KA-BOOOOOOM
LET'S ALL HAVE OUR KIDS AT THE SAME TIME SO THEY CAN BE CLASS-MATES!!
YAY!!
WHAT-IF SQUAD!! FULL RE-TREAT!!
YAAA-AARGH!!
OUR LOVE LIVES AREN'T THE KIND OF THING YOU DISCUSS AT A CAFÉ,
SITTING UNDER THE BRIGHT SUNLIGHT STREAMING THROUGH THE TREES...
...EATING CUTE PANCAKES COVERED WITH FRUIT...
...WHILE GAZING AT THE HEARTS DRAWN IN OUR CAP-PUCCINO FOAM...

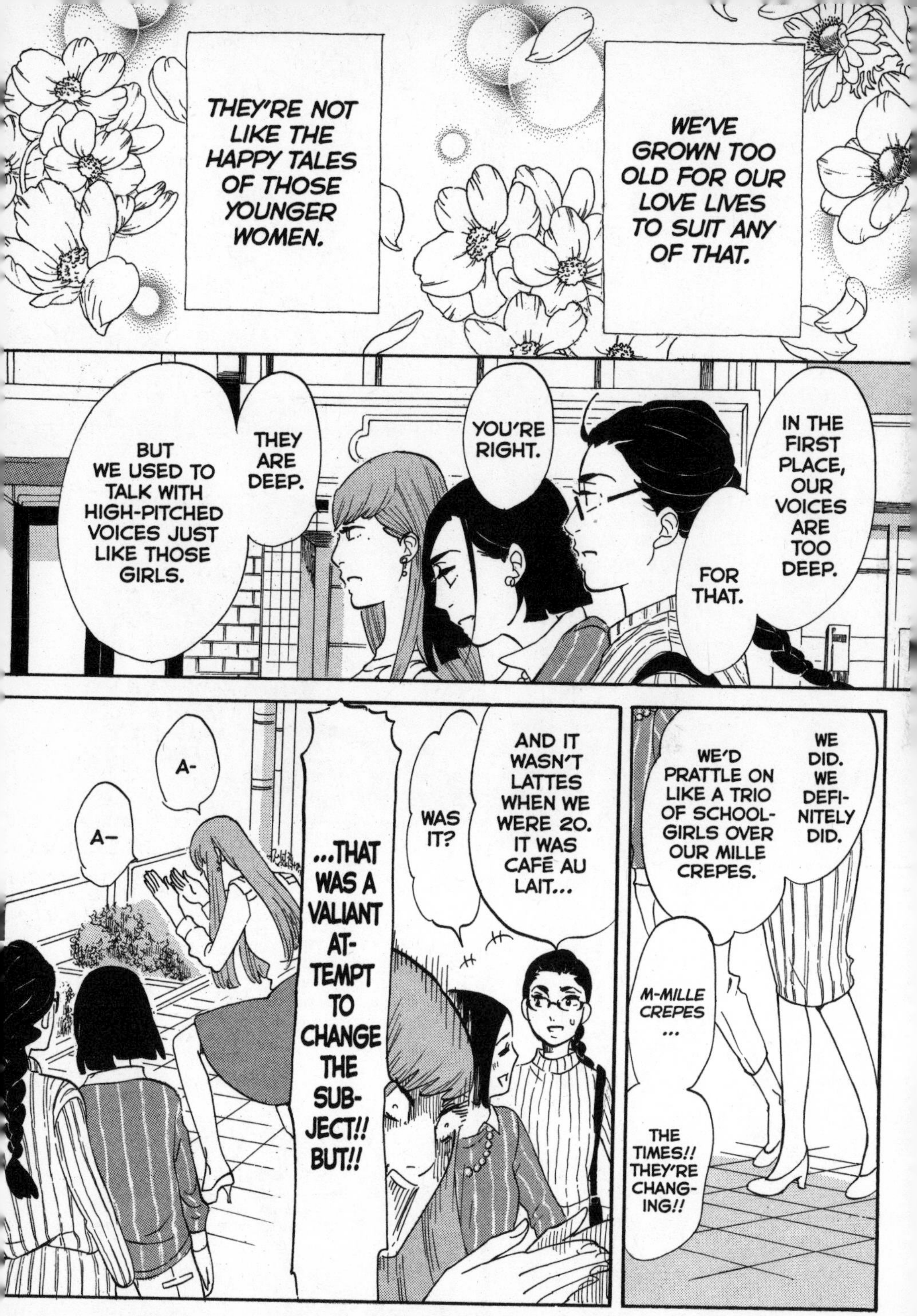
WE'VE GROWN TOO OLD FOR OUR LOVE LIVES TO SUIT ANY OF THAT.
THEY'RE NOT LIKE THE HAPPY TALES OF THOSE YOUNGER WOMEN.
IN THE FIRST PLACE, OUR VOICES ARE TOO DEEP.
FOR THAT.
YOU'RE RIGHT.
THEY ARE DEEP.
BUT WE USED TO TALK WITH HIGH-PITCHED VOICES JUST LIKE THOSE GIRLS.
WE DID. WE DEFINITELY DID.
WE'D PRATTLE ON LIKE A TRIO OF SCHOOL-GIRLS OVER OUR MILLE CREPES.
M-MILLE CREPES...
THE TIMES!! THEY'RE CHANG-ING!!
AND IT WASN'T LATTES WHEN WE WERE 20. IT WAS CAFÉ AU LAIT...
WAS IT?
...THAT WAS A VALIANT AT-TEMPT TO CHANGE THE SUB-JECT!! BUT!!
A-
A–

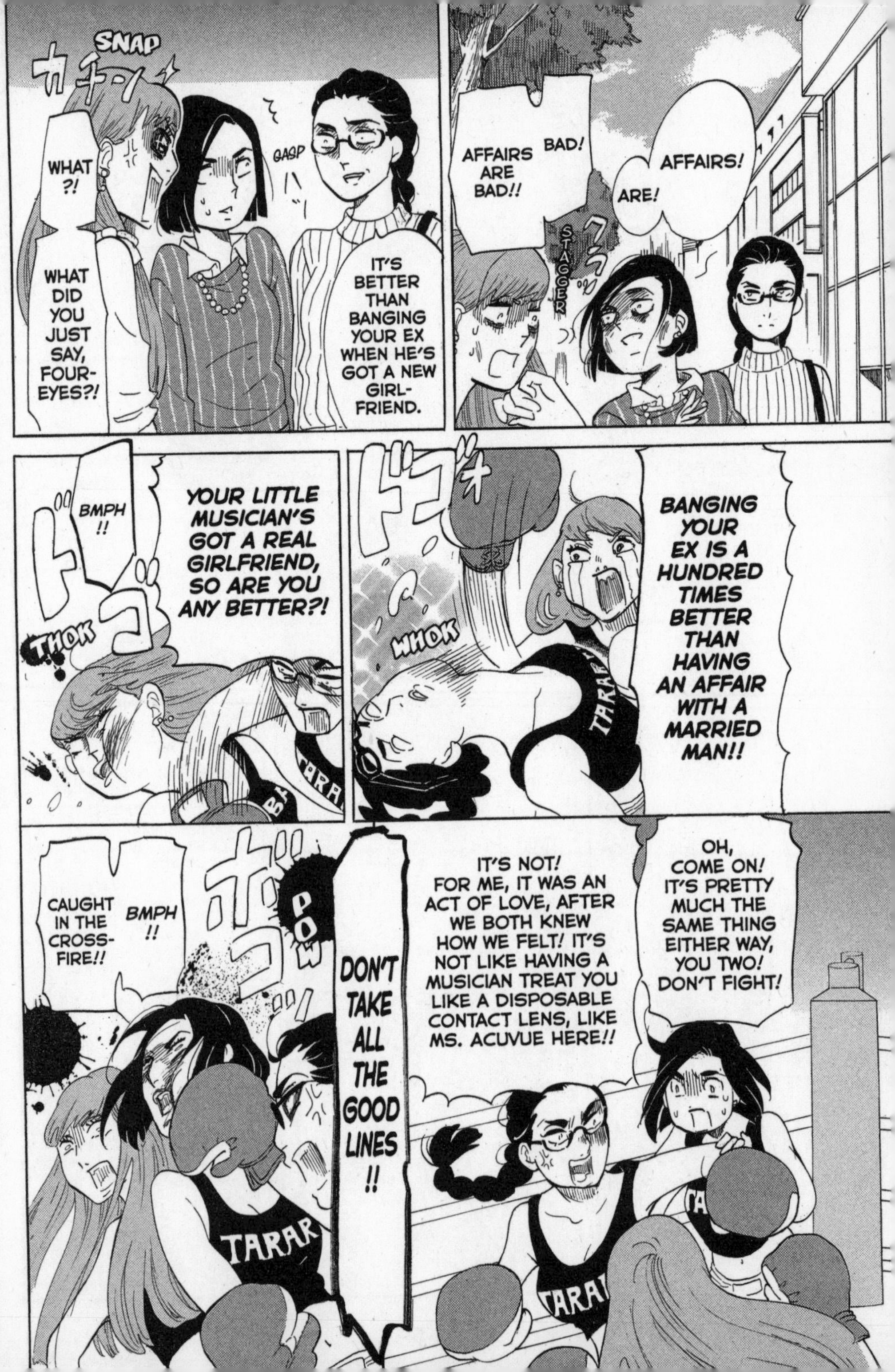
AFFAIRS!
ARE!
BAD!
AFFAIRS ARE BAD!!
STAGGER
GASP
IT'S BETTER THAN BANGING YOUR EX WHEN HE'S GOT A NEW GIRLFRIEND.
SNAP
WHAT ?!
WHAT DID YOU JUST SAY, FOUR-EYES?!
BANGING YOUR EX IS A HUNDRED TIMES BETTER THAN HAVING AN AFFAIR WITH A MARRIED MAN!!
WHOK
YOUR LITTLE MUSICIAN'S GOT A REAL GIRLFRIEND, SO ARE YOU ANY BETTER?!
BMPH !!
THOK
OH, COME ON! IT'S PRETTY MUCH THE SAME THING EITHER WAY, YOU TWO! DON'T FIGHT!
IT'S NOT! FOR ME, IT WAS AN ACT OF LOVE, AFTER WE BOTH KNEW HOW WE FELT! IT'S NOT LIKE HAVING A MUSICIAN TREAT YOU LIKE A DISPOSABLE CONTACT LENS, LIKE MS. ACUVUE HERE!!
DON'T TAKE ALL THE GOOD LINES !!
POW
BMPH !!
CAUGHT IN THE CROSS-FIRE!!

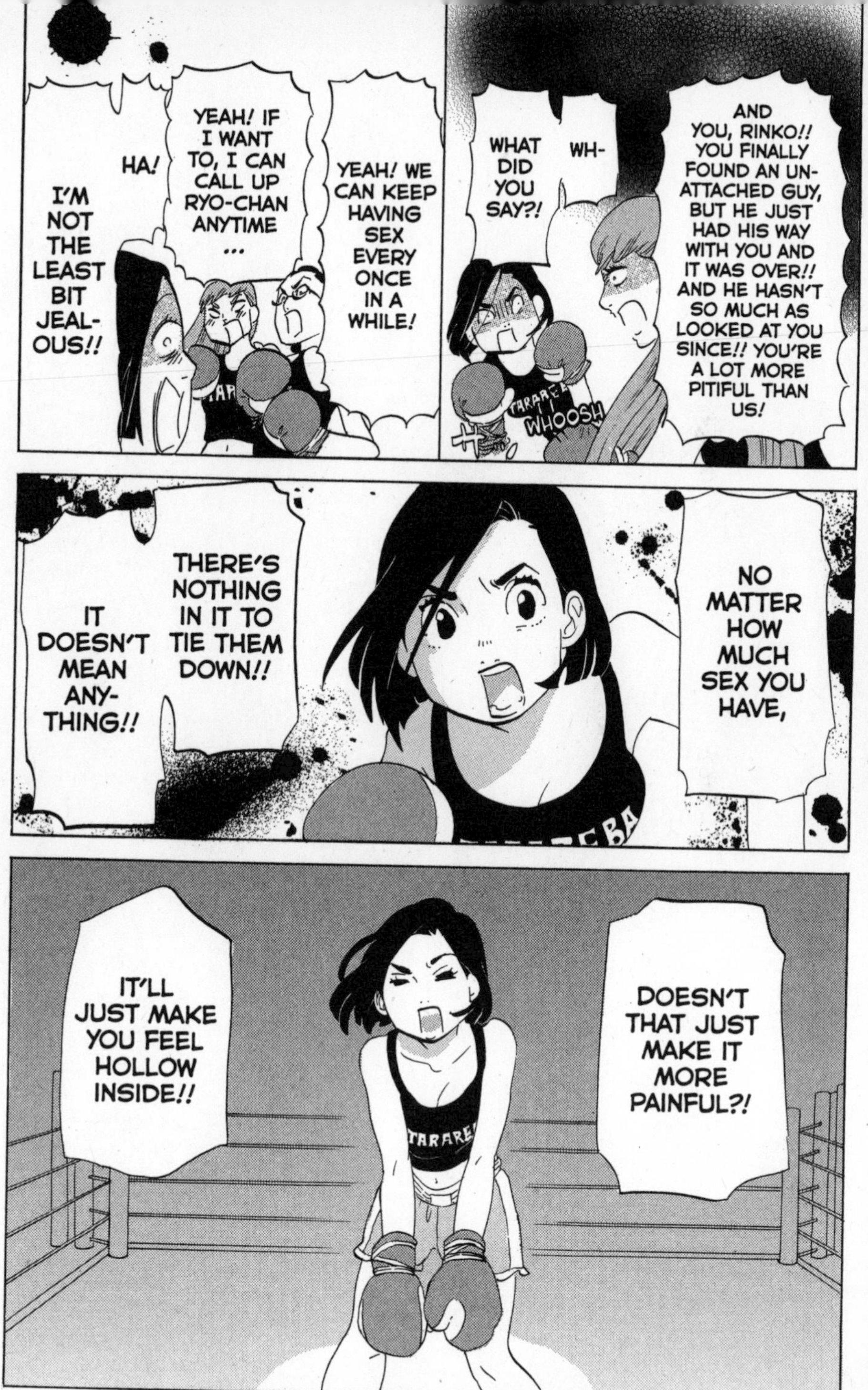
AND YOU, RINKO!! YOU FINALLY FOUND AN UN-ATTACHED GUY, BUT HE JUST HAD HIS WAY WITH YOU AND IT WAS OVER!! AND HE HASN'T SO MUCH AS LOOKED AT YOU SINCE!! YOU'RE A LOT MORE PITIFUL THAN US!
WH-
WHAT DID YOU SAY?!
WHOOSH
YEAH! WE CAN KEEP HAVING SEX EVERY ONCE IN A WHILE!
YEAH! IF I WANT TO, I CAN CALL UP RYO-CHAN ANYTIME ...
HA!
I'M NOT THE LEAST BIT JEAL-OUS!!
NO MATTER HOW MUCH SEX YOU HAVE,
THERE'S NOTHING IN IT TO TIE THEM DOWN!!
IT DOESN'T MEAN ANY-THING!!
DOESN'T THAT JUST MAKE IT MORE PAINFUL?!
IT'LL JUST MAKE YOU FEEL HOLLOW INSIDE!!

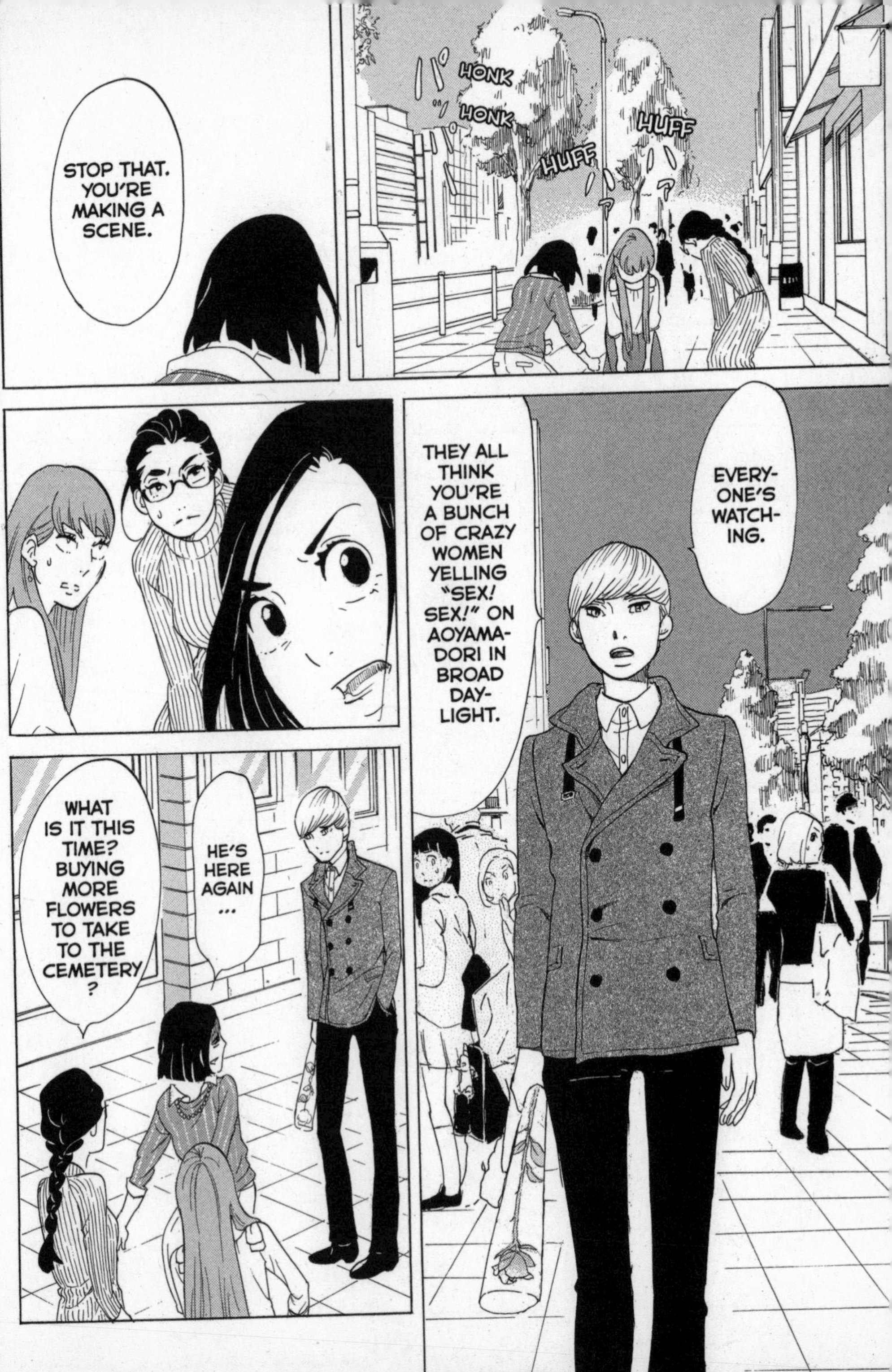
HONK
HONK
HUFF
HUFF
STOP THAT. YOU'RE MAKING A SCENE.
EVERYONE'S WATCHING.
THEY ALL THINK YOU'RE A BUNCH OF CRAZY WOMEN YELLING "SEX! SEX!" ON AOYAMADORI IN BROAD DAYLIGHT.
HE'S HERE AGAIN...
WHAT IS IT THIS TIME? BUYING MORE FLOWERS TO TAKE TO THE CEMETERY?

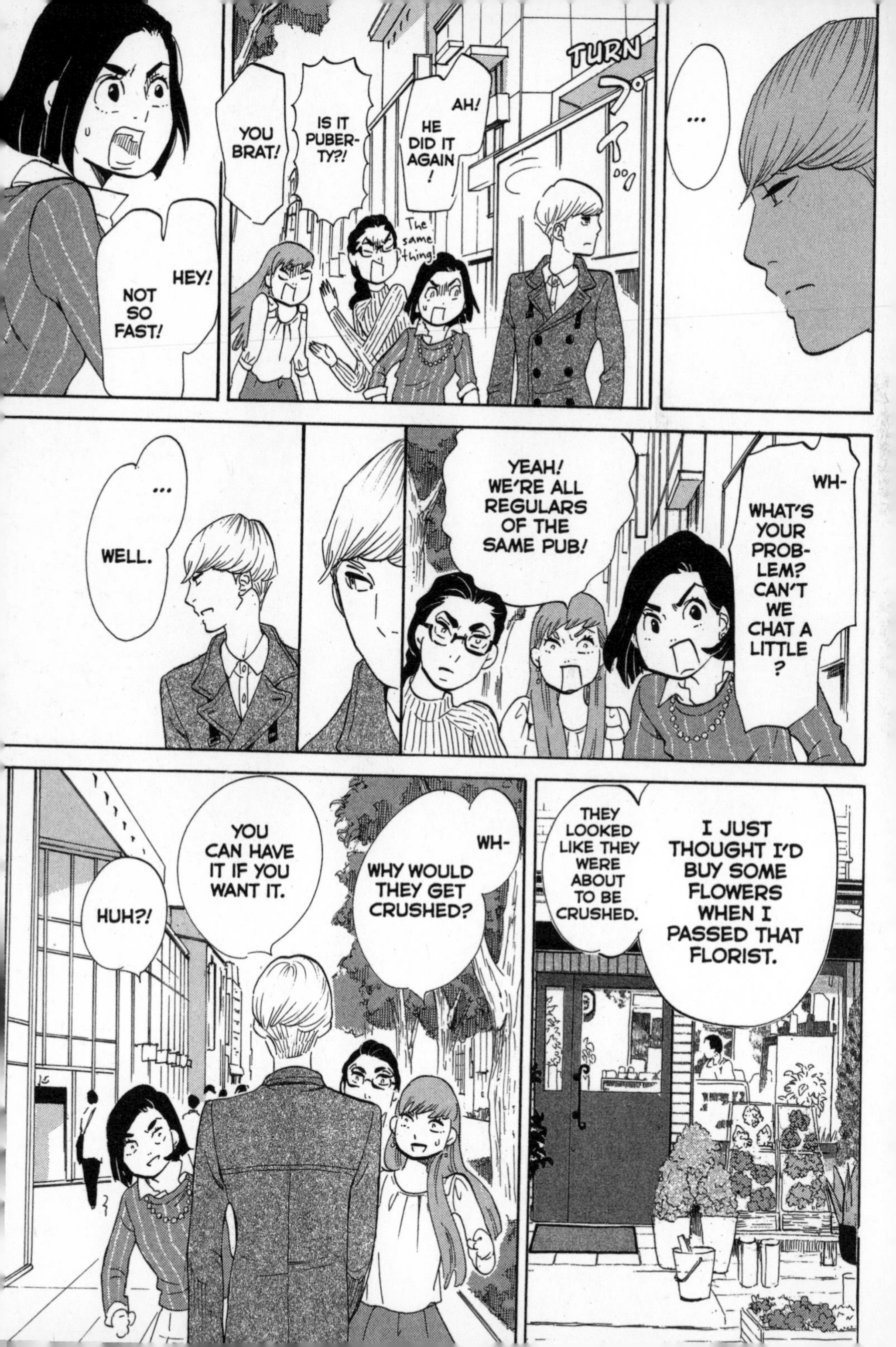
...
TURN
AH! HE DID IT AGAIN!
The same thing!
IS IT PUBERTY?!
YOU BRAT!
HEY! NOT SO FAST!
WH- WHAT'S YOUR PROBLEM? CAN'T WE CHAT A LITTLE?
YEAH! WE'RE ALL REGULARS OF THE SAME PUB!
... WELL.
I JUST THOUGHT I'D BUY SOME FLOWERS WHEN I PASSED THAT FLORIST.
THEY LOOKED LIKE THEY WERE ABOUT TO BE CRUSHED.
WH- WHY WOULD THEY GET CRUSHED?
YOU CAN HAVE IT IF YOU WANT IT.
HUH?!

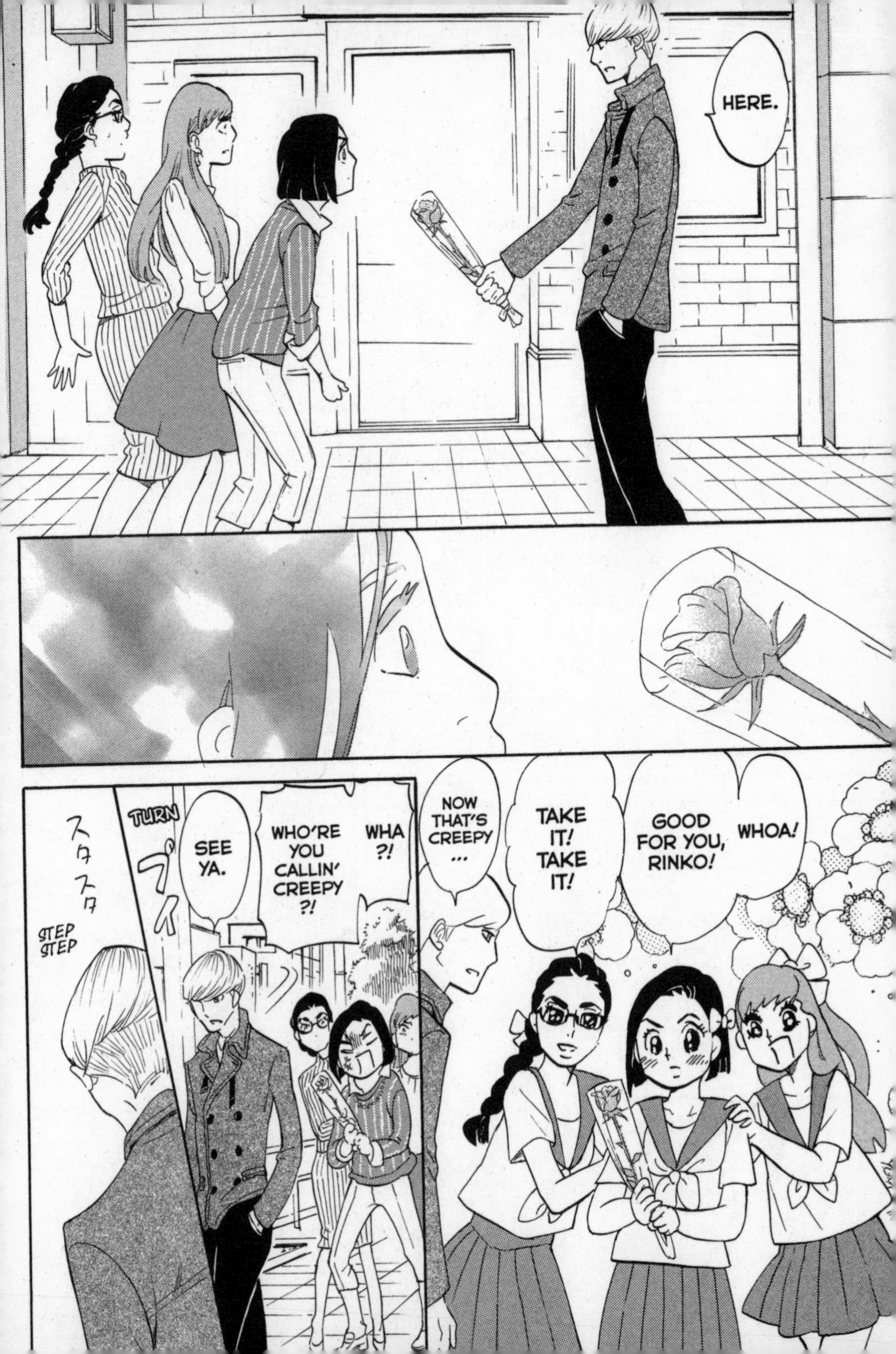
HERE.
WHOA!
GOOD FOR YOU, RINKO!
TAKE IT! TAKE IT!
NOW THAT'S CREEPY...
WHA?!
WHO'RE YOU CALLIN' CREEPY?!
TURN
プイ
SEE YA.
スタスタ
STEP STEP

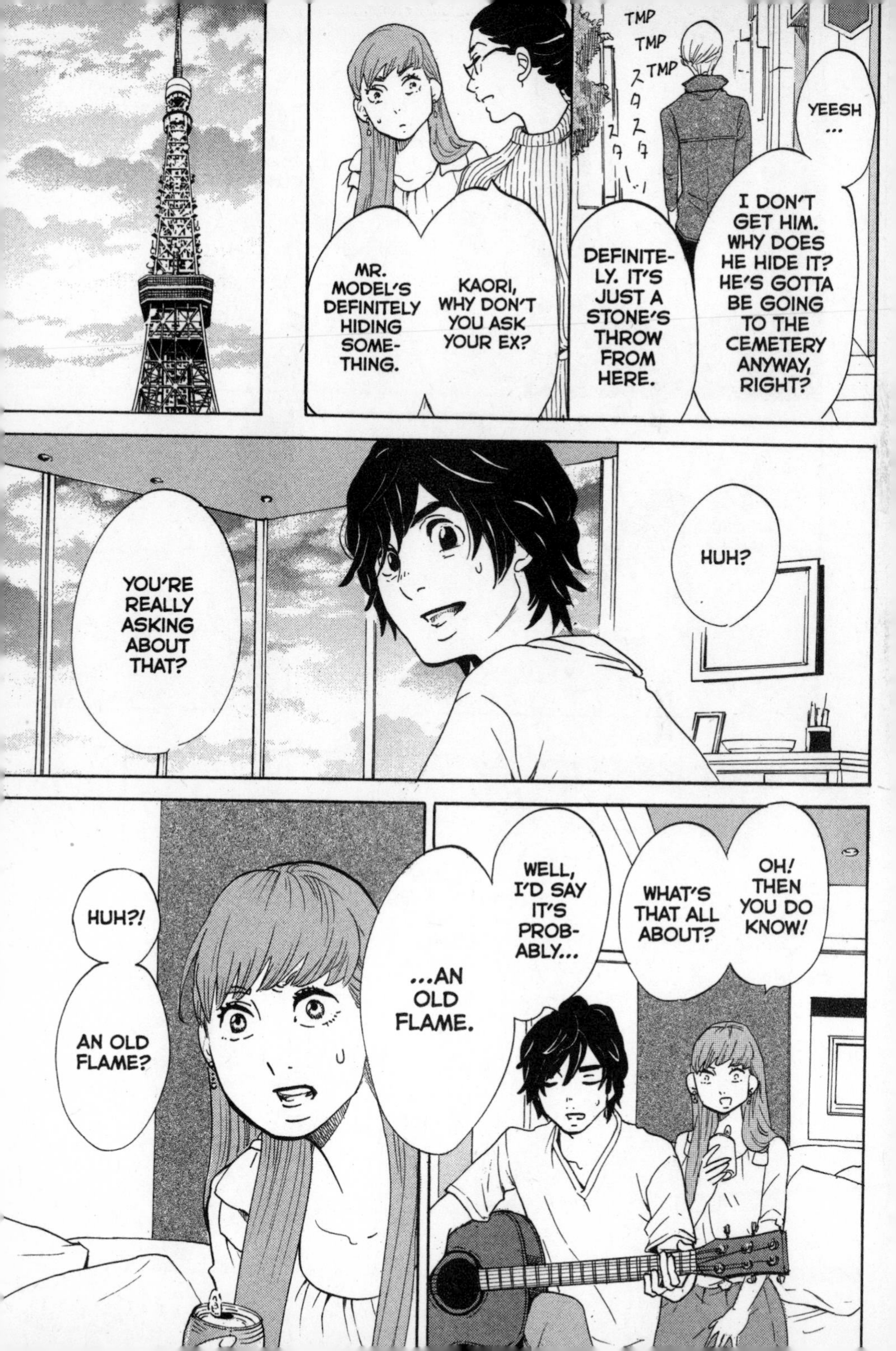
TMP
TMP
TMP
スタスタ
YEESH...
I DON'T GET HIM. WHY DOES HE HIDE IT? HE'S GOTTA BE GOING TO THE CEMETERY ANYWAY, RIGHT?
DEFINITELY. IT'S JUST A STONE'S THROW FROM HERE.
KAORI, WHY DON'T YOU ASK YOUR EX?
MR. MODEL'S DEFINITELY HIDING SOMETHING.
HUH?
YOU'RE REALLY ASKING ABOUT THAT?
OH! THEN YOU DO KNOW!
WHAT'S THAT ALL ABOUT?
WELL, I'D SAY IT'S PROBABLY...
...AN OLD FLAME.
HUH?!
AN OLD FLAME?

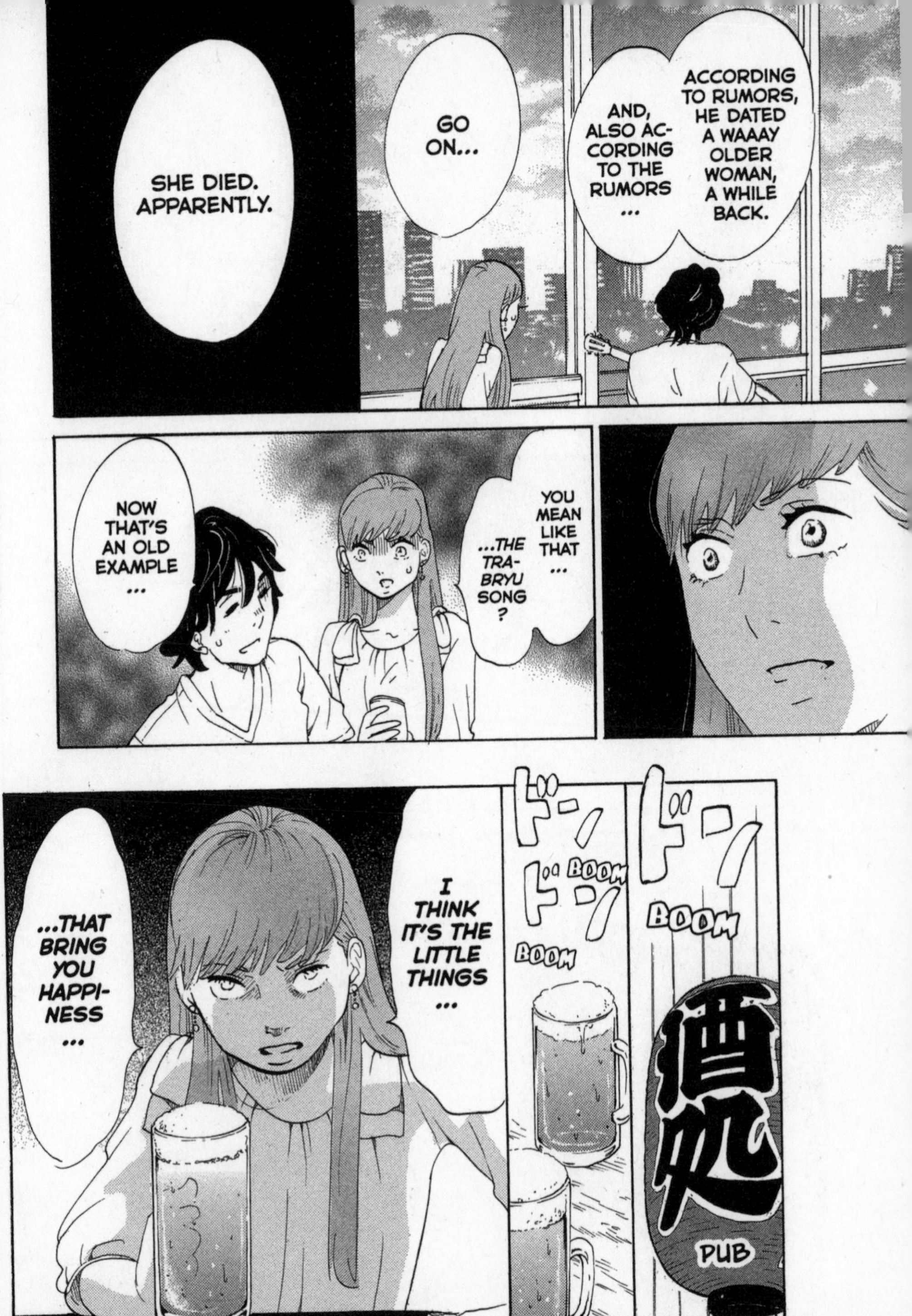
ACCORDING TO RUMORS, HE DATED A WAAAY OLDER WOMAN, A WHILE BACK.
AND, ALSO AC-CORDING TO THE RUMORS...
GO ON...
SHE DIED. APPARENTLY.
YOU MEAN LIKE THAT...
...THE TRA-BRYU SONG?
NOW THAT'S AN OLD EXAMPLE...
ドーン
BOOM
ドーン
BOOM
ドーン
BOOM
酒処
PUB
I THINK IT'S THE LITTLE THINGS...
...THAT BRING YOU HAPPI-NESS...

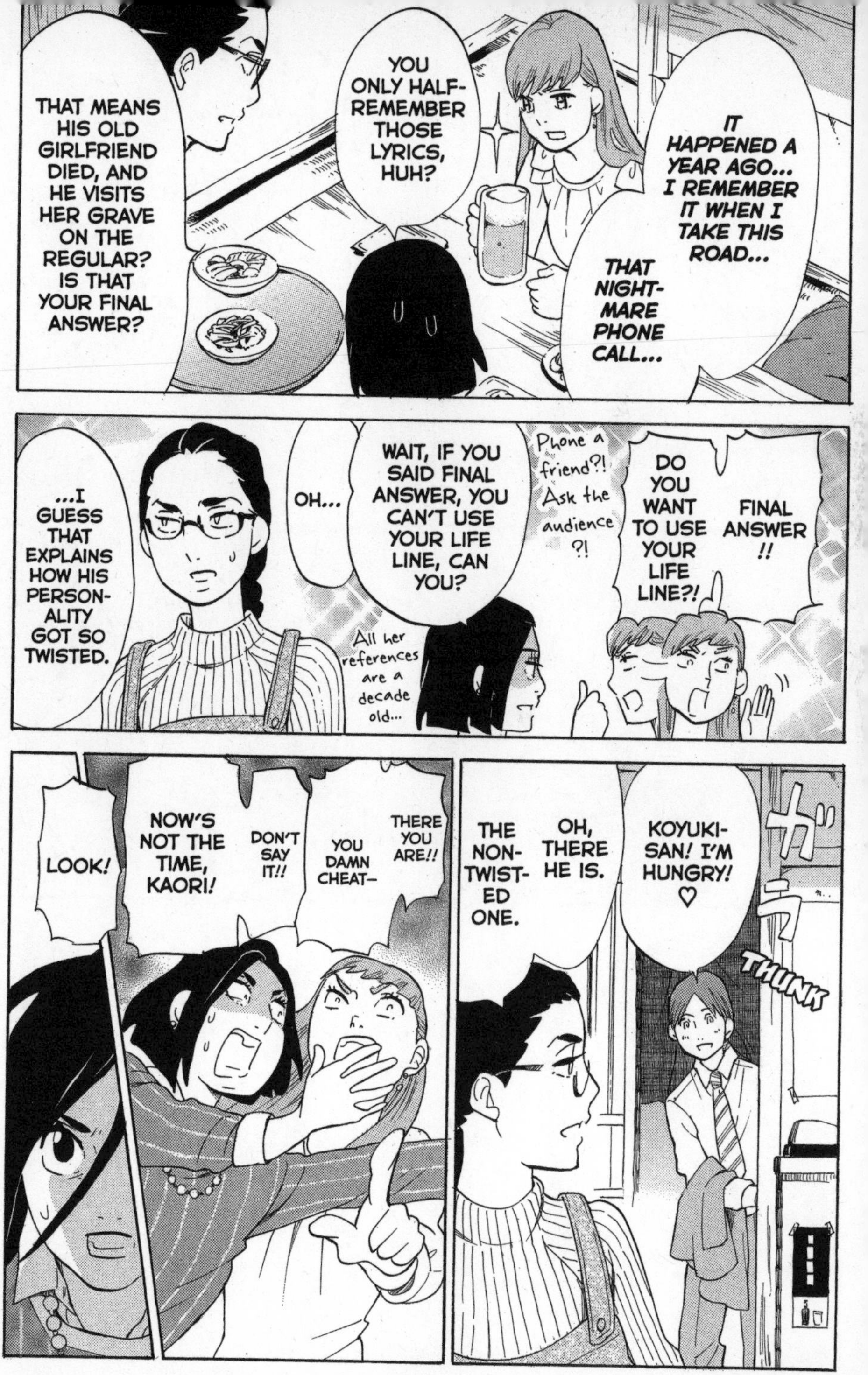
IT HAPPENED A YEAR AGO... I REMEMBER IT WHEN I TAKE THIS ROAD...
THAT NIGHTMARE PHONE CALL...
YOU ONLY HALF-REMEMBER THOSE LYRICS, HUH?
THAT MEANS HIS OLD GIRLFRIEND DIED, AND HE VISITS HER GRAVE ON THE REGULAR? IS THAT YOUR FINAL ANSWER?
FINAL ANSWER!!
DO YOU WANT TO USE YOUR LIFE LINE?!
Phone a friend?! Ask the audience?!
WAIT, IF YOU SAID FINAL ANSWER, YOU CAN'T USE YOUR LIFE LINE, CAN YOU?
OH...
All her references are a decade old...
...I GUESS THAT EXPLAINS HOW HIS PERSONALITY GOT SO TWISTED.
ガラ
KOYUKI-SAN! I'M HUNGRY! ♡
THUNK
OH, THERE HE IS.
THE NON-TWISTED ONE.
THERE YOU ARE!!
YOU DAMN CHEAT—
DON'T SAY IT!!
NOW'S NOT THE TIME, KAORI!
LOOK!

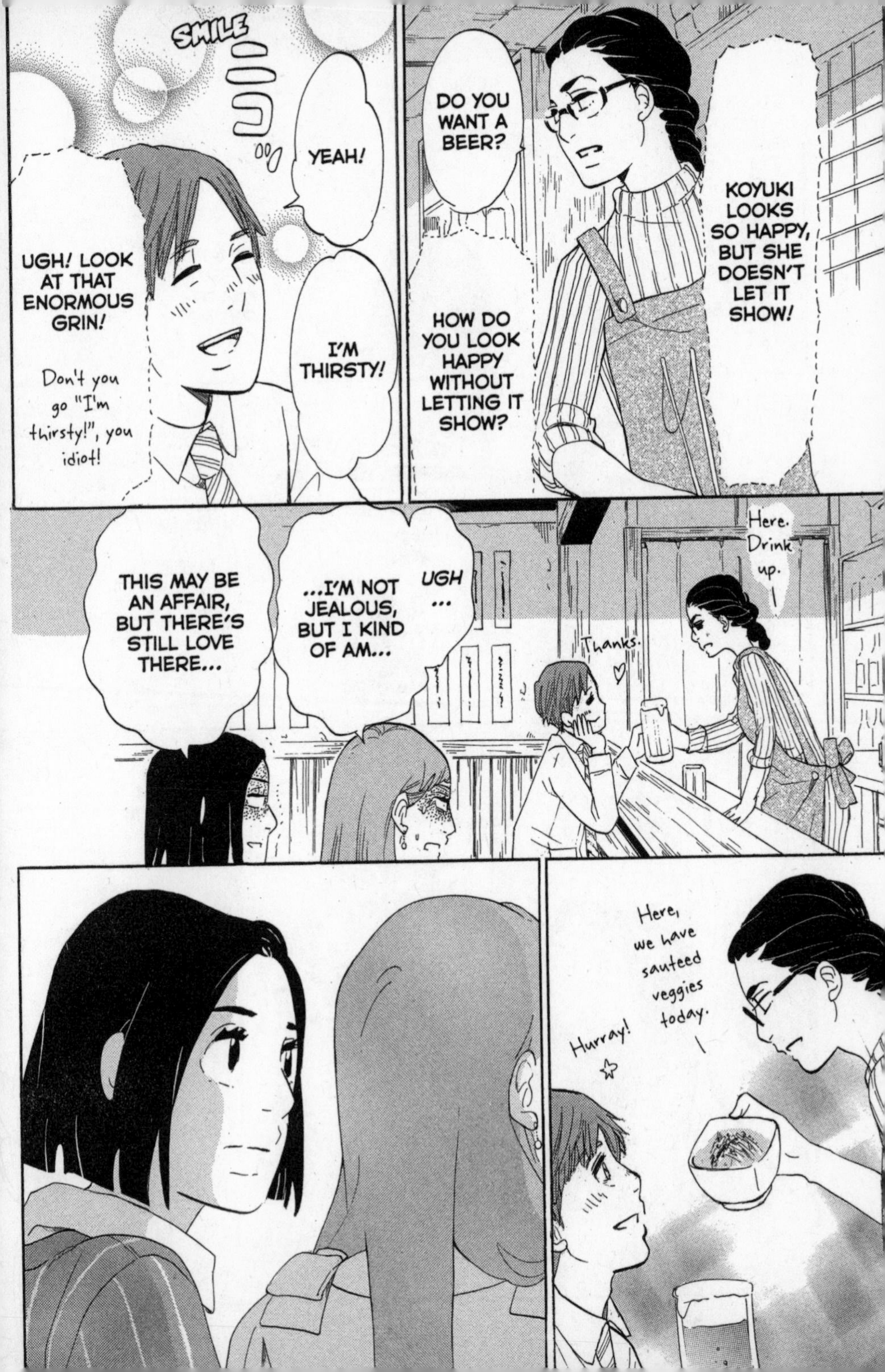
DO YOU WANT A BEER?
KOYUKI LOOKS SO HAPPY, BUT SHE DOESN'T LET IT SHOW!
HOW DO YOU LOOK HAPPY WITHOUT LETTING IT SHOW?
SMILE
YEAH!
I'M THIRSTY!
UGH! LOOK AT THAT ENORMOUS GRIN!
Don't you go "I'm thirsty!", you idiot!
Here. Drink up.
Thanks.
UGH ...
...I'M NOT JEALOUS, BUT I KIND OF AM...
THIS MAY BE AN AFFAIR, BUT THERE'S STILL LOVE THERE...
Here, we have sauteed veggies today.
Hurray!

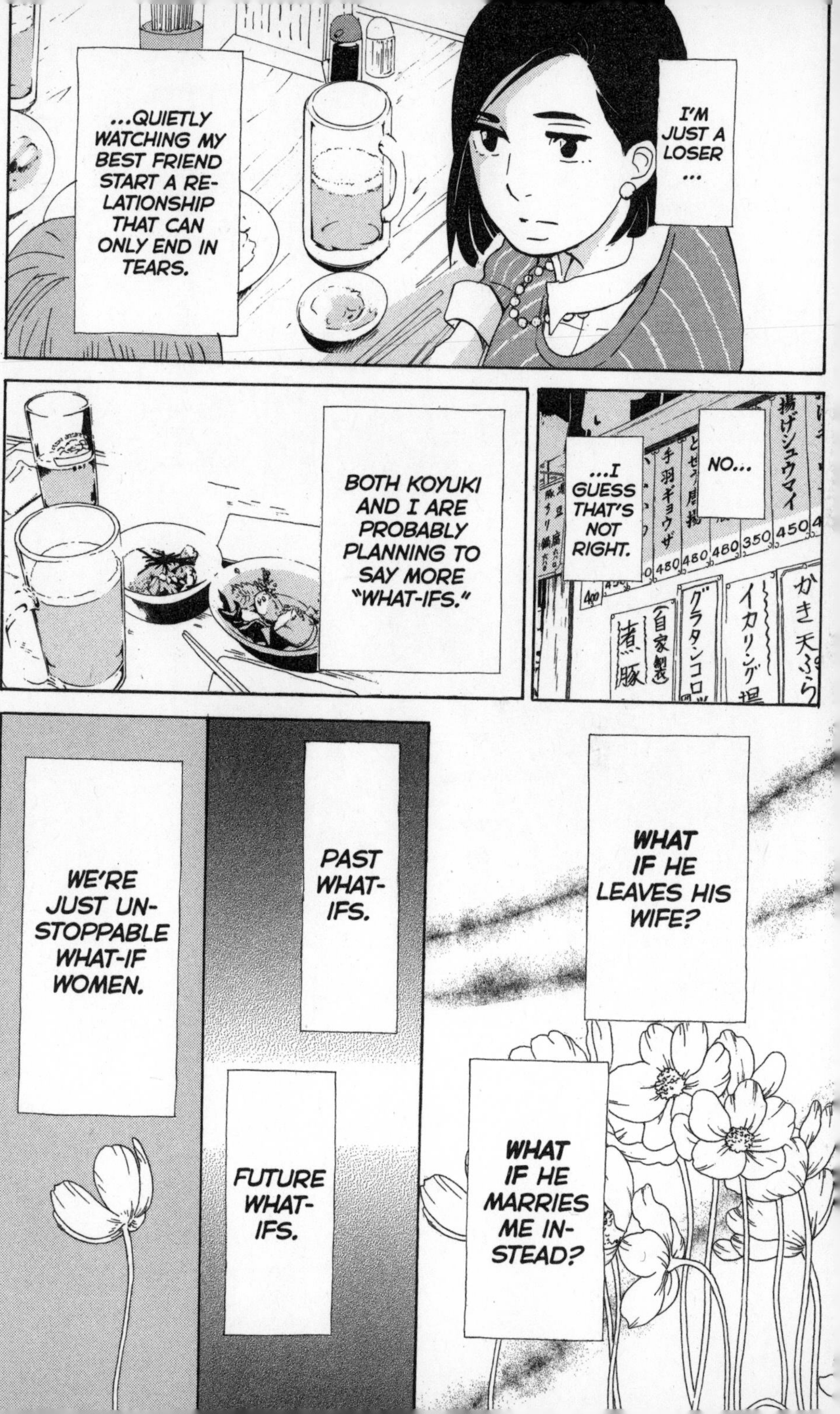
I'M JUST A LOSER ...
...QUIETLY WATCHING MY BEST FRIEND START A RELATIONSHIP THAT CAN ONLY END IN TEARS.
NO...
...I GUESS THAT'S NOT RIGHT.
揚げシュウマイ
手羽ギョウザ
かき天ぷら
イカリング揚
(自家製)
煮豚
BOTH KOYUKI AND I ARE PROBABLY PLANNING TO SAY MORE "WHAT-IFS."
WHAT IF HE LEAVES HIS WIFE?
WHAT IF HE MARRIES ME INSTEAD?
PAST WHAT-IFS.
FUTURE WHAT-IFS.
WE'RE JUST UNSTOPPABLE WHAT-IF WOMEN.

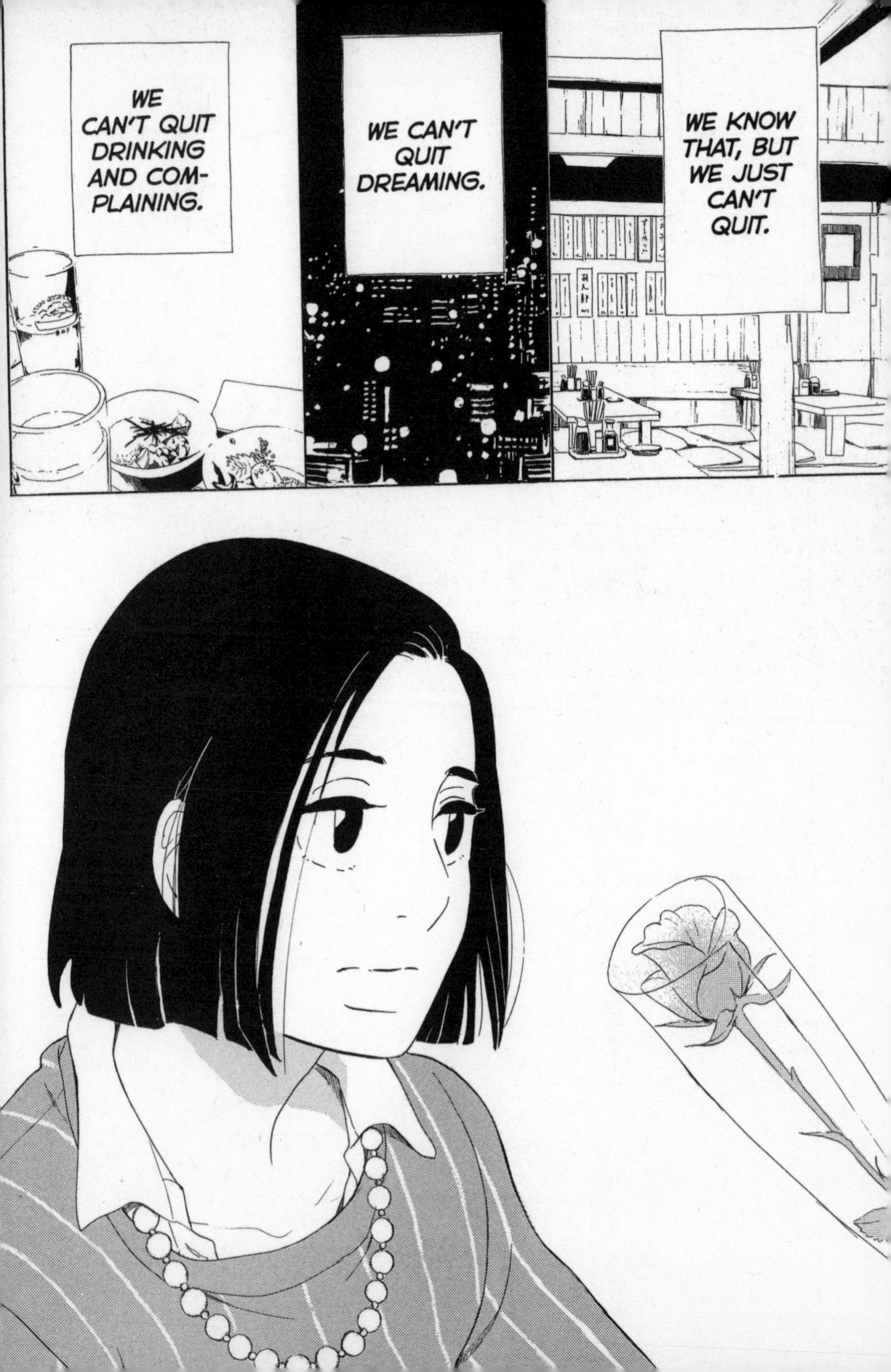
WE KNOW THAT, BUT WE JUST CAN'T QUIT.
WE CAN'T QUIT DREAMING.
WE CAN'T QUIT DRINKING AND COM-PLAINING.

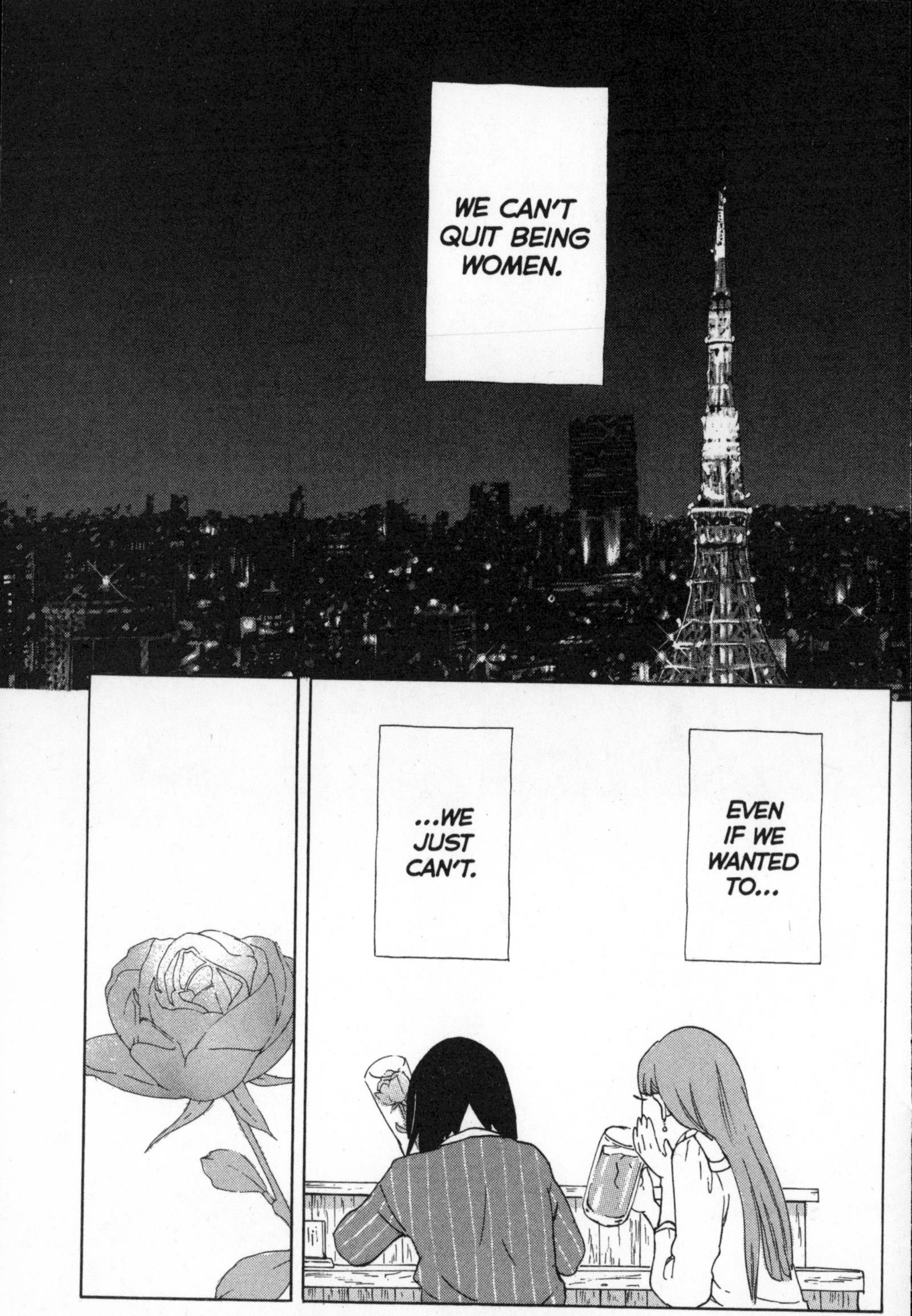
WE CAN'T QUIT BEING WOMEN.
EVEN IF WE WANTED TO...
...WE JUST CAN'T.

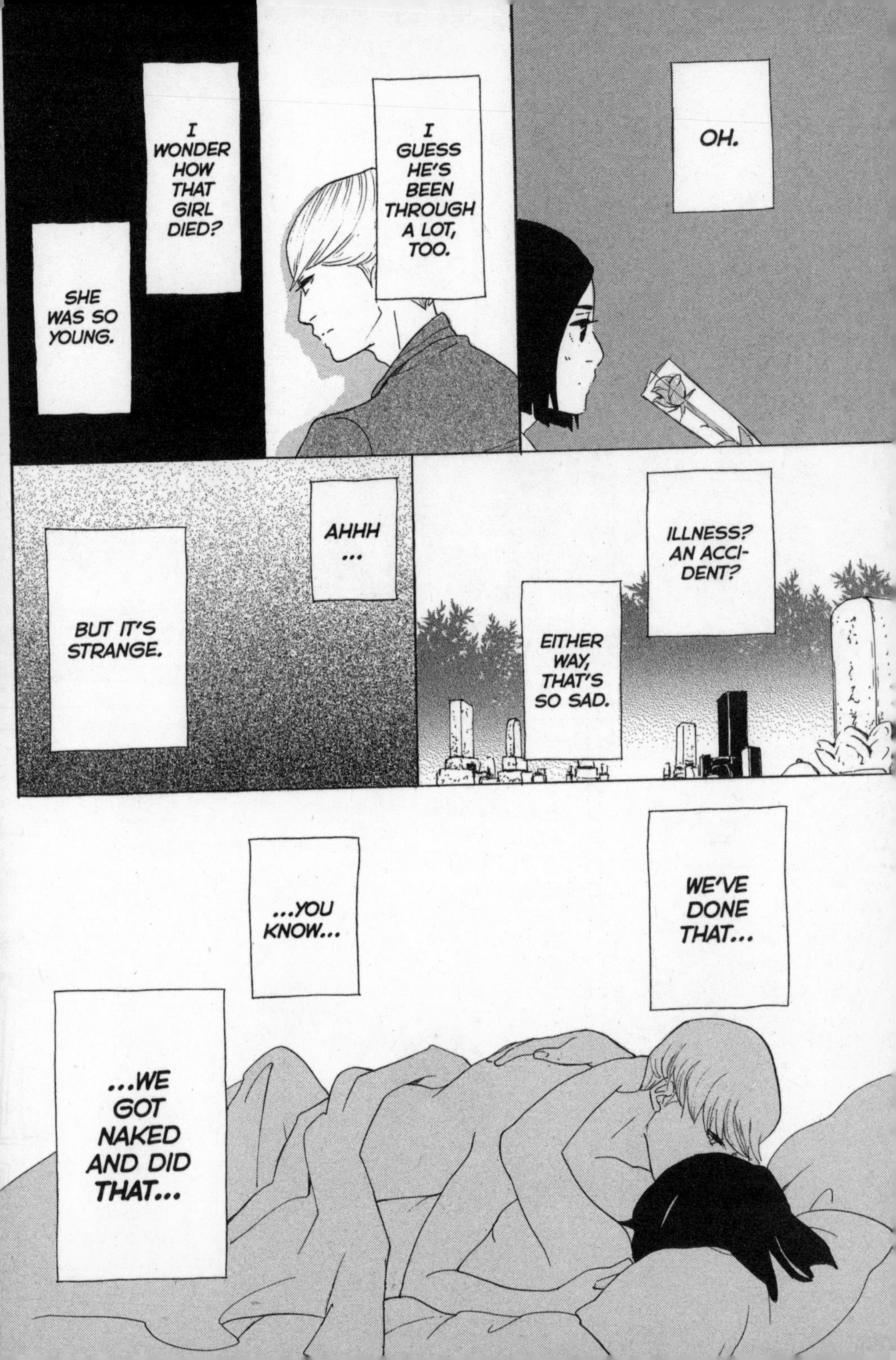
OH.
I GUESS HE'S BEEN THROUGH A LOT, TOO.
I WONDER HOW THAT GIRL DIED?
SHE WAS SO YOUNG.
ILLNESS? AN ACCIDENT?
EITHER WAY, THAT'S SO SAD.
AHHH...
BUT IT'S STRANGE.
WE'VE DONE THAT...
...YOU KNOW...
...WE GOT NAKED AND DID THAT...

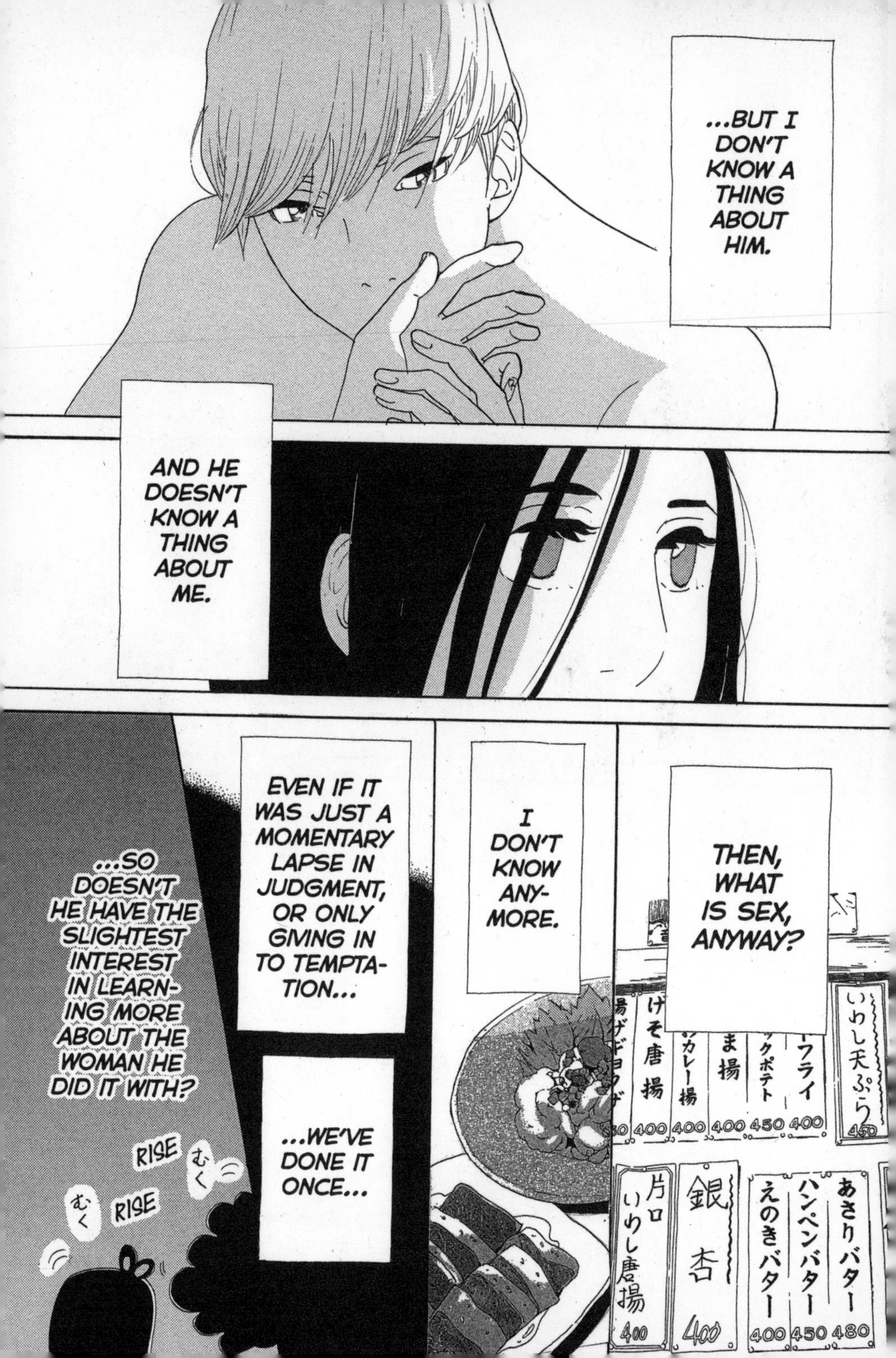

...BUT I DON'T KNOW A THING ABOUT HIM.
AND HE DOESN'T KNOW A THING ABOUT ME.
THEN, WHAT IS SEX, ANYWAY?
いわし天ぷら 450
あさりバター 480
ハンペンバター 450
えのきバター 400
銀杏 400
片口いわし唐揚 400
I DON'T KNOW ANY-MORE.
EVEN IF IT WAS JUST A MOMENTARY LAPSE IN JUDGMENT, OR ONLY GIVING IN TO TEMPTA-TION...
...WE'VE DONE IT ONCE...
...SO DOESN'T HE HAVE THE SLIGHTEST INTEREST IN LEARN-ING MORE ABOUT THE WOMAN HE DID IT WITH?
RISE むく
RISE むく

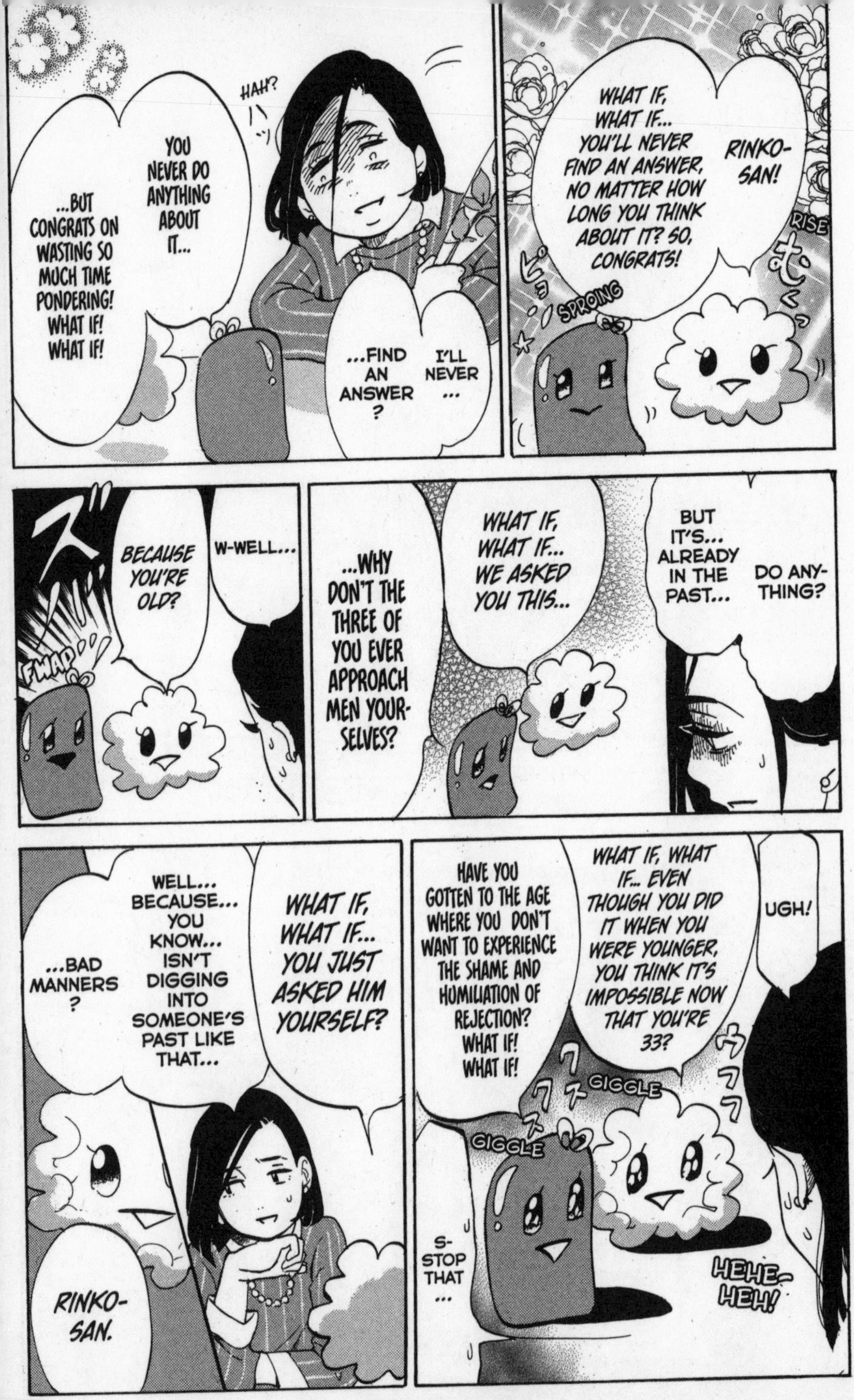
RINKO-SAN!
WHAT IF, WHAT IF... YOU'LL NEVER FIND AN ANSWER, NO MATTER HOW LONG YOU THINK ABOUT IT? SO, CONGRATS!
RISE
SPROING
YOU NEVER DO ANYTHING ABOUT IT...
...BUT CONGRATS ON WASTING SO MUCH TIME PONDERING! WHAT IF! WHAT IF!
HAH?
I'LL NEVER...
...FIND AN ANSWER?
DO ANY-THING?
BUT IT'S... ALREADY IN THE PAST...
WHAT IF, WHAT IF... WE ASKED YOU THIS...
...WHY DON'T THE THREE OF YOU EVER APPROACH MEN YOUR-SELVES?
W-WELL...
BECAUSE YOU'RE OLD?
FWAP
UGH!
WHAT IF, WHAT IF... EVEN THOUGH YOU DID IT WHEN YOU WERE YOUNGER, YOU THINK IT'S IMPOSSIBLE NOW THAT YOU'RE 33?
HAVE YOU GOTTEN TO THE AGE WHERE YOU DON'T WANT TO EXPERIENCE THE SHAME AND HUMILIATION OF REJECTION? WHAT IF! WHAT IF!
GIGGLE
GIGGLE
HEHE-HEH!
S-STOP THAT...
WHAT IF, WHAT IF... YOU JUST ASKED HIM YOURSELF?
WELL... BECAUSE... YOU KNOW... ISN'T DIGGING INTO SOMEONE'S PAST LIKE THAT...
...BAD MANNERS?
RINKO-SAN.

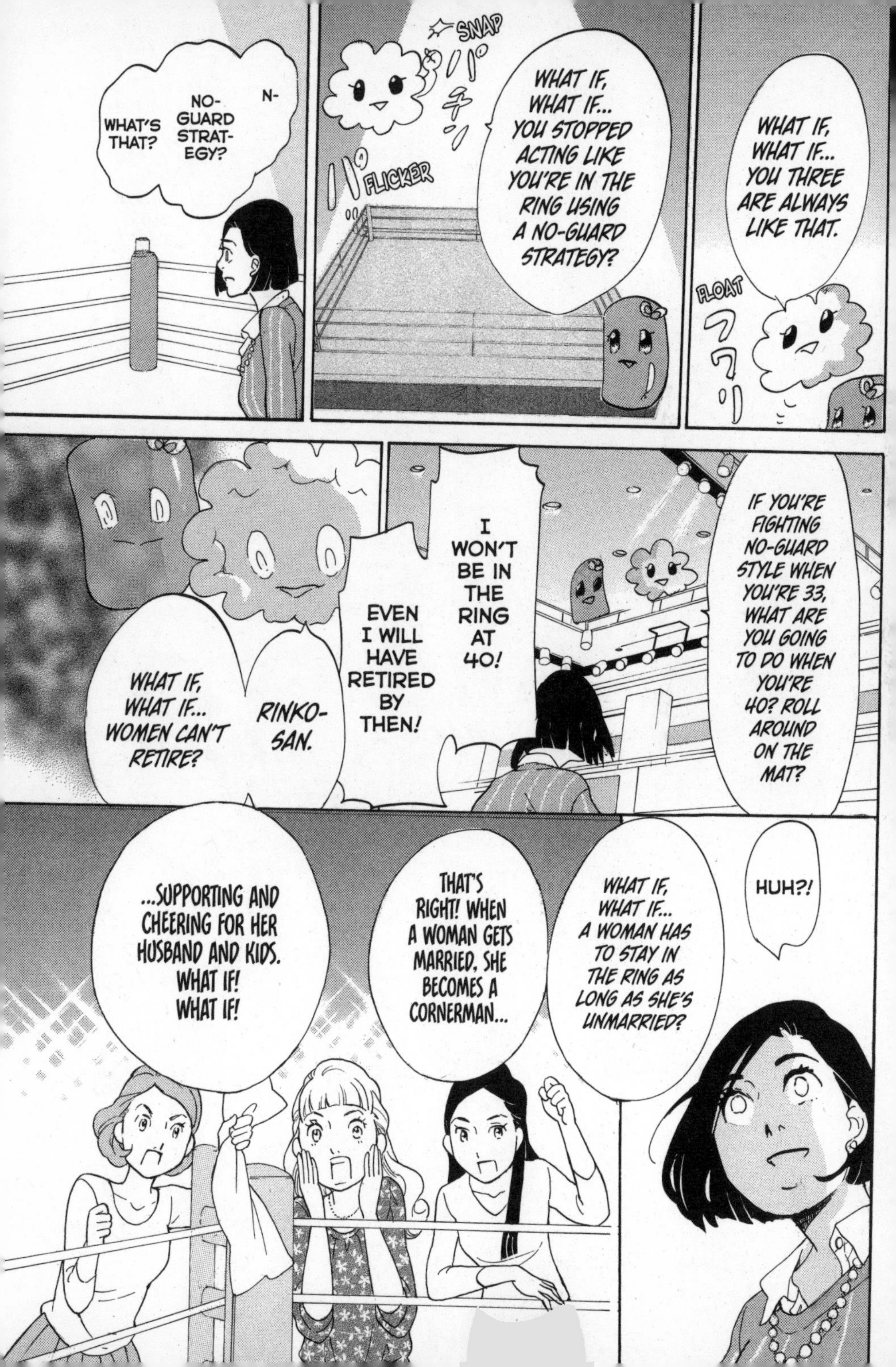
FLOAT
WHAT IF, WHAT IF... YOU THREE ARE ALWAYS LIKE THAT.
SNAP
FLICKER
WHAT IF, WHAT IF... YOU STOPPED ACTING LIKE YOU'RE IN THE RING USING A NO-GUARD STRATEGY?
N-
NO-GUARD STRATEGY?
WHAT'S THAT?
IF YOU'RE FIGHTING NO-GUARD STYLE WHEN YOU'RE 33, WHAT ARE YOU GOING TO DO WHEN YOU'RE 40? ROLL AROUND ON THE MAT?
I WON'T BE IN THE RING AT 40!
EVEN I WILL HAVE RETIRED BY THEN!
RINKO-SAN.
WHAT IF, WHAT IF... WOMEN CAN'T RETIRE?
HUH?!
WHAT IF, WHAT IF... A WOMAN HAS TO STAY IN THE RING AS LONG AS SHE'S UNMARRIED?
THAT'S RIGHT! WHEN A WOMAN GETS MARRIED, SHE BECOMES A CORNERMAN...
...SUPPORTING AND CHEERING FOR HER HUSBAND AND KIDS. WHAT IF! WHAT IF!

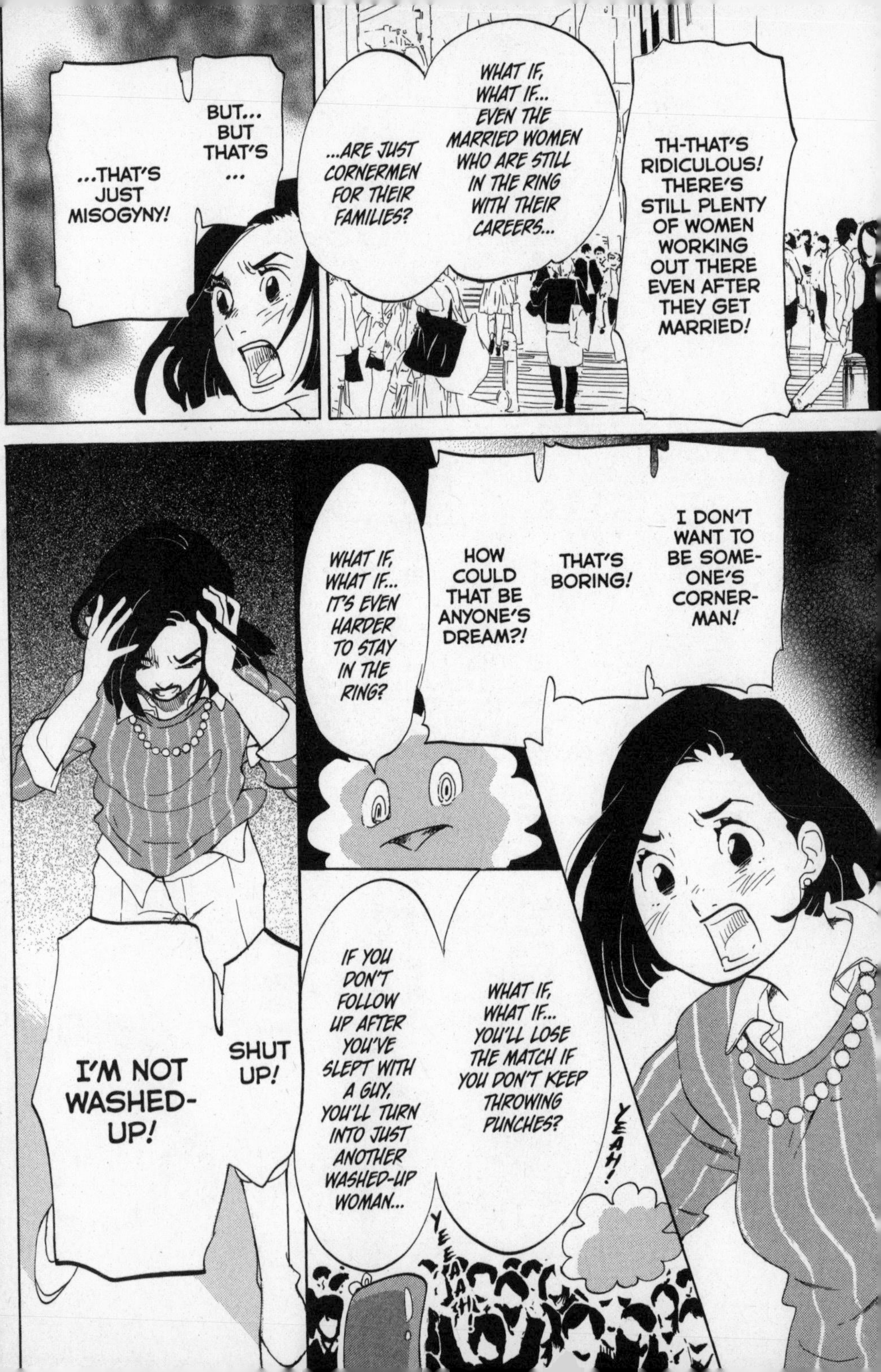
TH-THAT'S RIDICULOUS! THERE'S STILL PLENTY OF WOMEN WORKING OUT THERE EVEN AFTER THEY GET MARRIED!
WHAT IF, WHAT IF... EVEN THE MARRIED WOMEN WHO ARE STILL IN THE RING WITH THEIR CAREERS...
...ARE JUST CORNERMEN FOR THEIR FAMILIES?
BUT... BUT THAT'S ...
...THAT'S JUST MISOGYNY!
I DON'T WANT TO BE SOME-ONE'S CORNER-MAN!
THAT'S BORING!
HOW COULD THAT BE ANYONE'S DREAM?!
WHAT IF, WHAT IF... IT'S EVEN HARDER TO STAY IN THE RING?
WHAT IF, WHAT IF... YOU'LL LOSE THE MATCH IF YOU DON'T KEEP THROWING PUNCHES?
IF YOU DON'T FOLLOW UP AFTER YOU'VE SLEPT WITH A GUY, YOU'LL TURN INTO JUST ANOTHER WASHED-UP WOMAN...
YEAH!
YEEAAH!
SHUT UP!
I'M NOT WASHED-UP!

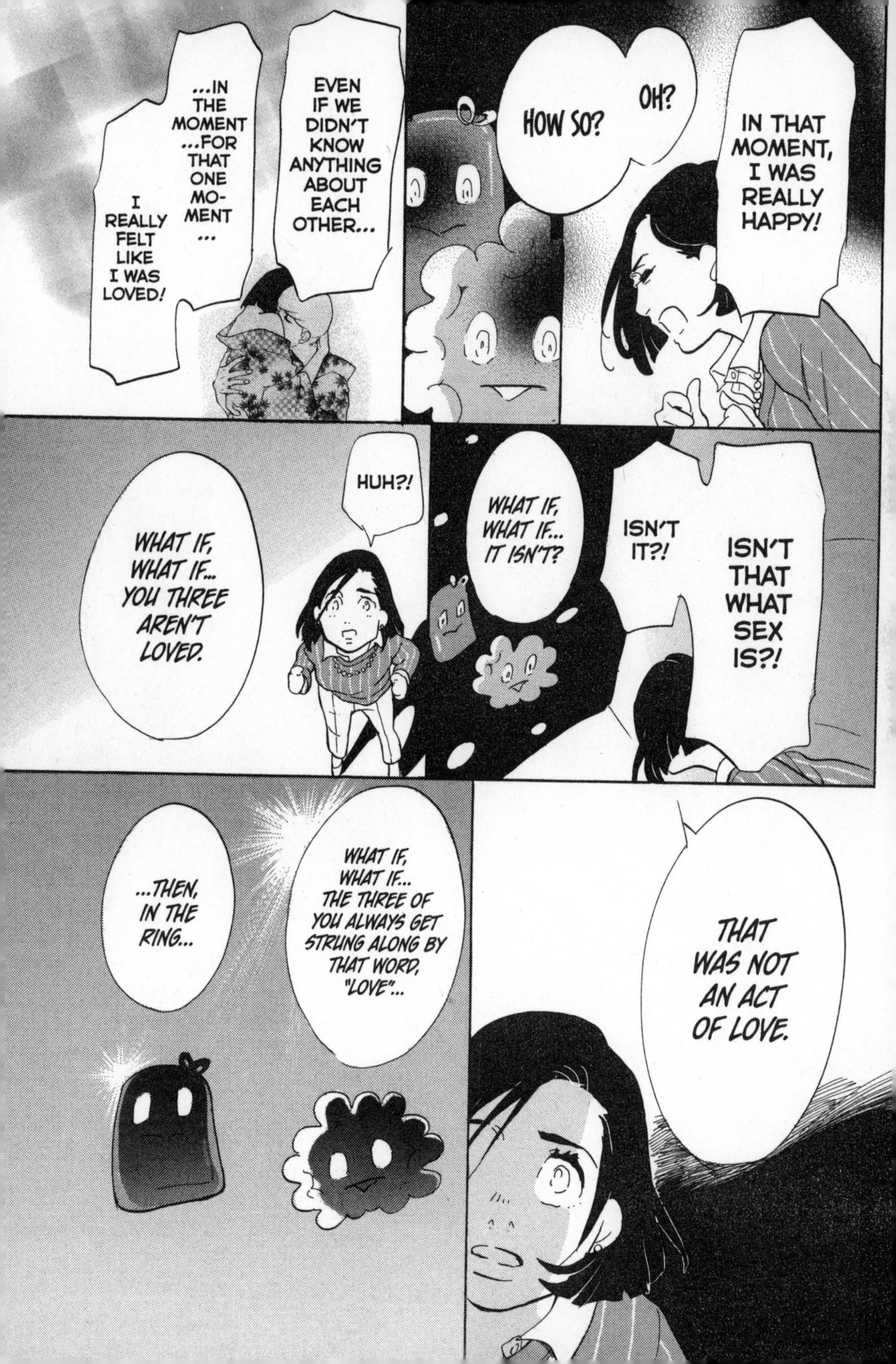
IN THAT MOMENT, I WAS REALLY HAPPY!
OH?
HOW SO?
EVEN IF WE DIDN'T KNOW ANYTHING ABOUT EACH OTHER...
...IN THE MOMENT ...FOR THAT ONE MO-MENT ...
I REALLY FELT LIKE I WAS LOVED!
ISN'T THAT WHAT SEX IS?!
ISN'T IT?!
WHAT IF, WHAT IF... IT ISN'T?
HUH?!
WHAT IF, WHAT IF... YOU THREE AREN'T LOVED.
THAT WAS NOT AN ACT OF LOVE.
WHAT IF, WHAT IF... THE THREE OF YOU ALWAYS GET STRUNG ALONG BY THAT WORD, "LOVE"...
...THEN, IN THE RING...

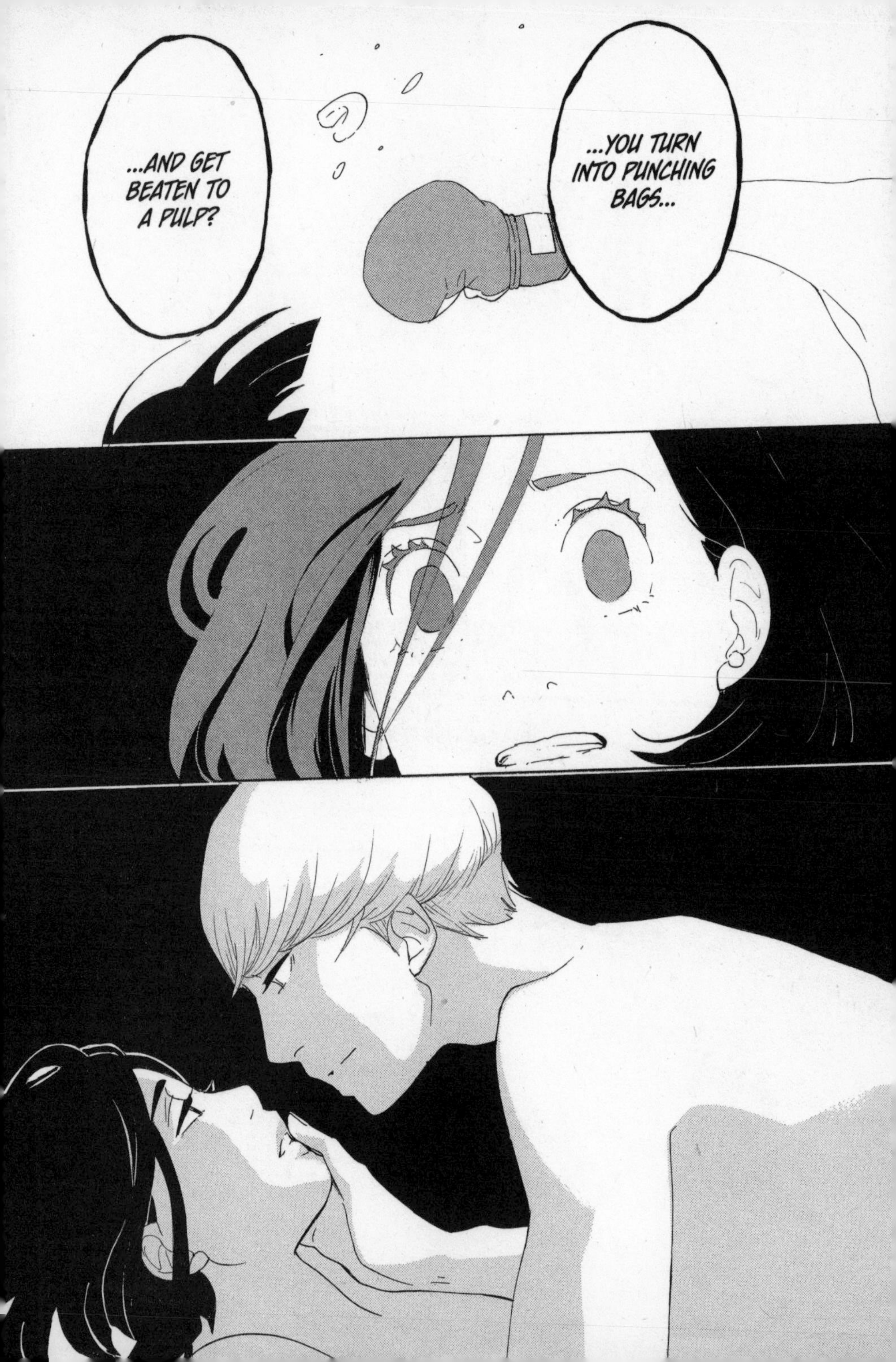
...YOU TURN INTO PUNCHING BAGS...
...AND GET BEATEN TO A PULP?

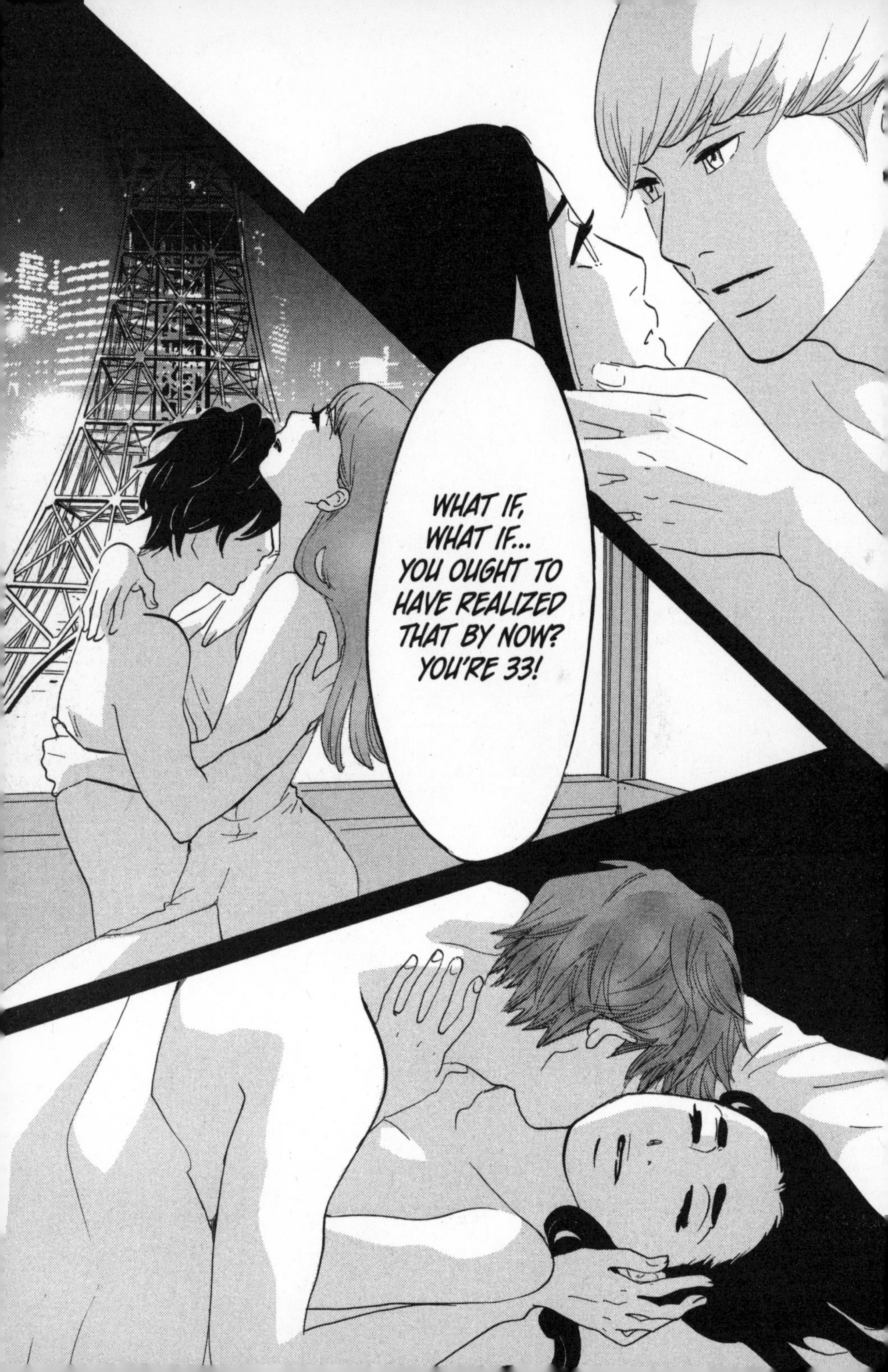
WHAT IF, WHAT IF... YOU OUGHT TO HAVE REALIZED THAT BY NOW? YOU'RE 33!

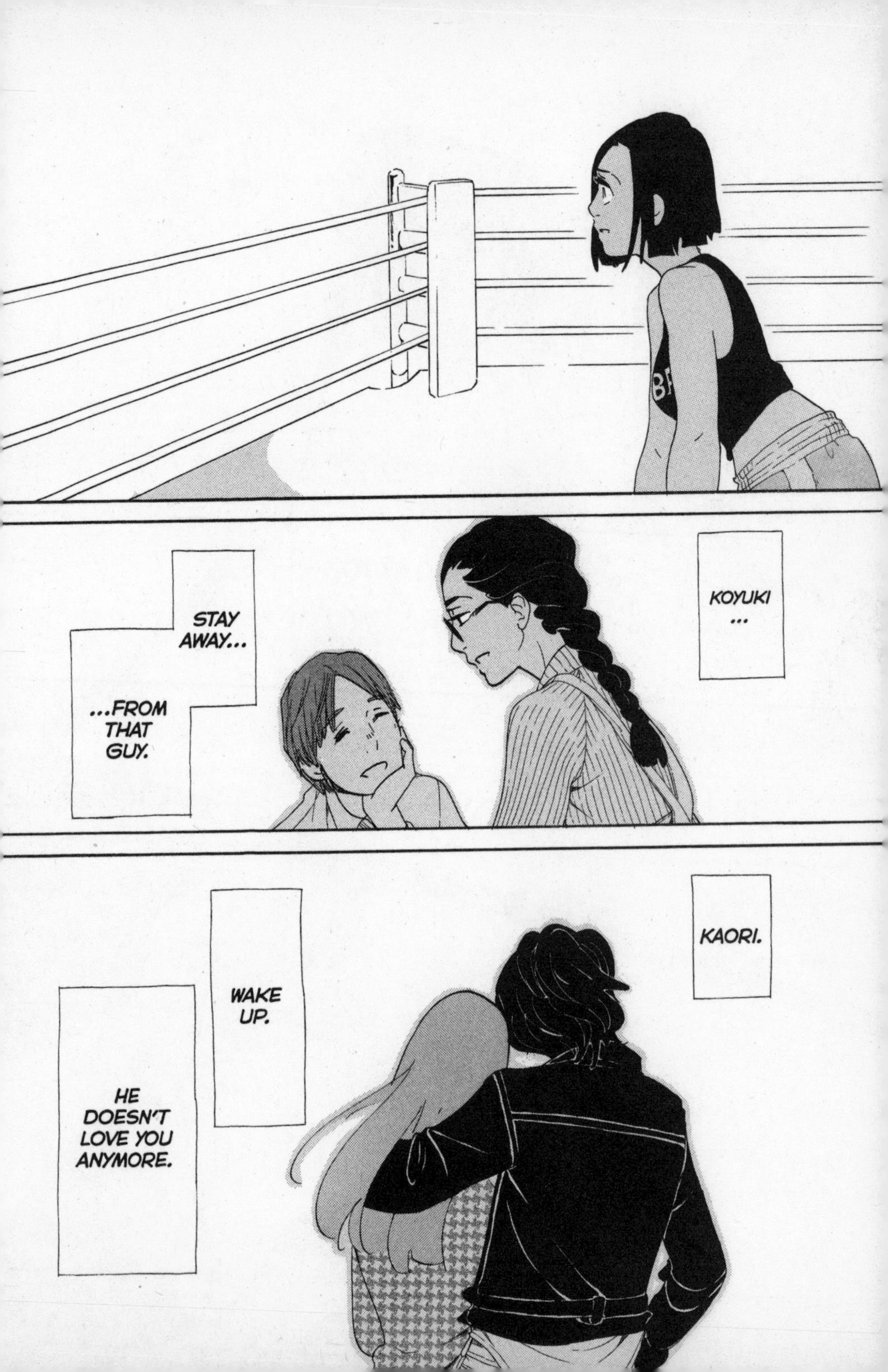
KOYUKI ...
STAY AWAY...
...FROM THAT GUY.
KAORI.
WAKE UP.
HE DOESN'T LOVE YOU ANYMORE.

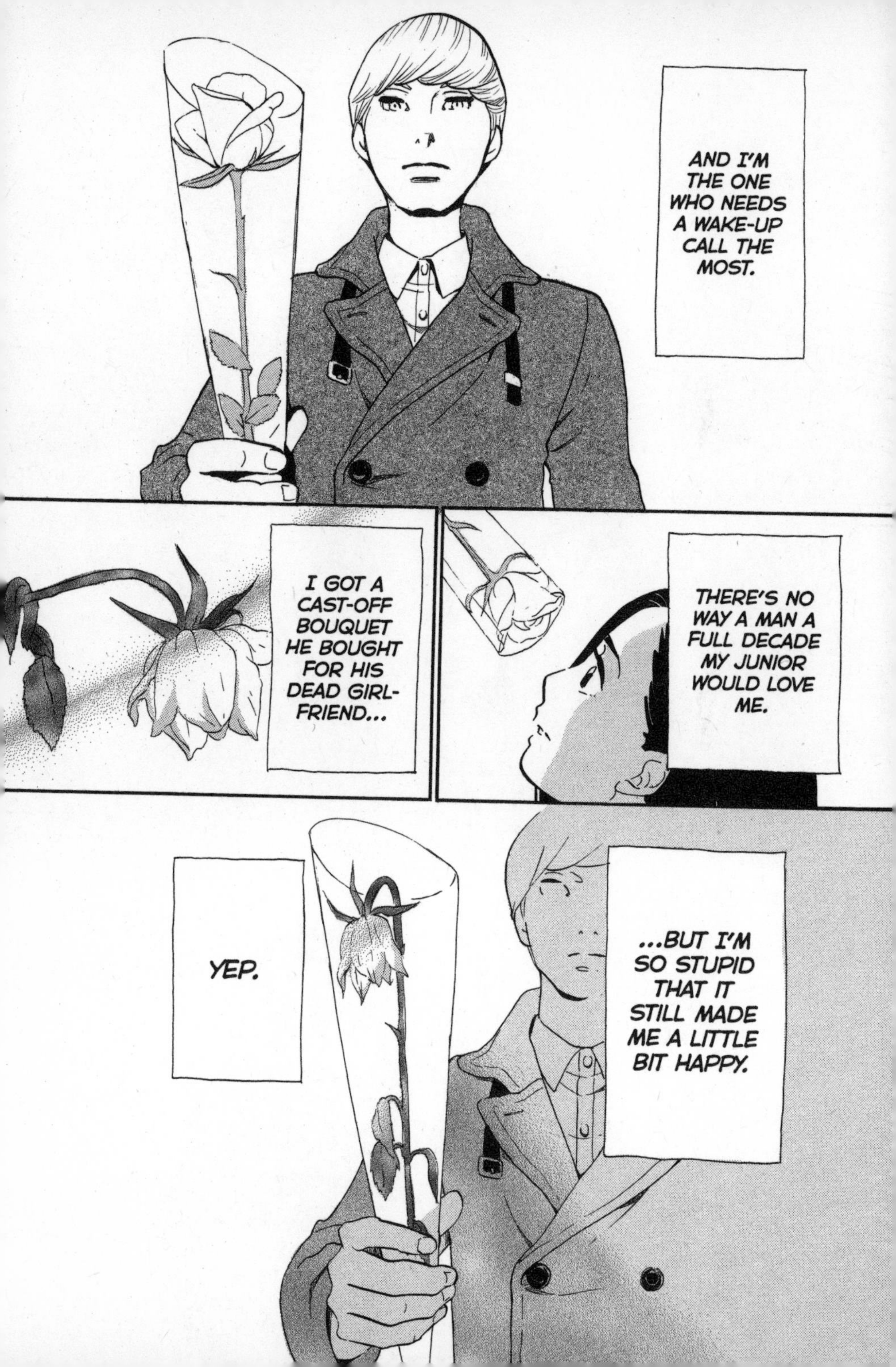
AND I'M THE ONE WHO NEEDS A WAKE-UP CALL THE MOST.
THERE'S NO WAY A MAN A FULL DECADE MY JUNIOR WOULD LOVE ME.
I GOT A CAST-OFF BOUQUET HE BOUGHT FOR HIS DEAD GIRL-FRIEND...
...BUT I'M SO STUPID THAT IT STILL MADE ME A LITTLE BIT HAPPY.
YEP.

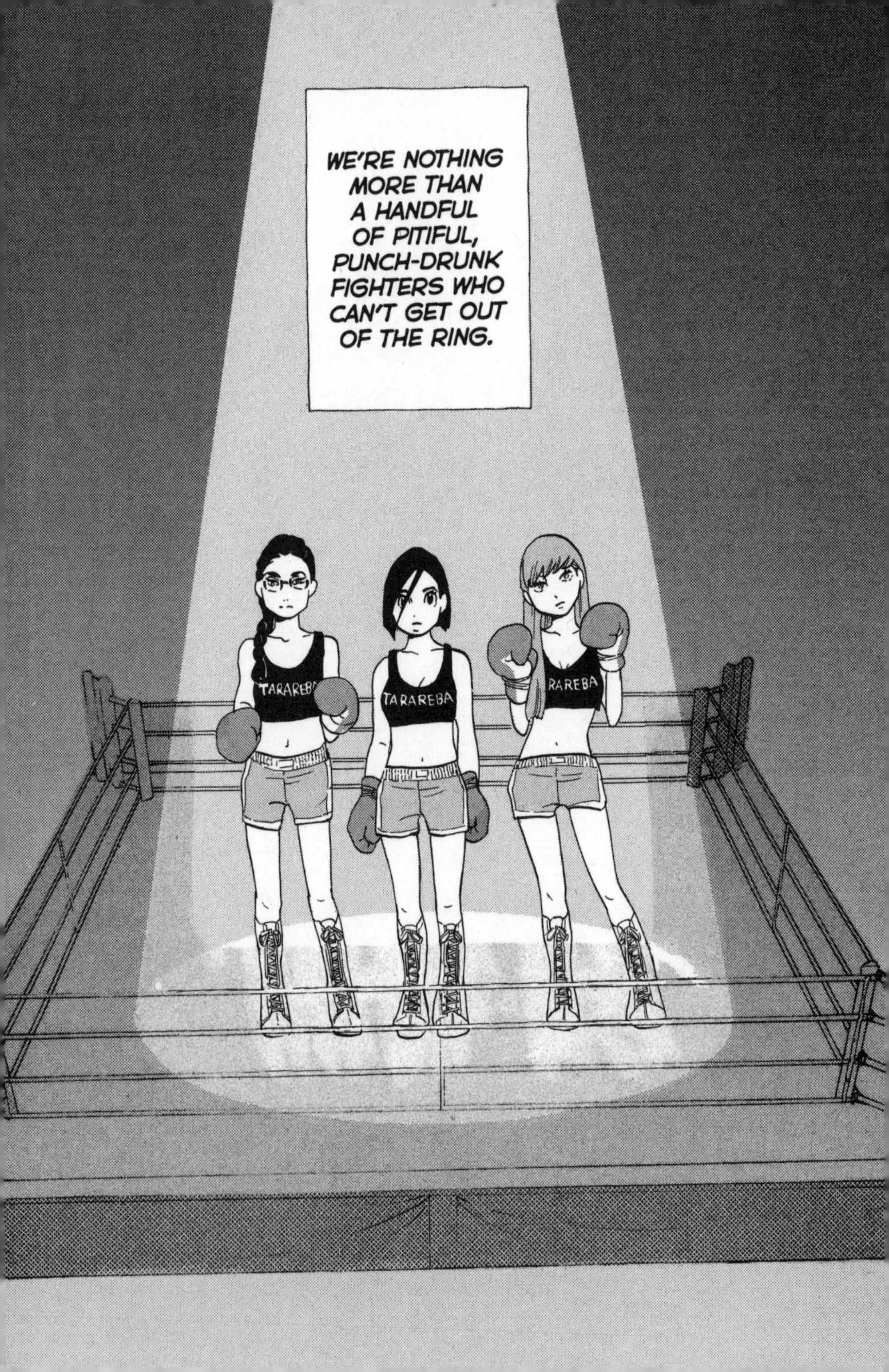
WE'RE NOTHING MORE THAN A HANDFUL OF PITIFUL, PUNCH-DRUNK FIGHTERS WHO CAN'T GET OUT OF THE RING.
TARAREBA
TARAREBA
TARAREBA

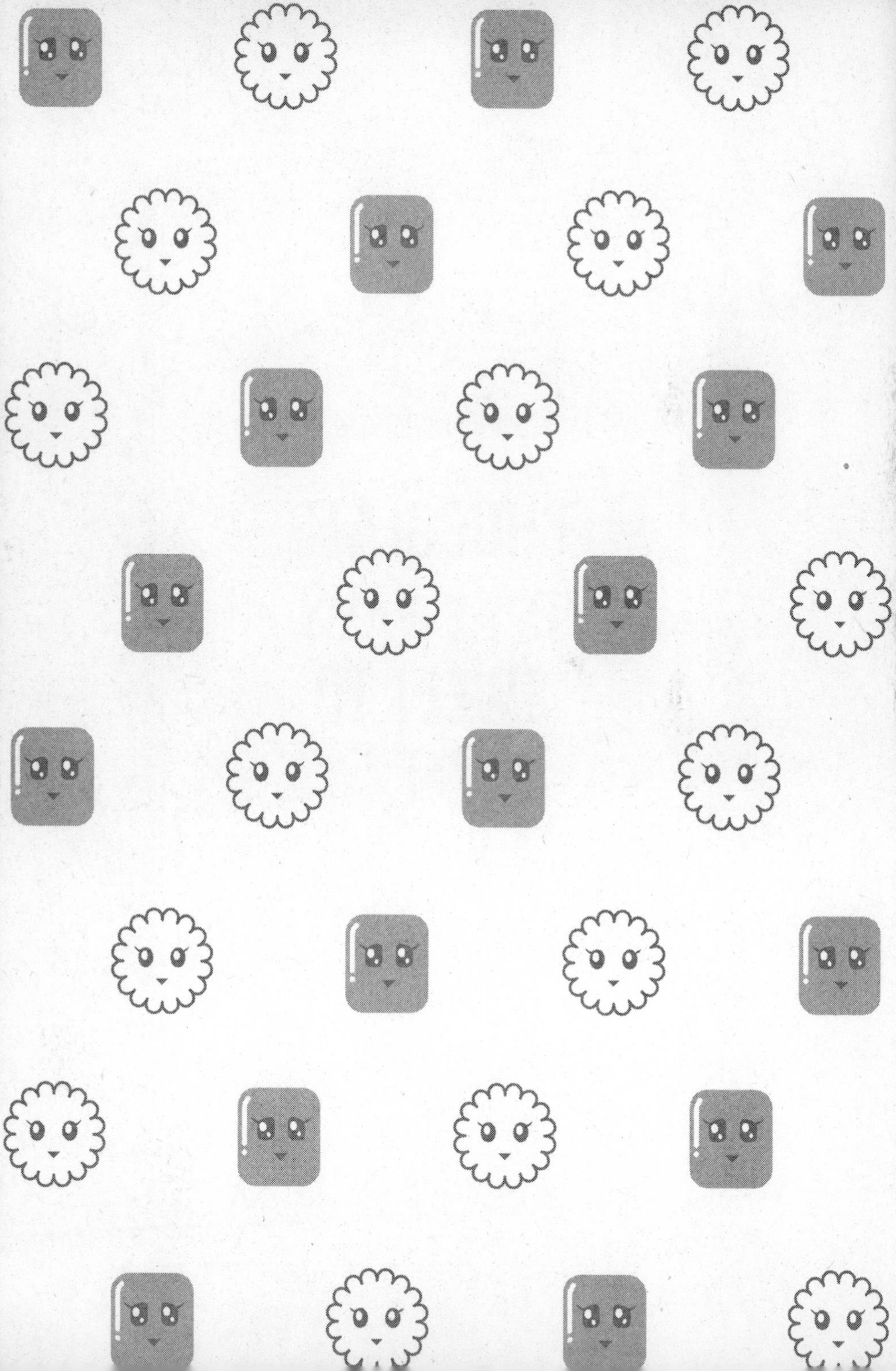

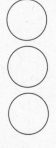

SPECIAL CHAPTER

# CHOCOLATE IS ALWAYS SWEET TO ME

*This comic was originally drawn for 2015 Takashimaya Amour du Chocolat!

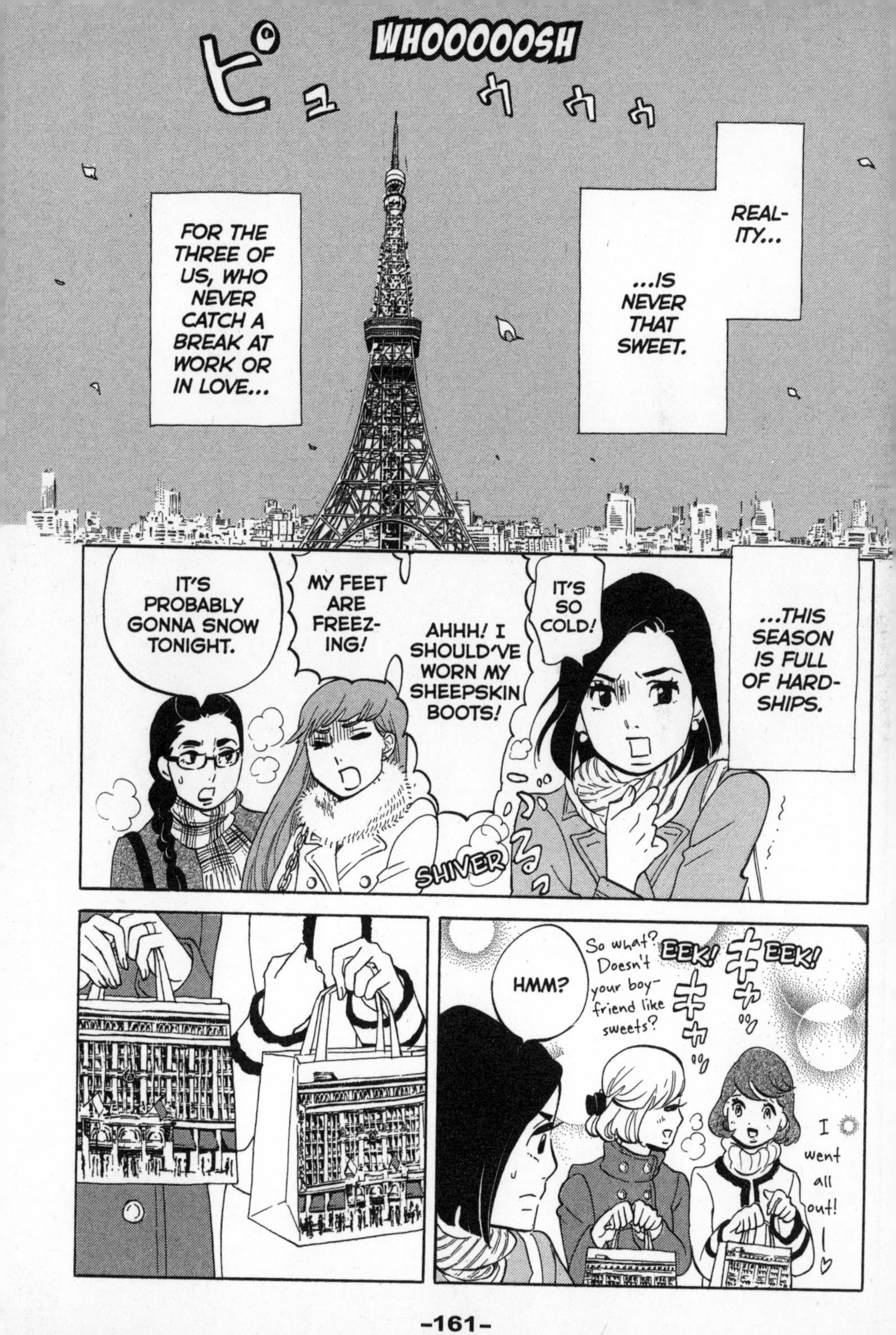

WHOOOOOSH
ピュウウウ
REAL-ITY...
...IS NEVER THAT SWEET.
FOR THE THREE OF US, WHO NEVER CATCH A BREAK AT WORK OR IN LOVE...
...THIS SEASON IS FULL OF HARD-SHIPS.
IT'S SO COLD!
AHHH! I SHOULD'VE WORN MY SHEEPSKIN BOOTS!
MY FEET ARE FREEZ-ING!
IT'S PROBABLY GONNA SNOW TONIGHT.
SHIVER
I went all out!
EEK!
EEK!
So what? Doesn't your boy-friend like sweets?
HMM?

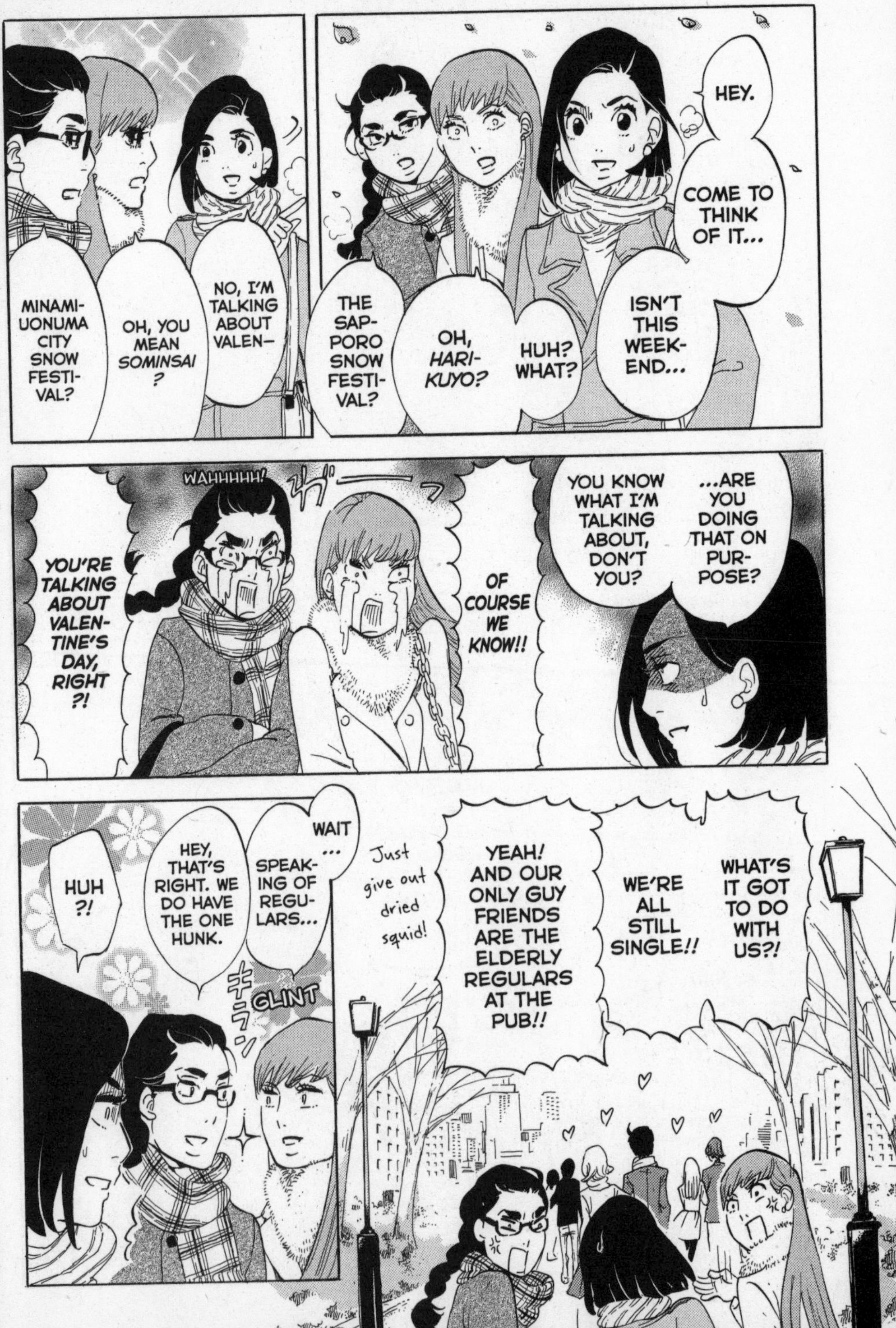
HEY.
COME TO THINK OF IT...
ISN'T THIS WEEKEND...
HUH? WHAT?
OH, *HARIKUYO*?
THE SAPPORO SNOW FESTIVAL?
NO, I'M TALKING ABOUT VALEN–
OH, YOU MEAN *SOMINSAI*?
MINAMIUONUMA CITY SNOW FESTIVAL?
...ARE YOU DOING THAT ON PURPOSE?
YOU KNOW WHAT I'M TALKING ABOUT, DON'T YOU?
OF COURSE WE KNOW!!
WAHHHHH!
YOU'RE TALKING ABOUT VALENTINE'S DAY, RIGHT?!
WHAT'S IT GOT TO DO WITH US?!
WE'RE ALL STILL SINGLE!!
YEAH! AND OUR ONLY GUY FRIENDS ARE THE ELDERLY REGULARS AT THE PUB!!
Just give out dried squid!
WAIT...
SPEAKING OF REGULARS...
HEY, THAT'S RIGHT. WE DO HAVE THE ONE HUNK.
GLINT
HUH?!

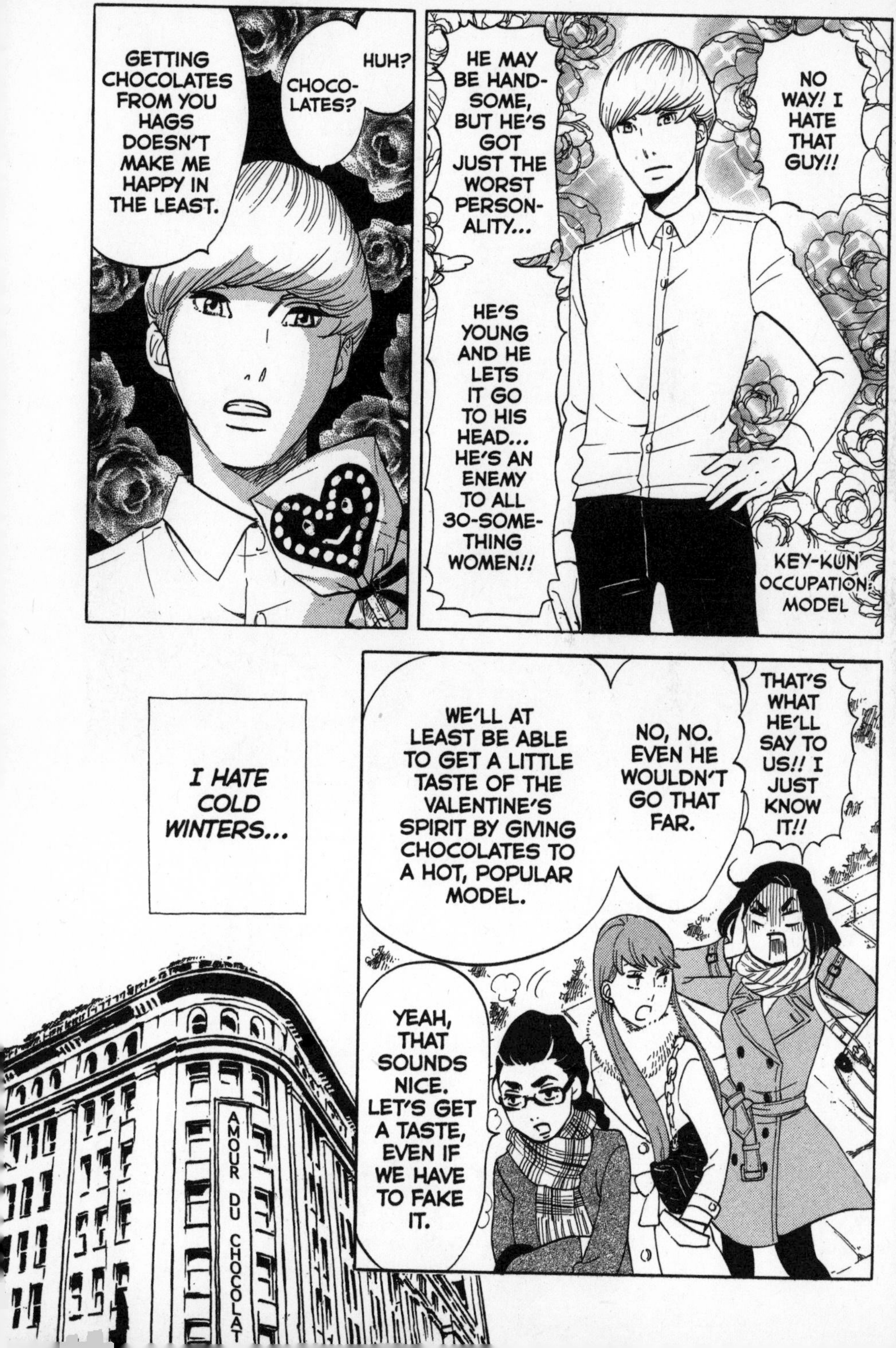
NO WAY! I HATE THAT GUY!!
HE MAY BE HANDSOME, BUT HE'S GOT JUST THE WORST PERSONALITY...
HE'S YOUNG AND HE LETS IT GO TO HIS HEAD... HE'S AN ENEMY TO ALL 30-SOMETHING WOMEN!!
KEY-KUN OCCUPATION: MODEL
HUH? CHOCOLATES?
GETTING CHOCOLATES FROM YOU HAGS DOESN'T MAKE ME HAPPY IN THE LEAST.
THAT'S WHAT HE'LL SAY TO US!! I JUST KNOW IT!!
NO, NO. EVEN HE WOULDN'T GO THAT FAR.
WE'LL AT LEAST BE ABLE TO GET A LITTLE TASTE OF THE VALENTINE'S SPIRIT BY GIVING CHOCOLATES TO A HOT, POPULAR MODEL.
YEAH, THAT SOUNDS NICE. LET'S GET A TASTE, EVEN IF WE HAVE TO FAKE IT.
I HATE COLD WINTERS...
AMOUR DU CHOCOLAT

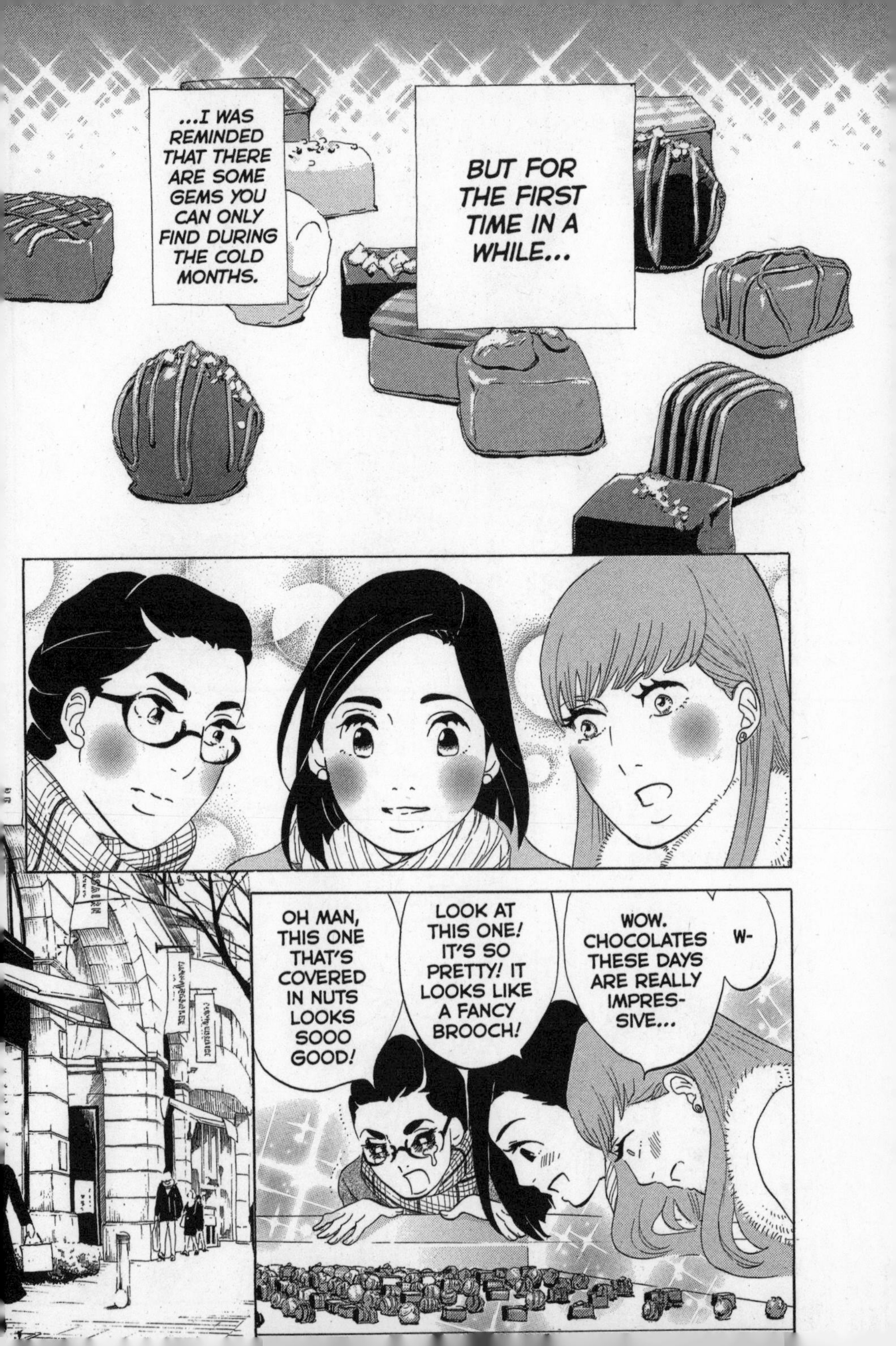
BUT FOR THE FIRST TIME IN A WHILE...
...I WAS REMINDED THAT THERE ARE SOME GEMS YOU CAN ONLY FIND DURING THE COLD MONTHS.
W-
WOW. CHOCOLATES THESE DAYS ARE REALLY IMPRES-SIVE...
LOOK AT THIS ONE! IT'S SO PRETTY! IT LOOKS LIKE A FANCY BROOCH!
OH MAN, THIS ONE THAT'S COVERED IN NUTS LOOKS SOOO GOOD!

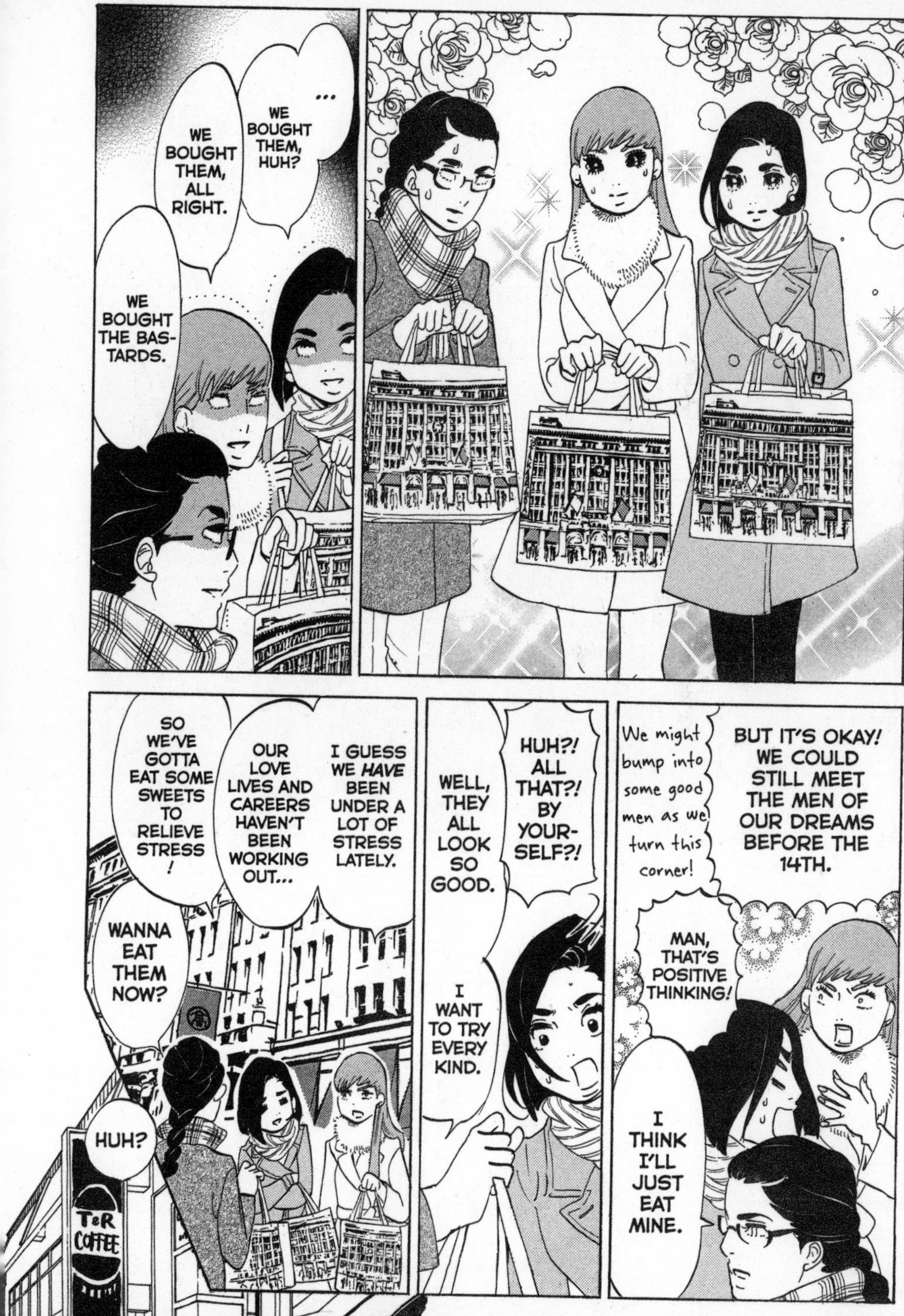
...
WE BOUGHT THEM, HUH?
WE BOUGHT THEM, ALL RIGHT.
WE BOUGHT THE BAS-TARDS.
BUT IT'S OKAY! WE COULD STILL MEET THE MEN OF OUR DREAMS BEFORE THE 14TH.
We might bump into some good men as we turn this corner!
MAN, THAT'S POSITIVE THINKING!
I THINK I'LL JUST EAT MINE.
HUH?! ALL THAT?! BY YOUR-SELF?!
WELL, THEY ALL LOOK SO GOOD.
I WANT TO TRY EVERY KIND.
I GUESS WE *HAVE* BEEN UNDER A LOT OF STRESS LATELY.
OUR LOVE LIVES AND CAREERS HAVEN'T BEEN WORKING OUT...
SO WE'VE GOTTA EAT SOME SWEETS TO RELIEVE STRESS!
WANNA EAT THEM NOW?
HUH?
T&R COFFEE

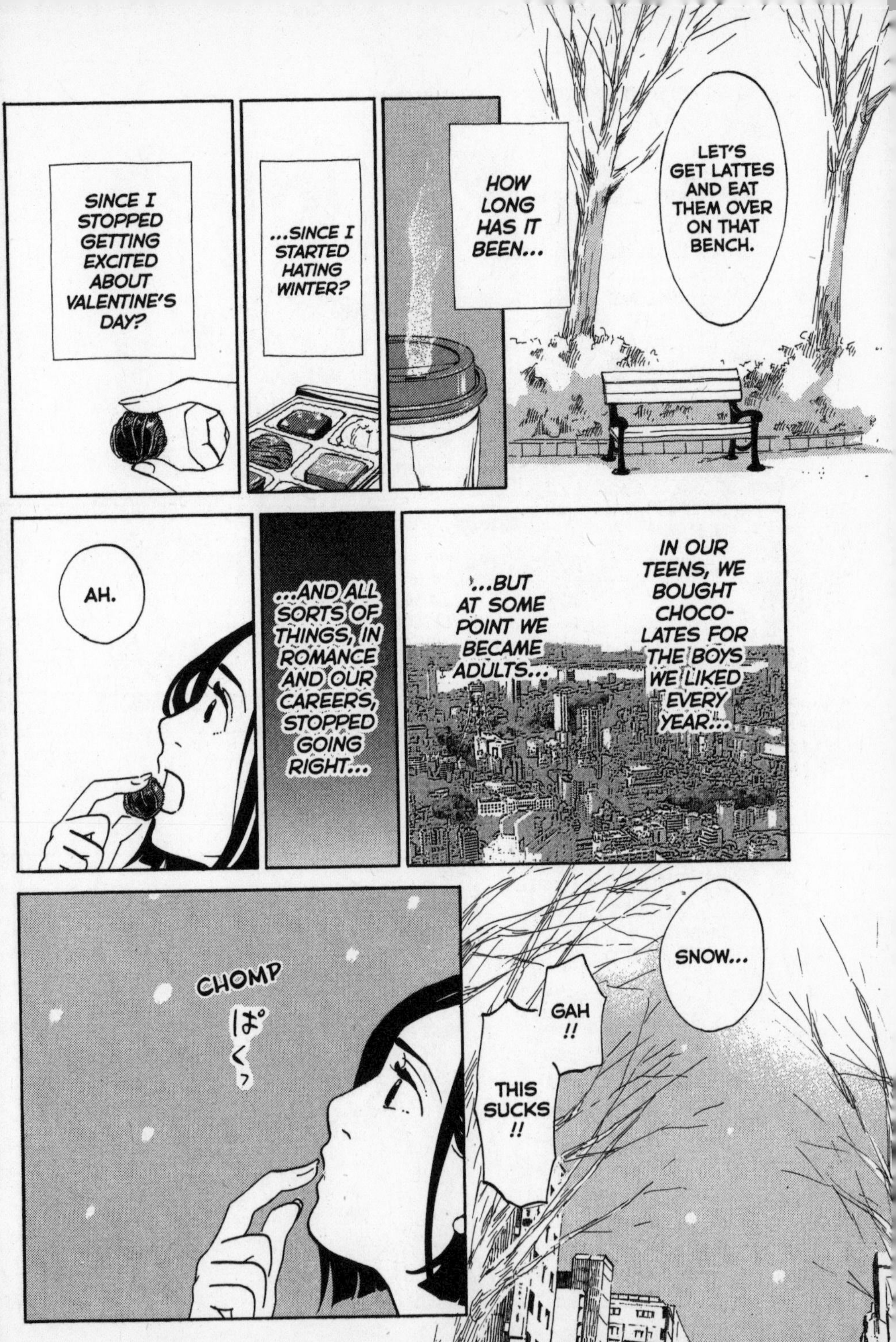
LET'S GET LATTES AND EAT THEM OVER ON THAT BENCH.
HOW LONG HAS IT BEEN...
...SINCE I STARTED HATING WINTER?
SINCE I STOPPED GETTING EXCITED ABOUT VALENTINE'S DAY?
IN OUR TEENS, WE BOUGHT CHOCO-LATES FOR THE BOYS WE LIKED EVERY YEAR...
...BUT AT SOME POINT WE BECAME ADULTS...
...AND ALL SORTS OF THINGS, IN ROMANCE AND OUR CAREERS, STOPPED GOING RIGHT...
AH.
SNOW...
GAH!!
THIS SUCKS!!
CHOMP
ぱくっ

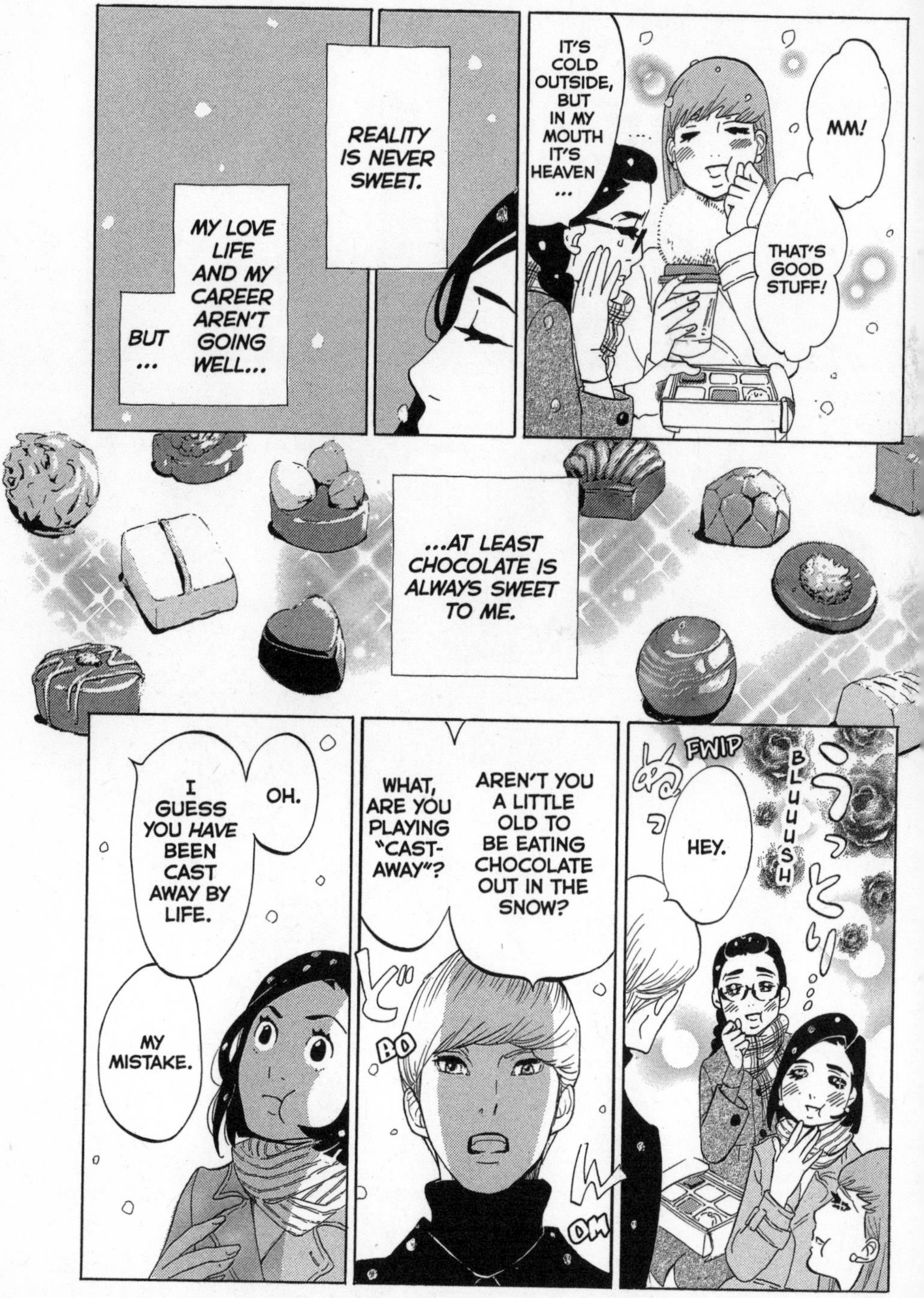
MM!
THAT'S GOOD STUFF!
IT'S COLD OUTSIDE, BUT IN MY MOUTH IT'S HEAVEN ...
...
REALITY IS NEVER SWEET.
MY LOVE LIFE AND MY CAREER AREN'T GOING WELL...
BUT ...
...AT LEAST CHOCOLATE IS ALWAYS SWEET TO ME.
FWIP
BLUUUSH
HEY.
AREN'T YOU A LITTLE OLD TO BE EATING CHOCOLATE OUT IN THE SNOW?
WHAT, ARE YOU PLAYING "CAST-AWAY"?
BO
OM
OH.
I GUESS YOU *HAVE* BEEN CAST AWAY BY LIFE.
MY MISTAKE.

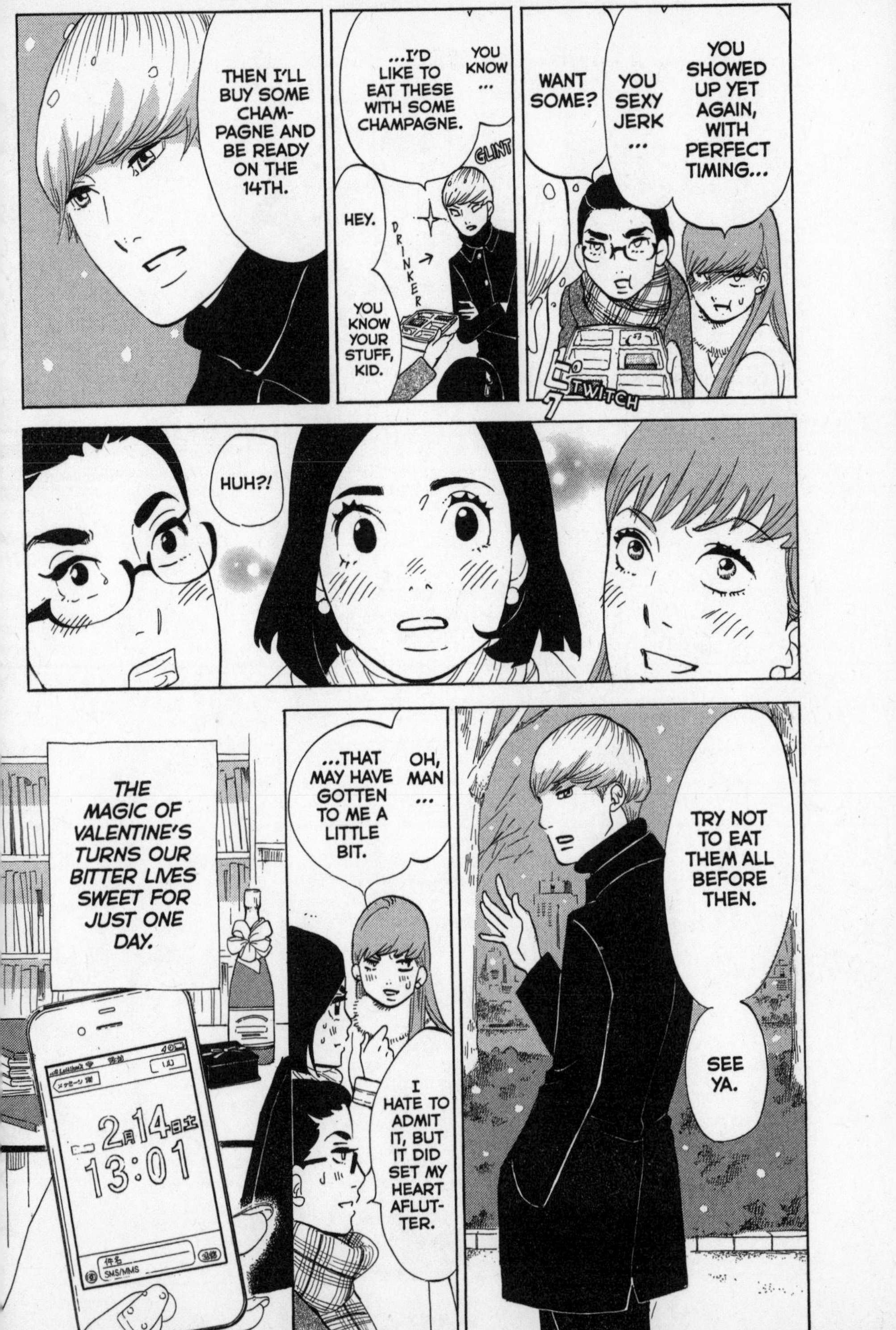
YOU SHOWED UP YET AGAIN, WITH PERFECT TIMING...
YOU SEXY JERK ...
WANT SOME?
TWITCH
YOU KNOW ...
...I'D LIKE TO EAT THESE WITH SOME CHAMPAGNE.
GLINT
HEY.
DRINKER
YOU KNOW YOUR STUFF, KID.
THEN I'LL BUY SOME CHAMPAGNE AND BE READY ON THE 14TH.
HUH?!
TRY NOT TO EAT THEM ALL BEFORE THEN.
SEE YA.
OH, MAN ...
...THAT MAY HAVE GOTTEN TO ME A LITTLE BIT.
I HATE TO ADMIT IT, BUT IT DID SET MY HEART AFLUTTER.
THE MAGIC OF VALENTINE'S TURNS OUR BITTER LIVES SWEET FOR JUST ONE DAY.
2月14日土
13:01
SMS/MMS

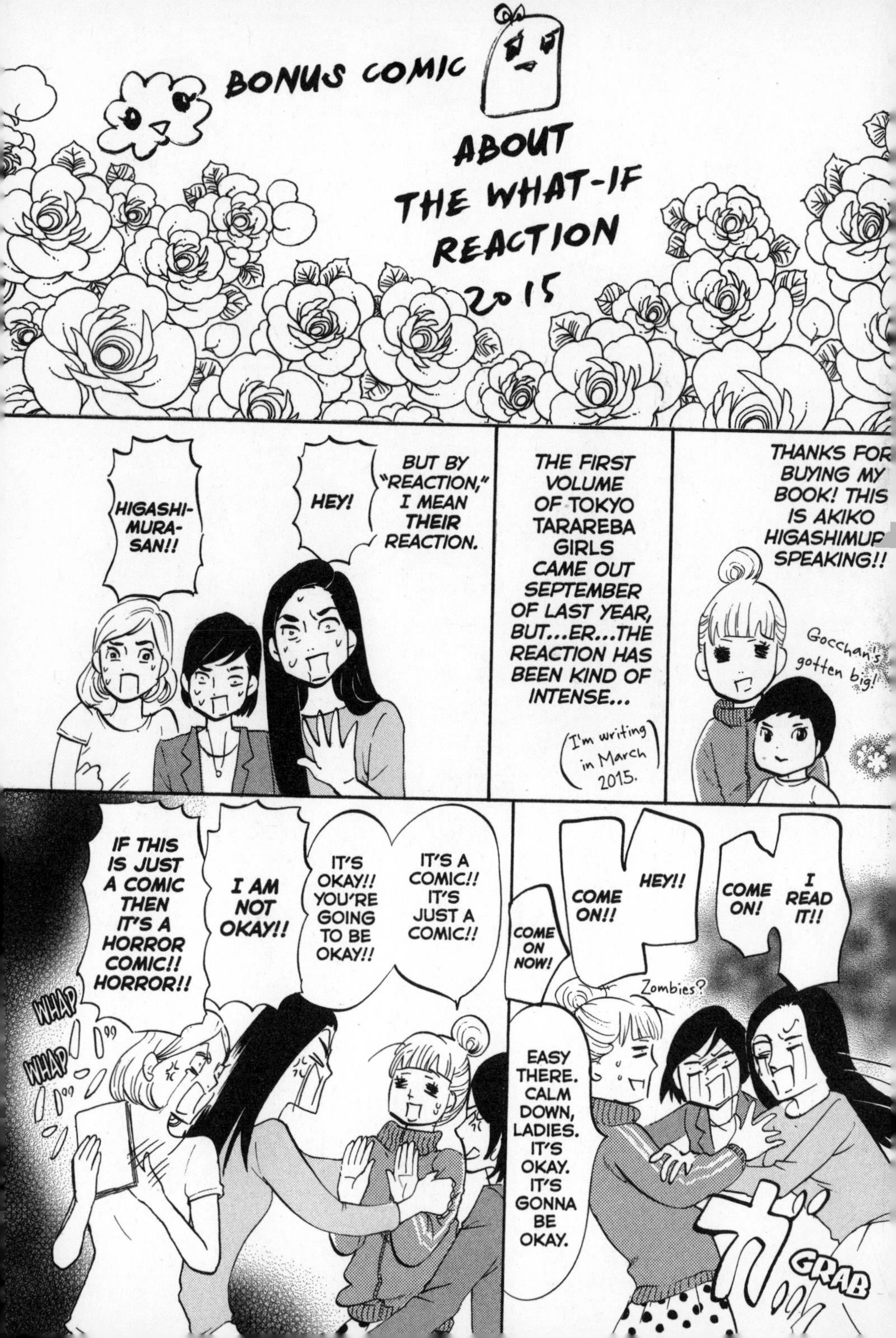

BONUS COMIC
ABOUT THE WHAT-IF REACTION 2015
THANKS FOR BUYING MY BOOK! THIS IS AKIKO HIGASHIMUR SPEAKING!!
Gocchan's gotten big!
THE FIRST VOLUME OF TOKYO TARAREBA GIRLS CAME OUT SEPTEMBER OF LAST YEAR, BUT...ER...THE REACTION HAS BEEN KIND OF INTENSE...
(I'm writing in March 2015.)
BUT BY "REACTION," I MEAN THEIR REACTION.
HEY!
HIGASHI-MURA-SAN!!
I READ IT!!
COME ON!
HEY!!
COME ON!!
COME ON NOW!
Zombies?
EASY THERE. CALM DOWN, LADIES. IT'S OKAY. IT'S GONNA BE OKAY.
GRAB
IT'S A COMIC!! IT'S JUST A COMIC!!
IT'S OKAY!! YOU'RE GOING TO BE OKAY!!
I AM NOT OKAY!!
IF THIS IS JUST A COMIC THEN IT'S A HORROR COMIC!! HORROR!!
WHAP
WHAP

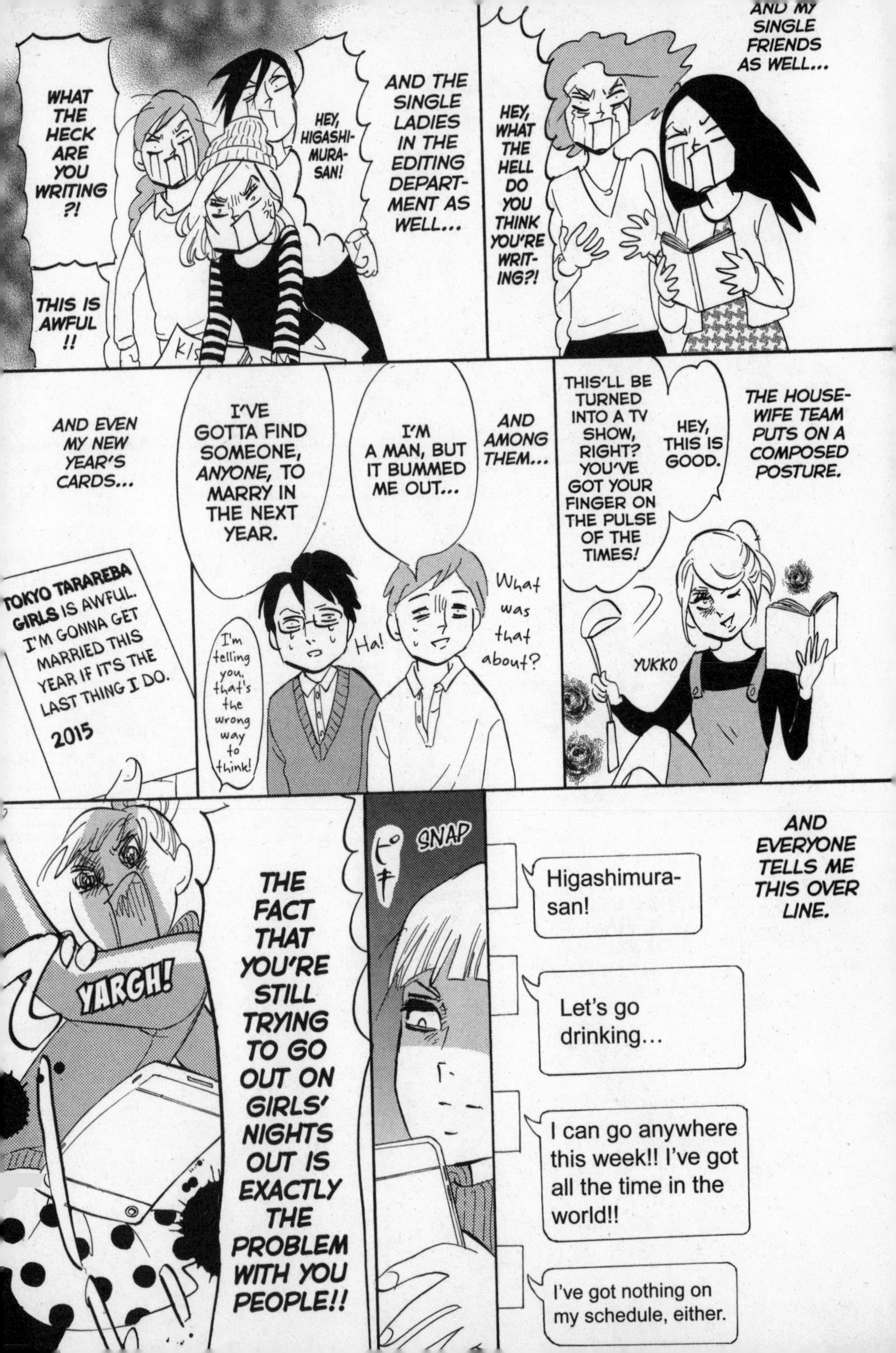
AND MY SINGLE FRIENDS AS WELL...
HEY, WHAT THE HELL DO YOU THINK YOU'RE WRITING?!
AND THE SINGLE LADIES IN THE EDITING DEPARTMENT AS WELL...
HEY, HIGASHIMURA-SAN!
WHAT THE HECK ARE YOU WRITING?!
THIS IS AWFUL!!
THE HOUSEWIFE TEAM PUTS ON A COMPOSED POSTURE.
HEY, THIS IS GOOD.
THIS'LL BE TURNED INTO A TV SHOW, RIGHT? YOU'VE GOT YOUR FINGER ON THE PULSE OF THE TIMES!
YUKKO
AND AMONG THEM...
I'M A MAN, BUT IT BUMMED ME OUT...
What was that about?
I'VE GOTTA FIND SOMEONE, ANYONE, TO MARRY IN THE NEXT YEAR.
Ha!
I'm telling you, that's the wrong way to think!
AND EVEN MY NEW YEAR'S CARDS...
TOKYO TARAREBA GIRLS IS AWFUL. I'M GONNA GET MARRIED THIS YEAR IF IT'S THE LAST THING I DO.
2015
AND EVERYONE TELLS ME THIS OVER LINE.
Higashimura-san!
Let's go drinking...
I can go anywhere this week!! I've got all the time in the world!!
I've got nothing on my schedule, either.
SNAP
THE FACT THAT YOU'RE STILL TRYING TO GO OUT ON GIRLS' NIGHTS OUT IS EXACTLY THE PROBLEM WITH YOU PEOPLE!!
YARGH!

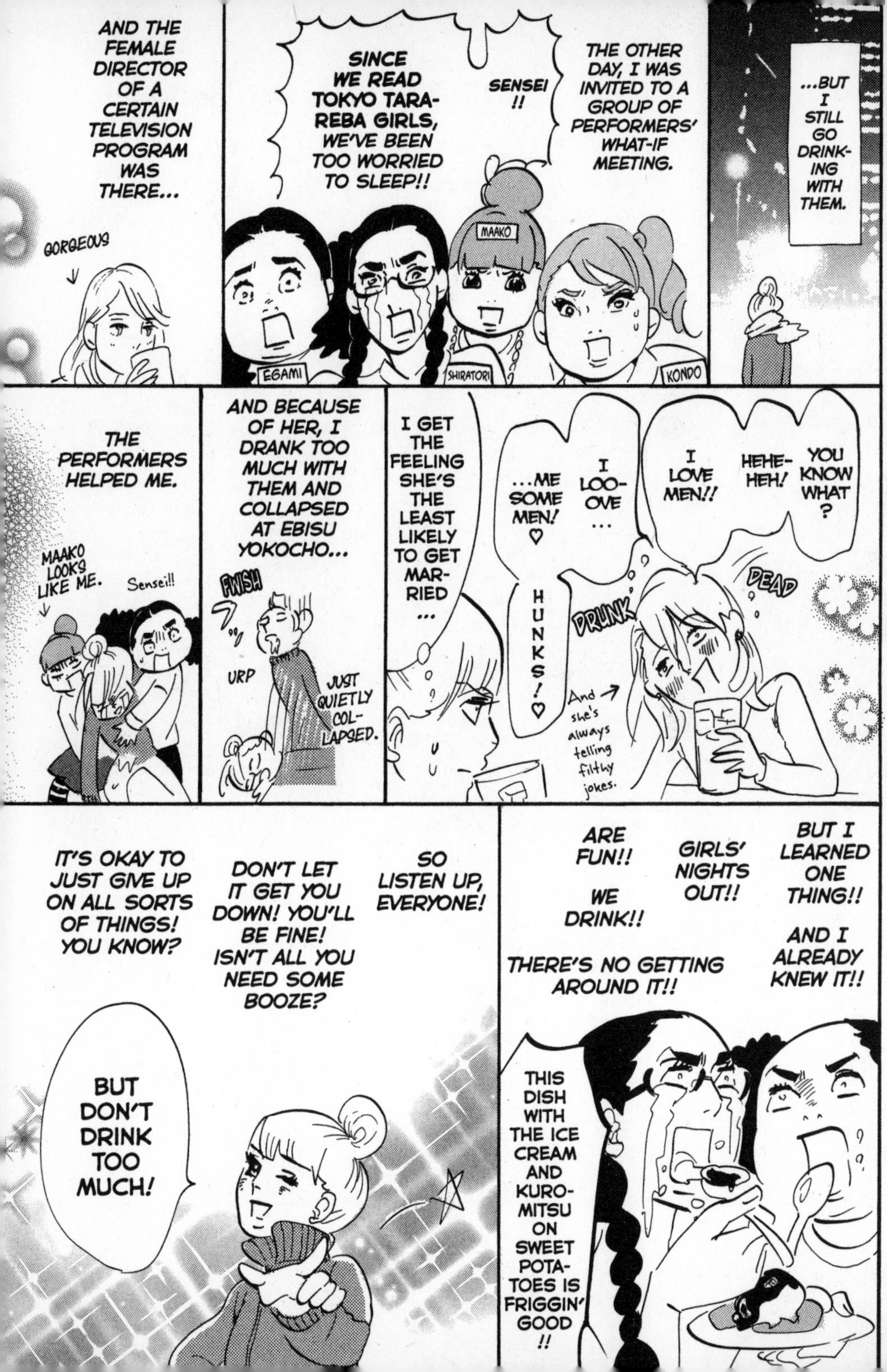
...BUT I STILL GO DRINKING WITH THEM.
THE OTHER DAY, I WAS INVITED TO A GROUP OF PERFORMERS' WHAT-IF MEETING.
SENSEI!!
SINCE WE READ TOKYO TARA-REBA GIRLS, WE'VE BEEN TOO WORRIED TO SLEEP!!
MAAKO
KONDO
SHIRATORI
EGAMI
AND THE FEMALE DIRECTOR OF A CERTAIN TELEVISION PROGRAM WAS THERE...
GORGEOUS
YOU KNOW WHAT?
HEHEHEH!
I LOVE MEN!!
I LOO-OVE...
...ME SOME MEN! ♡
HUNKS! ♡
DEAD
DRUNK
And she's always telling filthy jokes.
I GET THE FEELING SHE'S THE LEAST LIKELY TO GET MARRIED...
AND BECAUSE OF HER, I DRANK TOO MUCH WITH THEM AND COLLAPSED AT EBISU YOKOCHO...
FWISH
URP
JUST QUIETLY COLLAPSED.
THE PERFORMERS HELPED ME.
Sensei!!
MAAKO LOOKS LIKE ME.
BUT I LEARNED ONE THING!!
GIRLS' NIGHTS OUT!!
ARE FUN!!
WE DRINK!!
AND I ALREADY KNEW IT!!
THERE'S NO GETTING AROUND IT!!
THIS DISH WITH THE ICE CREAM AND KUROMITSU ON SWEET POTATOES IS FRIGGIN' GOOD!!
SO LISTEN UP, EVERYONE!
DON'T LET IT GET YOU DOWN! YOU'LL BE FINE! ISN'T ALL YOU NEED SOME BOOZE?
IT'S OKAY TO JUST GIVE UP ON ALL SORTS OF THINGS! YOU KNOW?
BUT DON'T DRINK TOO MUCH!

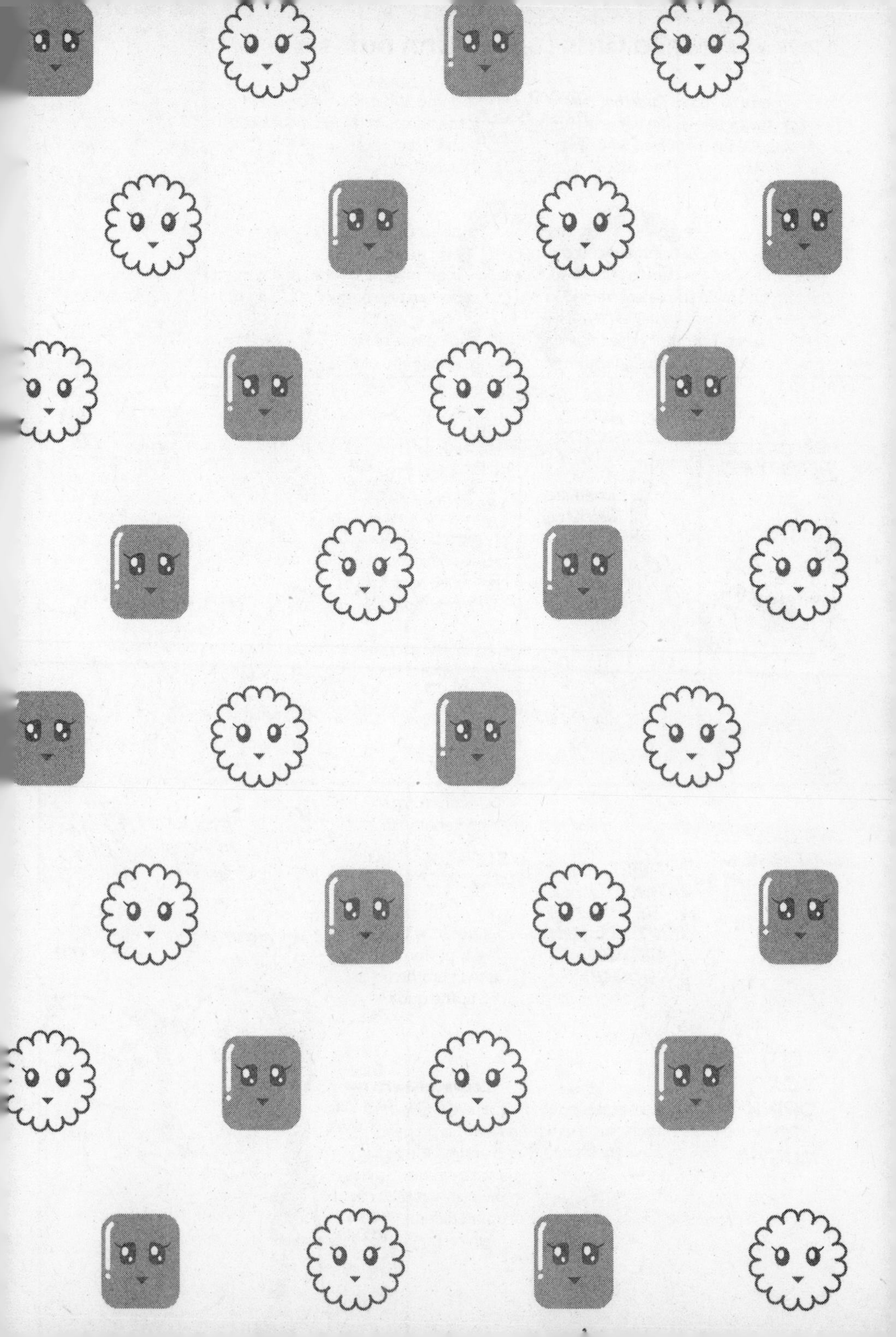

# Tokyo Tarareba Girls Translation notes

**Tokyo Tarareba Girls:** *"Tarareba"* means "What-if," like the "What-if" stories you tell yourself about what could be or could have been.The name is also taken from the names of the two food characters in the series, *tara* (codfish milt) and *reba* (liver) who always say *"tara"* and *"reba"* respectively at the end of their sentences in Japanese, referencing the "what-if" meaning of *"tarareba."*

**Suffixes:** In Japan, it is polite to use suffixes after a person's name or title. Commonly used suffixes include:
-san: This is the most commonly used suffix, and is akin to "Mr." or "Ms."
-chan: This is usually used to refer to someone younger than the speaker, and is mostly used for women and children (the male equivalent being "-kun"). This suffix can also be used playfully, or to indicate closeness (such as how Kaori calls her ex "Ryo-chan").
-sama: This was historically used to refer to lords and people of high status, but is now most often used for addressing letters and on signage (as on Ryo's dressing room) or to refer to someone on whom the speaker wants to confer honor. It can also be used sarcastically, as Koyuki does about Key on page 57.

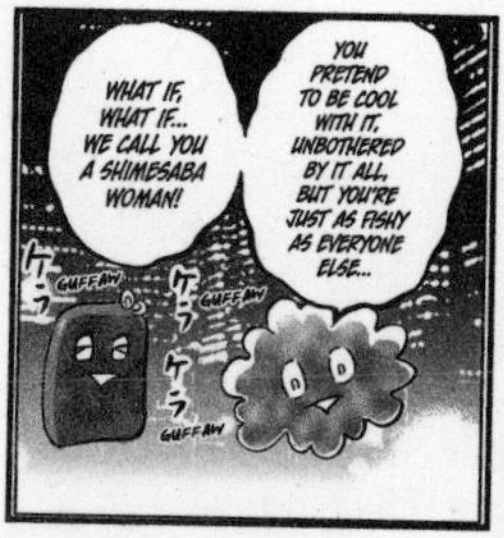
YOU PRETEND TO BE COOL WITH IT, UNBOTHERED BY IT ALL, BUT YOU'RE JUST AS FISHY AS EVERYONE ELSE...
WHAT IF, WHAT IF... WE CALL YOU A SHIMESABA WOMAN!
ケラ ケラ
GUFFAW
ケラ
GUFFAW
GUFFAW

**Shimesaba Woman, page 118**
When the chapter opens, Koyuki refers to herself with the phrase *saba-saba*, which is used to refer to women who are a combination of cool, down-to-earth, easygoing, unbothered, frank, and upfront. Though the origins of the term *saba-saba* are unclear, for a Japanese reader, the word *saba* (mackerel), *sabakeru* (to be sociable), or *sabaku* (to cut) would come to mind. *Shimesaba* (cured mackerel) is a common sushi preparation in Japan made by marinating mackerel in salt and rice vinegar to help it keep longer. By calling Koyuki a "*shimesaba* woman" at the end of the chapter, Tara and Reba are further insinuating that she may not be as unflappable and chill as she thinks herself to be.

***Katakoizake*, page 29**
From a famous pop song by Kana Nishino, who debuted in 2008.

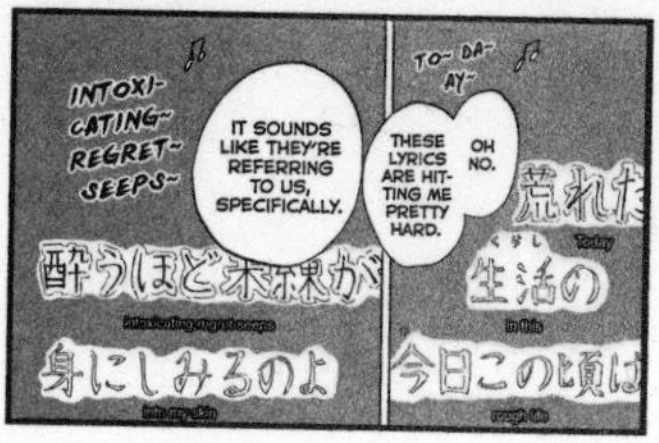
TO- DA-AY-
OH NO.
THESE LYRICS ARE HIT-TING ME PRETTY HARD.
荒れた
生活の
今日この頃は
IT SOUNDS LIKE THEY'RE REFERRING TO US, SPECIFICALLY.
INTOXI-CATING-REGRET-SEEPS-
酔うほど未練が
身にしみるのよ

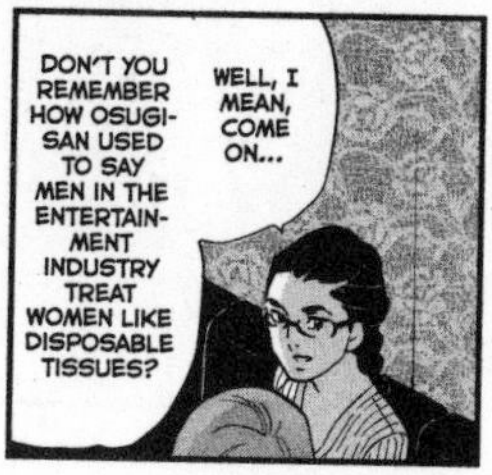
WELL, I MEAN, COME ON...
DON'T YOU REMEMBER HOW OSUGI-SAN USED TO SAY MEN IN THE ENTERTAIN-MENT INDUSTRY TREAT WOMEN LIKE DISPOSABLE TISSUES?

**Don't you remember how Osugi-san used to say, page 30**
Osugi is a famous gay performer and movie critic who also performs with his twin brother, Peeco. Both are known for being rather blunt, as the quote suggests.

**Conveyor-belt sushi, page 40**
Conveyor-belt sushi as a trend is popular in Japan, and is catching on in the U.S. At these restaurants, sushi of various kinds is prepared a la carte, and is placed on a conveyor belt that takes it around the restaurant. Patrons can simply take the plates of sushi they want from the conveyor belt, and their tab is calculated based on counting the plates at the end of the meal. Usually the plates are color-coded for price, and different kinds of sushi are typical for different price levels.

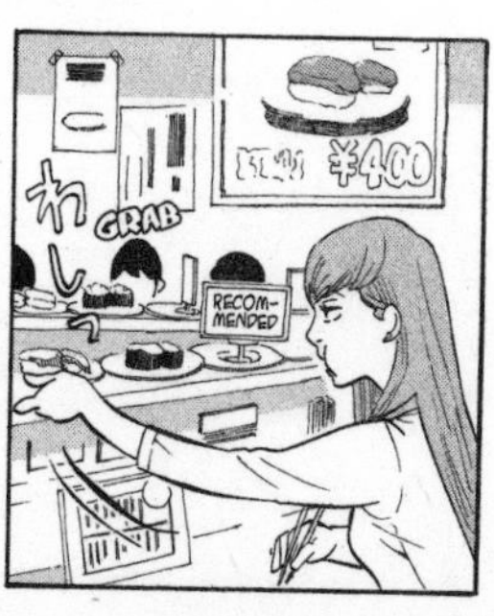
¥400
わし
GRAB
RECOM-MENDED

THEN I COULD JUST PICK THE ONE WITH THE HIGHEST SALARY.
HERE'S OUR FREE LUNCH SPECIAL, ARAJIRU.

***Arajiru*, page 41**
*Arajiru* is a type of fish broth made from *ara*, or various fish scraps such as fish heads and bones, which gives it a deep flavor. The soup made from it can vary from being a clear broth soup to being combined with other flavors, like miso.

IF THE AJI MAKES IT BACK TO ME AND I'VE STILL GOT ROOM, I'LL EAT IT THEN.
FWIP

***Uni* and *aji*, page 42**
These two kinds of fish are common in sushi restaurants. Mackerel sushi takes many forms, and *aji* (horse mackerel), is a popular variety. *Uni* (sea urchin) is always considered a high-priced item.

...WOULD WRITE BRILLIANT SONGS WITH THE POWER OF LOVE, AND FILL UP BUDOKAN ARENA.
BUDOKAN OR BUST!!

**Budokan, page 52**
The Nippon Budokan is a world-famous arena, originally built for the 1964 Summer Olympics in Tokyo. Bands such as the Beatles, Led Zeppelin, Prince, Malice Mizer, Utada Hikaru, and AKB48 (among many, many others) have released recordings made at Budokan.

WELL, ISN'T IT AT THE LIQUIDROOM EBISU?
The venue.
WE CAN STOP BY EBISU YOKOCHO ON THE WAY HOME.
GLINT
OH, THAT PLACE!

**Liquidroom Ebisu and Ebisu Yokocho, page 57**
Two famous spots in Ebisu. Liquidroom Ebisu is a well-known concert hall for live music, and Ebisu Yokocho is a long alley crowded with fantastic food stalls and bars.

I DON'T WANT TO BECOME THE TYPE OF WOMAN WHO DILIGENTLY COOKS NIKUJAGA FOR HER MAN.

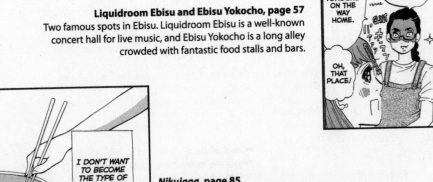

***Nikujaga*, page 85**
*Nikujaga* is a traditional Japanese comfort food made by simmering beef and potatoes in sweetened soy sauce. In Japanese, *niku* means "meat" and *jagaimo* means "potato." The dish is synonymous with home cooking, and here, Koyuki associates it with being tied down by marriage.

**Kagitani, page 111**

Key's last name in Japanese is written 鍵谷, a combination of the words 鍵 (*kagi*, meaning "key," "lock") and 谷 (*tani*, "valley"). By porting the meaning of the first character into English, he (apparently) arrived at his stage name, Key.

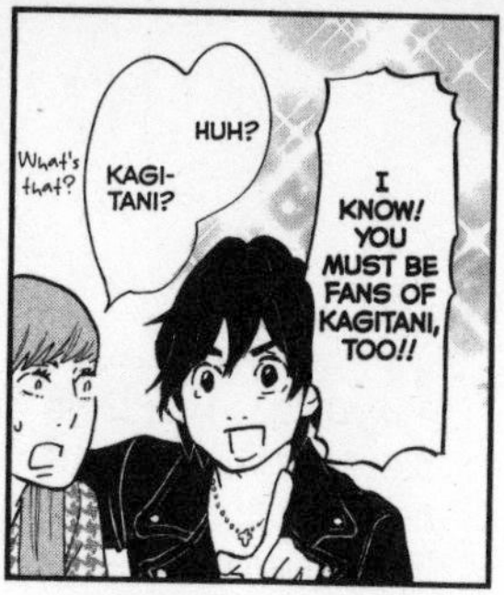
I KNOW! YOU MUST BE FANS OF KAGITANI, TOO!!
HUH?
KAGI-TANI?
What's that?

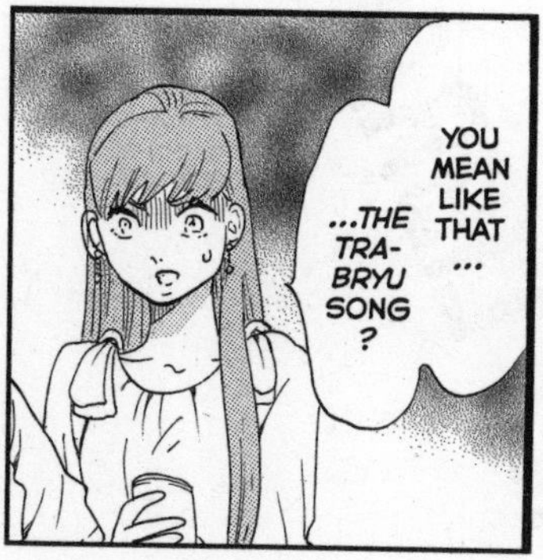
YOU MEAN LIKE THAT...
...THE TRA-BRYU SONG?

**THE TRA-BRYU, page 142**

Lyrics from the 1993 single "Road" by the rock band THE TRA-BRYU, which debuted in 1982, but is still around today.

***Harikuyo*, Sapporo Snow Festival, page 162**

Harikuyo is the Festival of Broken Needles, celebrated in February in the Kanto region. The festival is a memorial to the sewing needles broken in the previous year. The Sapporo Snow Festival is a world-renouned event, bringing in masses of tourists to the city every year. The festival is famous for its multitude of gigantic snow and ice carvings, and also features live performances on stages built from snow.

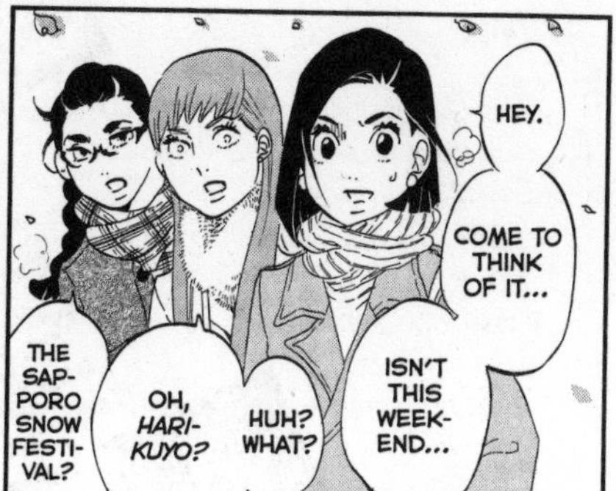
HEY.
COME TO THINK OF IT...
ISN'T THIS WEEK-END...
HUH? WHAT?
OH, HARI-KUYO?
THE SAP-PORO SNOW FESTI-VAL?

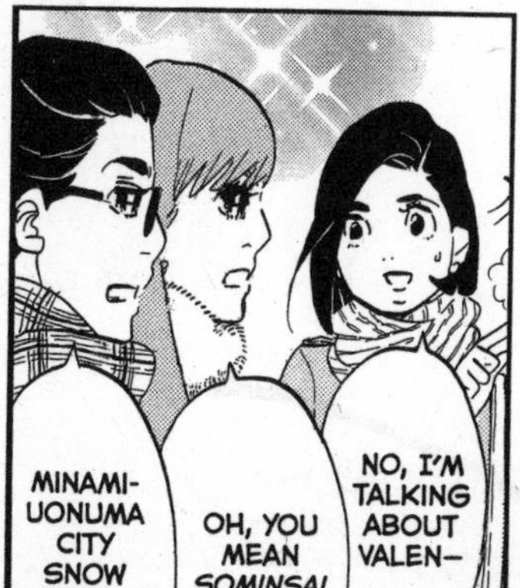
NO, I'M TALKING ABOUT VALEN–
OH, YOU MEAN SOMINSAI?
MINAMI-UONUMA CITY SNOW FESTI-VAL?

***Sominsai*, Minami-Uonuma City Snow Festival, page 162**

*Sominsai* is a "naked festival" held in Iwate during winter. Men strip down, splash themselves with water, and climb the local mountain. Despite the name, many participants wear a *fundoshi* loincloth. The Minami-Uonuma City Snow Festival is another annual event at which the people enjoy playing in the snow.

*Tokyo Tarareba Girls* volume 2 is a work of fiction. Names, characters, places, and incidents are the products of the author's imagination or are used fictitiously. Any resemblance to actual events, locales, or persons, living or dead, is entirely coincidental.

A Kodansha Comics Trade Paperback Original.



Published in the United States by Kodansha Comics, an imprint of Kodansha USA Publishing, LLC, New York.

Publication rights for this English edition arranged through Kodansha Ltd., Tokyo.

First published in Japan in 2015 by Kodansha Ltd., Tokyo, as *Tokyo Tarareba Musume* volume 2.

ISBN 978-1-63236-686-3

Printed in the United States of America.

www.kodanshacomics.com

9 8 7 6 5 4 3 2 1

Translation: Steven LeCroy
Lettering: Rina Mapa
Editing: Sarah Tilson and Lauren Scanlan
YKS Services LLC/SKY Japan, INC.
Kodansha Comics Edition Cover Design: Phil Balsman